Ethnonationalism and Political Systems in Europe

Ethnonationalism and Political Systems in Europe

A State of Tension

MARTIJN A. ROESSINGH

AMSTERDAM UNIVERSITY PRESS

The author and publisher gratefully acknowledge the assistance of the Netherlands Organization for Scientific Research (NWO).

Typesetting: teGiffel *Publishing Services*, Amersfoort
Cover Design: Marjolein Meijer, Beeldvorm, Leiden

ISBN 90 5356 217 6

Contents

Preface

In writing this book I benefitted from the support of many. Foremost among them are Hans Knippenberg and Herman van der Wusten, who guided me through this study and corrected my unmistakable talent to start at the wrong end of the analysis. Several others also read the whole or parts of this book, and corrected errors and suggested improvements; in particular I would like to thank Virginie Mamadouh, Petr Dostál, André Mommen, T.E. Puister, Anssi Paasi, Agnes Roessingh, and Robin Fetchko for their comments. Hans de Visser and Christian Smid (BRON) created the maps as beautifully as ever. Much support, often less tangible but even more crucial, has come from my colleagues. First of all, Jeroen van der Veer and Karin Meulenbelt, who were involved in this strange venture on a day-to-day basis; it must have been trying at times, but I hope they enjoyed my company as much as I did theirs. I likewise would like to thank Lucy Bloemberg, Marianne Bronkhorst, Annemarie Dekker, Aart Jan van Duren, Frank Hoogewoning, Els van der Meer, Caroline van der Meer, and the other colleagues at the Department of Human Geography. Thanks go to NETHUR for improving my practical skills, and to the Netherlands Organization for Scientific Research (NWO) for financially supporting this publication. Very special thanks, however, go out to Willy Francissen for her remarkable patience and endurance.

1

Nationalism and Ethnic Groups in Europe

In the winter of 1989–1990, Zbigniew Brzezinski, the former national security advisor of President Carter, published an article on the problem of nationalism in the post-communist world. He used ominous words: "This long dormant issue is now becoming, in a dynamic and conflictual fashion, the central reality of the once seemingly homogeneous Soviet world. Indeed, where Marx once described the tsarist Russian empire as the prison of nations, and Stalin turned it into the graveyard of nations, under Gorbachov the Soviet empire is rapidly becoming the volcano of nations" (Brzezinski, 1989:1). Subsequent events illustrated his point. By the time the article was published, the Berlin Wall had tumbled, setting the stage for a unified Germany and for radical changes across Eastern Europe. The failed coup in the Soviet Union in August 1991 signalled the independence of the Baltic states, after which the other Soviet republics followed. Some of them soon experienced further fragmentation and bloody civil wars. Former Yugoslavia in particular has been the scene of some of the worst violence experienced in Europe since World War Two.

I began my research in October 1990, before the fragmentation started. The dynamics of nationalism and ethnic conflict became all too apparent in subsequent years: one of my cases, Czechoslovakia, fell apart; another case, Belgium, went much further along the road to fragmentation. For Europe as a whole, we have seen the arrival of 15 new political entities and the disappearance of five.

Indeed, the complexity of ethnic conflict has often eluded even the most perceptive of observers. Thus, although Brzezinski was clearly aware of the danger of nationalism and of the need for the West to base its policies on the strength of nationalism in Eastern Europe and the Soviet Union (or Soviet disUnion, as he pointed out), he did not foresee everything. For Yugoslavia, for instance, he considered the Albanians in Kosovo to be the most severe threat to stability; although this was correct to a certain extent, the conflict nevertheless developed in quite different directions as we now know. For Czechoslovakia he considered the most pressing point the country's relationship with Poland, while the German drive for unification proved far stronger than he expected. However, this merely shows the strength of nationalism in politics, not any particular weakness in Brzezinski's perception. Some crystal balls are better than others, and Brzezinski's ball was clearly among the better ones.

1

Several recent publications have stressed the intractable nature of ethnic nationalism. For instance, US Senator Moynihan shows – in his book on the subject with the telling title 'Pandaemonium' (1993) – how his own crystal ball has always been finetuned to the ethnic dimension in politics. The book discusses 25 years of research on ethnic conflicts, and it reflects Moynihan's firm conviction that ethnicity is there to stay. In a similar evaluation of earlier work, Connor (1994) republished his articles on ethnic relations, some of which first appeared 25 years ago. In the collection he displays an unrelenting drive to make politicians as well as scientists aware of the pervasiveness of the ethnic cleavage; in doing so he often stands in direct confrontation to the prevailing theories of political integration at the state level. Both books, like numerous others, show that ethnicity is an important, pervasive and, politically speaking, highly relevant form of identity. Moreover, it is certainly not a phenomenon restricted to Eastern Europe, but equally present in Western Europe and on all other continents. According to Nielsson (1985:32), no fewer than 119 countries out of the 164 states he examined were multi-national states and thus at risk of an actual or potential ethnic conflict. Connor (1972) even concludes that less than 10% of the world's states can reasonably be described as nation-states.

In this book I do not intend to make that same point again. The book's geographical scope is restricted to Europe, and its main emphasis will be on the post Second World War period. Moreover, although the next section will very briefly introduce the ethnic map of Europe, I do not pretend that the book will be a comprehensive overview of ethnic conflict even on that single continent. Indeed, although some words will be said on the subject in this chapter, neither do I intend to come to grips with the individual's continuing affinity to his or her ethnic background. The crucial psychological dimension of ethnicity, the reason why it exists at all, is ably explored in other works, some of which will be discussed below.

What I do intend then is to look comparatively into the dynamics of ethnic relations once the groups exist at a basic level. Indeed, although the evidence is abundantly clear that ethnicity remains a foremost dimension of identification, it is equally clear that the relevance of this identification is highly variable. As Horowitz (1985:684) puts it in his thorough analysis: "Even in the most severely divided society, ties of blood do not lead ineluctably to rivers of blood." I believe that the perspective taken in this book adds to the comparative studies on ethnic conflict published thus far. It is the main argument of this book that while the interaction of specific groups is often discussed extensively, the crucial role of the form of the state in the mobilization and structuring of ethnic activism is generally considered only briefly, let alone analyzed systematically. Most of the time, as I will argue in chapter two, the state is either seen as a neutral broker in ethnic relations, or as simply responsive to ethnic demands. Therefore, the central role of the state machinery in strengthening or weakening the relevance of the ethnic sentiment deserves much more attention.

The rest of the book explores the dynamics of ethnic conflict in Europe from this perspective. First of all, in the remainder of this chapter, I will give an introduction to the prevailing theories on nationalism and ethnicity. After a brief overview of groups on European soil, the discussion will turn to the debate on the meaning and history of ethnic groups, nations and nationalism, and on their interrelationship and blurred boundaries. I will end this chapter by relating ethnic activism to the modern state. In the next chapter I will deal with the growth of the modern state and with the interaction between states and ethnic groups; in that chapter I will argue for a perspective that treats states as an autonomous force in the mobilization and institutionalization of ethnic sentiment. Building on that argument, I will use two dimensions that differentiate the collection of European states. The third chapter sets up the various case studies, which follow in chapters four to seven. In the final chapter I will then compare the cases by looking at the different forms of the states and by analyzing the impact they have had on the ethnic groups in the state's territory and on their interrelationship.

1.1   THE ETHNOPOLITICAL MAP OF EUROPE

Until the recent political changes in Europe – the unification of Germany and the collapse of the Soviet Union, Yugoslavia and Czechoslovakia – Europe counted 33 states (including the dwarf states Andorra, Monaco, Liechtenstein, San Marino and Vatican City). Recent events have increased this number by 10 (15 new states and 5 disappearances), not counting the political units on the slopes of the Caucasus[1]. Despite these changes, the number of groups living in Europe still clearly exceeds the number of states. In an attempt to provide a comprehensive overview, Krejčí and Velímský (1981) use criteria such as territory, political status, language, culture, history and subjective sentiment to distinguish a total of 72 groups in Europe, again excluding the peoples of the former Soviet Union who live in the Caucasus (see table 1.1). It should immediately be stated that this list is far from complete and is subject to much discussion, but it nevertheless gives a good impression of European ethnic diversity. Moreover, as the borders of European states do not match the living areas of the peoples involved, there has emerged a seemingly endless list of European minority situations. To say that the complexity of the ethnic mosaic could lead, and does lead, to enormous problems in all corners of Europe is therefore to understate the issue.

---

1   The 15 new states are the Russian Republic, Estonia, Latvia, Lithuania, Belorussia, Ukraine, Moldavia, small Yugoslavia (Serbia and Montenegro), Croatia, Slovenia, Macedonia, Slovakia, and the Czech Lands. Bosnia-Hercegovina is also counted as a state, although this is of course very contested, and so is Germany. Several other political units are not counted because of their unclear status (e.g., the Dnjepr-Republic, Chechnya, and so forth).

Ethnonationalism and Political Systems in Europe

Table 1.1 Ethnonational groups in Europe (in thousands)[1]

Name	Number	Name	Number	Name	Number
Western, Northern and Southern Europe		Lapps	50	Romanians	18,500
		Luxembourgers	350	Serbs	8,500
		Maltese	320	Slovaks	4,500
Allemanic Swiss	4,200	Manx	60	Slovenes	1,700
Alsatians	1,400	Norwegians	4,000	Sorbs/Lusatians	70
Austrians	7,500	Portuguese	9,000	Turks[6]	4,500
Basques	900	Romand Swiss	1,200		
Bretons	1,000	Romansh	60	**Former Soviet Union**	
Bruxellois	1,000	Sardinians	1,200	*European part, excluding the Caucasus)*	
Catalans	6,500	Scots	5,500		
Channel Isl	120	Spaniards	25,000		
Corsicans	250	Swedes	8,000	Bashkirs	1,200
Danes	5,000	Walloons	3,000	Belorussians	9,100
Dutch	13,000	Welsh	2,700	Chuvash	1,700
English	45,000			Estonians	1,000
Faroese	30	**Eastern and Central**		Jews	2,100
Finns	4,300	**Europe**		Kalmyks	130
Flemings	6,000			Karelians	150
French[2]	50,000	Albanians	3,600	Komi	500
Frisians	600	Bulgarians	7,700	Latvians	1,400
Furlanians[3]	500	Croats	4,500	Lithuanians	2,700
Galicians	1700	Czechs	9,600	Mari	600
Germans	77,000	Gypsies	2,000	Moldavians	2,800
Greeks	8,600	Hungarians	12,300	Mordovians	1,300
Icelanders	200	Macedonians	1,200	Russians	129,000
Irish[4]	3,500	Montenegrins	500	Tatars	5,900
Italian Swiss	800	Muslims[5]	1,700	Udmurts	700
Italians	53,000	Poles	33,000	Ukrainians	40,700

Source: Krejčí and Velímský, 1981:50–55

Notes:

1 The list is certainly not exhaustive. The Minority Rights Group (1990) for instance explicitly mentions the Pomaks, Åland Islanders, Valachs, and Azoreans as separate groups. On the other hand, the inclusion of some of the groups is certainly open for debate (e.g., Bruxellois, see chapter six), while the drawing of borders is often difficult. Instead of Albanians, for instance, it might be better to include Gegs and Tosks. If Moldavians are included, why should not Finnish Swedes be included? If Flemish are considered separate from Dutch, why not distinguish between Tyroleans and Austrians? Krejčí and Velímský were certainly aware of the difficulties involved. The figures should be treated as a rough indication only.

2 Including Occitans.

3 Including 20 thousand Ladins.

4 Including Catholics in Northern Ireland.

5 In former Yugoslavia.

6 European part of Turkey plus Turkish minorities in Greece, Bulgaria and former Yugoslavia.

4

Because of the wide distribution of (potential) ethnic trouble, academic interest in the subject has surged since the 1960s; entrances in the Library of Congress with the term 'ethnicity' in the title increased from 9 in the period 1968–1974 to 116 between 1975 and 1980 (Ryan, 1990:xxiv). In the general theoretical discussion on the subject three concepts are pivotal: 'nationalism,' 'ethnic group,' and 'state.' The three concepts are related. In fact, as Connor has noted, the concepts are generally mixed-up to the detriment of improved understanding: "In this Alice-in-Wonderland world in which nation usually means state, in which nation-state usually means multination state, in which nationalism usually means loyalty to the state, and in which ethnicity, primordialism, pluralism, tribalism, regionalism, communalism, parochialism and subnationalism usually mean loyalty to the nation, it should come as no surprise that the nature of nationalism remains essentially unprobed" (Connor, 1978:394–395). In this chapter the first two concepts, nationalism and ethnic group, will mainly be discussed. The third concept, the state, will be treated more extensively in the next chapter, although a certain overlap cannot be avoided.

1.2   NATIONALISM

There are as many definitions of nationalism as there are scholars on the subject (see, e.g., Smith 1991:73, Kamenka 1976:15, Seton-Watson, 1977:3, Snyder, 1990:247). Both the geographical reach of the phenomenon and the diverse impact it has had on the world political map are responsible. Indeed, nationalism can be seen as a two-faced coin, used in the context of two different kinds of historical processes. One face of the coin describes the attempt of states to homogenize the populace of their territory. The other face of the coin describes the political program that is used by movements to claim more political autonomy, or even to claim their own state. Nationalism thus describes either "the ethnicization of the polity" or "the politicization of ethnicity" as Grillo (1980:7) has so nicely put it. However, as coins go, the second face is closely connected to the first face and vice-versa, with earlier examples of one side of the coin giving rise to the emergence of varieties on the other side of the coin. Clearly, nationalism is a highly contagious political doctrine.

One of the most useful recent approaches to the subject has been suggested by Gellner (1983). His formulation is centred around the nationalist's idea that the geographical borders of the nation and the state should be coterminous: "Nationalism is primarily a political principle, which holds that the political and the national unit should be congruent. Nationalism as a sentiment, or as a movement, can best be defined in terms of this principle. Nationalist sentiment is the feeling of anger aroused by the violation of this principle, or the feeling of satisfaction aroused by its fulfilment. A nationalist movement is one actuated by a sentiment of this kind" (Gellner,

1983:1). The recent origin of nationalism is very much emphasized by Gellner. According to him, this principle is not at all part and parcel of human politics: "... nations, like states, are a contingency, and not a universal necessity ... Moreover, nations and states are not the same contingency. Nationalism holds that they were destined for each other, that either without the other is incomplete, and constitutes a tragedy" (Gellner, 1983:6). To put an end to this tragedy, nationalist movements formulate political programs which contains the following three assertions (Breuilly, 1982:3, see also Smith, 1991:74): 1) there exists a nation with an explicit and peculiar character; 2) the interests and values of this nation take priority over all other interests and values; and 3) the nation must be as independent as possible. This usually requires the attainment of political sovereignty. Not surprisingly, however, the fulfillment of the political program generally runs into problems; nationalism is not a doctrine that is automatically successful (see Wusten 1988).

Despite the variation in success-rate, the spread of nationalism has been all encompassing. This is not to say that its shape and impact were similar across the globe. To start with, the period in which nationalist ideology took root in the region influenced the character of the nationalism that developed. A traditional distinction in this respect has been the one between nationalism in Eastern Europe and Western Europe. Thus, Smith, following Kohn (1971), sees a Western European type of nationalism – the oldest in kind, and based on rational and associational grounds, promoted by the middle class [although Smith has some reservations on that point], more of a civic-territorial kind, and closer to state-nationalism – and an Eastern European type of nationalism – more mystical and organic, promoted by 'vernacular' intellectuals, more an 'ethnic-genealogical' kind, and closer to a emancipatory nationalism (Smith, 1991:80–82). Here we can return to the two sides of the nationalism mentioned above. Whereas nationalism originally emerged in Western Europe as a tool to fill the societal content of existing political units (ethnicizing the polity), it became a tool in Eastern Europe to adapt the political units to presumed social realities (politicizing the ethnicity). Nationalism reached the region before substantial industrialization was achieved, and the mix of populations and cultures was much more comprehensive and complex (see, e.g., King 1973, Hroch 1985, Gellner 1990). Nationalist movements in Eastern Europe were based on local languages and religions, and myths and histories became central devices in the process of national emancipation. According to several observers there are strong consequences attached to this difference in timing. Brzezinsky (1989:4) for instance argues that because of "... the historical immaturity of Eastern Europe's nationalisms ... [they] still tend to be more volatile, more emotional and more intense than those in the West."

The East-West distinction is certainly not the only difference in kinds of nationalism. Orridge in fact distinguishes five types of nationalism (1981:41–52). He considers Western Europe as the breeding ground and starting point of *state nationalism*, meaning the attempt to centralize the state and to achieve a high degree of cultural homogeneity on the territory of the state. The power and dynamics of Western European states inspired writers and philosophers such as Rousseau and Herder to consider the bonds of communities and the progress these communities could make. *Unification nationalism*, which then emerged in reaction to the first type (for example among German and Italian speaking people), intended to unify a particular culture under one political roof (a modern variety, though slightly different, is pan-nationalism). Nationalism became politically explosive with the rise of *reaction nationalism or separatism*, which emerged especially among the peoples under Habsburg and Ottoman rule. Its political importance and success derived to no small extent from the Wilsonian principle of self-determination. President Wilson declared in Congress, to the horror of some of his advisors, that "National aspirations must be respected; peoples may now be dominated and governed only by their own consent. 'Self-determination' is not a mere phrase. It is an imperative principle of action, which statesmen will henceforth ignore at their peril" (quoted in Moynihan, 1993:78–79). The political problem is what constitutes the self here, and who determines what to what extent; clearly the situation was such that the principle was to apply only for groups under the rule of the defeated powers (Hannum, 1990:28).[2]

Self-determination was definitely not meant for the colonies of the European powers. The ideology of nationalism nevertheless came to span the earth with the growth of *anti-imperial nationalism*, emerging among the peoples in Asia, Africa and Latin-America precisely in resistance to colonial rule.[3] Finally, with the state map starting to reach all corners of the earth, there emerged, or reemerged, *cultural nationalism or renewal nationalism*, meaning the attempts by cultural groups to separate from supposedly unitary states on the basis of former, real or perceived, greatness on the part of

---

2   The two reports on the Åland Islands, prepared by commissions of the League of Nations, are illuminating: "Although the principle of self-determination of peoples plays an important part in modern political thought, especially since the Great War, it must be pointed out that there is no mention of it in the covenant of the League of Nations". And, one year later: "Is it possible to admit as an absolute rule that a minority of the population of a State, which is definitely constituted and perfectly capable of fulfilling its duties as such, has the right of separating itself from her in order to be incorporated in another State or to declare its independence? The answer can only be in the negative. To concede to minorities, either of language or religion, or any fractions of a population the right of withdrawing from the community to which they belong, because it is their wish or their good pleasure, would be to destroy order and stability within States and to inaugurate anarchy in international life; it would be to uphold a theory incompatible with the very idea of the State as a territorial and political unity" (quoted in Hannum, 1990:29–30).
3   As Hannum (1990:24) points out, in that phrase, the "self" in question were groups less defined by ethnically, linguistically or otherwise homogeneous groupings, but by territorially and politically demarcated bundles of people. The use of the term 'statism' instead of 'nationalism' might therefore be more correct, although it should immediately be added that the homogeneous character of prior 'nations' was also questionable.

the group. Others have called it substate nationalism, minority nationalism, ethnic nationalism, regionalism, primordialism, and so forth. It is this latter type of nationalism that is at the centre of this book.

1.2.1 Nations and ethnic groups

The enduring presence and the wide spread of nationalism shows that the moral image of the nationalist ideal is very appealing. However, if nations are pictured as the natural units of society, then the problem is to define what a nation is. Generally several characteristics are mentioned that 'objectively' differentiate one people from another, such as language, religion, culture, territory, common ancestry, and so forth. A typical example is the definition by Josef Stalin, who described the nation as "a historically evolved, stable community of people, formed on the basis of a common language, territory, economic life, and psychological make-up manifested in common culture" (in Connor 1994:73). The problem is of course who makes the decision whether these characteristics are in fact 'common'. Safran points out an obvious but nonetheless crucial aspect, when he emphasizes that "[i]t is political power that determines the difference between culture and folklore, language and dialect, literature and oral tradition, history and legendry, law and custom, functional and primordial relations, religion and sect, and faith and superstition" (Safran, 1991:7). Moreover, the differentiating characteristics in one case are often not the important ones in other cases. Thus, whereas religion defines the Bosnian Muslims, it did not divide the Dutch into two nations. Whereas language defines the Flemings and Walloons, it is not what makes the Germans and the Austrians or German-speaking Swiss different. Moreover, differentiating characteristics can disappear over time, religion losing its importance, or knowledge of language being lost.

Therefore, for understanding the concept of nation, the sentiment in particular is crucial. Ultimately, the nation is "the largest community which, when the chips are down, effectively commands men's loyalty, overriding the claims both of lesser communities within it and those which cut across it or potentially enfold it within a still greater society" (Emerson, 1960:95–96). The psychological process that differentiates between 'us' and 'them' does of course make use of the characteristics to 'justify' the sentiment, so to speak, but it does not always need them. Nations are therefore especially subjective groups. However, since at least two groups are involved when national differentiation is stressed, this sense of otherness of a group is at the same time ascriptive and self-descriptive (see, e.g., Barth 1969, Horowitz 1975, Amersfoort 1991). On the one hand individuals may voluntarily opt for one group or another (although there are limitations to this), and on the other hand they may be forced to identify with a group by outsiders. Throughout modern history individuals have been labelled member of one national group or another, without them wishing so; recently this process could again be observed in Bosnia.

Much of the literature on recent nationalism uses the concepts of 'ethnic group' and 'ethnicity', but generally the characteristics that are connected with the concept of 'nation' can also be found when the subject is called an 'ethnic group' (see, for instance, discussions in Snyder 1983, Wolf 1986, and Symmons-Symonolewicz 1985).[4] Despite some nuances, therefore, ethnic groups and nations have in common an emotional bond and a clear self-perception of difference from neighbouring groups. Moreover, a traditional view which considers ethnic groups to be an early stage in the development of nations cannot be upheld when modern forms of cultural nationalism are discussed; in particular in the European context it is justified to use interchangeably the terms 'ethnic group' and 'nation,' implying that in Europe we are all ethnics of one kind or another. In fact, I will use the (strictly speaking) pleonasm 'ethnonationalism,' following Connor, to describe the sentiment that activates a political movement of ethnonational groups within multi-ethnic states for more autonomy or independence[5].

What further complicates the discussion is the fact that ethnonational groups are often minorities. Indeed, the term minority itself may cause confusion: whereas it usually describes a numerical situation, it sometimes indicates a socio-political situation[6]; and whereas it can describe both a group which is a 'spill-over' of the dominant group into a neighbouring country (e.g. Elzas-Germans), it may also be a separate ethnonational group in its own right (e.g. Bretons). Most literature on minorities and minority-state relations deals with all of the above possibilities.[7] Regarding the latter point, it should be noted that in cases of a 'spill-over' minority, the question

---

4   The meaning of 'ethnicity' in fact has evolved over time: it has been used to describe a racial grouping, but has now taken on a much more cultural dimension. To add to the confusion, the term 'ethnic group' is also used to describe immigrant communities that still hold in esteem their cultural and geographical background, and have some experience of psychological commonness and organization. It is not used in that sense here, although a comparison of the variety and dynamics of ethnic activism of territorially based groupings and immigrant groupings is in itself very interesting (see, e.g., Gurr 1993, Esman 1985, and Amersfoort 1993).

5   Connor uses the term to avoid confusion between nationalism as a sentiment connected with the nation or ethnic group, and nationalism as a sentiment connected with a state. The latter use he considered wrong, making ethnonationalism thus a clarification of his use of the term 'nationalism' (see Connor 1972 and 1978).

6   Most of the time it is used to describe both. The definition given by the influential London-based Minority Rights Group (1990) states that a minority is "a group numerically inferior to the rest of the population of a state, in a non-dominant position, whose members being nationals of the state possess ethnic, religious, or linguistic characteristics differing from those of the rest of the population and show, if only implicitly, a sense of solidarity directed towards preserving their culture, traditions, religion, or language".

7   A strict distinction between types of groups is difficult to uphold. In the large project undertaken by Gurr, for instance, Bretons, Catalans, South Tyroleans, and Jurassiens are classified as ethnonationalist groups, but the Muslim Greeks, the vast majority of whom are Turkish-speaking, are classified as a militant sect (Gurr 1993).

always remains of whether the minority in question considers its bonds with the 'mother-culture' more important than its separate identity as a minority group in another state. In other words: how will the individuals making up the group (minority) identify themselves when 'the chips are down'. Indeed, even these days former 'spill-over minorities' have surprised observers by taking an extremely independent stance, which may (or may not) cause them to develop into another branch on the European ethnic tree (e.g., Moldavians, Bosnian Serbs). How different are they, in the long run or under specific circumstances, from, say, Flemings, Walloons, German-speaking Swiss, or Swedish-speaking Finns? Moreover, the question is whether the dynamics of mobilization will be different, and if so, to what extent? More will be said on the issue in the next chapter and in chapter eight.

1.2.2 Territory and ethnonationalism

It is worthwhile exploring a little further the linkages between nations and one of the characteristics: territory. Successful nationalism, of course, always results in the creation of new political territories. This may occur either through unification, or by separation of regionally based groups within existing states; the latter process aptly called 'radical surgery' (Horowitz, 1985:588, see also Waterman 1989). The large amount of often conflicting claims, however, raises the question of to what extent the fragmentation of territories can continue or at what geographical level political self-determination is 'justified'. Indeed, as Williams (1985:334) notes, a minimum size of a nation as a social group is hard to define, and the self-determination of Malta, Iceland, and Luxembourg in Europe alone indicate that size is not really a decisive issue. The question is further complicated by the notion that different geographical levels of identity can be combined (Knight, 1982:515). However, as much as some would like multiple identities to be the solution to conflicting identities, inherent in every discussion on nationalism is the notion that the political importance of one specific level of identification, the nation, takes priority over all others.

There is more to link nationalism to territory than just the changing configuration of the world political map: territory plays a central role both in nationalist identity and in nationalist strategy. Indeed, despite the fact that territory figures in many of the definitions of nationalism and the nation, Anderson (1986,1988) has correctly pointed out that the role of territories for nationalist ideology has often been underestimated. He argues that "[n]ations, like states, are not simply located in geographic space – which is the case with all social organizations – rather they explicitly claim particular territories and derive distinctiveness from them." The concepts of motherland, fatherland, homeland, and other expressions of territorial affiliation show the psychological importance of territory to the nation. Where in a cultural sense the concepts of 'us' and 'them' have been central to the development of national groupings, this translates quickly into spatial terms: nationalism is ultimately a territorial ideology which is internally unifying and externally divisive; looking inward nationalism seeks to unify the nation and its constituent territory, and looking outward it tends to divide one nation and territory from another (Anderson 1988). Both approaches are involved in the process of nation-building.

In fact, as Knight (1982:516) notes, the power of territory is such that individuals are often classified according to their location in space more than according to their cultural markers. In nationalist strategy, therefore, a crucial role is played by territoriality, having been defined by Sack as "the attempt by an individual or group to affect, influence, or control people, phenomena, and relationships, by delimiting and asserting control over a geographic area" (Sack, 1986:19). The combined effects of territorial classification, the delimitation of boundaries and internal control and homogenization enable the development of large scale communities like nations. Moreover, the use of territoriality gives the nation an absolutist and historically continuous presence, and provides it with a basis of power and access to resources, including population. As Sack points out, the use of territory in itself also reifies political power, making it impersonal by identifying it with a place instead of with power relations. Therefore, the nationalist strategy to obtain a (part of the) state combines with the attempt by the leadership of the group to obtain political control; for them it necessitates a successful claim over a specific territory[8]. The central role territory plays in nationalism has prompted many scholars to describe nationalist groups as regionalist.

In sum, the phenomenon that is the subject of this book is one of the varieties of nationalism in one of the continents of the world. Ethnonationalism, as Connor called it, is studied from various perspectives: a large body of literature deals with nationalism in general, and an equally large body of literature deals with ethnicity, ethnic groups, and minorities. In order to create a firm theoretical foundation for this study, the remainder of the chapter deals with some of the main discussions in both strands of literature.

---

8   Not surprisingly, cartography plays a major role. See for instance the fascinating account by H.R.Wilkinson (1951) on the ethnographic cartography of Macedonia, which clearly illustrates the political uses and mental effects of cartographic representation.

1.3   THE HISTORICAL ROOTS OF NATIONS

In political reality, the cultural and territorial demands that nationalists put forward are based on the historical roots of the nations they claim to represent. Smith has put forward extensive argumentation which supports that claim. Many pre-modern examples of nationalist-type identities are provided by him to show a more or less continuous development from pre-modern cultural organization to nationalism. He uses the French term *ethnies*, aimed to describe "named human populations with shared ancestry myths, histories and cultures, having an association with a specific territory and a sense of solidarity" (Smith, 1986:32). He considers the 'religious complex' of a group as the 'pivotal element' in crystallizing and maintaining ethnic identity in the long term, especially when the religion and the religious stratum renews itself often enough and when the religious stratum succeeds in spreading and transmitting the holiness and salvation to the ordinary people (Smith, 1986:120). To Smith it is wrong to see nations and nationalism as purely modern phenomena: "Not only in spirit but in structure, modern nations and not only nationalism, turned out to be Janus-headed – and this is necessary. If there was no model of past ethnicity and no pre-existent *ethnies*, there could be neither nationalism nor nations. There would only be states and *étatisme* imposed from above, a very different phenomenon. The role of the state in homogenizing the populations and stimulating their cultures and sentiments was considerable, but could never have produced the results it did without ethnic cores and ethnic models for mobilizing grass-roots aspirations and solidarities" (Smith, 1986:213).

In recent academic debate, however, these historical roots have seriously been questioned, both in individual cases and with regard to the phenomenon of 'the nation' as such. The Marxist historian Hobsbawm argues that in the Middle Ages and before, the enormous gap between educated people ('hegemonic culture') and uneducated people ('popular culture') stood in the way of the kind of group-identity which could compare in any sense with the group sentiment of modern nations. Modern languages, for instance, he considers to be "almost always semi-artificial constructs and occasionally, like modern Hebrew, virtually invented. They are the opposite of what nationalist mythology supposes them to be, namely the primordial foundations of national culture and the matrices of the national mind" (Hobsbawm, 1990:54). In a similar vein he treats other national characteristics such as ethnicity, religion, and a common history, to conclude that "the modern nation, either as a state or as a body of people aspiring to form such a state, differs in size, scale and nature from the actual communities with which human beings have identified over most of history, and makes quite different demands on them" (Hobsbawm, 1990:46). As a

12

consequence, Hobsbawm denies that proto-nationalism can be legitimately identified with the modern nationalism, mainly because they had or have no necessary relation to the unit of territorial organization which is a crucial criterion of what we understand as a 'nation' today (Hobsbawm, 1990:47). Others take up similar positions. Gellner, for instance, points out that nationalism has only very limited roots in pre-modern society: "nationalism is not the awakening and assertion of these mythical, supposedly natural and given units. It is, on the contrary, the crystallization of new units, suitable for the conditions now prevailing, though admittedly using as their raw material the cultural, historical and other inheritances from the pre-nationalist world" (Gellner, 1983:49).

1.3.1 Modernization and nationalism

Gellner's remarks point at the rather paradoxical nature of modern nationalism. Whereas we can agree with Hobsbawm and others that the factual bases for the claims of common historical roots may often be inadequate, the resulting sense of belonging and political relevance is no less concrete, while the 'raw material' is certainly used (see, e.g., Kohn 1971, Seton-Watson 1977, Kamenka 1976). The context in which this 'raw material' became the basis of modern nations has been summarized as 'modernization'. The term covers various aspects, such as increasing means of communication, large-scale education, industrialization, and so forth. In this context of modernization, group sentiment was forged between individuals previously unaware of their common bonds. Anderson (1983) coined the now well known term 'imagined communities' to describe these new sets of individuals who obviously don't know each other, but still started to consider themselves to be members of that limited and sovereign group, and are even willing to die for it. According to Anderson, central in mending these communities was the printing press.

In fact, which aspects of the modernization process are most central to this emergence of imagined communities is the subject of heated debate. Generally, community formation is explicitly linked to industrialization and to the rise of the modern market economy. As Deutsch argued, for instance, social and technological change have "uprooted" people, have exposed them to the risks of economic competition, and have taught them to "hunger for success"; he called this process *social updraught*, leading people to look for support. "For almost any limited group within a competitive market, both security and success can be promoted by effective organization, alignment of preferences, and coordination of behaviour. Vast numbers have felt a need for such a group and have answered it by putting their

trust in their nation" (Deutsch, 1966:101).[9] In that context a common culture has become the central binding agent of modern society, a "necessary
shared medium, the life-blood or perhaps rather the minimal shared atmosphere, within which alone the members of the society can breathe and survive and produce"; this single medium is necessary to enable every individual to move in a flexible way in the labour market (Gellner, 1983:37–38).
Education is central in creating this single cultural-linguistic medium shared
by all citizens in a state. Gellner agrees with Deutsch on the fast growing
importance of communication in modern society, because of "the complexity, interdependence and mobility of productive life, within which far more
numerous, complex, precise and context-free messages need to be transmit-
ted than had ever been the case before." However, he adds the democratization of high culture as a totally new and crucial social fundament of post-
agricultural society (Gellner, 1983:74).

The impact of modernization on nationalism has also been studied by
Marx and his followers, although they have been somewhat reluctant
because of the basic theoretical incompatibility between loyalty to the
nation and loyalty to class (see the next chapter). However, social reality
has been rather convincing, and when the political relevance and strength of
the nationalist doctrine became obvious, it prompted an increasing number
of writings; in fact, the share devoted to the issue in the works of Marx,
Lenin, and Stalin increased from 3 to 10 to a solid 50 percent, respectively
(Wright, 1981:149).[10] Modern Marxist theories see nationalism as closely
connected to the rise of capitalism, in which the nationalist appeal is used

---

9   Deutsch has been the first and arguably most influential of the modernization theorists.
To him, nations are the direct result of major changes in the possibilities for social communication. He pictures the world as consisting of culture communities bounded by relative barriers of communication instead of the more traditional view of boundaries made
up by one particular ingredient of nationality (e.g., language); the cultures produce, select
and channel information and therefore are made up of "a common set of stable, habitual
preferences and priorities in men's attention, as well as in their thoughts and feelings ... In
so far as a common culture facilitates communication, it forms a community" (Deutsch,
1966:89). The level of communication complementarity is heightened by the process of
social learning, which can be called assimilation if it takes place at a higher rate than the
increase in the economic cooperation of men and in the "limited but direct communication which this entails"; in other words, if community is growing faster than society
(Deutsch, 1966:125). In contrast to some of the conclusions drawn by several of his
severest critics (e.g., Connor), he qualifies it by allowing for cases where assimilation fails
because society grows faster than the sense of community (see also the discussion in
Lijphart 1977a).

10   According to Marx, the least interested, the rise of nationalism was closely connected to
the rise of capitalism, and capitalism would also ensure its demise (see discussion in
Wright, 1981:150). Nevertheless, nationalist sentiment was considered by him as a tacti-
cal tool to achieve certain political objectives. Thus, Marx favoured Polish independence,
for instance, because of its economic viability (and coined the phrase "right of self-determination" in the process), but opposed the Czech, Croatian and other Slavic nationalisms because they had helped to defeat the progressive Viennese and Hungarian revolu-
tions of 1848–1849 by siding with the monarchy (King, 1973:15). Lenin also expected
nationalism to die with capitalism, when it transformed into socialism. Inevitable as that

by the bourgeois and the working class to free themselves of traditional rulers and create the basis for further capitalist development (see, e.g., Hroch 1985, and discussions in Connor 1984, Breuilly 1982). For more recent varieties of nationalism, Marxist scholars have focused on the unequal development of capitalism, and its effect on peripheral groupings that are better understood as territory-based classes. Their theories and insights will be discussed in the next chapter.

Since nationalism is ultimately a political ideology that holds that the political and the national should coincide, the links between the rise of the modern state and the rise of nationalism need special emphasis.[11] Breuilly (1982) in fact argues that before we can come to grips with the meaning and purpose of nationalism – the economic, social, cultural or psychological basis of nationalism – we must first understand the political workings of nationalism. He points out that nationalism must be seen as a form of politics and can make sense only in terms of the particular political context; the modern state both shapes nationalist politics and gives those politics its major objective, namely possession of the state. Overall, then, it is the political context which the modern state provides that is crucial for the emergence of nationalism as a form of politics: "The modern state centralizes and specializes significant political action. Political opposition in turn engages in centralized and specialized political action which builds upon the institutions provided by the state. In certain situations, such as with political opposition originating from outside the core territory of a multinational empire, nationalist ideology seems best to describe and promote that political opposition" (Breuilly, 1982:370).

Nationalism should therefore be seen primarily as a form of opposition politics, taking one of three forms: it can seek to break part of the state territory away from the state (separation nationalism); it can seek to take the state over and reform it (reform nationalism); and it can attempt to unite it with other states (unification nationalism). Nationalism is therefore a distinctively modern phenomenon, because only "under the modern state system could a political opposition see its objective as possession of sovereign,

---

was, it was also desirable. "In place of all forms of nationalism, Marxism advances internationalism, the amalgamation of all nations in the higher unity" (quoted in King, 1973:21). He nevertheless considered nationalism of use in furthering the cause of the revolution. Finally, Stalin was pressured into dealing with nationalism and his definition of a nation has become well-known (see above).

11   Most modernizationist theories of nationalism somehow take the emergence of the modern state into account, although their main emphasis is on cultural or economic explanations. Gellner, for instance, argues that "[t]he existence of politically centralized units and of a moral-political climate in which such centralized units are taken for granted and are treated as normative, is a necessary, though by no means a sufficient, condition of nationalism" (1980:3). However, most explicit in the link between nationalism and the emergence of the modern state has been Breuilly (1982).

territorial state power and justify that objective in the name of the society ruled by the public state. Only in the context of competing territorial sovereign states could this objective be seen as the possession of a state like other states on the basis of representing a nation like other nations" (Breuilly, 1982:360). Breuilly makes an obvious but no less important point when he concludes that the success of nationalism depends on the distinction between the state and the society: "... an effective nationalism develops only where it makes political sense for an opposition to the government to claim to represent the nation against the present state" (Breuilly, 1982:382). Therefore, if nationalism is seen as a form of opposition politics, each nationalism ultimately strives for the abolishment of the distinction between state and society; it will only remain popular as a distinctive form of politics as long as it is not successful in that ambition.

Whereas Breuilly's approach to nationalism is particularly fruitful, several remarks must be made. First of all, Breuilly's emphasis on nationalism as opposition politics downplays the extent to which nationalism is at the basis of current state policies. In a way this only shows its success, of course, but, to say the least, the impact is no less. Directed outward, nationalism may bolster the state against foreign threats. Directed inward, as will be discussed in the next chapter, nationalist state policies may in fact be responsible for the emergence of new ethnonational movements. Secondly, national movements may support the state against outsiders. Whereas this point in itself is an important addition, the focus in this book is on modern ethnonational movements, and the depiction in this context of nationalism as a form of opposition politics seems particularly useful as it stresses the need for a careful analysis of the political context in which the movement is created and takes shape. A third comment that should be made concerns Breuilly's focus on the political form. While he certainly has paid attention to the social basis of nationalist movements, his definition of the subject precludes careful analysis in that direction. However, these additions in no way detract from his basic argument.

It is therefore clear that for any kind of national movement, including ethnonationalism, the state is central to the movement's dynamics as well as its goals. Before I expand on this point in chapter two, I will end this chapter by discussing the basic approaches to recent ethnonationalism.

1.4   EXPLANATIONS OF ETHNONATIONALISM

To many scholars the recent upsurge in ethnonationalism came as a surprise. Indeed, many theorists of nationalism tend to expect the phenomenon to whither away over time.[12] Given the political reality – even in highly developed Europe – they can be criticized for underestimating the strength of the ethnonational bond and its persistence under the homogenization processes that flow from modernization (see Connor 1972, Lijphart 1977a). Reanalysing the effects of modernization, like Connor suggested, has therefore been one of the main avenues of research, and on the one hand it has therefore been argued that the character of ethnonational groups may be far more fixed than previously assumed under this process of modernization – the so-called primordialist approach (see, e.g., Shils 1957, Geertz 1963, Smith 1984). The rise of inter-ethnic conflict is a result of 'cultural incompatibility' of groups, coupled with a sudden rise in awareness of one's identity *vis à vis* another ethnic group; conflict is ultimately inevitable and revolves around right-wrong dichotomies. The recent events in former Yugoslavia have shown the general public as well as the media to be very susceptible to this particular point of view (see contrasting discussions in Meštrović et al. 1993, and Donia and Fine Jr 1994).

However, whereas the emotional nature of ethnic bonds is clear, the dynamics displayed necessitates more subtle explanations, taking into account the economic and political context in which the ethnic conflict is taking place. As discussed above, ethnic groups and the boundaries between them are not fixed, but "a matter of social definition, an interplay of the self-definition of members and the definition of other groups" (Horowitz, 1975:113, see also Barth 1969). Moreover, other interests are indeed generally bound up with ethnic differences to account for the dynamics of ethnic identification. A second perspective, called the instrumental approach, therefore stresses the dynamics of competition and change in modern society, including the roles of class and class conflict (see, e.g., the volumes edited by Glazer and Moynihan 1975a and Olzak and Nagel 1986; also Regowski 1985, Knight 1982). Various contributions deal with the capability of ethnic groups of "renewing and transforming themselves", with the impact of competition on the labour market and the housing market, with the need for local reassertion in light of increases in scale, and so forth. Unfortunately, instrumentalist theories have equally been unable to explain in a satisfactory way the timing and strength of ethnonational movements. There is often no clear correlation between the strength of ethnic movements and the presence of certain political, economic and political conditions, while most models are confronted with (too) many deviant cases. Sec-

---

12   Hobsbawm, for instance, explicitly considers nationalism past its peak, and at best "a complicating factor, or a catalyst for other developments" in the near future (Hobsbawm, 1990:181). In Deutsch's view nationalism is a stage in the process towards ever larger communication units: "Thus far, the age of nationalism has grouped people apart from each other, and may for a time continue to do so. But at the same time it is preparing them, and perhaps in part has already prepared them, for a more thoroughgoing world-wide unity than has ever been in human history" (Deutsch, 1966:191).

17

ondly, whereas instrumentalists correctly point to the goals of a movement which could explain the mobilization of the groups, they overestimate the homogeneity of the groups with respect to these political, economic and social goals. In general, severe internal strife and competition can be seen (see for example Williams 1985, and the contributions in Watson 1990). Thirdly, instrumentalists underrate the influence of emotional bonds on human behaviour and exaggerate the influence of materialist motivations on human behaviour.[13]

The study of ethnonationalism indeed needs to take into account both aspects; ethnic tension or conflict which is purely ideal or purely material constitutes a minority of all cases (McKay, 1982:402, see for a discussion Douglas 1988, Amersfoort 1991). Given the discussion on nationalism in general, however, it should be concluded that – disregarding some important exceptions that will be discussed in the next chapter – both approaches have discussed the reemergence of ethnonationalism without taking a systematic look at the political-institutional context in which it takes place. Thus, where theories on political integration and on the state in general have tended to ignore the existence of different ethnic groups, theories on ethnic conflict have tended to ignore the existence of completely different kinds of states. This is of course not to say that the state has completely been disregarded as a factor. Indeed, many authors have pointed to the fact that ethnonational movements take their cue from the existence of states as such, while case studies have often paid attention to the political arena the group had entered.

Nevertheless, the state as a structuring and mobilizing factor in the emergence of ethnonationalist tension deserves much more explicit, extensive, and comparative treatment. Recent analysis of ethnic conflicts (e.g., Keating 1990, Gleason 1990, Roeder 1991, Roessingh 1991) has indicated that the state does not just attract ethnonational interest because of the appeal of the nationalist ideology and the quality of the state's mere existence (causing the subsequent desire for control of (a part of) the state), but is a major autonomous influence regarding the definition of ethnicity itself, the ethnic homogeneity of the groups, the claims the ethnic national movement produces, and the chances of success of the ethnonational movement in achieving its goals and fulfilling its claims. Nationalism being a form of politics, there is every reason to look at the variety of states in Europe to analyze how ethnonationalist tension has been created, countered, conditioned and guided by the different political structures that are found on the continent. In the next chapter, therefore, the role of the state, its autonomous influence on ethnonational conflict, and the variations between states will be reviewed.

13 Horowitz (1985:104) therefore bashes the ones who consider "ethnicity ... not the collective will to exist, but the existing will to collect".

2

The State and Ethnonationalism

In the previous chapter I introduced the concept of ethnonationalism and discussed its theoretical background. Ethnonationalism was considered a sentiment that may activate a political movement of an ethnonational group for more autonomy or independence. In this chapter the relation between the state and ethnonationalism will be the central subject of the discussion. The main argument will be that although the political nature of ethnonationalism has found expression in several studies on the interaction between ethnic groups and the state, the autonomous influence of the state on the development and dynamics of ethnonational activism needs more careful examination. After a short introduction to the phenomenon of the state, the interaction of ethnonational groups and the state will be discussed. In the third section of this chapter I will look into the differences between European states that may influence the emergence and structuration of ethnonationalist activism. That section will also contain several propositions regarding the effects of these differences.

2.1 INTRODUCTION: THE GROWTH OF THE MODERN STATE

Despite some challenges, the modern state is now the single accepted model of politico-territorial organization world-wide. Unfortunately, characterizing the state is just as awkward as characterizing 'nations' and 'nationalism'. A valid attempt was made at the 1933 Montevideo Convention on Rights and Duties of States, where the state was defined as "a person of international law [which] should possess the following qualifications: a) a permanent population; b) a defined territory; c) government; and d) capacity to enter into relations with other states" (in Hannum, 1990:15 – 16). The state is considered sovereign, meaning that it has the ability to determine its relations with outside states by itself and that no other state interferes in the affairs that take place within its territorial boundaries. This sovereignty is, of course, ultimately protected by the willingness and ability of the state to prove it by force. Apart from being a sovereign partner in interstate relations, however, the state is also the embodiment of political power in a particular society; control over internal affairs is just as central to the state's functioning as sovereignty among its peers (see, e.g., Giddens, 1987:20; Badie and Birnbaum, 1983:105).

The type of state that has been most successful in claiming control over territory has been called the national state (Tilly 1992). Along the way it proved more successful than political alternatives, such as the city-state and the feudal state. Central in the emergence of the national state has been the use of violence and coercive power, both externally (waging war) and internally (pacification) (see in particular Tilly 1975, Giddens 1987, Poggi 1990). Nevertheless, the rise of the state has certainly not resulted solely from the concentration of coercive power. After all, it emerged amidst the rising tide of capitalism, which fundamentally changed the relationship between the rulers and the ruled. The ruled – in particular in the cities where the most capital was accumulated – could provide the rulers with funds, either through fiscal extraction or through loans. With these funds armies and bureaucracies could be maintained which, in turn, improved the state's capacity for fund raising. Overall – and despite much diversity in the process – the state, its bureaucracy and capitalism developed in "mutual association" (Badie and Birnbaum, 1983:21; see also discussions in, e.g., Johnston 1982; Johnston 1989; Taylor 1989; Finer 1975; Giddens, 1987:148–160, Tilly 1992).

The increasing demands the state made on its population increased the need to use means, other than pure force, to legitimate these demands. Needless to say, after chapter one, nationalist ideology was a particularly powerful argument, nicely combining ideology with the increasing need for standardized languages, state-wide uniform educational systems, and state-wide recruitment of soldiers (Breuilly, 1982:53). By extending control, and legitimizing it by the idea of the 'nation,' the connections between state and society became more and more intense, with increasing claims from groups not previously involved in the political process. Along the way the importance of violence-related officials in the modern state diminished, and the state's machinery became more diversified and complex. The widening of tasks resulted in an enormous increase in the share of the state in social life; for example, government expenditure as a percentage of gross national product can nowadays reach as high as 55% in some cases in Western Europe (see Poggi, 1990:110; Lane and Ersson, 1991:325ff).

The state's power *vis à vis* society and aspects of the internal operation of the state are generally written down in the constitution. Constitutions, or 'Power Maps' as they are called by Duchacek (1973), regulate the relations among state institutions and between the state institutions and (specific parts of) the society. Moreover, constitutional law and constitutional arrangements are an important example of the context the state provides for the relations *within* society, not only structuring relationships between civil society and the state in a polity but also structuring many crucial relationships within civil society (Palley, 1978:3). Constitutionalism has become the generally accepted way of describing not only the various central, regional and local agencies in charge of legislation, administration and adjudication, but also the way of describing the ideology of the state's leaders and the legitimacy of a new revolutionary regime (that will often introduce a new constitution). In former colonies, the constitution sometimes even forms the surrogate common history of the population (Duchacek, 1973:9). The state's policies are guided by the state's political system, the main elements of which are usually contained in the constitution. A wide array of myths and symbols are used to strengthen the legitimacy of the state, stressing the unity of the people and of the state's territory.

In sum, the state has grown to be a powerful centralized political unit, enveloping and controlling previously autonomous localities, often inhabited by culturally distinct communities (Kirby 1989, Tarrow 1977). It attempts to maintain a stable society – if possible by peaceful means, but if necessary by coercion – under the pretence of the unity of the state, both cultural and territorial. However, the state's legitimacy depends heavily on the population's perception of the political system as reflecting its ethnic and cultural identity. At this point tension clearly arises because in most states the image of unity does not reflect social reality. Largely due to the dominance of liberal, Marxist and organic-statist (corporatist) views on state-society relations, for too long this tension between ethnic diversity and state unity has been neglected (Kauppi 1984). The next section deals with this tension, and with several theoretical approaches that have been developed since the beginning of the 1970s.

2.2   THE STATE AND ETHNONATIONALISM

If the process of state-building is regarded as the institutional penetration of territory originating from a centre, the remaining resistance by cultural communities to this penetration may best be analyzed and described as a (set of) core-periphery structure(s). Hechter (1975), for instance, explains the reemergence of inter-ethnic conflict in Great Britain by analyzing specifically the unequal capitalist development on British territory, which had lead to a 'cultural division of labour', or a geographical overlap between cultural differences and the relative position in the capitalist system. This exploitation of cultural groups by other cultural groups, called internal colonialism, can lead to the resistance of the exploited ethnic group.[1] How-

---

1   A variant of this is the analysis by Nairn (1977), who stresses the uneven development of cultural regions under capitalism, causing the development of ethnic-based nationalist movements both in advanced regions and less advanced or declining regions. His perspective leaves room for cases like the Basque movement that do not fit the internal colonialism model well. Critiques of both models can be found in, e.g., Esman 1977, Williams 1980, Agnew 1981, Orridge and Williams 1982, and Connor 1984.

ever, the empirical basis of this perspective is limited, ethnonationalism being supported by movements too diverse in class content and located in regions too diverse in economic development. Moreover, as will be discussed in the chapters on Czechoslovakia and Belgium, economic equalization, which should cause the disappearance of ethnic activism, in practice does not diminish its relevance.

The incorporation of peripheries nevertheless remains an important process that may trigger ethnic activism. Fundamental theoretical work in this respect has been undertaken by Rokkan and Urwin (1982, 1983), who show, however, that in the process of state-building, centre-periphery polarity on cultural, economic and political dimensions at the same time is unlikely to occur. Moreover, the territorial diffusion of economic development, cultural standardization and political incorporation usually follows quite different paths, and the circumstances of mobilization for each group are therefore very different. The impact is only similar to the extent that the regionalist basis of most ethnic political movements in the state's territorial periphery means that they have a claim on the state which is distinct from claims by other types of groups: they "identify with, and make claims upon the central government on behalf of territories and groups that are not coincident with state boundaries and national populations" (Rokkan and Urwin, 1982:8).[2] The exact avenue towards politicization is thus variable, and the politicized ethnicity surfaces and hardens along the most accessible and yielding fault line of potential cleavage available (Rothschild, 1981:96, see also Brass 1985).

From a bird's eye view ethnonationalism can therefore be explained as an immediate backlash from unfulfilled promises explicitly or implicitly phrased by the state. Political impotence, or even total disappearance of the decision-making power of the state, may cause the state to lose its legitimacy with part of the population and account for its increasing image of being quite dispensable. There is however a much wider range of possibilities that can trigger dissatisfaction with the state's performance. Of particular importance, because it is a central function of the state as we have seen, is when the state appears incapable of resolving problems of internal or external security, or of providing for equal distribution of resources over its territory.[3] Clearly, the ethnonational group, with its usual territorial basis,

2 It is interesting to note in this respect, as Murphy argues convincingly, how territories are used by subnational groups in these circumstances. He points out that territories, as human constructs, serve to change social relations and to redefine the depth and scope of social problems (Murphy, 1988b:147, see also Murphy 1988a).

3 Indeed, Urwin (1982) therefore suggests that ethnonational activism in Western European peripheries may very well be part of a greater wave of resistance against unequal territorial redistribution of resources under the welfare state; distinctive cultural threats can serve as an easy base for mobilization. See extensive discussions in Glazer and Moynihan 1975b, Esman 1977, Lijphart 1977a, Williams 1980, Rothschild 1981, Orridge 1982, Keating 1991, Watson 1990, Amersfoort 1993.

provides a particularly good example of a group for which an unsatisfactory level of status on various dimensions can easily be found.[4] Moreover, although the failure of state performance might and in fact does trigger all sorts of group protest that do not have an ethnic content (e.g., class), the pervasiveness of ethnonational sentiments must be found in the fact that, in contrast to other types of groups, ethnonational communities combine both socio-economic and cultural-political reasons for political mobilization against the state (Rothschild, 1981:235).

The political elite that mobilizes the groups because of this real or perceived mismatch of cultural, economic and political geographies have been dubbed 'ethnic entrepreneurs' (Smith 1981, 1982).[5] Indeed, as many argue, the problematic entrance of ethnic intelligentsia into the state machinery may by itself provide enough incentive to spark off ethnic mobilization. Ethnonationalism is therefore connected with prestige and with the political struggle for prestige by ethnic elites (Horowitz 1985). The concept of prestige links the individual attachment to ethnic identity to the political struggle of ethnic elites for a piece of the political pie, because "[i]f the need to feel worthy is a fundamental human requirement, it is satisfied in considerable measure by belonging to groups that are in turn regarded as worthy" (Horowitz, 1985:185). A test of the worthiness of an ethnic group is the extent to which it gets political affirmation, politics becoming the "allocation of prestige," and power becoming indeed a goal in itself. This political affirmation of prestige may stretch from the language of the group becoming a official language to a fair share of the positions in the civil service. Relations between ethnic groups turn into continuous comparisons in which relative positions within the state become litmus tests.

In sum, whereas ethnonational conflict is often described in terms of tension between groups, the state plays a central role in striking a new balance between modern identities and ethnonational roots. The state is, because of its increasing importance and visible penetration, increasingly checked to determine whether it represents all sections of the population and whether its distributive policies are satisfactory. If they are found wanting, dissatisfaction will lead to demands directed at the state. Moreover, and fundamental for understanding ethnonationalism as a form of politics, the state has itself become a central object of comparison: a prize for the taking, and

4 However, as Rothschild (1981) argues, even without the territorial component, the patterns of differences between groups can be sufficient to have a group perceive their ethnic ties as systematically affecting their place and fate in the political and socio-economic structures of their state and society.

5 Indeed, the recent developments in the Soviet Union indicate that the influence of the various intelligentsia in the development of nationalism in the republics has been considerable. The intelligentsia not only helped develop the ideology of national self-consciousness, but influenced the process of the realization of national interests as well, by which the different stages in nationalist development of the movements can be linked to the different types of elites that get involved because of their frustration over the distribution of resources, power, and so forth (Dobrizheva 1991, see also Dostál 1991).

an indicator of group status. The type of demands ethnonational groups put forward reflect this central role of the state.

2.2.1 Ethnogeographical make-up and the generation of demands

Whereas the state may be central to all ethnonational groups, it is highly unlikely that they will put forward the same demands. The ethnonational geography of a group – including such basic components as size, concentration and location – partly determines the range of options open to a group. Thus, a large, concentrated ethnic group (but a minority nonetheless) which is living at the edge of the state's territory is much more likely to raise far-reaching political and territorial demands than small, scattered minorities that are found throughout the country. The ethnogeographical situation can be analyzed for the states as a whole, as well as for constituent republics in federations, if the ethnonational tension plays out at that level (see Anderson 1990, Anderson 1989, Dostál 1991). However, systematic comparison of cases has generally not been undertaken (for an important exception, see Gurr 1993).[6] A further important aspect concerning the geography of the group is its location in relation to the main centres of the state (Mikesell and Murphy, 1991:586). This not only involves the centre of the country in a political, cultural or economic sense, but also the central nodes of the group itself. In fact, Murphy (1990a) concludes that no ethnic groups have succeeded in successfully articulating demands that do not have a major city located in the group's living area.

The character of demands is also influenced by the 'cultural distance' to competing groups and to the general character of the state. 'Cultural distance' is of course a rather indeterminate qualification, but denotes the great variety in cultural differences between groups that can be found. Language is often a major issue, because of its visibility (or audibility), but religion is sometimes considered to be more pervasive and enduring, while social customs, historical origin, and urban versus rural residence also define the span of the cultural gap (Gurr, 1993:38ff).[7] However, the internal

---

6   The position the group finds itself in is of course subject to change. For example, differences in demographic growth, often inversely related to the differences in economic growth, add their own dynamics. Thus Kosovo, while lacking severely in economic growth compared to Slovenia, almost doubled in population between 1955 and 1983, while Slovenia experienced only 25% demographic growth in the same period (Stanovi, 1992:361). Needless to say the processes of internal and external migration are also of great importance, thoroughly changing the circumstances for the group or groups in question. This not only poses a problem for comparison, but it is also a major political variable because migration might be precisely the irritant that sparks off ethnonational mobilization.

7   Gurr also uses ethnicity or nationality, because his interest is in cultural groups in general.

Table 2.1   Possible demands by ethnic groups

1) Exit:	e.g., union with kindred, independent state, control of own land and resources
2) Autonomy:	e.g., religious freedom, political autonomy, cultural autonomy, subsidies to sustain autonomy
3) Access:	e.g., power sharing, civil and political rights, cultural rights, economic rights, equal opportunities, compensation
4) Control:	e.g., reversal of power, privileged access to state power, protection of economic privileges

Source: based on Gurr 1993

Note: in his 'Minorities at Risk' project Gurr distinguishes six types of communal groups (ethnonational, indigenous, ethnoclasses, religious militant sects, advantaged communal contenders, and disadvantaged communal contenders) that voice partly different, partly similar demands. The table is a compilation of these demands.

cultural unity of each group in itself is often questionable as within each group other characteristics and loyalties often cut across the one that is considered salient by observers.

A great variety of demands may therefore be found in reality. Mikesell and Murphy (1991) make a very useful distinction between demands that are directed at inclusion in the state and its machinery, and demands that are directed at exclusion from the state. Dissatisfied groups will often demand a combination of both, the latter category having territorial implications and therefore more serious consequences for the state.[8] The classification in table 2.1 offers the basic types of exit from the state, autonomy within the state, access to resources from the state, and control over the state. Each category involves several subvarieties, and, due to the diverse circumstances and backgrounds of groups, not all groups will be able to put forward all kinds of demands. Indeed, neither are the demands brought to the attention of the state in a similar fashion. Use of violence is usually restricted to a small section of the group, but the high visibility of violent actions may have a great impact on the subsequent negotiations between states and ethnic groups (Zariski 1989). The problem with all sorts of activism, however, is to what extent the movement (which it then becomes) represents the population that forms the ethnic group, with its usually complex ethnogeographical distribution, blurred ethnic borders, and unclear pattern of real and perceived socio-economic and political deprivation. A quite intricate

---

8   The categorization by Mikesell and Murphy underplays possibilities for non-territorial forms of autonomy, however (see Roessingh and Sytsema 1993).

and highly dynamic triangular relationship between groups, movements, and the state emerges. In fact, the state has the option of finding solutions for the movement itself, or for part of the movement, or for the group as a whole. It will question the movement's legitimacy in representing the group, favour some factions over others, support some differentiating characteristics but not others (e.g., economic improvement, but not linguistic autonomy), and so forth. The question then becomes whether the movement is able to keep its internal homogeneity in interests and goals, as well as in methods. This triangular relationship forms a major complicating factor in the analysis of state – ethnic group interaction, and I will return to it in the next chapter.

2.2.2 The state's response

From the perspective of the state, the activism of ethnonational movements is clearly somewhat of an anomaly. The challenge to unity – both in an ideological sense as a challenge to state nationalism, as well as in a territorial sense in the case of autonomy demands or separation movements – is usually not welcomed by states. The territorial integrity of the state mentally and politically inhibits the implementation of flexible answers to the demands. This is true in particular when spill-over groups are involved.[9] Nevertheless, certain elements of ethnicity are hard to pass by for the state, even if only for reasons of control and surveillance; in particular language, because "the state can pretend to be blind, but it cannot be deaf mute" (Zolberg, 1977:140). The expanding bureaucracy and mass education have in fact necessitated active language policies by the state, and new ethnic demands raise the same kinds of questions from time to time. What is true for language is also true for most other aspects of cultural diversity.

Basically the state can follow two options: it can attempt to eradicate the ethnic differences in its territory, or it can choose to accommodate the demands that stem from these differences (McGarry and O'Leary, 1993:4).

---

9   In Eastern Europe, many newly independent countries were forced to sign treaties regarding their spill-over minorities after World War One, to protect these minorities against the viciousness of local nationalism. The treaties focused on the right to equality of treatment and non-discrimination, on citizenship, on the use of minority languages, on the establishment and control of charitable, religious, and social institutions, on 'equitable' financial support to minority schools (in which instruction at the primary level would be in the minority language) and other institutions, and on recognition of the supremacy of laws protecting minority rights over other statutes. A certain degree of territorial autonomy was, besides the Åland Islands, officially provided for Ruthenia in Czechoslovakia, the Valachs in Greece, and the Transylvanian Saxons and Szeklers in Romania; these territorial arrangements were very much an exception (Hannum, 1990:52–5). However, the new states offered only piecemeal implementation. In Western Europe there are now interstate treaties on South-Tirol, on the Danes in Germany and the Germans in Denmark, on Croats and Slovenes in Austria, on Northern Ireland, and on the Åland Islands (Minority Rights Group 1990).

Belonging to the first category, options such as genocide, expulsion, and population exchanges have been widely practised. Horrifying examples of genocide are of course those perpetrated by the Nazis and by Stalin, but it is certainly not a thing of the past; witness Rwanda and former Yugoslavia.[10] It may be noted that the passive acceptance by the state of genocide inflicted by one group on another falls within the same category. Only slightly less horrifying is mass expulsion and regulated expulsion or population exchanges, which can result from civil wars or from deliberate policies. The recent examples of 'ethnic cleansing' (sic) in former Yugoslavia fall within this category. International endorsement has at times been found, starting with the Greek-Turkish exchanges in the beginning of the 1920s. Migration policies can also be used the other way around, in order to 'minorize' the population in the 'target area' and assimilate them. A third solution to eradicate differences is to allow secession of the group. This does occur sometimes peacefully (e.g., Norway from Sweden in 1905, Iceland from Denmark in 1944, Slovakia from Czechoslovakia in 1992), but this is rare. Of course, lack of central state power or the unwillingness to use it may also create this result (e.g., former Soviet Union). Given the ethnogeographical complexity often found, secession is generally hampered by the creation of new minorities that are related to the former dominant group; this makes secession even more unacceptable for the original state. A final solution to eradicate differences is by the state to encourage assimilation. There are many ways in which the state can attempt to do so, including internal forced migration (speeding up mobilization so to speak), the forced eradication of ethnic markers, and so forth. The policies by the Bulgarian government in the 1980s fall within this category (see chapter four), but examples are abundant. As has been said in the previous chapter, however, even if objective differences disappear, psychological assimilation may still be far off. All these solutions can be propelled by ethnic demands, although, as will be discussed further down, the state may initiate them for other reasons. If the state does not want to eradicate ethnic differences, this still does not necessarily spell good news from the perspective of the minority ethnic group. The state can use hegemonic control to keep ethnic demands at bay, for instance by coopting part of the ethnic elite but leaving out further measures. Ignoring the differences is also a favourite strategy, although this is hard to keep up in the fase of sustained demands.

If the state wants to deal with the demands in more positive ways, some form of accommodation or autonomy is needed. As Hannum puts it: "Personal and political autonomy is in some real sense the right to be different and to be left alone; to preserve, protect, and promote values which are beyond the legitimate reach of the rest of society" (Hannum, 1990:4, see

---

10   In a thorough analysis, Bauman (1989) argues that the Holocaust was in fact distinctively modern and "not an irrational outflow of the not-yet-fully-eradicated residues of pre-modern barbarity" (p.17).

overviews in Hall 1979, Hannum 1990, and Gurr 1993). Autonomy can be personal-based or explicitly territory-based. As McRae (1975) illustrates for language policy, the personal principle means that everyone, throughout the territory of the state, is entitled to the use of their own language, for instance, in dealing with the state or in pursuing education. Other forms of this non-territorial type of accommodation include concessions that deal with improved access to the economy (preferential treatment, subsidies), to the state (e.g., proportional representation in the bureaucracy), and to the political arena (e.g., ethnic seats in parliament). Cultural group rights, to be implemented in the whole territory of the state, also fall within this category. This is the kind of autonomy propagated by the Austrian socialists Renner and Bauer (see Ra'anan et al. 1991). An intricate method of non-territorial accommodation in the political field is consociational power sharing. As described in Lijphart (1977b), this involves close cooperation in the decision-making process by the elites of the cultural groups, each of which has veto power.[11]

Much attention is usually paid to territorial forms of state concessions (Murphy 1989). Part of this attention stems from the idea that a territorial arrangement is somehow superior to non-territorial forms; as Ben Gurion put it, in the absence of territorial autonomy personal autonomy is groundless in every sense of the word (in Dinstein, 1981:293). In the field of language policies, a territorial solution means in its extreme form that everybody within certain geographical limits is forced to speak that language. In general, autonomy involves territorially based concessions involving specific rights that the group can exercise in a delimited territory. Further along the path are cantonization or federalization on an ethnic basis, partitioning the machinery of the state itself. This differs from autonomy in the sense that in a genuine federation there are separate tasks set apart for both levels of government, while there are also some shared tasks; moreover, the constituent republics have direct influence on the decision-making process at the central level, in particular with respect to changes in the constitution. Territorial concessions are stretched to the limit in a confederation, which basically means a treaty between nominally independent countries. However, a confederation is usually the start of cooperation instead of the result of devolution of power by the centre.

In practice, the state will often use several approaches simultaneously. It is for instance difficult to picture a successful implementation of group rights without some form of consociational decision-making, in particular on cultural issues or education. Moreover, individual rights are often a *sine qua non* for successful accommodation of demands by ethnonational

---

11   The power sharing arrangement is combined with the existence of separate and autonomous cultural segments in society. However, the usefulness of this arrangement for cleavages that are more ascriptive and intense remains very much debated. More on this form of accommodation will be said in chapters six and eight.

groups: if minority members do not enjoy civil and political rights as individuals, one can hardly expect sufficient accommodation in the cultural or political fields at the group level; indeed, their imminent subjugation and even assimilation are very likely (Stanovčić 1992:364). Of course, official policies do not tell everything, even if written down in the constitution, and the notions regarding the accommodation of ethnic diversity on the state's territory are often just propaganda intended for (part of) the population of the state or for other countries.[12]

2.2.3 The effect of solutions and non-solutions upon ethnonational movements

It is clear now why the state is often the goal of the mobilization by ethnonational groups and how the state may respond to demands by those groups. However, whereas the above analysis is perhaps illuminating and shows the almost infinite range of possibilities in state responses, there are still many questions that remain unanswered. The reason for this is that in the context of ethnic group – state interaction, state policies are not just reactive.

Indeed, recent theoretical contributions to the social sciences have increasingly regarded the state as an autonomous force in the shaping of society (see discussions in Mann 1984, Skocpol 1985, Stepan 1978, Clark and Dear 1984, Taylor 1989, Caporaso 1989). This role stems in particular from the state's ability to centralize its resources territorially.[13] This centrality enabled the state to use the logistical advantages of centralized power, which could be mobilized effectively against any particular civil group in society, or any outside aggressors, even though the state in itself may have been inferior in overall resources (Mann, 1984:204). By combining multiple functions in the most efficient way – such as the maintenance of order, military aggression, the maintenance of communication structures and economic redistribution – the state created room to manoeuvre between the various interest groups in society and could play them off against each other. Since civil groups were unable to centralize themselves in a similar

---

12   Many authors have discussed solutions and state responses more extensively. Recent discussions are for instance found in Stanovčić 1992, Coakley 1992b, Gurr 1993, Esman 1992, Hannum 1990, McGarry and O'Leary 1993, Mikesell and Murphy 1991, and Roessingh 1991. Of earlier date, but very useful, are Connor 1980 and Palley 1978. A separate method that falls somewhat outside the scope of this book is arbitration by third parties, either within the state, or, most common, by outsiders. This may involve active intervention, peace-making, peace-keeping, and so forth (see Ryan 1990, Zartman 1990, Gottlieb 1993).

13   As Mann puts it: "Unlike economic, ideological or military groups in civil society, the state elite's resources radiate authoritatively outwards from a centre but stop at defined territorial boundaries. The state is, indeed, a *place* both a central place and a unified territorial reach" (Mann, 1984:198).

fashion, they were actually forced to endorse the increase of autonomous state power. Over time, the autonomous power of the state has developed from the despotic power of the state elite – defined as the range of actions which the elite is empowered to undertake without routine, institutionalized negotiation with groups in civil society – to also include, for modern states, infrastructural power – the capacity of the state to actually penetrate civil society, and to implement political decisions logistically throughout the realm (see Mann 1984).

The autonomous role of the state operates both through the 'goal-oriented actions of state officials,' and through the 'structural configurations' that set the political agenda and stimulate or hamper the organization of societal groups and interests (Skocpol, 1985:21). Whereas the first appears rather straightforward, the latter needs more explanation. In particular the institutionalization of the state and its elements – meaning by institutionalization the tendency of patterns of behaviour, norms or structures to persist through time – tends to constrain and structure the lives and actions of groups and individuals, often stretching beyond the institution's initial purpose (Krasner 1989).[14] Powerful examples of institutions are such diverse elements as laws, tax privileges, and educational regulations, but also the institutions that regulate political decision-making such as parliament, and the territorial elements in the state organization. The institutional permanence of the state structure, both in form and in policies, has long-range effects.

It is to be expected, therefore, that the state has a clear autonomous impact on the development of ethnonationalist sentiment and ethnonationalist movements through its policies and institutional structure. The reactive approach, however, fails to systematically question the consequences, in terms of the resulting level of ethnonationalism, of state policies that deal with ethnonational demands. Thus, although all the policies described above may be used by central governments to alter the context for ethnic group – state interaction, the impact of these policies is usually not discussed. For instance, high-handed policies directed at the cultural identity of the ethnic group that fall short of total suppression, no matter how unfair or intentionally repressive, are likely to have the opposite effect. In fact, as Murphy puts it, "[t]he story of ethnonationalism is in many ways the history of the development of a sense of a common threat by a people who are made to feel as one because the threat focuses attention on some shared attribute" (Murphy, 1989:415). The non-response of the government, on the other hand, may lead to violence in the long run. For instance, Gurr

---

14 Krasner even takes it one step further by arguing that the character of the individual himself is to some extent derivative from the existing institutional structure, including the existence of the state as a whole. As he points out, citizenship itself is bestowed on the individual by the state without which it would have no meaning, but it influences his identity to such an extent that he actually wants to die for this political unit.

argues that for European ethnonational movements that resort to violence no less than an average of thirteen years passed between the moment the first demands were raised and the moment the violence started (Gurr, 1993:145; see also Zariski 1989:263–4, Hannum, 1990:71–73).

Paradoxically, a genuinely accommodating response may equally turn out to be counterproductive, in the sense that it fails to lead to the eradication of ethnonationalist tension or to the abatement of group aspirations (Rudolph and Thompson 1985, Rabushka and Shepsle 1972).[15] Indeed, the institutional ways in which the state deals with regional demands may encourage and transform ethnic movements.[16] It may be expected that territorial policies and demarcations are of particular relevance in this respect, due to the importance of territory in both state formation and nation formation. Creating a territorially demarcated kind of autonomy, or perhaps even an administrative subdivision, may profoundly alter group identification and segmentation in society; this may work both to the advantage and the disadvantage of the group (see Murphy 1989, Roessingh 1991). Related to this is the notion that there could be all sorts of token concessions turned into real effects. There are of course many examples of differences between the letter and the initial spirit of the constitution and the practice of the political system, but the presence of constitutional guarantees may ultimately produce unintended self-fulfilling prophecies; most famous is no doubt the secession option in the Soviet constitution (see the next section for further discussion). In that sense, institutional plurality may form an unexpected problem in particular for a state in crisis, as it forms a well-defined framework within which ethnonational demands can be articulated and the tensions can build up (Amersfoort 1993). Finally, states may even willingly stress ethnonational differences for their own purposes.[17]

15 Rabushka and Shepsle (1972) for instance are very sceptical on this point and argue that the resolution of ethnic conflict in a democratic framework is extremely difficult if not impossible. The logic of party systems that have their base in ethnic differences have also been extensively discussed by Horowitz (1985:346–363), who shows how and why ethnic parties have a tendency to crowd out other types of parties. As he points out, electoral systems cannot manufacture ethnic and sub-ethnic divisions, but they can certainly help sustain them once they have crossed the threshold of political relevance. However, see the comments by Amersfoort and Wusten (1981), who argue that ethnic party systems are not more prone to degenerate into violence than systems based on other cleavages.

16 Comparing the Basques and the Andalusians, Greenwood (1985) for instance argues that the Basques have developed a strong sense of separateness as a result of central state attempts to reduce tax privileges; this helped to create Basque identity. Andalusian regionalism emerged as a result of the 1978 constitution, merely lagging in time the Basque's sense of separateness. Indeed, as Tarrow points out, centre-periphery relations are regulated by the centre through the same organizational structure that provides a channel for the periphery to influence the centre (Tarrow, 1977:29).

17 Enloe (1980b) has for instance analyzed how the state can use ethnicity in forming and deploying military units in order to increase control. A similar point is made by Coakley (1992b), who suggests the possibility of unsolicited support for ethnic groups by a state that desires to counter demands by other groups. By making similar concessions to other groups the state of course hopes to diminish the advantage for the first group, but it can result in major backlashes against the state.

Moreover, ethnonationalism may thrive as a result of the institutional context the state provides apart from the specific question of state – ethnic group relations. It is to be expected that groups mobilize not just on the basis of their complaints, but also on the basis of the possibilities that are provided by the political structure of the state. In a liberal democracy, for instance, mobilization can occur through a regionally based ethnonational party, in an alliance with a state-wide party, through a cross-party umbrella organization, by negative mobilization (non-voting or protest voting), or, of course, through extralegal action (see, e.g., Williams 1985). In contrast, as will be discussed below, the possibilities for voicing demands under authoritarian systems are of course severely limited. The institutional structure of the state has often been in place long before tension arises, and this has presented the ethnonational movements in Europe with completely different contexts in which to work, and with different sets of policies against which to react. Furthermore, similar mobilization may yield substantially different results. In the nineteenth century, for instance, the ultimate impact of rather weak movements on the Ottoman Empire was much more serious than that of more dynamic movements on the Habsburg Monarchy, mainly as a result of the differences in internal political structure of the two empires (Breuilly, 1982:90–110).

In fact, state autonomy and state power are not at the same level everywhere and at all times. Not only do the incentives for autonomous action by state officials differ over time, but also "the very *structural* potentials for autonomous state actions change over time, as organizations of coercion and administration undergo transformations, both internally and in their relations to societal groups and to representative parts of government" (Skocpol, 1985:14). As a result then, the degree of autonomy of the state *vis à vis* society varies in space, with different countries experiencing different levels in the saliency of the state in society (see, e.g., Nettl 1969, Badie and Birnbaum 1983, Wusten 1993). It is therefore useful to look specifically and systematically at different states to analyze how they affect ethnonationalist activism, or, in the words of Rothschild, what is "... the potency of political institutions and political decisions in affecting the configuration of ethnic groups, the cutting edge of ethnic conflict, and the very content of ethnicity per se" (Rothschild, 1981:99). Thus, whereas ethnicity may be present under all sorts of political systems, it will not have the same relevance and dynamics under all types of systems.

2.3   DIVERSITY IN POLITICAL SYSTEMS

Where the relation between state and society is concerned Duverger (1973) sees two general categories of states: liberal states that weaken the authority of the state to the advantage of the freedom of its citizens, and authoritarian states that, in contrast, increase the authority of the state at the expense of the freedom of its citizens.[18] Both kinds of autonomous power will be much more important in authoritarian systems than in liberal systems.

In fact, there is a basic difference in philosophy about individuals and groups that lies behind this distinction between authoritarian and liberal states, emphasizing either the collective or the individual as the central unit in society (Duverger 1973; Berki 1979). Thus, on the one hand groups (or even society as a whole) are considered to be the central unit, of which individuals are only the building blocks that derive their meaning from their membership in the group. This *transcendentalist* perception emphasizes that man primarily belongs to a moral community; the interests of this community go beyond the interests of its members, and public interest not only delimits but also morally defines the proper pursuits of individuals who belong to it. This, as Berki concludes, is "an idealistic principle, since it understands men not as they are, but as they ought to be" (Berki, 1979:3). State power needs not to be limited, as it represents the interests of the group (society) itself, for instance when acting against maladjusted individuals. The liberal approach on the other hand holds that individuals form the central elements in society. Every organization in society, including the state itself, should result from their combined interests. This *instrumentalist* perception holds that man belongs primarily to an interest community, which exists and functions beyond the individual, is not directly related to his moral feelings and aims, and which can be joined voluntarily and when deemed most profitable for the individual's private aims. The public interest, then, is the sum of individual interest and nothing beyond that, and the community is not based on uniformity, but on diversity and conflict.[19]

18   This main distinction is reflected in the following elements: 1) how (and whether) rulers are elected by the population; 2) how the state is organized with regard to the division of powers between the various organs of the state; and 3) how the state's power over society is limited. Although Duverger's discussion of these three dimensions is admirably clear in itself, they are certainly related. In fact, the complexity of any analysis of the variety of political systems in this way shows in his final classification, which is based more on the historical evolution of the political systems than on his own formal discussion. Thus, he distinguishes between systems that followed the British example, those that followed the example of the United States, and those that followed the example of the Soviet Union. Other attempts at classification more or less run along similar lines, with formal and historical argumentation intertwined (see Van Damme 1984). More recently, separate attention has also been paid to political systems that have emerged in developing countries and that are considered to contain specific elements of their own.

19   Corporatism (or organic-statism) is often considered as a third way of describing state-society relations; the constituent parts are considered to originate from the division of labour that follows industrialization, each party forming a particular kind of interest.

These philosophies result in highly divergent perspectives of the relation between states and societies. In Duverger's terms, in authoritarian systems, on the one hand the state's limitation of power over society will be lessened, while on the other hand the population's influence on decision-making within the state will be minimalized; put in an extreme way, one can differentiate between state-led societies and society-led states. Although they have now disappeared among the European family of states, the most influential form in which the transcendentalist perception of state-led societies has been implemented politically in twentieth-century Europe has of course been the communist states, i.e., the Soviet Union from 1917 onwards and in Eastern Europe after the Second World War. It is therefore useful to differentiate between European states by using a first dimension that distinguishes communist from liberal-democratic political systems; this may be called a politico-economic dimension, although it is particularly the political side of the power balance between state and society which will be central in this study.[20]

Of course, the distinction between communist and liberal-democratic systems is not the only meaningful differentiation between European states. A second distinction is the one between unitary and federalized states. In federalized states, the division of powers not only follows functional lines (e.g., the executive, the legislative, the judiciary), but also a geographical one. The basic idea is that federalism is an exercise in territorially based pluralism: by constitutionally dividing state power across various geographical layers of government, the democratic character of the state is improved and the defence of society against central state power is better guaranteed. However, whereas organized and guaranteed pluralism in itself may prevent the concentration of power in the hands of a few, this dimension remains somewhat ambiguous when it comes to differences in the autonomous power of the state; after all, the constituent republics are themselves part of the state machinery. Moreover, in the context of this study it must be noted that federations in many cases are meant to reflect in the political system the geographical diversity within society itself. In other words, seen from this perspective it is as much a technique to organize politically the geographical diversity within society as it is a technique to divide power within the state. There is a danger of confusing cause and effect, and of confusing solutions to ethnonational diversity with the impact of that same solution on ethnonational diversity. I will return to this problem in section 2.3.2.

---

20 It may be added that this dimension is not only of interest because it distinguishes between political systems in terms of the power relation between the state and the society, but also details in the case of communist states two conflicting examples of the transcendentalist approach; as has briefly been touched upon in chapter one, there is a clear tension between group conceptions based on class identity and group conceptions based on ethnonational identity. I will return to this tension in the next section.

In this study then, states are distinguished on the basis of their power *vis à vis* the society in their territory, as operationalised by two dimensions. On the basis of a politico-economic dimension, which distinguishes between communist and liberal-democratic political systems, we can analyze how differences in institutional form and policies that emanate from completely different political ideologies affect the relation of the state to ethnonational groups in society. On the basis of a territorial dimension, which distinguishes between unitary and federalized states, we can analyze how the differences in the geographical division of power within the state affect this same relationship. It should be pointed out, however, that the two dimensions do not completely derive from the same kind of reasoning. Whereas both indicate a difference in the capacity of the state to mobilize power in relation to society, the first dimension concentrates on the state suppressing or not suppressing forms of alternative power in society, whereas the second is based on the facilitation or non-facilitation of pluralism in society within the state. I will return to this problem in the last chapter of this book. In the remainder of this chapter I will discuss the two dimensions more extensively.

2.3.1 Dimension 1: differences in political-economic organization

As follows from the discussion thus far, the states on the two poles of this dimension have quite a different organization, and quite different roles to fulfil in society. Two aspects can be distinguished that illustrate the diverse perceptions on the role of the state in society and that reflect the difference in state power *vis à vis* society. First of all, under communism no separate existence of ideological and economic power was allowed in society. This meant that all the means of production, and all ideological life, was to come under control of the state (or under control of the Party that was supposedly controlled by the proletariat and which in turn controlled the state). However, local circumstances have not always made this possible, and differences existed between communist states to the extent to which they collectivized agriculture and planned economic enterprise (see, e.g., Staar 1982). In liberal-democratic systems the basic principle is that economic life operates more or less independently of central state control.[21] A second aspect is that the ideological content and 'scientific truth' of communist politics was accompanied by strict control over the population to ascertain its reliability in keeping the correct course. This stood of course in stark con-

---

21 The precise distance between state and economic life varies, of course, while all European liberal-democratic states have to some degree developed arrangements to redistribute wealth among the population.

trast to the official ideal in which wealth would be shared voluntarily and enthusiastically, in which opposition would be non-existent, and in which the coercive state would have lost its purpose. In particular members of the elite were subject to extensive surveillance, for which an elaborate secret police system was invented. Both aspects illustrate the penetrating and directive nature of communist states. Liberal-democratic states have less pervasive claims and quite different programs, although the state may still have substantial obligations.

This difference in state power is reflected in the general organization of the state. In liberal democracies, an organizational context is guaranteed for the variety of societal forces to arrive at political decisions through democratic procedures. The most important institution in this context is the parliament, in which the members (of at least one chamber) are elected directly by the public. The parliament is the legislative force in the political system, deciding on the political issues at hand and ordering other elements of the state to execute these decisions. These other branches are in particular the bureaucracy (organized in the various ministries), other layers of government (e.g., local councils and provinces), the judiciary, and the army and police. Selection for the most important political office can be done by the direct election of a president by the public, or by the choice of a prime-minister by the other members of parliament. Differences between liberal-democratic states are of course substantial.

Communist systems developed historically in such a way that they differed in one major aspect from liberal-democratic systems: only one single political party, the Communist Party, was allowed to exercise political power (Ionescu 1967, Hill 1990). If other parties were present, their lack of autonomy was sufficient to warrant their treatment as clones of the Communist Party itself, and voting was merely an exercise to substantiate the claim that the whole society was united behind the leadership of that party; it was the party for the working class, officially 85% of the population. In communist countries only the working class interest officially existed, since conflicting class interests were theoretically eliminated after only a short period of communist rule. Moreover, the Party represented the general will in society, which in theory enabled it to arbitrate any dispute that emerged in the society; it was organized parallel to the formal institutions of the state, which therefore functioned more as tools by which the Party could impose its will rather than as autonomous decision-making institutions in their own right. The most important political office in the communist system was thus not the chairman of the presidium of the supreme soviet, but the Secretary-General of the Communist Party. The internal organization of the Party followed the principle of 'democratic centralism', which meant that its members could participate in the discussion until a decision was made; the decision was then binding for all. In daily practice the centralist element generally triumphed over the internal party democracy.

The ideological view that in communist systems the state is supposed to lead society on its way to transformation called for the state to fulfil more functions in society than in the case of its liberal-democratic counterpart. As a result it was larger, and more people were employed by the state. Thus, for instance, besides the ones found in liberal-democratic systems there also existed ministries organized around various sectors in the production process (the ministry of the aviation industry, and so forth). The bureaucracy necessary for the effective centralization of decision-making and for the control of economic development was large and extremely powerful, because its influence was neither checked by competing private bureaucracies (of large industries, for instance) nor by organized masses of citizens. This was especially true for the bureaucracy of the Communist Party itself; since the Party controlled the institutions of the state, the Party's bureaucracy was considered by some to wield the ultimate power (see Šik 1981).

Because of the differences in the policy-making processes between the two systems, it is only to be expected that there were different ways in which the European states on both sides of the Iron Curtain shaped, generated, or discouraged ethnonationalist activism. However, that these ways were different does not follow directly from the underlying philosophies, because, as has been said above, neither approach as it has been worked out in the European context has an immediate place for ethnonational organization in the political system. Liberalism doesn't because it considers individual action as central to political life, and liberal theories of political integration therefore argued for the superfluousness of the ethnonational phenomenon. Neither does Marxist-Leninism allow for ethnonationalism because it considers classes to form the basis of all kinds of political life and the only politically and historically relevant way in which humans are divided.[22]

Political reality, however, has forced both types of states to take ethnonationalism into account. For liberal-democracies this did not necessarily imply the development of an explicit program; the liberal-democratic political system allows for multiple forms of group formation to combine individual interests, including ethnonational ones. Thus, even though nationalism itself served to cement a form of political unity among the population of the state at large, the political system and underlying philosophy as such does not support or prohibit mobilization on an ethnonationalist basis.[23] As regards Marxist-Leninist theory and practice, however, ethnonationalism is so much an antithesis to its basic assumptions that some sort of polit-

---

22 Of course, transcendentalist philosophy as such would have place for ethnonational sentiments, or nationalism in general (see Berki 1979),
23 Nevertheless, practical politics in Western European states has led to a more active approach towards ethnonationalist sentiment. Many of the solutions discussed above have been put into practice in liberal-democratic environments to counter the implicit threat that ethnonationalism poses to the system as such. With mixed results, however, as is illustrated by the numerous studies on ethnonationalism in the 'developed West'.

ical program had to be developed to deal with ethnonational groups. As with other elements of Marxist theory, the location of the revolution in Russia necessitated some major adaptations to the general theory, and they were particularly developed by Lenin and adapted by Stalin (see Connor 1984, King 1973). Lenin's strategy in dealing with nationalism in Russia consisted of three components and was later, completely or in part, imitated in other countries:

1)   prior to the assumption of power by the Communist Party, all national groups were to be promised the right of self-determination, expressly including the right of secession, in order to gain their support. They were also to be offered a position of equality if they wished to remain within the state;

2)   following the assumption of power the right to secession was to be terminated – if not in fiction, then certainly in fact – while a process of cultural integration was to be started by a dialectical route of territorial autonomy for all compact national groups;

3)   the Communist Party itself was to remain centralized and to be kept free of all nationalist elements.

Lenin argued that the nations would slowly converge if they were given an equal position. This process would continue until a complete blending was achieved, and a single identity had emerged. Assimilation would certainly not occur, as that was the end result of capitalist national oppression and coercion; besides, assimilation too clearly would benefit dominant groups in communist states, such as Russians, and later Serbs, Han-Chinese, and so forth. The blending or merging was therefore to create a new socialist man, the Soviet man, the Yugoslav, and so on. In order to arrive at that stage ethnonational cultures were at first to be supported in their development, in particular in languages. This would provide the channels to transfer the socialist message and avoid the image of socialism as a political program that the dominant ethnic group was using to control and incorporate the other groups. To describe the purpose of this cultural pluralism, Stalin coined the phrase "nationalist in form, socialist in content." Since education was in the hands of the communists, this approach would prove effective and sufficient (Connor, 1984:202–204).

Over time, the states in Eastern Europe developed their own solutions, and national specifics became more and more apparent (Rothschild 1989, King 1973, Banac 1990). Further discussion of the policies of communist states towards ethnonational groups can be found in chapters four and five.

In sum, it is likely that the general differences between the two political systems will have important bearing on the dynamics of interaction between states and ethnonational groups. This will supposedly show up in three distinctive elements. First of all, the general set of policies that is developed by the state to regulate and arrange society will differ. Secondly, it is expected that the political structure of the state will result in differences in the extent to which ethnonational movements are enabled and induced to mobilize. Thirdly, the centralized character of the state will be an important explanatory element with regard to the extremity of ethnonational desires.

Regarding the first element, economic policies and cultural policies appear particularly important. Economic policies because the liberal-democratic program is less encompassing and prescriptive, even though the state in liberal-democratic systems is still substantially involved in the regulation of the economy; cultural policies (in the sense of social culture) because of their immediate importance for the ethnonational markers of the groups involved. The character of communist systems is such that there will not only be a more extensive program in these fields, but also a more powerful attempt at implementation due to the centralized control. In liberal-democratic systems the multiple checks and balances will diffuse many of the efforts.

The second element particularly concerns the main structural difference between the two systems, the number of political parties that have access to political power. Furthermore, the political system of the liberal-democratic countries is more open to other forms of accepted activism by ethnic groups than the communist political system. Thus, ethnonational movements can become successful if they are able to organize themselves into an effective pressure or interest group, or into a political party. This is true even though the chances for success probably depend on several other conditions as well, such as the capability to combine ethnic with other interests, access to the mass media, the level of party discipline, the territorial distribution of the ethnic group, and so forth. Given the discussion in this section, it is useful to point out that, although the competition of interests will be present in both liberal-democratic systems and communist systems, the stakes of the competition in communist systems will be much higher; this increases the need for (partial) control of the state organs (especially the Communist Party and the bureaucracy) on the part of ethnic groups. It is therefore within the state (and especially within the Communist Party and the bureaucracy) that ethnic strivings will most likely be fought out.

The third element does justice to the psychological dimension that is central to ethnonationalism as a phenomenon. The centralised organization of the political system under communism did not enable (and could not tolerate) the existence of alternative centres of power and loyalty, since these centres presented a potential challenge to the functioning of the system as such. Moreover, policies had to focus on the state as a whole. For instance, in the practice of centralist economic planning there was no room for the special preferences of particular localities, since the planning system was especially equipped for looking at the well-being of the entire country. This could lead for example to planned regional specialisation instead of intra-regional diversified development, and could entail the establishment of industries by the state that needed large numbers of specialized workers from other ethnic and regional origins. It is likely that the central state would be held responsible by the local community. A further possible effect of centralist organization is that while for a dominant group failures appear to simply be the consequence of authoritarianism and bureaucracy, the non-dominant ethnic group will consider these failures as a violation of eth-nonational rights and a confirmation of the hegemony of the dominant group. Due to a lack of regulated access and open debate on these kinds of issues, movements that choose the opting out variety of ethnic demands will emerge sooner. Thus, not only will the state be held accountable, the intention of leaving the state will develop sooner as ethnic interest is perceived, rightly or wrongly, behind the state's action.

2.3.2 *Dimension 2: differences in territorial organization*

As has been discussed in the first chapter, central to the identity of ethnona-tional groups is their perceived homeland. A distinct territory helps to define groups, and provides them with resources. Because of this, it can be expected that the territorial organization of the state will have distinctive effects upon the development of ethnonationalism. As has been pointed out above, however, this dimension is slightly more complicated than the previous one, because a federative form of the state is often used as a solution to ethnonational problems; it is thought that by constitutionally laying down guaranteed authority in specific fields for various territorial layers of government, the potential for ethnonational conflict at the level of the state as a whole is reduced. Nevertheless, as will be discussed in this section, due to the subsequent effects this arrangement can have on the state's interaction with the ethnonational groups and between the ethnonational groups themselves, federalism may be both a solution and, at the same time, a new problem.

Within federalized states, power is shared by various layers of government, each of which has a distinct set of competencies, and none of which is considered subordinate to the other. It should be clear that in this book *the state, the federal state* or *the federation* is meant to describe the political system as a whole, *the central state* or *the central government* is meant to be the 'upper layer' of this political entity, whereas a *federal republic* is meant to be one of the constituent parts or the 'lower layer' of this political entity. The constituent republics not only have their own competencies aside from those of the central government, they also take part in the affairs of the central government by forming one of the organs of the central state, normally the second chamber of the parliament. In this way a federation differs from an autonomy arrangement; in that case the central state only grants certain specific rights to a specific part of the population, or limits state involvement in specified fields, while the ultimate authority remains with the central state (Bernhardt, 1981:24–26). However, federations come in all sorts and sizes, and often the legal competencies do not quite compare with political realities. Some authors make a distinction between quasi-federations and true federations (Paddison, 1983:98; Bennett, 1989:11–12). In all, the range of possibilities may run from states where the federal republics are just allowed to 'implement' political decisions made by the central government (resembling straightforward decentralisation of central government), or can interpret decisions made by the central government, or can even possess their own rule-making institutions (Duchacek 1986; Elazar 1991).[24]

Whereas there may be substantial differences between federations, it should also be clear that constitutional arrangements as such do provide demarcated territories that potentially may be used as building blocks for the group's identity. It remains therefore an open question as to what extent different kinds of federations wield different results in this respect. I will return to this question in the next chapter. A second comment that should be made is that the territorial boundaries of the federal republics may or may not follow ethnic lines. This question becomes particularly important when the federation is considered to have resulted from an attempt by the state to counter ethnic diversity in its territory. Examples can be found of federations where boundaries have nothing to do with ethnic diversity (e.g., USA, Austria), where the relation to ethnic borders is ambiguous (e.g., Switzerland, Canada), or where political and ethnic territories show a close, though still imperfect fit (e.g., former Yugoslavia, former Soviet Union). Horowitz (1985:603–605), for instance, shows how diverse configurations work out quite differently in this respect in the case of Nigeria. Although the analysis of the impact of different kinds of political-territorial arrangements will be instructive (and something more will be said on the subject in chapter eight), for the purpose of this study the last category in which ethnic and political territories more or less coincide will be the most useful. It shows the clearest difference with unitary states in providing a territorial arrangement that may have a distinct impact on ethnonational sentiment and conflict. In this book, therefore, a federation is a political system of which the constituent territories are based on ethnonational living areas.

24   Three sets of questions are important in determining the precise relationship between the layers of government: 1) How are the competencies divided across the levels of government?; 2) In what way is control by the republics over the centre guaranteed?; 3) Are there special conditions included in the constitution that enable the central state to undermine the federal character of the state, such as for example special powers in case of war and foreign policy powers, or powers to prevent internal chaos? Moreover, the territorial organization of a federation comes under pressure from social changes, such as for instance the continuing urbanization that causes metropolitan areas to overflow the borders of the federal republics, economic and technological changes that alter the way in which efficient government should be organized, and changes in the ethnic composition of a republic as a result of migration or differences in birthrate. These changes may necessitate the redefinition of the rights of the different layers of government, keeping questions on the division of authorities a constant issue on the political agenda of federal states.

For a long time, it was expected that federal states would gradually develop into more centralized states later on, the result of ever increasing mobility and interaction within the entire federation (Paddison, 1983:107).[25] A short look at the former Soviet Union shows some evidence to the contrary, however. Of course, the Soviet federation hardly became a 'true federation' because of the centralized power of the Communist Party and the ability of the centre to alter the constitution unilaterally. Nevertheless, the federation remained in place as a concession by the new regime in order to keep political control over the state's vast territory. As Roeder has argued, this was not intended as a concession to the ethnonational groups, because whereas the republican borders followed some national lines, the basic strategy of the Soviet regime was to develop political institutions to control the process of mobilization and economic transformation of the population, rather than deal with the issue of national identity. The local ethnic elites were encouraged by the centre to pursue the regime's economic interests and were deterred from following primordial ethnonational strategies. Although this tactic resulted in temporary inter-ethnic peace and relative control by Moscow over the politicization of ethnicity, it resulted at the same time in "autonomous homelands" that in the 1980s provided the essential resources for the collective mobilization of the ethnic communities. The institutions of the federal republic (in particular the bureaucracy), and the local elite that ran it, provided the main possibilities for ethnic mobilization and played a critical role in the conjunction of primordial and instrumental interests, the shaping of ethnic communities, and the politicization of ethnonational sentiment (Roeder, 1991:230, see also Knippenberg 1991, Gleason 1990, Smith 1989; Smith, 1990:86).[26]

It may be useful to stress at this point that though this is a communist case, the territorial dimension is expected to operate independently from the politico-economic dimension. This is not to say that the two do not interact. In fact, as will be discussed in chapter eight, this interaction may produce some interesting insights into the interplay of political systems and ethnonationalism. The example of the former Soviet Union illustrates how the balance between the central government and the federal republics is under constant pressure. These dynamics are even more interesting in the case of more recent federations in Europe that have more clearly been established

25 Strong republics were considered more suitable only in the early stages of development of states, when the economic and political differences between the constituent units were more apparent. Early federations were also not primarily intended to reconcile different ethnic demands, but were designed to service governmental efficiency and ensure a proper working of democracy.

26 Indeed, apart from the identitive value of the republican territories, barriers could be raised against the assimilation of the titular group into the other groups, in particular the Russians. Dostál and Knippenberg (1992) showed that the status of the territorial unit correlated with the level of assimilation of the group over the years; the higher the political status, the less assimilation took place.

to accommodate ethnic demands and where the territories of the republics coincide with the living areas of the ethnonational groups in question.

Overall then, it can be expected that unitary and federalized systems will provide different contexts for the development of ethnonational activism, and will pose different demands on the organization of this activism. It is also to be expected that federalism, if it is intended to accommodate ethnic diversity, raises its own problems and sets off developments that may run counter to the original intention of the system. Federalism may therefore influence the development of ethnonational movements and identity in three ways: with regard to identity, with regard to political access to the centre, and with regard to ethnonational homogenization.

First of all, a federalized political system can be expected to play an important role in the definition of ethnic identity through its geographical expression. This role may result in confirmation of ethnic identification and in an increase of ethnonational activism. It is expected that in unitary systems both the policies of the central state and the lack of an institutionalized territorial base will hamper the development of ethnic identity and ethnonational activism. In a federalized state, on the other hand, the institutionalized territorial base will stimulate the development of ethnonational sentiment, and may lead to severe challenges to the *raison d'être* of the system as a whole.

Secondly, a federation may provide political channels for the expression of group interests to the political centre, by which the exact possible uses of these channels necessarily depend upon the distribution of powers across the two levels of government. Nevertheless, in any federation of the kind discussed the organization of ethnic interest will occur on a territorially institutionalized basis. The existence of a federal republic provides the ethnic group with its own permanent channel of interest articulation and increases the possibilities for successful ethnonational activism *vis à vis* the centre. In unitary political systems on the other hand, ethnonational groups lack an institutionalized and separate political channel to the political centre, which seriously hampers the successful development of an ethnonational movement.

Thirdly, the federalized state can be expected to allow the ethnic group to protect its characteristics by the competencies that are given to it in certain fields. However, the level of protection federal institutions provide for the ethnic identity of the group will probably depend strongly on the exact power distribution in the federation. If this distribution simply resembles decentralisation (the regionalization of central state organs), then the central state only enlarges its penetration of the territory and improves its grip on the state's population. Nevertheless, for ideological reasons, in unitary states special policies to institutionalize the ethnic differences in society are less likely to be developed, and if they do develop they will not be likely to have a territorial expression. This diminishes the importance of territorial characteristics of ethnonational groups to the development of ethnic nationalism. In federalized states, special policies towards ethnonational groups are more likely to be formulated (both by the central and by the republican government), and this helps to strengthen the ethnonational characteristics of the groups.

2.4   SUMMARY AND CONCLUSION

This chapter focused on the relation between the state and ethnonationalism. I argued that the general emphasis on state responses to ethnonational demands underplayed the autonomous role of the state in society, which it exercises both in its policies and through its institutional structure. In order to explore the usefulness of this, two dimensions were introduced that differentiate between the political systems in Europe. One dimension is constructed around the politico-economic characteristics of the state; the other dimension looks at the territorial organization of the state. It has been argued that political systems may enable or disable, and encourage or discourage, the development of ethnonational characteristics, the articulation of ethnic interests, and the occurrence of violent ethnonational conflict. For both dimensions, several propositions were formulated regarding this general argument, which will direct the analysis of the various cases in chapters four to seven; the cases will be compared in chapter eight. In chapter three, however, further attention will be given to the design of this study.

3

The Design of the Study

In this chapter the design of the study will be discussed. I will comment shortly on the methodology and possible pitfalls of the use of case studies (3.1), and I will then select the cases following an overview and discussion of the political systems in the countries of Europe since the Second World War (3.2). The differentiating characteristics will be the two dimensions that have been discussed in the previous chapter. In section 3.3 I will give more attention to the ethnonational movements and the features that characterize their organization and strength. In the final section of this chapter I will provide a short framework for the study of the cases in the rest of this book.

3.1 THE METHOD OF RESEARCH

For the comparative research of political phenomena, statistical methods as well as the case study method can be used. According to Yin (1989:23), a case study can be defined as an empirical inquiry that investigates a contemporary phenomenon in its real-life context, in which the boundaries between phenomenon and context are not clearly evident, and when multiple sources of evidence are used to study the case. Thus, while other research methods may be better equipped in other types of research, particularly where generalization towards populations is needed (see Yin, 1989:16–21), the case-study method is particularly apt for adding information to the present body of theory. In the context of this research the case-study method therefore has some advantages over the statistical method as the purpose of this study is to explore the influence of different types of political systems on ethnonational mobilization. Furthermore, it should be noted that the European family of states lacks sufficient cases for a satisfactory use of the statistical method.[1]

An ideal multiple case study may for instance be based on eight cases: four cases to produce equal results and to support the theoretical model, and four cases to produce contrasting results, also to support the theoretical model underlying the research. This ideal set up cannot be completely fulfilled in this study, for three reasons. The first reason is the lack of sufficient comparable cases in Europe. Although I will try to overcome this limitation by extending the framework of research over time, this clearly remains a problem. The second reason is theoretical and concerns the often paradoxical nature of the ethnonational phenomenon that makes it difficult to formulate straightforward expectations regarding the cause-effect relationships. This has partly to do with the close interconnectedness of ethnonationalism as a political movement and the state as a political entity. The third reason is more practical and concerns the limitation of time that has to be set for any kind of research.

Figure 3.1 Dimensions of political systems

		Territorial organization	
		Unitary	Federalized
Politico-economic organization	Communist	I	II
	Liberal-democratic	III	IV

1 The case-study method has of course its own specific difficulties and pitfalls. First of all, a strict research design must be used in which, for all cases, the initial research questions are connected with the empirical data found in the cases (and with the conclusions following from the analysis of the data) in a similar way. These connections clearly can pose serious problems for the researcher, because of the technical features of the case-study approach (Ragin, 1989:51–52). The general goal is to uncover patterns of invariance and constant association, whereby the designation of cause and effect is accepted as definitive only if all deviating cases are accounted for in some way. Therefore the method is, secondly, relatively insensitive to the frequency distribution of types of cases, because a single case may cast doubt on that presumed cause-effect relationship established on the basis of many observations. Thirdly, the method forces investigators to consider the cases as whole entities, and not as collections of variables but as causal complexes. Finally, a constant dialogue is needed between ideas and evidence, since few simplifying assumptions are made at the beginning. Because of these characteristics the number of cases has to remain limited, since the number of complex comparisons between the cases increases exponentially with each case added. Having too few cases, however, makes it more difficult to connect the research results with the theoretical framework; it should be attempted to select cases that are predicted to either replicate the results of other cases (literal replication), or to produce contrasting outcomes (theoretical replication) (Yin, 1989:53).

The choice of the four cases in this research is based on the variation in the conditioning factor, the state, of which the two sets of differences are considered important for the development of the ethnonational movements. It is expected that in each cell of figure 3.1, the autonomous role of the state in the development of ethnonational movements takes a specific form and that in each context movements are confronted with different opportunities and incentives and with different chances of success. Apart from this differentiation, it is attempted to use cases that are as similar as possible in the European context. This will be further discussed in the next section. The four cases together will then allow for three sets of comparisons. First of all, it will be possible to compare them on the effects of the politico-economic structure; secondly, they can be compared on the effects of the territorial organization of the state; and thirdly, they can be compared on the combined effect of the two dimensions. It is indeed to be expected, given their theoretical origin, that this combined effect might produce some interesting and perhaps contrasting sets of conditions. Thus, as has been discussed at the end of the previous chapter, in principle the effect of the two dimensions is analyzed separately; to add further insights into the dynamics at work, their combined effect will receive separate attention in chapter eight.

3.1.1 The time span of the research

The main time frame of the research is the period after the Second World War because of two reasons: firstly, as discussed in chapter one, the interest in this research lies in particular with the recent ethnonational activism as experienced in the last twenty five years; secondly, the communist takeover in Eastern Europe took place after the Second World War. Nevertheless, whereas the emphasis in the cases will indeed be put on the more recent period, it should also be clear that the historical basis of ethnonationalism as a phenomenon necessitates some careful scrutiny of the earlier experiences of the group and the movement. Ethnonationalism has its roots in mythology and historical traumas, and the movements usually cannot be discussed in isolation from this history. Moreover, as the previous section has indicated, the analysis of earlier time periods also has the advantage of adding new quasi-cases to the comparison which should add further insight into the relationship under study.

3.1.2 Data gathering

The data for this research have predominantly been gathered from the literature. Although this certainly has limitations, it nevertheless has the advantage of enabling thorough comparison of the different analyses and opinions that have been formulated by the specialists on the respective countries. In fact, the existing literature has been based on a variety of research methods, which can be used in addition to each other to provide a more or less complete picture of the case regarding this subject. Furthermore, the literature has been supplemented by news reports and statistical material for more recent developments, while several experts, in particular on Eastern Europe, have added their insights into specific elements of the cases.

3.2   SELECTION OF THE CASES

3.2.1   *Types of political systems in European countries*

For the period since World War Two the European countries can be divided over the four cells of figure 3.1 (see table 3.1). To make the categorization useful, the political history of European states has been slightly simplified. First of all, the mini-states of Andorra, Liechtenstein, Monaco, Malta, San Marino, and Vatican City are excluded. Secondly, the countries in Eastern Europe were categorized as communist immediately after the Second World War; neither is the end of the communist rule in 1989 reflected in the table. Unified Germany is therefore not included, neither is the dissolution of Yugoslavia, the Soviet Union, and Czechoslovakia; the status of the successor states is also not discussed.[2] The remaining problems concerning the categorization will be discussed below.

Table 3.1   Political systems of Europe

I   *(communist/unitary):*
  Albania, Bulgaria, Czechoslovakia (until 1968), East Germany, Hungary, Poland, and Romania.
II   *(communist/federalized):*
  Soviet Union, Czechoslovakia (after 1968), and Yugoslavia.
III *(liberal-democratic/unitary):*
  Belgium (before 1970), Denmark, Finland, France, Greece, Iceland, Ireland, Italy, Luxembourg, the Netherlands, Norway, Portugal, Spain (before 1978), Sweden, and the United Kingdom.
IV *(liberal-democratic/federalized):*
  Austria, Belgium (after 1970), Spain (after 1978), West Germany, and Switzerland.

---

2   These exclusions do not mean, of course, that the influence of these events will not be treated later on. In fact, they will be, both in the study of the cases and in the concluding chapter.

The categorization of many countries is rather problematic. The inclusion of Spain (before 1978), Greece and Portugal with the liberal-democratic states is debatable due to the periods of authoritarian rule in those countries. Belgium, Italy, Spain (after 1978), United Kingdom, and Denmark are difficult cases to categorize with regard to the territorial dimension. The first three countries have taken substantial strides towards devolution of power from the centre. For Belgium the turning point came in 1970, when constitutional reform created the possibility of allowing large-scale devolution of decision-making powers to sub-state units, both cultural and economic; the changes were subsequently implemented in the following years and in the reform laws of 1980. Although the line is difficult to draw, the constitutional specialist Senelle considers Belgium to have started its road to a federation from then on; the official step in that respect was only taken in the summer of 1993 (Senelle 1989). The 1947 constitution in Italy created the possibility for extensive regionalization, and nowadays several regions in fact have a high degree of autonomy.[3] However, overall the state remains unitary in structure, in particular because of financial regulations (Lane and Ersson, 1991:210). The regionalization of Spain has proceeded along a similar path, with four of the seventeen regions (Catalonia, the Basque Country, Galicia and Andalusia) now having substantial autonomy with constitutional status, each region negotiating its own level of autonomy with Madrid (Riezebos and Tang, 1992:17). However, even though there are arrangements for self-government, the institutions remain ultimately controlled by national bodies. Of these three countries with quasi-federative arrangements, Belgium can be considered to have proceeded farthest along the path in the 1980s (Lane and Ersson, 1991:224).

Denmark and the United Kingdom are states that have politically distinguished several territories, but are still generally governed in a unitary way. Thus, the United Kingdom is governed from London, but has separate judicial arrangements for Scotland, has special assemblies for the Channel Islands and the Isle of Man, and had home rule for Northern Ireland until 1972. Denmark has a separate arrangement for Greenland and the Faroe Islands, each of which has its own executive and legislative power. Of course, in this respect there are difficulties in the classification of other countries as well, mainly because of special autonomy arrangements for small parts of the territory or outlying islands. Indeed, some countries had colonies during part of the post-war years, and some still do. Thus, Portugal and the Netherlands have special arrangements for island populations, some of which lay outside European territory. Finland has a home rule arrangement for the Åland Islands that have a Swedish-speaking population. France has had an autonomy statute for Corsica since 1982 and has

3   The regions are Sicily (since 1946), Sardinia (since 1948), Valle d'Aosta (since 1948), Trentino-Alto Adige (since 1948, consolidated in 1972) and Friuli-Venezia Julia (since 1963). Separate arrangements exist for Vatican City and for San Marino.

49

several separate constitutional articles for its overseas territories. The range of special regulations is therefore substantial, in particular in Western Europe.

However, classification of some of the communist countries also runs into difficulties. Romania had, for a short period of time (the first few years after World War Two), an autonomy arrangement for the Hungarian part of the population in Transylvania. However, by the time a separate "Autonomous Hungarian Province" was installed in 1952 the political wind changed to Stalinism. Since 1953 the autonomy was gradually cut down, and the province was abolished in the 1960s (Paul 1991). Czecho-slovakia had had a separate arrangement for Slovakia, the Slovak National Council, before the federation, although this did not in practice reduce any of the centralized power of Prague. In general, as pointed out in the previous chapter, the federalist nature of communist states is a matter of dispute, due to the centralized nature of the Communist Party. However, this should not hamper the analysis, because what is considered to be important is not so much the original intention of the creators of the federalist constitutions, but the fact that the institutions created under the constitutional arrangements in reality could have succeeded in enlarging their relative power position towards the central government.

3.2.2 Ethnonational diversity in European countries

A second limitation to the availability of countries for study is the necessary presence of various ethnonational groups in the territory of the state.[4] It can be assumed that a certain threshold needs to be passed before an ethnonational movement can develop any momentum, and before a relevant and comparable interaction of states and ethnonational movements can take place. This threshold can be a certain percentage of the population of a country, here put arbitrarily at 5%, or an absolute number, put arbitrarily at 100,000. In general, however, good data on ethnonational groups are hard to find, since often their mere existence is politically sensitive. This has particularly been the case in Eastern Europe. As Shoup (1981:13) points out, the measurement of the group is often based on different criteria (language, or ethnicity, or religion) and this can differ between censuses, just as the wording of the main questions can differ. In fact, complete groups have disappeared or reappeared between censuses, as happened with the Macedonians in Bulgaria (their number dropped from 188,000 in 1956 to 9,362 in 1965), or the Muslims in Yugoslavia (their number increased from 972,000 in 1961 to 1,729,932 in 1971). Even though both examples are

---

4   As mentioned in chapter one, only autochthonous and territorially based movements are the subjects of this study. Recent immigrants are not discussed, nor are groups like Jews and Gypsies; some remarks will be made on them in due course, however.

from the Balkans, data problems are definitely not restricted to that region, as the next chapters will show.

Table 3.2 lists all countries in Europe that have substantial ethnonational groups in their territory. Only ethnonational minority groups of a hundred

Table 3.2   Ethnonational groups in European states in the 1980's

State	Group	Size (thousands)	% estimate	Alternative	Source
Albania	Greeks	-	6.8%	200[1]	MRG
Belgium	Flemish	5,676	57.5%		
	Walloon	3,206	32.5%		
	Bruxellois[2]	977	9.9%		
Bulgaria	Macedonians	-	2.5%	250	MRG
	Pomaks	-	1.5%	150	MRG
	Turks	-	9.0%	900	MRG
Czechoslovakia	Czechs	9,805	63.3%		
	Hungarians	593	3.8%		
	Slovaks	4,888	31.5%		
East Germany	Sorbs	100	0.6%	70	MRG
Finland	Swedish-Finns	298	6.1%		
France	Basks	150	0.3%	200[3]	MRG
	Bretons	1,450	2.6%	2,500[4]	MRG
	Catalans	300	0.5%	200	MRG
	Corsicans	200[5]	0.4%		
	Elzas-Germans	1,200	2.2%	1,900	MRG
	Flemish	200	0.4%	100	
Greece	Muslims	-	1.2%	120[6]	
Hungary	Germans	200	1.9%		
	Serb-Croat	100	0.9%		
	Slovaks	100	0.9%		
Ireland	Protestants	-	3.3%	115	MRG
Italy	Germans	300	0.5%		
	French	200	0.4%		
	Friulians	550[7]	1.0%		
	Sardinians	1,500	2.6%		
Netherlands	Frisians	200	1.4%	700[8]	MRG
Poland	Germans	200	0.5%		
	Ukrainians	180	0.5%		
	Belorussians	170	0.5%		
Romania	Germans	270	1.2%		
	Hungarians	-	8.1%	1,850	MRG
Spain	Basks	900	2.3%	1,100	MRG
	Catalans	6,000	15.5%	5,700[9]	MRG
	Galicians	2,500	6.4%	3,000	MRG
Switzerland	Germans	4,140	63.4%		
	French	1,172	17.9%		
	Italian	622	9.5%		

Table 3.2 continued on page 52

State	Group	Size (thousands)	% estimate	Alternative	Source
United Kingdom	Cath. Irish	-	0.8%	415	MRG
	Prot. Irish	-	1.9%	1,068	MRG
	Scots/Gaels	-	9.9%	5,500[10]	KreVel
	Welsh	-	4.9%	2,700[11]	KreVel
Yugoslavia	Albanians	1,730	7.4%		
	Croats	4,428	19.0%		
	Hungarians	427	1.8%		
	Macedonians	1,340	5.8%		
	Montenegrins	579	2.5%		
	Muslims	2,000	8.6%		
	Serbs	8,140	35.0%		
	Slovenes	1,754	7.5%		
	Turks	101	0.4%		
	Yugoslavs	1,219	5.2%		

General comment:
The majority ethnonational groups are not listed, and outlying island populations (population of the Azores, Greenland, etc.) are not included.

Specific comments:
1   MRG reports an official Albanian number of 50,000 Greeks. Kraas-Schneider gives a number of 200,000 Greek-Orthodox. The distinction between Gegs and Tosks is not further discussed here.
2   The figures for Belgium are based on territorial criteria; whether the Bruxellois should be included as a separate group is doubtful. There are also 70 thousand German speakers in Belgium.
3   There are approximately 80 thousand speakers of the Basque languages.
4   Approximately 500 thousand speakers of the Breton language. There is a great variation in the estimates.
5   Including Italian speakers.
6   The majority is Turkish-speaking, others are Albanians and Pomaks. There is a great variation in estimates, and there are no reliable estimates on the number of Valachs and Macedonians.
7   Includes 30 thousand Ladins.
8   Approximately 400 thousand speak the language. There is a great variation in the estimates.
9   Approximately 80% are Catalan speakers.
10   Approximately 80 thousand speakers of Gaelic.
11   Approximately 500 thousand speakers of Welsh.

Sources: Kraas-Schneider 1989, Krejčí and Velímský 1981 (KreVel), Minority Rights Group 1990 (MRG)

thousand or more are listed, as well as groups that live in multi-ethnic states where no group constitutes a clearly dominant position. The Soviet Union is not included.[5] The numbers are taken from Kraas-Schneider (1989) and are compared with and supplemented by figures from the Minority Rights Group (1990), Krejčí and Velímský (1981), and Lane and Ersson (1991). The figures still remain as estimates for many groups, and if the differences are too large, they will be commented upon separately.

As can be seen from the table, only ten European countries have ethnonational groups that are big enough to cross the threshold value of 5% of the total population. They are Albania, Belgium, Bulgaria, Czechoslovakia, Finland, United Kingdom, Romania, Spain, Switzerland, and Yugoslavia. France, Italy, and the Netherlands, however, have very substantial groups in a numerical sense. If these three countries are also included, we get the possible cases for further research displayed in table 3.3.

The communist unitary states Romania and Bulgaria are roughly comparable in political system (as defined by the two dimensions) and in their ethnonational diversity: a large-sized Hungarian and Turkish spill-over group, respectively, combined with other, smaller sized, minorities. For both countries, there are serious data problems connected with studying ethnic conflict and the development of ethnonational movements. This is exemplified by the differences in the official statistics and the estimates by the Minority Rights Group and authors like Shoup (1981). Czechoslovakia (before 1968) is the weaker choice in this category because of the shorter period of time, while Albania seems too different in terms of its regime and the degree of its isolation. Overall, therefore, Bulgaria seems a good choice as a typical unitary communist state, with a slight advantage over Romania, with its personalized communist regime under Ceauçescu and its temporary autonomy arrangement for its Hungarian minority after World War Two.

Of the communist federal states only former Yugoslavia and Czechoslovakia (after 1968) remain as options. There are two reasons why Yugoslavia

5   For this study, I consider the former Soviet Union to be too different from the other European countries primarily because of its size. Not only does the country stretch over two continents, but also the amount and size of the ethnonational groups in its territory sets it apart. For instance, the largest non-Russian group, the Ukrainians, numbered more than 42 million in the census of 1979 and was thus larger than all other European groups except the Russians, the French, the Germans, the Italians, and the English (only just). Almost 50 groups number more than 100 thousand people, of which 23 (including Russians) number more than 1 million (Knippenberg, 1991:45). Therefore, the kind of problems faced by both the central state institutions and the ethnonational groups necessitate separate attention, instead of inclusion in a general discussion on the development of ethnic national movements in Europe (see Gleason 1990, Nahaylo and Svoboda 1990, Hajda and Beissinger 1990, and Kolossov et al. 1992). A second reason for the exclusion from the comparison has been the specific position of the former Soviet Union in the world political arena. Both in size and in political status the other Eastern European countries are much more similar to the countries in the western part of Europe.

Table 3.3   Possible cases

I *(communist/unitary)*	II *(communist/federalized)*
Albania	Czechoslovakia (after 1968)
Bulgaria	Yugoslavia
Czechoslovakia (until 1968)	
Romania	

III *(lib-dem/unitary):*	IV *(lib-dem/federalized):*
Belgium (until 1970)	Belgium (after 1970)
Greece	Spain (after 1978)
France	Switzerland
Finland	
Italy	
The Netherlands	
Spain (until 1978)	
United Kingdom	

is not the best choice. First of all, Yugoslavia resembles the complexity of the Soviet Union, albeit on a smaller scale; the ethnic mosaic in the country and the history of ethnic strivings before and during the Second World War is such that it is to a large extent incomparable with other European countries (see Banac 1984, Glenny 1992). Secondly, the communist system in Yugoslavia is different from other communist countries; this might also hamper the comparison. The main problem with Czechoslovakia, of course, is its change from a unitary to a federalist state halfway through the period of research. Nevertheless, the country has still experienced 20 years of communist federalism, and it seems therefore the better choice of the two communist federalized political systems.

Belgium forms a good liberal-democratic federalized counterpart, because of its similarities with Czechoslovakia in ethnic make-up and the construction of its federalized state. Unfortunately it has the disadvantage of having gone through a state reform late in the research period that, moreover, has only in recent years resulted in formal federalism. Nevertheless, of the other options, 'Spain since 1978' has no general advantage over Belgium, because the Spanish state reform started even later than in Belgium, while the ultimate depth of its reforms is not as striking; moreover, the character of the ethnonational diversity does not compare well with the Czechoslovakian case. Switzerland, on the other hand, does form a true federal state. The character of its ethnonational diversity, of course, does not quite mirror the Czechoslovakian situation (63 - 18/10/1 instead of 63 - 31/4). However, much more important is the fact that the territorial shape of the federal republics is not at all comparable with Czechoslovakia (26 units against 2); as has been argued in the previous chapter, for this research a more or less complete overlap of federal republic and ethnonational living area would be ideal. Switzerland is indeed in many respects a notorious exception, and although some remarks will be made on the country in chapter eight, a comparison involving Belgium and Czechoslovakia promises to be more fruitful.

There is a wide range of choices for a unitary liberal-democratic state. As has been said above, 'Spain before 1978', is not a good choice because of the authoritarian nature of the Spanish regime until 1975. This is also the case with Greece, certainly between 1967 and 1974. In particular Italy compares unfavourably with France, the Netherlands and Finland in strength and duration of their unitary system. Italy has, since the Second World War been on its way to 'regionalization', even though for a long time this did not affect the basic principle of its unitarism. The Netherlands is a good example of a unitary state, although the ethnonational diversity is less comparable with Bulgaria because no irredenta is involved. Both France and Finland have irredenta groups on their territory (German speakers, Dutch speakers, and Italian speakers (besides Basques and Catalans) in France and Swedish speakers in Finland), while both countries also have other types of minorities. The United Kingdom is somewhat of a special case, because the separate institutions for Scottish people and the separate parliament for Northern Ireland until 1972 partly obscures its otherwise clear unitary character. Also unfavourable in the context of the comparison, however, is the country's size, its geographic peculiarity, and its political status as a world power. The problem of the large size and political status also applies to France. Belgium before 1970 was certainly a unitary state, even though there had been linguistically-defined territories since the 1930s. However, its ethnonational diversity does not compare well with Bulgaria. Overall, given these arguments and the comparison of the main minority as a percentage of the total population, Finland seems, of all unitary liberal-democratic states, to be most comparable with Bulgaria.

In sum, the dimensions formulated in chapter two led to the choice of cases that will be discussed in the next four chapters; the cases are Bulgaria, Czechoslovakia, Belgium, and Finland. As has become clear from the above discussion, the cases chosen are not just different with respect to the 'type of territorial organization,' and the 'type of politico-economic organization.' First of all, even though an attempt to limit the differences has been made, they also differ in their ethnogeographical structure; both unitary countries have a main minority that forms 10% or less of the populations, whereas in both federations it is at least 30% of the population. A second difference is that the groups in both unitary cases are spillover groups, whereas this is not the case in Czechoslovakia; the status of the Flemish and the Walloons is debatable. Lack of sufficient cases to choose from makes these kind of complications unavoidable, but I will try to partly overcome these problems by looking at the smaller spillover groups in the two federalized countries, by analyzing the two Eastern European cases after the fall of communism, and by analyzing the two federations before their political system changed. This adds several quasi-cases that can be used to check on the analysis made in the four main cases. Thirdly, it is unclear to what extent the political systems are comparable with others of the same category; for example, the assumption that all liberal-democratic countries are equal except for their federalist nature or unitary nature is of course not tenable. A fourth problem is that the four cases are located in four separate regions of Europe. As this may affect the 'nature' of local nationalisms, as discussed in chapter one, this may be important. However, in an international comparison these kind of difficulties are inevitable and they will be taken into account when the comparisons are made. I will therefore return to these points in the last chapter.

3.3   THE ETHNONATIONAL MOVEMENTS

The most important phenomenon within the cases for this study is the ethnonational movement, and it is useful to discuss some aspects before turning to the cases. Indeed, as has been mentioned in chapter two there is a complex relationship between the ethnonational group (the potential base of the movement), the movement, and the state. Not only can the movement as such take many forms, with any level of support possible, but the policies that the state develops autonomously or in response to the movement normally affect the group as a whole; this then feeds back to the movement. Clearly, part of the problem of analyzing ethnonational activism is that movement and group are not coterminous, although they are of course related: a movement will have a hard time expanding beyond its base (apart from an irredenta), and the claims a movement can put forward depend, at least partly, on the size of the group, on its ethnogeographical characteristics, on its financial potential, and on its cultural cohesiveness. In fact, one of the goals of the movement may indeed be to improve the cohesiveness of the group, in order to strengthen its political base, and important differences may occur between the different factions of the movement precisely because of this goal.

However, the existence of a potential base is not sufficient. Ethnonationalism of course depends on signs of support during demonstrations and mass rallies, but it is unlikely that ethnic nationalism will continue to flourish if it merely depends on occasional displays of support. Organizations are therefore crucial. This institutionalization does not necessarily have to take place in political organizations that explicitly strive for the representation of the ethnic group in the political system (such as political parties or factions within parties); illegal political institutions, like terrorist groups or underground movements, are also an option. Other possibilities are organizations that function to strengthen the socioeconomic base of the ethnic group (such as labour unions or welfare organizations), and organizations that are central to the group's ethnic distinctiveness (such as churches, cultural organizations, and specific educational institutions). Around these types of organizations the support for the ethnonational movement can be mustered and made more permanent, even if no official representation is possible yet. Therefore, it is clear that the borderline between a cultural and a political organization is a very thin one.

Of course, an organization in itself does not set any political wheels in motion. The successful change (or defence) of the present arrangements depends on the actions and claims a movement can put forward and can get implemented. Thus, the organizations become much more relevant when they initiate actions and demands that have some kind of support. Different numbers of people will be involved in different kinds of organizations, and the relative importance of the different modes of organization and support is hard to evaluate. Three aspects of this support appear to be important: first of all, the absolute level of support of the ethnic movement as expressed through voting behaviour and presence at rallies, demonstrations, and so forth; secondly, the relative support of the movement as part of the ethnic group as a whole; and thirdly, the uniformity of this support or the question of whether any counterclaims are formulated. The absolute support for the national movement is important because of the possibility for the state (and for competing ethnic groups) to ward off the group's demands or, on the contrary, to meet those demands without having to fear harmful effects on the overall structure and identity of the state. The relative support on the other hand is more crucial for the legitimacy of the movement's demands and for the conviction with which these demands can be brought forward. As has been pointed out in the previous chapter, the same reasoning applies to the uniformity of the support, because the state can play the different factions against each other and grant concessions to parts of the movement(s) only. Nevertheless, the support for an ethnonational movement as shown at demonstrations, mass rallies, or through individual political actions (violence) and voting behaviour remains one of the few ways to measure the strength and political momentum of ethnonational sentiments.

As has already been discussed in chapter two, the range of possible demands open to movements is quite extensive, ranging from exit options, to demands for autonomy, access or control (see table 2.1). National movements, however, may thus be described not only by the extremism of the goals they wish to achieve, but also by the means through which they are prepared to strive for those goals. It is not immediately clear as to what is the effect of a violent campaign on the potential following of the ethnic movement. Violence may alienate the majority of the potential supporters instead of attracting them, again dividing the group as well as the movement itself. Moreover, extremity in itself can sometimes be considered as a political weakness, if the only way for a faction of a national movement to obtain more support is by using dramatic and forceful means. It can therefore weaken the credibility of the movement.

The various aspects of ethnonational movements discussed in this section will all surface during the study of the cases. They will be further commented upon in chapter eight.

3.4   THE FRAMEWORK FOR THE STUDY OF THE CASES

The framework for the study of the cases reflects the various issues that have been discussed in this chapter and chapter two. I will start the discussion of each case by providing the general background and introducing the political system of the country. In the second section I will pay attention to the ethnogeographical make-up, with information on the size of the group and on their distribution over the country. The third section deals with the interaction between the state and the ethnonational movement, the activism it has generated, and developments with regard to identity formation. Although I will place emphasis on the period for which the case has been selected, other periods will be treated as well. In a fourth section I will evaluate the influence of the political system on the development of ethnonational activism in that country and will draw some conclusions.

In the next four chapters I will therefore look at the interaction of states and ethnonational groups under four different types of political systems: chapter four deals with Bulgaria, chapter five with Czechoslovakia, chapter six with Belgium, and chapter seven with Finland. From the propositions discussed at the end of the previous chapter it may be expected that the first case will differ severely from the last in terms of the state of tension that is generated by the political system. The two federalized cases fall somewhere in between. Following the four cases, the last chapter will contain the comparison of the cases to see whether this expectation was justified. That chapter also contains the main conclusions of this study.

4

Bulgaria
The Denial of Ethnonational Diversity

The Bulgarian case will be analyzed to explore the dynamics of the interaction between a unitary communist political system and the mobilization of ethnonational movements. The main emphasis will be on the largest minority in the country, the Turks. Some attention will also be given to the periods before World War Two and after the opening of the Iron Curtain. The chapter will follow the outline provided at the end of the previous chapter. It starts with a very short general political history of the country (4.1). This is followed by a description of the ethnogeographical characteristics of the minorities in Bulgaria, with specific information on the Turkish minority (4.2); following this the interaction between the state and the minority is discussed extensively in section 4.3. In that section I will devote the most attention to the period of communist rule, but the years before 1946 and after 1989 will also be treated. The chapter ends with an evaluation of the impact of unitary communism on ethnonational mobilization as exemplified by this case (4.4).

4.1   GENERAL INTRODUCTION

4.1.1 Bulgaria until 1944

Before 1878 Bulgaria formed part of the Ottoman Empire. With the treaty of San Stefano in March of that year, which followed the Russian-Turkish war of 1877–1878, Bulgaria was created on a large piece of land that stretched from the Danube to the Aegean and from the Vardar and Morava valley in Macedonia to the Black Sea; the new political unit was given an autonomous status close to complete independence. However, only a few months later, the Treaty of Berlin reduced the territory of Bulgaria by two-thirds, following concern by the other Great Powers over too much Russian influence on the peninsula; Macedonia was returned to the Turkish Empire, while Eastern Rumelia (the southern part of San Stefano-Bulgaria) was given a separate status under Ottoman rule. Within this reduced territory, a constitution was passed in 1879 and a German prince was invited to lead the country. In the next 35 years much effort was put into the return of the lost territories. The first area to be reclaimed was Eastern Rumelia, over which Bulgaria gained effective control in 1885. Bulgaria's full independence from the Ottoman Empire came in 1908.

However, union with Eastern Rumelia was also the start of the conflict with two neighbours, Greece and Serbia, both of whom rejected Bulgarian control over Rumelia and competed with Bulgaria over Macedonia and Thrace (see Wilkinson 1951). Serbia was defeated on the battlefield in 1885, but conflicting aspirations again came to the fore during the Balkan Wars of 1912 and 1913. Bulgaria's conflict with both contenders revolved around territorial ambitions as well as the character of the national cultures in Macedonia. Regarding the Greeks, under Ottoman rule Bulgarian nationalism had developed almost as much in opposition to Greek dominance in the Orthodox millet as to the Turkish overlords, and both Orthodox Churches competed in Macedonia (Raikin, 1989:354–356). Bulgaria's conflict with its other rival, Serbia, was rather fought over the pretence of the linguistic character of the Macedonian people. The situation in the region was further complicated by the emergence of the Internal Macedonian Revolutionary Organization (VMRO, under that name since 1906) that from 1893 onwards attempted to cause a popular uprising in Macedonia. The VMRO would trouble internal Bulgarian politics at least until the 1930s.

The continuous tension over Macedonia and the attempts by Greece, Serbia, Bulgaria, and the VMRO itself to gain as much control as possible over the areas still under the rule of the declining Ottoman Empire culminated in the Balkan Wars. The substantial territories that Bulgaria gained in Macedonia and Thrace during the First Balkan War were lost almost completely during the Second Balkan War. The Treaty of Bucharest of August 1913 and the Treaty of Constantinople one month later left Bulgaria with only the eastern part of Macedonia (Pirin-Macedonia), the Kărdžali district and a small part of Thrace. An attempt to undo this turn of events by allying with the Central Powers during World War 1 cost the country further territories, in particular Thrace. The Treaty of Neuilly also imposed large war reparations, to be paid to Greece, Yugoslavia and Romania, which put a severe burden on economic development in Bulgaria during the interwar years.

Between the two World Wars political life remained as volatile as it had been since independence. Embittered Macedonian refugees created an atmosphere of instability that not only plagued internal politics but also created difficulties for Bulgaria's foreign relations, in particular with the new Kingdom of Serbs, Croats, and Slovenes (Yugoslavia). The rule, by the Agrarian Stambolijski immediately after the war was ended by a coup in 1923, organized by VMRO, part of the military, and some oppositional political groupings; their coup resulted in a decade of unstable coalitions that were characterized by factional infighting and by large-scale distribution of spoils. With the signing of the Balkan Entente in 1934 by Greece, Romania, Turkey, and Yugoslavia, the isolation of Bulgaria on the peninsula was again clearly illustrated. Internal and international uncertainty played into the hands of right-wing members of the military (part of an elite pressure group called Zveno) and the King; a coup was staged in May 1934 by Zvenari, followed by a crackdown on the VMRO, the dissolution of all political parties, and an attempt to speed up the modernization process in the country. Reorganization of education and administration and the stress on cultural and political unity became central themes in the government. The Zveno regime lacked support, however, and it was followed in 1935 by a regime of personal rule by King Boris III. His rule of 'controlled democracy' lasted until the Second World War.

The depth of Bulgarian frustration over the loss of territories again became clear in 1941. Similar to World War 1, the alignment with the Axis powers appeared to be the best guarantee for territorial gains, and it was made easier by the Molotov-Ribbentrop pact that provided the certainty that alignment with Germany could be combined with the pro-Russian sentiments among the Bulgarian population (Crampton, 1987:121). Occupation of large parts of Macedonia, Thrace and the Dobrudža region followed. The political opportunism of this policy and the lack of conviction in Nazi policies as such showed in the lack of implementation of anti-Jewish policies, at least in Bulgaria proper.[1] However, as in World War 1, the fruits of war were only to be kept for a very short period of time. After the German attack on the Soviet Union had ended the comfortable correlation of political objectives with popular sentiment, the government was forced to retreat. The death in August 1943 of Boris III, who had succeeded in keeping Bulgaria out of the war on the Eastern Front by inventing all kinds of reasons for not being able to fight the Soviet Union, made the Bulgarian position even more awkward, and Allied bombing on Bulgarian cities rapidly caused the erosion of public morale. Nevertheless, the Bulgarian government hesitated until September 1944 before actually severing relations with the Germans, by which time the Soviets had declared war on the country. With the entrance of Soviet troops, the alliance with the Soviet Union became inevitable. The borders of Bulgaria were fixed at their 1940 positions, which included the Dobrudža region in the northeast but excluded the territories in Macedonia and Thrace.[2]

---

1   In the occupied territories practically all Jews were handed over to the Germans (see Hoppe 1986, and Georgeoff, 1981:64–65). The Bulgarian regime also continued to attempt large-scale bulgarization of the Macedonians in the areas that Bulgaria held occupied during the war, which alienated the local population (Franz, 1991:84).
2   The Dobrudža region had been returned to Bulgaria in 1940 under the Second Vienna Award. The population in the region was mainly of Bulgarian (38%) and Turkish (34%) background, with only 21% Romanians (King, 1973:48–49). In total, no fewer than 150 thousand Muslims were added to the Bulgarian population (Kettani, 1988:13; Jackson, 1987:79).

The Macedonian prize thus again eluded the Bulgarians, and the conflict was not diminished by the arrival of the 'internationalist' movement. Indeed, whereas the Comintern had talked about the possibility of creating a Balkan Federation including both Macedonia and Bulgaria, a rift had already emerged between the Yugoslav communists and their Bulgarian counterparts over the question. Each communist party, despite its formal commitment to internationalist solidarity, attempted to achieve nationalist goals by the construction of the federation (see King, 1973:58–71). When Stalin decided to give Tito control over the Macedonian communist resistance during the war, mainly for practical reasons, this was a blow to Bulgarian aspirations. Whatever disagreements there were in the years immediately after the war, the federation ultimately became impossible following the expulsion of Yugoslav communists from the Cominform in 1948 (Bell, 1986:64–66).

In Sofia, a 'Fatherland Front' – a coalition of communists with part of the Zvenari, Agrarians and Social Democrats that had existed since 1941 – staged a coup on the same night that the Russians entered the country. It set the stage for a large-scale purge of the bureaucracy and the army, and an intense power struggle between the communists and the other political factions in the Front.[3] The most important resistance came from the Agrarians who, under the leadership of Dr. 'Gemeto' Dimitrov and later Nikola Petkov, gained substantial support among the population and struggled on until 1948.[4] This was not surprising given the overwhelmingly agrarian character of the Bulgarian economy and the distrust among many farmers of any plans for collectivization (see below). However, communist tactics – under the direction of Georgi Dimitrov, Traicho Kostov, and Vasil Kolarov – to obtain control of the ministry of Interior and Justice, and the presence of the Soviet army on Bulgarian soil proved to be too big an opposition. The communists eliminated their last opponents, most notably Nikola Petkov, when the ratification of the peace treaty by the US Senate removed the last means of external pressure (Crampton, 1987:160; Bell, 1990:66, Höpken, 1990a:210–214).

4.1.2 Bulgaria under communist rule

For over 40 years Bulgaria was a People's Republic. Two constitutions gave shape to that notion: the so-called Dimitrov constitution of 1947, modelled

---

3   By the end of 1944 over 30 thousand officials were discharged. Ultimately over 11 thousand people were tried officially, although some estimations have reached as high as 100,000, with 2700 condemned to death (Bell, 1990:59–60; Crampton, 1987:148–149). A similar fate befell the army.
4   The membership of the Agrarians had grown even faster after September 1944 than that of the Communist Party (Bell, 1990:57).

on the 1936 constitution of the Soviet Union, and the 1971-constitution that contained some small reforms and explicitly certified the leading role of the Bulgarian Communist Party (BKP) in society (Bell, 1986:129). It can be said that from 1947 the basic elements of the Bulgarian political system remained unchanged until the sweeping events of 1989. During the whole period political life in Bulgaria was closely linked to the Soviet Union, to the extent that General Secretary Todor Živkov commented that the two countries shared "a single circulatory system" (in Bell, 1990:81). As in other Eastern European countries the rift between Tito and Stalin had a substantial impact: in 1950 Vulko Chervenkov succeeded Georgi Dimitrov (who had died in 1949) by eliminating his main opposition through accusations of Titoïsm. The main victim of this was Traicho Kostov, who had been crucial along the communist road to power in Bulgaria, but who was ultimately executed in December 1949 (Bell, 1990:70). Chervenkov himself, aptly called 'Little Stalin,' in his turn stepped down from the position of General Secretary after the death of Stalin in 1953, and was replaced by Todor Živkov (who was called First Secretary). Although Chervenkov kept his position as Minister President until 1956, his retreat from power was accompanied by destalinization. Živkov himself, who was supported by Khrushchev, indeed proved to be somewhat of an exception in surviving the fall of his Soviet mentor; he was able to adapt to the changing circumstances until 1989, and he became the longest ruling communist leader in Eastern Europe. By the end of the communist era, Bulgaria was the only country in the region not to have had a major conflict with the Soviet Union. The close link further showed in Bulgaria's trade with Comecon countries, which at 80% was the highest in Eastern Europe.

Not surprisingly therefore, the communist political system also much resembled the Soviet example. The BKP was the 'governing force' in society and in the state; its legitimacy stemmed from its declared ability to interpret Marxist-Leninist theory and find the way to socialism and communism (Luchterhandt, 1990:137). The leading concept in the BKP, and also in the rest of Bulgaria's political system, was 'democratic centralism,' which stood for the attempts to combine the notions of top-down centralized decision-making and bottom-up democracy. The BKP, founded in 1919, had as its highest organ the Party Congress, which gathered once in every five years. This Congress elected the Central Committee, the General (or First) Secretary, and the Politburo; the Central Committee gathered officially once every four months and generally had between 100 and 200 members and a smaller number of candidate members. The membership of the Central Committee changed rapidly during the fifties and sixties, when Živkov had not yet secured his position, but the stability of its membership increased markedly from then on; generally, between 60% and 90% of the members were re-elected (Höpken, 1990a:188). It led the country in the periods between the Party Congresses. The practical leadership of the BKP, however, rested with the Politburo, and in particular with the General (or First) Secretary.

Every Bulgarian citizen above the age of 18 could become a member of the BKP, as long as he or she subscribed to the statutes of the BKP, and actively supported and participated in the building of Socialism. From 1945 until 1958 membership fluctuated between 400 and 500 thousand people; this fluctuation was mainly caused by the regular cleansing of socially undesirable groups, especially farmers (Höpken, 1990a:181). From the beginning of the 1960s the membership rose steadily to over 900 thousand at the end of the communist era. The social profile of the party members changed from more farmers (51.9% in 1944) to more labourers (44.4% in 1986) and intellectuals (39.3% in 1986), which reflected social changes within the country and the desire by the party leadership to maintain a high level of blue-collar membership (Bell, 1986:130). The territorial organization of the BKP was based on the territorial-administrative system of the country as a whole, each level sending representatives to higher levels.

A particular feature of the Bulgarian political system was the existence of the Bulgarian National Agrarian Union (BZNS), which was the only other party allowed to function in the political system after the communist takeover. It had about 120 thousand members, a steady share of 25% of the seats in the National Assembly, and was always represented by four or five members in the State Council and by four or five ministers (Höpken, 1990a:191–201). BZNS was not allowed to develop any policies of its own, but proved functional in broadening the political basis of the regime in agrarian Bulgaria. In the words of communist historian Hristo Hristov (1987:5), "the Bulgarian Communist Party pursued a policy of lasting, strategic cooperation with the Agrarian Union. Taking into account the political realities and the inner possibilities of [BZNS] to make a genuine contribution to the process of the country's socialist construction, the BKP continued to follow this principle after the victory over fascism." BZNS's role was exemplified by the use of Agrarian leaders in 1953, including the son of Stambolijski, who was released from prison to quell the unrest amongst the farmers that resulted from the acceleration of the collectivization process (Bell, 1990:72).

The main legislative body in which the two political parties acted was the National Assembly, the Sābranie, which was composed of 400 members after 1966 (until 1966 between 239 and 416 members). Its members were elected on the basis of a single list system, half of them by single candidacy, and the other half by a majority decision. There were elections in 1945, 1946[5], and once every four years from 1949 onwards. The Sābranie met three to four times each year and delegated its power outside those periods

---

5   This year also included a referendum on the monarchy in which over 90% of the populations rejected the monarchy in favour of the republic (Crampton, 1987:154).

to the State Council (25 members), which it chose from its own members. The Sābranie also elected the Council of Ministers, headed by the Minister President who was the main executive authority of the Bulgarian state. The Council of Ministers fell under the State Council in the hierarchy, making it politically rather unimportant (Luchterhandt, 1990:148). However, the most important ministers were also member of the Politburo, such as the ministers of Defence, Foreign Affairs, Internal Affairs and of course the premier and vice-premier. The main function of the Council of Ministers was therefore to implement the directives of the BKP and the legislation by the Sābranie and the State Council by formulating detailed laws. The executive institutions fell into two categories: on the one hand, the ministries and the institutions of similar importance, and on the other hand, the special organs. The first category was represented in the Council of Ministers and appointments were made by the Sābranie. The second category, which included such institutions as the Central Statistical Agency and the Bulgarian National Bank, did not have representation in the Council of Ministers but were directly subordinate to the State Council.

The unity of the state machinery that is central to unitary communist rule was also reflected in the organization of the local government in Bulgaria. Before the reorganization of 1959 there were three levels of local administration: around 2000 village and municipal communities (obštini), around 100 districts (okolii), and 15 provinces (okrāzi). Over the years various reorganizations have altered this system, first in 1959 by abolishing the districts and creating 28 provinces (including Sofia city); then, in 1977–1978 by introducing so-called settlement systems;[6] and finally, in 1987, by grouping the provinces together into nine regions and by reducing the number of settlement systems (or counties) to 248 (excluding the counties in Sofia). The various reorganizations had as their goal the improvement of the integration of the economic and the political administration, and the decentralization of part of the economic administration away from the central branch ministries to the local government. This was thought to improve the possibilities of regional equalization under a political system in which the economic role of administrative centres had become crucial (Luchterhandt, 1990:155; Bell, 1986:129, Koulov, 1992:394). However, true decentralization did not take place. After the fall of communism the provinces were again subdivided in a total of 28 districts. Interestingly enough, all the terri-

6   The settlement systems were considered to enable not only a more effective infra-structural planning, but also a closer connection between the agrarian sector and the industrial sector. A total of 291 settlement systems were created, to which the municipalities were adapted to fit. The new territorial entities were in fact intended to constitute social communities in themselves, with closely connected territories both economically and socially; they should in particular function to eradicate differences between rural and urban areas (Koulov, 1992:396). Since the urbanization process was considered as proceeding too quickly, this new territorial arrangement hoped to stem the migration flow to the cities. It did not work, however, and some additional measures had to be taken.

torial modifications produced an administrative system with provincial level administrative units of roughly the same size as the ones existing a century ago (see Koulov 1992).

In summary, over the years, communist rule attempted to provide a perfect fit between economic and administrative regions; it was considered to have almost been achieved after 1987 (see Popov and Demerdjiev 1989). However, decentralization of power did not really take place under any of these attempts, and territorial reorganization was also implicitly used several times to destroy the power of local officials (Bell, 1990:82). This use of territorial reorganization in part reflected the tension in communist systems between branch organizations and territorially based executive institutions; the first generally kept the upper hand as they received their orders immediately from the Council of Ministers (Luchterhandt, 1990:160). The centrality of the system was further increased by the fact that control over the various levels of local government, as well as over the other parts of the administration, was mainly exercised by the 'Institutions for State and Peoples Control'. This 'special administrative institution' was constructed in a hierarchic fashion to match all levels of local government and branch administration and was also directly subordinate to the Council of Ministers. Moreover, it was directly responsive to the Central Committee of the BKP and worked together with local representatives of the BKP. They had the task of ensuring that the directives of the party and the decisions of the highest state organs concerning (especially) economic, (but also) social, cultural and juridical policies were implemented, and to check whether the attitude within the administration was as desired. It was the main tool of the BKP in use over the country's state administration and over its officials (Luchterhandt, 1990:164–165).

The state thus acted in a highly unified way, and opposition was almost non-existent. In fact, the strict control of the BKP over the state and its machinery meant that opposition could, besides within the party itself, only take place in such organizations as the Orthodox Church. In the Law on Religious Denominations of 1949 the Bulgarian Orthodox Church was declared to be the traditional Church of the Bulgarian people, but its Patriarchs were carefully checked (or even replaced) and paid by the state. Over several decennia the highest Church officials were seated more at the back of the hall, which reflected their decline in political influence and importance (Raikin, 1989:376). Also the Church lost ground in relation to the population at large, while the international links were disconnected by upgrading the Exarchate in 1951 to a Patriarchate; this effectively meant the disconnection from the Orthodox hierarchy in Istanbul. Not surprisingly, the other churches, such as the Catholic and Protestant Churches and the Islamic institutions, fared even worse (see section 4.3.2.2) (Pundeff, 1984:345–46). Because of its reduction in competencies the Church concentrated mainly on its role as guardian of Bulgarian nationalism, including Bulgaria's claim on Macedonia (see Raikin 1989, Pundeff 1984).

The consolidation of communist power was further effected by the disposal of private ownership. In an agrarian society such as Bulgaria, one of the most important projects in this respect was the collectivization of land.[7] In Eastern Europe in general, land reform was functional in consolidating communist political power and was less intentioned for preparing for the collectivization that was to follow (Wädekin, 1982:32). In Bulgaria there was less need for an extended land reform, but the country was, together with Yugoslavia, the first country to start the collectivization process in full. Of course, because of the sheer mass of agricultural labour, in 1948 still making up 82.1% of the total labour force, the communists were intent on starting the collectivization process early to reinforce their control over the population. The number of traditional cooperations, 579 in the autumn of 1944, was, during this process, increased through various methods, by which farmers were directed towards cooperation: unequal pricing and taxing, obligatory deliveries, restricted access to fertilizer, machinery, and so forth (Wädekin, 1982:36). During the whole process, the land was not nationalized, but only collectivized, which meant that the farmers remained the owners of (a share of) the land. The first phase of collectivization in 1946 and 1947 was indeed more or less voluntary and did therefore not have much effect: in 1948 only 6.2% of the arable land was organized in collective farms, a small increase from the 3% in 1945 (Whitaker, 1990:462). In 1949, after Stalin's orders to increase pressure on the farmers, the percentage grew to 43%, and this phase had, for instance, great impact in the Dobrudža region where most of the land was owned by Turkish farmers. Ever more mechanisms now started to work towards collectivization, such as, for example, the increase in state control over internal agricultural trade (from 43% in 1947 to 87% in 1949) and the use by local officials and party members of extra-legal pressures (Lampe, 1986:148). At the end of 1952 the percentage of arable land in collective farms reached 61%, and the collectivization process was completed in Bulgaria in 1958, after some stag-

---

7   Two major land reforms had already preceded the collectivization of land under communism. First of all, in the period directly after independence the land of estate holders of Turkish origin (who had fled to Ottoman territory in fear of revenge) was taken and redistributed to small peasants (Dovring, 1965:254, Lampe, 1986:24). On the whole, this land reform in the 1880's was very advanced and contained, among other features, the availability of credit to break the hold of money-lenders and the introduction of various forms of collective holdings such as the 'zadruga' (a loose neighbourhood or village association for common landholding, founded in one way or another upon previously existing tribal, kinship, or settlement groups) (Dovring, 1965:164). This type of cooperative farming existed mainly before World War One, with no less than 1123 cooperatives in 1908, its facilities making it the best system of agricultural credit in the pre-1914 Balkan states (Lampe, 1986:31). A second wave of land reform came in the 1920's under Stambolijski, but just 2% of the arable land in Bulgaria was affected by it. From then on the land was further fragmented, and accordingly in 1934 no less than 40% of the arable land was in need of consolidation. They were in large majority private plots: in 1934, when a major farm census was taken, 90% of the land was owner-operated, as were 92% of the farms (Dovring, 1965:169).

nation (as in the rest of Eastern Europe) in the wake of Stalin's death. Of all the significant changes introduced in Bulgaria after the BKP assumed power, the most important no doubt was this "assault on the tradition of private farming, which was at the very core of the pre-socialist peasant social-structure" (Whitaker, 1990:462).

In contrast to most other socialist countries, only collective farms of the kolkhoz-type and hardly any state farms were created (Grosser, 1990:349). Over the years, the average size of these farms increased tremendously, and after some initial neglect large investments were made in the sector. Between 1960 and 1970 this led to the highest growth in the agricultural sector in Eastern Europe. Although in part an attempt to decentralize some of the decision-making to lower levels, the introduction of 170 'agricultural complexes', and later of the about 300 'settlement-systems', could not prevent a downfall in agricultural productivity. In 1988 the overall agricultural production was 8% lower than in 1982 (Grosser 1990). In the communist period, the relative importance of the agricultural sector for the Bulgarian economy was sharply lowered; between 1948 and 1987 the share of agrarian labour in the total labour force declined from well over 80% to just above 20% (Grosser, 1990:336). As will be discussed below, this decline substantially increased the importance of the Turkish minority in this sector. In fact, the policies implemented by the Bulgarian government towards the Turks, which will be discussed in section 4.3, have partly been responsible for the difficulties in the agricultural sector.

4.1.3 The recent political changes

Although Todor Živkov had attempted to adapt to the changing circumstances that came with Gorbatchov's rise to power (the so-called pseudo-strojka), the winds of change ultimately proved too strong even for him. Opposition started to organize in all sorts of ways, including in particular an ecological organization (Eco-glasnost), an alternative trade union (Podkrepa), human rights organizations (e.g., Independent Association for the Defence of Human Rights in Bulgaria), including organizations of ethnic Turks (see below), and the so-called 'Discussion clubs for the support of Glasnost and Perestrojka,' led by the dissident Želju Želev. On 10 November 1989, amidst this pressure for change, the position of Živkov was taken over by foreign minister Petăr Mladenov. It meant the beginning of the end of communist rule, and in January of the next year the leading role of the BKP was officially removed from the constitution (see, e.g., Gehrmann and Naydenov 1993, Bell 1993).

The various opposition groups (though not the ethnic Turks) cooperated in the Union of Democratic Forces (SDS). In round table negotiations with the (reformed) communists it was agreed to elect a Grand National Assembly of 400 deputies that would design a new political system and write a new constitution. To the surprise of the opposition, and amidst accusations of unlawful pressures by local officials, at the first free elections in June 1990, the renewed Communist Party, the Bulgarian Socialist Party (BSP), succeeded in winning more than half (211) of the seats in the Sābranie. The SDS ended up with only 144 seats, and a party that represented in practice the Turkish minority, the Movement for Rights and Freedom (DPS), gained 23 seats; these were more seats than the (reformed old agrarian party) BZNS-PN (see Höpken 1990b). The election showed a strong contrast between rural areas, where the BSP was very strong, and the cities, where the SDS gained most of the seats. Besides a strong animosity between rural culture and urban culture in Bulgaria (Creed 1993), this also reflected the fears of many smaller communist officials for a wholesale purge once the opposition came to power. Moreover, the nationalist card was widely played, in particular by the BSP in the rural regions where Turks and Bulgarians lived intermixed (Höpken, 1990b:437). The elections and subsequent political debate nevertheless also showed the new limits for the reformed communists. In July 1990 the oppositional candidate, Želju Želev, became the first non-communist president of Bulgaria, and amidst severe economic contraction the government under the communist Lukanov resigned in November 1990, and a care taker government took over.

After another year of prolonged negotiations and conflicts, a constitution was passed in the summer of 1991. The process as a whole was characterized by intense political debate and fragmentation, and heightened nationalist tension (see Gjuzelev 1992, Troebst 1992). New elections took place in October 1991, in which the BSP and the SDS won roughly an equal number of seats in the (shrunken) Sābranie (106 versus 110, respectively), and in which the DPS gained no less than 10% of the seats (24 out of 240). No other party succeeded in passing the 4% threshold, giving the DPS a crucial balancing position between the two main parties. A government was formed under Filip Dimitrov, with the support of the DPS, and Želev was reelected as president three months later. When at the end of 1992 the Dimitrov government was forced to resign, the DPS sided with the BSP. With the help of president Želev, it in fact put together a new care taker government under Lyuben Berov consisting mainly of technocrats. This government survived until October 1994. The elections in December 1994 turned into a victory for the BSP, which gained 125 seats against 69 seats for the SDS, and the increased fragmentation of the Bulgarian political landscape put an end to the balancing position of the DPS (down to 15 seats).

During the political debate the attempts to privatize the economy proceeded only very slowly. In 1992 private firms produced only 16% of the GDP, and in December of that year just 10% of the land had been returned to its owners. Moreover, after the economy had completely crashed in 1990 (under the short rule of Lukanov alone the economy contracted by 10.7%), it continued to contract by 20% in 1991 and by 7.7% in 1992. This created tremendous social problems. Nevertheless, while the tension several hun-

Table 4.1   Ethnonational groups in Bulgaria (in thousands)

	1934[1]	%	1946	%	1956	%	1965	%	1992	%
Bulgarians	5,173	85.1	6,073	86.4	6,507	85.5	7,231	87.9	7,271	85.7
Turks	618	10.2	675	9.6	656	8.6	781	9.5	800	9.4
Macedonians	–	–	–	–	188	2.5	10	0.1	–	–
Roma	81	1.3	–	–	198	2.6	149	1.8	313	3.7
Pomaks	ca. 102[2]	1.7	–	–	–	–	–[4]		–	–
Others	104	1.7	281[3]	4.0	65	0.8	57	0.7	103	1.2
Total	6,078		7,029		7,614		8,228		8,487	

Sources: Georgeoff 1985, Troebst 1990, National Census Bulgaria 1992.

Remarks:
1   For this year the nationality was determined by native tongue, but for the other years by ethnic affiliation.
2   This figure was given in the census eight years prior. In 1934 approximately 134 thousand Muslims spoke Bulgarian; the majority of these were Pomak (Georgeoff 1985:281).
3   Mainly of undetermined ethnic affiliation.
4   Troebst (1990) mentions the number of 170 thousand for 1970, which is the last official information regarding the Pomaks during the communist period.

dred kilometres further away in the Balkans culminated in fierce civil war, Bulgaria appeared to be an island of peace and calm by comparison. More extensive treatment of this period is to be found in section 4.3.3, where particular emphasis will be placed on the role of the Turkish minority in the new political system.

4.2   THE GEOGRAPHY OF ETHNICITY IN BULGARIA

The majority of the minorities in Bulgaria are Muslims who ended up in Bulgarian territory upon the redrawing of Balkan borders. Some of them had arrived there following the conquests by the Ottomans, while others had already lived there and had been converted to Islam during Ottoman rule (see Popovic, 1986a:67). Although many Muslims fled during the first couple of years of the Bulgarian state – between 1878 and 1900 their share in the total Bulgarian population declined from 26% to 14% – large numbers nevertheless have always remained. The majority of the Muslims are Turkish-speakers, but there are substantial numbers of Bulgarian-speakers and Roma (Gypsies) as well. Table 4.1 lists the numbers of the main minorities in Bulgaria at various times during this century.

The numbers displayed in the table have to be treated with caution. Throughout the period the number of Turks is probably the most reliable, although any judgement of that is made very difficult by the enormous emigration flows that have taken place since the Second World War, particularly from 1989 onwards.[8] The last census seems to provide a reasonable count of the Turkish minority, even though protests had been voiced, both that they were too high and that they were too low (Puister, 1994:133). The numbers for the Roma, the Pomaks, and the Macedonians are either not given or are very questionable. The last census which gave the numbers of national minorities under communism was taken in 1965. All minorities taken together in that period constituted between 15% and 20% of the population. The changes in the numbers partly indicate the differences in treatment of the various minorities during different periods. However, this magic with numbers is one of the usual tactics applied to the region's nationality conflicts. Bulgaria is in this respect not too different from, for example, Greece, Turkey, or Romania.

Before I discuss the Turks, some brief information on the other groups is in order. Unfortunately, very little information is available about the second largest minority, the Roma (or Gypsies or Tsigani). Their numbers dropped in the official statistics from 197,865 in 1956 to 148,874 in 1965, but both figures can be considered too low. Since then, an official number of 233 thousand was reported in the mid–1980s, but very different numbers were reproduced in the publication by Konstantinov et al. in 1991 (see note 8). Their information showed that the Roma lived in all parts of the country, often in separate settlements around urban centres (see also Carter, 1994:9–10). The 1992 census roughly confirmed this pattern of generally even spread and slight concentrations, even though the total numbers were much lower. The communist regime started around 1953 with a 'settlement program,' and a name-changing campaign for the Islamic Roma, to assimilate this group. However, as a whole it appears not to have been very successful (Poulton, 1991:116). A major share of the Roma are Muslims (estimates ranging from 40% to 75%), and according to the census of 1965, 42.6% spoke Bulgarian, 34.2% Romani, and 22.8% Turkish (Troebst, 1990:481). Konstantinov et al. (1991), however, mention the possibility that over half of the Roma is 'Turkish-oriented.'

8   As will be discussed extensively below, in 1989 over 310 thousand Turks left the country and only half of them returned, while the flow to Turkey did not really stop between 1990 and December 1992 (the month of the census) (RFE/RL, 5 Feb. 1993). Another problem is that the number of Roma is in reality probably much higher and a large number of them and of the Pomaks have probably registered as Turks. This compares with the results that Konstantinov et al. (1991) gathered from local officials and the Ministry of Interior. They arrived at no less than 577 thousand Gypsies and 269 thousand Pomaks; they also arrived at 848 thousand Turks at the time (Konstantinov et al., 1991:103–104). For the number of Gypsies and Pomaks similar numbers are quoted by Troebst (1994). After the exodus of 1989, the total number of remaining Turks could therefore be lower than the 800 thousand mentioned.

The third largest group are the Pomaks, a Muslim group that speaks a Bulgarian dialect and lives in the western part of the Rhodope mountains on the border with Greece (and in Greece itself (Seyppell 1992)). Their origins are unclear; one suggestion is that they are the descendants of a Turkish group, the Cumens, who arrived in Bulgaria in the 11th and 12th centuries; others consider them to be Islamized Bulgarians who were converted to Islam by the stick and the carrot of Ottoman rulers (Karpat, 1990:7, Crampton, 1987:7). Because the census-takers consider them as Bulgarian they have not been categorized as a separate group since World War 2. Various estimates have been made of their size in 1956 and later, ranging up to 300 thousand (Konstantinov et al. 1991, Kettani 1988, Troebst 1994). Before the First World War they were among the groups with the lowest literacy rates, with very little intellectual life, and they remained isolated and separated from the Bulgarian and Turkish communities alike. They married mainly amongst themselves and were almost solely occupied with agriculture and forestry (Popovic, 1986a:105). The Bulgarian government has always tried to separate the Pomaks from the Turkish minority by a variety of means, and their position has not been very enviable. At various times during Bulgarian history the government attempted to change their Muslim names, for instance during World War 2 (see Konstantinov 1992). Their problems still remain; in recent negotiations about the reversal of forced name-changing the Bulgarian government initially suggested restricting the reversal to the period after 1984, thereby obviously excluding the Pomaks from that process (Poulton, 1991:168). However, they ultimately were included in the reversals of the name-changing as well.

Many observers have long considered the assimilation of the Pomaks into the Bulgarian group only a (short) matter of time, because of the strength with which the Bulgarian government attacked the separate identity of the Pomaks (e.g., Popovic, 1986a:97). However, at the moment it remains to be seen whether they will survive as a distinct group, assimilate into the Bulgarian group, or even assimilate into the Turkish group. Recent research indeed suggests that the Turkish identity is currently favoured, due to the present status of the Turkish minority and of Turkey (see Konstantinov et al. 1991), but there also seems to be a relationship with the ethnic mix in the region; since ethnicity feeds on adversity the Turkish identity is stressed in situations where Pomaks live among Bulgarians, whereas the Bulgarian side of the Pomak identity is stressed where Pomaks live among Turks (Troebst, 1994:35–36). The actions of the group are carefully observed by Bulgarian politicians. In this context it is somewhat disquieting that the Bulgarian parliament started an investigation into allegations of turkification just before the census of December 1992 (Puister, 1994:143).

The importance of the fourth group in size (in all probability) has already been discussed above. There were 187,789 Macedonians counted in 1956, but this number dropped dramatically to 9,632 in 1965, giving rise (in Yugoslavia) to the term 'administrative genocide'. The drop was the result of a drastic 'reduction' in the number of Macedonians living in the Pirin region bordering Yugoslavia, which has Blagoevgrad as its main town. The decrease was preceded by a turn in policy in 1958, only two years after the census of 1956. In the historical journal of the central committee at the end of that year, the new Bulgarian position was formulated as follows: "there is no foundation for the recognition of the population of the [Pirin] region as a separate nationality. Such a distinction would be artificial. ... There are no differences in language, culture, or economy between the population of the Pirin-region and the Bulgarians, nor are there legal or political differences. It would be an act of oppression to force on the inhabitants of the Pirin-region the half-Serbian literary language that has been invented in Skopje" (in Bell, 1986:118).

As has been described above, Macedonia has been, and still is, one of the major problems of the Balkan Peninsula, and a source of irritation between Greece, Serbia (or Yugoslavia), and Bulgaria. The friction during and after World War Two between the two communist parties from Bulgaria and Yugoslavia was only temporarily stalled by the agreement in 1946 to give a substantial amount of cultural autonomy to the region (the so-called Dimitrov years). For Bulgaria this implied the recognition of the separate nationality of the Macedonians and the teaching of the Macedonian language. Because of this around one hundred teachers (and, of course, propagandists for Macedonian unification) came from its Yugoslavian counterpart. Although, as has been said above, this initiative over the question proved short lived because of the rift between Tito and Stalin, there remained some cultural autonomy during the 1950s. During the 1970s and 1980s large investments were directed to the region, in part to diminish the attraction of the Yugoslavian Federal Republic of Macedonia (Troebst, 1990:481; Poulton, 1991:108–109). In the last couple of years, however, the Macedonian Question has re-emerged on the political agenda. Recent estimates of the number of Macedonians put the number at slightly over 200 thousand, but the position of this minority remains extremely complicated, both in terms of ethnonational characteristics and of international intricacies.

Numerous other, smaller-sized minorities live in Bulgaria as well, such as Armenians, Russians, Greeks, Tatars, Jews, Romanians, Karakatchanis, Koutsovlachs, and so forth. I will not discuss them further. Good overviews are found in Troebst (1990, 1994) and Carter (1994).

Map 4.1 Turks in Bulgaria (1992)

4.2.1 The Turks of Bulgaria

By far the largest group, the ethnic Turks, live mainly in two areas: in the Arda river basin in the south of Bulgaria, around the city of Kārdžali, and in the Dobrudža region in the northeastern part of the country, near the towns of Razgrad and Šumen. According to the last census they form the majority in the district of Kārdžali and are a very substantial minority in the districts of Tārgovište, Šumen, Silistra and Razgrad. Map 4.1 shows the regional distribution of the Turks according to the census of December 1992. It should be noted that the living areas of the Turks extend somewhat beyond the five districts marked on the map, but in those districts their share in the total population does not exceed 15%. Moreover, in those regions it is likely that many non-Turks have registered as Turks (see note 8).

The rural character of the Turks has been a persistent characteristic of the group, not only before the Second World War, but also after. At the end of the war 70% of the ethnic Turks lived in the provinces Kolarovgrad (Šumen), Haskovo (including Kārdžali) and Ruse (including Razgrad), and within these provinces they were mainly concentrated in purely Turkish villages. In 1956, 92.7% of the Turks in Kolarovgrad still lived in rural areas, just like 94.6% in Haskovo and 88.5% in Ruse (Höpken, 1987a:261). Figures for the mid–1970s showed that even after 30 years of communist rule 56.1% of the Turkish labour force was still involved in agriculture, almost twice as many as the figure for the total population (28.4%) (Höpken,

1987a:266). As Karpat (1990:15) describes, the "occupational change from agriculture to industry and services resulted in the movement of large numbers of Bulgarians from villages and towns to cities. Meanwhile, the Turkish population in particular, and the Muslims in general, with the exception of those from a few areas around Plovdiv, Burgas, etc., stayed in their village and remained involved in agriculture ... There they now form half of the agricultural labour force" (Karpat, 1990:15). Whereas the Turks also migrated to smaller regional towns, their dominance in the rural areas in some parts of Bulgaria was indeed a continuing one. The importance of the Turkish population to agriculture in Bulgaria could also be shown by the decrease in agricultural productivity in the 1980s, which could very well have had something to do with the treatment of the Turkish minority in that period (Grosser, 1990:339). Thus, for example, the total production of tobacco, in which the Turks play an important part, between 1985 and 1989 fell from 113 thousand tons to 60 thousand tons (RFE/RL, 17/9/1993).

Not just in occupational structure, but also in demographic characteristics, the Turks clearly differed from the Bulgarians. Indeed, as can be derived from table 4.1, Bulgaria as a whole faces some severe demographic problems. Population growth has slowed down during the last decades, causing the total number of Bulgarians now to still be significantly lower than the 10 million Georgi Dimitrov predicted in 1948 for the early 1950s (Oschlies, 1986:3).[9] Including out-migration the period since 1970 has hardly seen any growth at all, and between 1985 and 1992 there has even been a decrease by 475 thousand (RFE/RL, 5/3/1993). During the 1970s, the number of Turkish families with more than three children was four times as high as the national average, and it was estimated that the population in Kārdžali would double in the 35 years between 1965 and 2000, while nationwide the increase would only be 17% (Höpken, 1987a:267–268). In Kārdžali, the birth rate between 1976 and 1984 was still 29.7‰ yearly against a national average of 15‰, with a natural growth of 14.8‰ against 4.2‰ (Troebst, 1990:476). The high birth rates have only been offset by significant out-migration (see section 4.3.2).

---

9   The main reason for the decline in population growth is the relatively low birthrate of 13‰ in 1987, which is caused by a variety of factors: the lack of adequate housing for large families, especially in the cities; the extremely high labour participation of women, forming almost half of the total workforce and caused as much by the long dominance of communist ideology as by the wish for higher living standards; the inadequacy of governmental stipends for pregnant women and the lack of guarantees that they can keep their jobs; the high number of abortions at 125 thousand a year; the high rate of divorce; and so forth (see e.g., Oschlies, 1986:12–18; Taaffe, 1990:444). It might be added that the speed of the urbanization process in Bulgaria (with a urbanization rate of 66.4% in 1987, against 46.5% in 1965 and 21.4% in 1934 (Taaffe, 1990:444–447)) has left the rural areas with an older population which generally has an excess of rural deaths over rural births. In 1986, only three regions had an excess of births over deaths in the rural areas (Smolîan, Blagoevgrad, and Kārdžali); two of them are inhabited by large numbers of Turks or Pomaks (Taaffe, 1990:452).

In summary, the Turkish minority in Bulgaria has remained large, mainly rural, and concentrated in a few regions. As can be seen from map 4.1, the living areas do not quite border Turkey. The next section deals extensively with the history of the Turkish minority in the Bulgarian state, with the main emphasis on the communist period.

4.3   THE BULGARIAN STATE AND THE TURKISH MINORITY

4.3.1 *Prelude: the Turkish minority until 1944*

As has been said above, many Turkish-speaking Muslims fled during the first years of the Bulgarian state. Among those who left were especially the administrative and commercial cadres in the cities, reinforcing the agricultural character of the Turkish community. In addition, many of the wealthier Turks in the rural areas left for Constantinople after the land reforms; their emigration further reduced the social power of the Turks in the countryside and increased the feeling of vulnerability that had followed the change in position from members of the dominant group to members of the subordinate group. Naturally, the Turks and other Muslims lost many of their public functions, and only small numbers of doctors (Turkish especially), journalists, teachers, and mayors remained (see Popovic 1986a). Generally speaking interaction with the Bulgarians and the Greeks was kept at a minimum; intermarriage did not even occur in the bigger cities (Mollahüseyin, 1984:141). Quite understandably, therefore, in 1927 one observer concluded that "conservative Islam still retains its hold on the hearts of the people. It is true that there are movements towards reform and signs of progress, but the general impression remains that for the most part these minority groups continue to be static, like little islands of Asiatic conservatism in the midst of the swift current and rising tides of European life" (Zwemer, 1927:332).

Despite this assessment, it was clear that the Turkish communities were forced to adapt to the new circumstances. Until then, even after the decline of Ottoman control and the emigration of the majority of the Turkish establishment, the institutions that had developed under Ottoman rule remained the backbone of the Islamic communities. Thus, the *vakufs* formed the most important financial institutions of the community, through which the buildings and agricultural lands of the community were managed. The *muftis*, the local Islamic clergy (which after 1909 included a *Grand Mufti* in Sofia) headed the administrative councils of the *vakufs*; they were elected by the local population and officially confirmed by the *Sheik-ül Islam* in Constantinople. The *muftis* had a number of other functions in the local communities as well, such as controlling and organizing the education of the local population, presiding over the Islamic council, and speaking justice in civil cases. There were also Islamic courts and a religious school in Šumen. The

Tărnovo Constitution and the Turco-Bulgarian Convention of April 1909, and the 'Law Concerning the Establishment and Administration of the Islamic Religious Community' of May 1919 all extended this tendency towards Muslim autonomy (Crampton, 1990:66).

Nevertheless, all Muslim communities on the Balkans became divided between leaders based in these traditional institutions and leaders having their base in more modern types of organization (see Roessingh and Sytsema 1993). The strongest growth in more progressive institutions occurred in the 1920s and the beginning of the 1930s. One of the main exponents was the 'Turan' Association that tried to organize the Turkish 'sportsclubs'; these had mushroomed in Bulgaria after the Kemalist takeover in Turkey in 1922. The association had a strong Kemalist stance and apart from sports activities also had libraries, reading rooms, and newspapers; it wanted to emphasize cultural studies, and unite and raise the social and educational level of the Turkish youth, thereby following closely the developments in Turkey (Şimşir, 1988:71–76). The Turks also attempted to voice their interests on the political scene; in 1929 representatives of the Turkish community held, with the permission of the Bulgarian government, the first 'National Congress of the Turkish Minority in Bulgaria'. The Congress produced a detailed list of demands concerning the administration, the local elections, the religious institutional structure and the religious and secular education. Concerning the elections for the local councils, for instance, they desired the exclusion of the Roma from the process (for more details see Şimşir 1988:78–83).

Despite these protests and demands, however, the Turkish community appears to have been quite satisfied with their status in those years. In particular during the rule of Stambolijski they experienced substantial autonomy and state support (Eminov, 1987:290). The emigration of Greeks after the First World War further facilitated an unqualified implementation of the minority laws. The animosity between Greeks and Bulgarians, the regional conflict over Macedonia, and the status of Macedonians on Bulgarian soil was at the time considered a more pressing problem than the problems between Bulgarians and Turks, and population exchanges in the 1920s therefore eased the tension in the country for the minority as a whole (Crampton, 1990:70). Moreover, in 1925 a Treaty of Friendship was concluded with Turkey which confirmed the autonomy of the Muslim minorities in Bulgaria and also settled for regulated, voluntary, and unrestricted emigration to Turkey. Understandably, therefore, the final document of the 1929 Congress stated that "The Congress notes with great joy and gratitude the fact that the Turkish people in Bulgaria enjoy broad cultural, educational, and religious freedoms and is happy to express publicly its thanks and respect to the Bulgarian state." However, the statement continued, "Notwithstanding this, the Congress feels obliged to observe with great sadness that, in spite of the firm orders of our government, some small officials, and also some persons and organizations who do not wield any

77

authority, are forcing the peaceful and loyal Turkish people to emigrate from Bulgaria by their hostile and unseemly behaviour and are hence causing the Turkish people to suffer tremendous economic losses" (in Şimşir, 1988:94).

None of the demands of the Congress were really met by the Bulgarian government. Instead, it started to crack down on the newly educated Turkish intellectuals, whom the government considered Kemalists and Turkish nationalists. The Bulgarian government thereupon sided with the conservative *Grand-Mufti* who had condemned the "modernist and abominable reforms" of the new regime in Turkey (in Popovic, 1986a:89). One of the most heated debates concerned the introduction of the Latin-Turkish script in education. In October 1928 the acting *Grand-Mufti* succeeded in making the Bulgarian government prohibit the use of the new alphabet, either because he thought that the new script would deprive the Bulgarian Turks of the spiritual guidance and enlightenment of the Holy Quran, or because he considered the fact that many Bulgarian Turks did not know any script other than Arab, with few also having the ability to read cyrillic (Şimşir, 1988:99). Naturally, protests came from the Turkish government which sided with the progressive Turkish Teachers Association which had initiated the attempts at educational reform in Bulgaria along the same lines as that of Turkey. After prolonged diplomatic exchanges between Bulgaria and Turkey the new script was introduced in 1929, and the use of Arabic script was forbidden in 1930. Aside from the printing of books and the publishing of modern education methods, the new script also began to be used for most newspapers. Nevertheless, internal divisions within the Turkish community continued to be used by the central government, which maintained a preference for the more conservative part of the Turkish community. Thus, in 1930 the Bulgarian government closed the secular school in Šumen which had been opened in 1921 and placed its pupils in the religious Nüvvab school. And four years later, the decisions concerning the Latin script were reversed, and the new schoolbooks and newspapers were banned.

The deterioration of the position of the Turks in 1934 started to accelerate unmistakably with the nationalist, centralizing, and modernizing policies of the Zvenari, who considered Bulgaria no place for 'archaic and traditionalist' sections like that of the Turks or the other Muslims. They changed, for instance, almost 2000 place-names to rid them of their Ottoman connotation (Crampton, 1990:62). Under the authoritarian rule of King Boris III the situation worsened further: the number of Turkish schools dropped from 1712 in 1934 to 545 in 1936 and continued to drop to a mere 400 in 1944; Bulgarian language education in Turkish primary schools started in the school year 1936-1937; the structure of Islamic Courts was abolished in 1938; and the last Turkish newspaper was closed in 1941 (Şimşir, 1990:165).

In general, until the Second World War the political influence of the Turks was very limited. The authoritarian governments saw them as nothing more than an irritating barrier to further economic and social development in Bulgaria, while the liberal governments, if anything, considered them as a means of securing a majority in the Grand National Assembly. In 1914, for example, the 'liberal' Vasil Radoslavov included the new territories in Macedonia and Thrace in his campaign, forbade the campaigning of opposition parties, and put the Muslim population under great pressure to vote for him in order to secure a workable majority in the parliament (Crampton 1987:63). At the time, most of the Muslim population in those regions did not even have Bulgarian citizenship. The communists also apparently found (or attempted to find) some support among the Turks, because they also published their magazine in Turkish between 1920 and 1923. Furthermore, there were some Turkish members (no Pomaks or Roma) in the Bulgarian parliament: Popovic (1986a:94) mentions 15 representatives in 1908, 9 (out of 246) in 1920, 10 in 1923, 5 in 1925 and 4 in 1933. In all likelihood their influence was minimal.

The developments up until the Second World War led to several waves of emigration. After the initial out-migration after independence a continuous flow of Turkish and other Muslim emigrants from Bulgaria arrived in Turkey. Although the exact number is hard to obtain it has been estimated that 350 thousand Turks left Bulgaria between 1880 and 1926, followed by another 110 thousand up to the Second World War (see e.g., Höpken 1992). While most of the Turkish elite had left the country immediately after Bulgarian independence, the waves of emigration in the second half of the 1930s again hit the elite; this time they involved most of the writers, teachers and other intellectuals who had tried to organize the community in the previous decades (Popovic, 1986a:70; Şimşir, 1990:165). During World War Two and shortly thereafter, emigration almost came to a standstill.

In summary then, the structure of the Turkish community remained largely intact at least until the coup by Zveno in 1934. The Turks were generally tolerated, and discrimination was not systematic but depended on the specific sentiments of the government or local officials in charge. The Turks for a long time kept much of their autonomy, although this partly could have resulted from the lack of state capacity to intervene (Eminov, 1987:29). The waves of emigration nevertheless were detrimental to the community, as it was at various times robbed of its potential leadership. By the time the communist regime was created, the Turkish minority was therefore rural, rather isolated, and on its own.

4.3.2 *The Turkish minority under communism*

As has been pointed out, the sometimes sudden changes in the numbers reported in the censuses reflected fluctuations in policy with regard to the various national minorities on Bulgarian soil. In general, it can be said that the policies of the communist regime have followed the Soviet example of the two-stage process that has been discussed in chapter two. At first, efforts were made to imbue ethnic culture with socialist elements. Various possibilities for teaching languages, for developing the arts, and even for practising religion were thus tolerated and stimulated. Article 71 in the 1947 constitution, for instance, specifically mentions that "[n]ational minorities have the right to be educated in their vernacular, and to develop their national culture" (Poulton, 1991:120). This attitude is still reflected as late as 1964 in the congratulations Todor Živkov presented to the Turkish magazine Yeni Hayat (The New Life) on its tenth anniversary: "All possible opportunities have been created for the Turkish population to develop their culture and language freely ... The children of the Turkish population must learn their [mother] tongue and perfect it. To this end, it is necessary that the teaching [of the Turkish language] be improved in school. Now and in the future the Turkish population will speak their mother tongue; they will develop their progressive traditions in this language; they will write their contemporary literary works [in Turkish]; they will sing their wonderfully beautiful songs [in Turkish]... Many more books must be published in this country in Turkish, including the best works of progressive writers in Turkey" (in Eminov, 1990:213).

Ethnic minorities were expected to reach the second stage, in which the separate identities of the groups would merge to form a common socialist identity (Eminov, 1983:144). This was implied by Todor Živkov, when in 1970 he stated that assimilation was not to be considered a term fit for the communist context, but a term fit only for a bourgeois context. Therefore, in Bulgaria there was only the convergence of all the workers in the country and their joint construction of the socialist and communist society. In that sense, according to Živkov, the Bulgarian nation in Bulgaria was assimilating into a socialist community (Troebst, 1990:489). It has, however, become clear from the policy changes since the Second World War that this expected second level was not easily reached, thereby causing the communist regime to alter its course. Though in the Dimitrov constitution the minorities were specifically mentioned, in the 1971 constitution only individuals, instead of groups were described as having rights; no guarantees were given stating that the state would provide for the implementation of the rights. Thus, article 45 only mentioned "citizens of non-Bulgarian extraction" (Georgeoff, 1981:50; Poulton, 1991:119). It was nevertheless stated, in article 35, that no citizen can be discriminated against on the basis of his 'nationality' and his 'religion.'

4.3.2.1 Turkish participation in the political system

It should be clear immediately that the participation of Turks in the communist system has on the whole remained very limited. The only specific political institution for national minorities was the special 'committee for the Turkish minorities' in the BKP (and before that in the OF), but it is not clear what influence and role it had and how long it existed (Troebst, 1990:479). In the lower branches of government immediately after the war, it was very likely that the Islamic clergy and teachers acted as the representatives of the Turks, because they were in general the only ones literate enough, certainly following the out-migration of Turkish intellectuals during the 1930s. Naturally, the communist regime tried to generate a new Turkish elite that could be expected to be more loyal to the socialist cause. This was supported by the publication of a Turkish version of the newspaper of the Fatherland Front, called Işik (Light). It is doubtful whether this new cadre acted accordingly in the first few years. The opening up of local branches of the BKP and of the state organs during the 1940s and 1950s attracted a "new, politically minded Muslim intellectual elite," that was surely under the direct supervision of Bulgarian chiefs, but apparently could occasionally voice the demands and defend the interests of their people (Karpat, 1990:16).

While the membership of Turks in the BKP was very low immediately after the war, in 1951 it was decided to increase their membership substantially (Poulton, 1991:121). Thus, in the beginning of the 1960s it was supposed to be 2.9% (against 6.5% of the ethnic Bulgarians), and it rose to 4.9% at the end of the 1960s (against 7.3% average); since then it has not been higher and has probably declined. BKP membership among ethnic Turks has thus always remained lower than for ethnic Bulgarians (Höpken, 1987a:276; Bell, 1986:131). The BKP particularly tried to incorporate the intellectuals of the various minorities in their ranks, but the Turkish intellectuals were generally not given any position of influence for the reason that they were considered to stay too strongly connected to the rest of their group. In fact, the Turks who had started to participate in party institutions were often criticized for their lack of discipline and socialist consciousness (Poulton, 1991:121). For the individual Turkish party member, the result was a position isolated both from the rest of the group, from the political leadership, and, as no group coordination of policy was made possible, also from their Turkish comrades in the party. The Pomak intellectuals, on the other hand, were apparently less attached to their ethnic kin and rose more easily to positions of influence.[10]

A few Turkish intellectuals nevertheless made it to the top. Although their level of participation in the higher state organs is unclear, it was even

10   Personal communication by Yulian Konstantinov.

lower than the rates for membership in the BKP (Höpken, 1990a:217–218). The number of Turks elected to parliament between 1949 and 1981 was somewhere between 2.5% and 4.3%, while between 1954 and 1962 the Turks were only represented by candidate members in the Central Committee; in other years they had one member and two to four candidate members. In the 1981 Central Committee there was one Turk, who was accompanied by three Jews and one Pomak; no Roma participated (Bell, 1986:131). Surprisingly, in light of the assimilation campaign (see further down), the share of Turkish CC members has actually gone up since 1984, when it became three members and four candidate members (Höpken, 1990a:188). A proportion of Turks similar to the share in the membership of the BKP was probably found for the youth organizations and for the local People's Councils, but no figures are available.

As for other institutions, it has been reported that the ethnic Turks were not allowed to make a career in the army or the police (Poulton, 1991:121). They nevertheless participated, as did large numbers of Roma and Pomaks, in the (semi-military) Construction Corps that was engaged in the construction of roads, railways, state buildings etc. The Construction Corps, created after the Balkan Wars to compensate for the restrictions on the size of the Bulgarian army, probably consisted in great majority of Roma.[11] It was also very difficult to work within institutions where many of the policies with regard to the Turks originated, such as the Ministry of Education. Whether any specific minority participation in BZNS was available is unclear, although this seems likely, given the function BZNS had for the implementation of agricultural policies of the communist regime and given the agricultural background of the Turks as a group.

Overall, the picture that emerges is one in which the participation of the Turkish minority in the state organs and in the BKP was very low. Moreover, it is unclear what function they had if they did participate. As Krasteva points out, whereas there may have been quotas in education or executive boards for minorities, this did not imply defence of the interests of the minorities or the articulation of their concerns. Generally, it was done to conduct the state's strategy towards them more effectively, whereby the state determined the position the community or minority had to take. Thus, paradoxically, "those 'representatives' were the most typical instance of integration, and not of difference ... The function of their inclusion was not the stimulation of activity in the civil society, but the integration into the system. In other words, the purpose was to strengthen the sense of Bulgarian affiliation without forming a citizen's position" (Krasteva, 1992:16–17). Because of this, they were on the one hand used to deflect the critique by the Turks of state policies. According to one observer, the lack of resistance against most of the measures regarding the education of ethnic

---

11 Personal communication by Yulian Konstantinov.

Turks (see below) was caused precisely by "the government practice of presenting regulations that affect the lives of Turkish speakers in the name of prominent Turkish-speaking party members. These regulations [were] also enforced by local Turkish-speaking party members. An impression [was] created that educational and cultural policies of the government [represented] the desires and aspirations of the Turkish-speaking community itself" (Eminov, 1983:142). On the other hand, the incorporation had a second function of isolating the intellectual leadership of the minorities; this discouraged the emergence of organized interest defence on the part of the minority outside control of the BKP. In sum, the limited numbers of Turks who did participate in the political system were hardly in a position to initiate or influence policies concerning their group, even though the government sometimes tried to portray it that way.

4.3.2.2 Collectivization

The Turks, having very few means to influence policies in Sofia, were therefore largely dependent on the whims of the communist leadership. As discussed above, initially the communist policies were not too detrimental to the group, and there was some improvement in comparison with the period immediately before the war. The Turks appear not to have been hostile towards the new regime, in particular after their treatment under the regimes of Zveno and King Boris III. In December 1944 a Turkish Minority Conference was organized in Sofia (by Turkish Fatherland Front committees), where support for the Fatherland Front was expressed and where new demands were raised regarding educational, religious and economic aspects of the minority's daily life (Şimşir, 1988:136–141). Some of the demands were met, such as those in education. The interest of the regime was clear in that respect, because in order to arrive at a socialist nation the Turks had to be 'uprooted' from their agricultural surroundings and 'backward' culture. Nevertheless, the close cooperation with the Bulgarian socialist nation was not forgotten. Thus, during the fifth Party Congress of the BKP in 1948, the policy of 'involvement' (*priobštavane*) in the construction of socialism was announced (Troebst, 1990:487). This involvement could be achieved through the upgrading of the Bulgarian language in the lower levels of education and through the simultaneous downgrading of education of minority languages in primary schools. The start of the collectivization process also meant more pressure on the minorities to interact with the Bulgarian part of the population in the building of socialism.

Because of the large number of Turks living in rural areas, the collectivization process was of particular importance to their economic and social position. It is certainly clear that during the first wave of collectivization at the end of the 1940s and the beginning of the 1950s, Turkish farmers resisted entrance into the collective farms. Moreover, even as late as 1957 only 42% of the Turkish farmers had found their way into the collective farms (Höpken, 1987a:263–264). Bulgarian sources blamed this resistance on the local Islamic clergy, and clearly the collectivization was, much more so than among Bulgarian farmers, seen by the Turks as a full-blown attack on their way of life. It is also likely that in the process their position as small farmers was often replaced by low status jobs within the collective farms, such as shepherds and cowherds, and garbage and fertilizer collectors (Mollahüseyin, 1984:138). On top of that, and perfectly in line with the intentions of the regime, social interaction between ethnic Turks and Bulgarians was created where none had existed before.[12]

Although the precise impact of the collectivization on Turkish life is as yet unclear, the new regime surely had a strong effect on the Turkish population. It is useful to look at two different fields of policy that were particularly central to the Turkish identity in a little more detail: education and religious life. In the final part of this section I will deal with the culmination of Bulgarian communist policy for its Turkish minority, the assimilation campaign of 1984–1989.

4.3.2.3 The education of ethnic Turks

For generations the education of ethnic Turks had been provided mainly by religious officials. Not only did these represent almost the only literate group within the Turkish communities, but the schools were also important tools for their religious mission (Eminov, 1983:137). Between the two World Wars, 90% of the funds for the schools came from the communities themselves, but the situation had already come under pressure from the authoritarian regimes in the 1930s.

---

12 It is conceivable that with each step in the enlargement of the agricultural units, local autonomy was further minimized and social interaction increased. Thus, where at first the local brigades may have acted as a means to defend local control, the reorganization into agricultural complexes may have further eroded local control. Therefore, by 1977 the member farms of most agricultural complexes had lost their independent identities and had turned into territorial subdivisions and production branches of the complex (Wädekin, 1982:250). In fact, a Romanian commentator on the subject of agro-industrial complexes indicated that in the long-term the complexes were considered to be very useful in achieving certain sociopolitical goals: "People belonging to different social classes, or groups, are employed in the agro-industrial economy, having different training and income levels as well as various forms of existing labour organization, etc. In the process of building up and developing the agro-industrial sector, these differences are reduced gradually; the social relations are being transformed. Within the framework of Romania's economy this process represents one of the fundamental principles capable of ensuring the gradual reduction of the existing differences both within the agricultural sector, as well as between this sector and the other material producing sectors" (in Wädekin, 1982:262). It remains obscure however as to what extent such goals were actually reached in the Bulgarian context.

In light of the general communist policy described above, it is not surprising that when the schools in Bulgaria were nationalized in September 1946, the separate identity of the Turkish schools was retained. In fact, their number almost doubled from 673 in 1946 to 1199 in 1950, and an intensive alphabetization campaign was started to diminish illiteracy (with modern books in Latin script of course). This education campaign was generally welcomed by the Turkish population and its leaders, because they considered it an improvement in the development of their own culture (Şimşir, 1990:166–168). As a result, illiteracy disappeared among the Turkish youth almost completely, even though Bulgarian sources accused the Islamic clergy of actively opposing the campaign; the effect on the older generations was markedly less, however (Eminov, 1983:139; Höpken, 1987a:262). Illiteracy, which was extremely high at the end of World War Two, was brought down to 36.2% in 1956 against a country-wide average of 13.1% (Troebst, 1990:479; Bachmaier, 1990:494). The goal of the education was of course to create a socialist-inspired Turkish culture.

In June 1960, the Turkish and Bulgarian schools were completely merged, both in an organizational sense and in their curricula. Of the 112,733 Turkish children who received education that year, only 800 received it in both languages, Turkish and Bulgarian (Mollahüseyin, 1984:141). For a few years Turkish children received two to four hours of Turkish language education, but after 1964 that ceased altogether. This was officially decided upon in 1974, and no Turkish education can be said to have existed from then on until 1989. Higher education was also curtailed. In 1974, the Turkish language department at Sofia University was closed down, after the entrance of Turkish students (70% of all students) had already been strongly discouraged in previous years. It was replaced by a department of Arabic Studies that was only accessible to children of diplomats and so forth. According to some, however, in the end this actually contributed to social improvement for the Turkish intellectuals, since they were forced to take jobs in other sections of the society, and their activities became more relevant to the day-to-day affairs of the Turkish minority (Poulton, 1991:121).

As discussed above, the official reason behind these changes was that only together with the Bulgarian children and in the Bulgarian national language could the Turkish minority develop into competent and equal builders of socialism; in April 1959, for instance, the Central Committee announced that separate Turkish education brought with it the danger of 'self-isolation' and 'estrangement' (Bachmaier, 1990:495). Another argument was that bilingual education placed too much strain on the Turkish students (in Eminov, 1983:141). However, a more realistic reason for the curtailment of Turkish education is probably that the speed by which the Turkish minority changed its language in daily communication was considered too slow, and that too many Turkish people, especially elderly people, totally refused to learn the Bulgarian language. In 1951 therefore, a separate and intensive literacy campaign was started among the Turks to speed up the reduction of illiteracy; among the measures taken were lower entrance grades for the Turkish youngsters and the involvement of teachers from the Soviet republic of Azerbaidjan in education in the regions of Šumen, Kārdžali, Razgrad and at the University of Sofia (Bachmaier, 1990:494). Moreover, it appears that the literacy campaign in the Turkish regions had to continue well into the 1960s to also reach the most outlying communities (Höpken, 1987a:270–271).

Article 45 of the constitution of 1971 declares only that "citizens who are not of Bulgarian origin have a right to learn their language, while the learning of Bulgarian is compulsory"; no guarantee is given that the state will provide for education in minority languages. It is not surprising that under communist rule the Turks have maintained a lower level of education than their Bulgarian counterparts, in part because of their inability to combine their educational language with their daily language (Eminov, 1983:141). Thus, the latest figures available, those for 1975, show that over seven years the proportion of the Turks who had received higher education (0.6%) was more than eight times lower than the percentage for the total Bulgarian population (5.0%); for secondary schools this percentage was 4.7% versus 16.4% (Höpken, 1987a:264).

4.3.2.4 The religious organization of the Turks

As has been mentioned in section 4.1, the Law on Religious Denominations was passed on March 1, 1949. In this law an important role was laid down for the Bulgarian Orthodox Church, for even an atheist regime had to take into account the important role of the Church for Bulgarian nationalism. Although the Bulgarian Orthodox Church could not escape the political purges of the 1940s and 1950s, the law nevertheless stated that "The Bulgarian Orthodox Church is the traditional religion of the Bulgarian People, associated with its history, and has such form, contents and spirit, that it may become the people's democratic church" (in Ramet, 1984:14). The Muslim community was therefore confronted with a coalition of the communist regime and the Bulgarian Orthodox Church, causing some observers to comment that the "deplorable situation of Bulgarian Muslims is more due to old conversion expectations of the orthodoxy than to the communist doctrine" (Balic, 1985:378).

The communist regime intended to reduce both the influence of the Islamic institutions, and of 'religious behaviour'. Therefore, the government undertook to lower the number of mosques and *imams* serving in them. The number of Turkish *imams* declined between 1956 and 1961 from 2393 to 462, while the number of Pomak *imams* declined in the same period from 322 to 95 (Popovic, 1986a:103). The *Grand Medresse* in Šumen, the religious school, was closed down in 1952, and religious education in schools disappeared altogether in the same year (Mollahüseyin, 1984:141). Furthermore, the *Grand Mufti* in Sofia lost his importance as a genuine representative of the Turkish community. Religious leaders were put under the control of the government, religious feasts were suppressed, and Islamic press was non-existent (imported and self-produced alike); no external contacts were allowed, let alone the pilgrimage to Mecca. Apparently no Bulgarian Muslim has had the opportunity to go to Mecca since 1945 (Popovic, 1986a:104). As mentioned above, the regime was eager to establish the differences between Turks and Pomaks, for instance by creating separate religious organizations for each (Popovic, 1986a:99).

The policies have undoubtedly had some effects on the religious feelings of the Turks, although it is of course impossible to clearly differentiate between secularization tendencies as a result of modernization and the separate effects of specific policies of the communist regime. Thus, for instance, the number of Turks describing themselves as religious declined from 80% in the beginning of the 1960s to 60% in 1973, while one observer called the religiosity of the average Bulgarian Muslim 'mediocre' in the mid–1980s (Popovic, 1986b:21). It seems nevertheless clear that Turks have held stronger religious beliefs than the ethnic Bulgarians. A survey taken in the mid–1970s indicated that almost 50% of the Turks were believers, against some 17% of the Bulgarians (Höpken, 1987a:241n33). Although the figures should be treated with much caution, they seem to indicate that, at a time when the anti-religion campaign had been well under way for two decades, religious life was still very much a central aspect of Turkish life. It was therefore clear that the Turks had not achieved the atheistic attitude ascribed to a socialist nation.

4.3.2.5 Towards a homogeneous state

The policy changes in education and religious life reflect the general development in minority policy of the communist regime. Overall, the tension between more involvement and the maintenance of a separate culture became apparent early. In the winter of 1950–1951 over 150 thousand Turks emigrated to Turkey, while 120 thousand more were surprised by the sudden closure of the border and failed to get out. Clearly the pressures caused by collectivization, by the nationalization of the educational system and by the controls on religious activity created a climate of weariness after the prewar regimes and World War Two had already caused much hardship (see Höpken 1992).[13] On the other hand, an exodus created the opportunity for the regime to rid itself of the two groups within the Turkish community it found least acceptable: the religiously devout Muslims and the relatively prosperous landowners from the Dobrudža region; the removal of these 'elements of uncertainty and unproductivity' was expected to diminish the resistance of the Turks against collectivization and against the economic chaos that accompanied the changes in the political-economic system (Irwin, 1984:220; Eminov, 1986:509).

Following this crisis, the situation initially improved; perhaps this was a conscious effort by the authorities to calm the situation. However, the tension increased further after 1956 when it became clear that the expected second phase of 'merging' was not taking place as expected. In a decision by the Plenum of the Central Committee of the BKP in April, it was established that Bulgaria was not a multi-national state and that the examples of Yugoslavia and the Soviet Union were not to be followed. A declaration by the Central Committee reads that the Turks resisted ideological re-education as well as unification with the Bulgarian People and, worse, sabotaged the construction of Socialism (Reuter, 1985:171). The increasing pressure showed itself primarily in the field of education, as discussed above, but use of the Turkish language became more difficult in other fields as well. Thus, for instance, Turkish-language newspapers slowly changed their Turkish pages into Bulgarian ones up to the point where Yeni Işik (New Light), in its last issue of January 29, 1985, contained only 10 percent Turkish text; after that date it was only published in Bulgarian (Şimşir, 1988:245; Poulton, 1991:136). It is also from this perspective that the increasing incorporation of Turkish intellectuals in the BKP must be seen, in order to have them transmit the new messages to the population at large and prevent them from organizing Turkish protests. In fact, the government, with similar intentions, allowed for the expansion of some cultural activities among Turks at the same time that Turkish education was being curtailed. This kept another section of the potentially vocal elite in check – the poets, the writers and the playwrights – and created the image of a blossoming socialist Turkish culture; this is exemplified by the encouraging words of Todor Živkov at the anniversary of Yeni Hayat. However, this period of cultural freedom also ended in 1969.

---

13 As some observers have pointed out, the emigration could also have been intended (by the Soviet Union) to upset the Turkish economy. In the climate of the Cold War this could have been a response to the fact that Turkey had just sent troops to Korea (see Kostanick 1957, Höpken 1987b). Naturally, because of the scale and character of the emigration, relations with Turkey turned sour. The Turkish treatment of the expelled Bulgarian Turks also showed signs of the Cold War fears. None of the immigrants were settled in the strategic areas because Ankara feared that there were communist spies being sent with them (Carter, 1994:5).

The new attitude was put into words by the introduction of the term 'unified socialist Bulgarian nation,' which included the notion that all minorities were 'remnants of the past' that hampered the socialist modernization of Bulgaria. Thus, it meant implementing with full force the ideas which had already been written down for the first time in 1956: Bulgaria was a mono-national state, it had a homogeneous population that was unified by a common socialist history, and there was no connection between religion and the ethnic character of parts of the population, meaning that no minority rights flow from the constitutional right to free religion (Troebst, 1990:488). The Pomaks and the Roma were the first groups to fall victim to this new approach, and most of them were forced to change names between 1971 and 1974; in the beginning of the 1980s the Tatars were to follow.[14] The Turks were as yet left untouched in this respect. Thus, although there were certain instances of attempts at forcible assimilation of the ethnic Turkish minority, this was not pursued by the authorities on a consistent countrywide basis before December 1984 (Poulton, 1991:130).

Increased suppression over the years translated itself into a continuous wish for emigration. Almost 400 thousand Turks petitioned the Turkish consulates and embassy in Bulgaria in the beginning of the 1960s (Şimşir, 1988:210).[15] In 1968 an "Agreement Concerning the Emigration from the People's Republic of Bulgaria to the Republic of Turkey of Bulgarian Citizens of Turkish Origin whose Close Relatives Emigrated to Turkey before 1952" was signed, enabling over 100 thousand Turks to emigrate in the decade that followed (see Höpken 1987b).

4.3.2.6 The ultimate policy: forced assimilation

In the winter of 1984–1985, the 'logical' continuation of the theses of a mono-national Bulgaria culminated in the start of an assimilation campaign intended to destroy the foundations of Turkish identity. The campaign only ended with the collapse of the communist regime in 1989. In response to growing international protests a 'scientific foundation' was formulated, which stated that the ethnic Turks were ethnic Bulgarians who had forcibly been converted into Turks under Ottoman rule, both linguistically and religiously, and who now voluntarily and gladly returned to their true identity;

---

14 The precise beginning of these campaigns remains unclear. Certainly for the Roma the settlement and name-changing campaigns started earlier, but it remains unclear how many of them actually suffered from the campaigns and to what extent Pomaks were already involved as well. See e.g., Franz (1991:92).

15 As Hannum suggests, population transfer was considered the best solution to the Bulgaro-Turkish problems after World War Two. He even mentions 600 thousand Turks who applied to leave the country in the 1960's (Hannum, 1990:57n196). A similar figure is mentioned by Reuter (1985:171) for the 1950's.

a so-called 'rebirth'. In defence of the policies 19th century sources were used, including a *mufti*, who claimed that all Turks were Bulgarians (see Zagarov 1987, Iliev 1989).[16] The 'rebirth' was rather dictatorial, however, as armed units accompanied the Bulgarian officials who came with the new identity cards and with the lists of official names to chose from. The Turkish villages were surrounded and the inhabitants were forced, sometimes at gunpoint, to adopt new names (see Amnesty 1986; Poulton, 1991:129–151; Eminov 1986). Around a hundred people were killed during the campaign and many more arrested and jailed. In the years that followed the wearing of Turkish clothing, religious expressions, and even conversations in Turkish were forbidden.

The exact motives for the 'rebirth' campaign are not very clear, and the documents concerning the decision have been declared missing (Vasileva, 1991:348). In fact, even after the fall of communism it remained obscure who, apart from Živkov himself, was responsible for the decision (RFE/RL, 10/7/1992). One of the main reasons for the campaign in all likelihood was the continuously high differential in birthrate between the ethnic Turks and the ethnic Bulgarians. This difference not only confirmed the lack of assimilation between the two groups, but also fuelled the fears of the Bulgarians of being 'outgrown.' On top of that, as has been indicated above, the fast growth of the Turkish community and the declining growth of the ethnic Bulgarian community was making the Turkish labour force more and more important for Bulgarian agriculture, which made the expulsion of the minority less preferable. In particular if the future workforce was taken into account, assimilation must have looked a far better option to the communist elite. Related to this is the possibility that the regime panicked under the deteriorating economic situation in the country and in this way tried to deflect attention from itself. Other possible 'rationales' are manifold. They include the depopulation of the border areas by ethnic Bulgarians because of urbanization (leaving only Turks in certain vital (and disputed) areas), the nearness of the next census (December 1985) so another administrative genocide could be sealed, the increasing restlessness among Turks and Pomaks under the conditions of political and cultural repression, the increasing influence and propaganda on the part of neighbouring Turkey, and the need for a strong southeast-wing of the Warsaw Pact (see for discussions, e.g., Eminov 1986, Eminov 1990, Höpken 1987b, Karpat 1990, Oschlies 1986, Reuter 1985, Bell 1993).

---

16   An official of the Balkan Department of the Bulgarian Ministry of Foreign Affairs put it as follows: "The forcibly converted part of the population has become aware of the historical truth about their national identity and has been regaining their national self-consciousness (as Bulgarians) in the whole course of a century after Bulgarian liberation in 1878 ... All this has found a final and categorical expression in the process of the restoration of Bulgarian names by the Muslim citizens of their own free will and on their own initiative" (in Eminov, 1986:508).

This ultimate policy led to a degree of resistance that had been unknown among the Turkish minority until then. There were even reports of bombing and terrorist attacks, and various group were organized that tried to attract international attention (see Gehrmann and Naydenov, 1993:8; Nationalities 1989). Many Turks, however, became convinced of the hopelessness of their situation and preferred to leave the country. By 1989, under increasing internal and external pressure, the communist regime came to the conclusion that expulsion could perhaps reduce the tension. By 1989, Turkey was certainly willing to accept them, as already in 1985 the Turkish president Özal had declared that his country was willing to receive between 300 and 500 thousand Bulgarian Turks (Höpken, 1987b:179). Not surprisingly therefore, when the borders were opened in 1989, almost 370 thousand Turks left for Turkey (Vasileva, 1991:347). Again, as in earlier waves of emigration, one of the first groups to be exiled was the leadership of the resistance that had been organized among the Turks. This time the flow was immediately very large because of the fear of a new closure of the border (RFE/RL, 1/12/1989). Emigration was only stopped by the closing of the border on the Turkish side. Although several months later the crumbling of the Berlin wall led to the demise of communism in Eastern Europe, and although within the next year over 150 thousand Turks returned, more than a quarter of the total Turkish population in Bulgaria chose to leave the country forever (Vasileva, 1991:348; see also Kirisci 1991, Franz 1991, and Höpken 1992).

4.3.3 Aftermath: the Turks in the new parliamentary system

As described in section 4.1, on November 10, 1989, Živkov was replaced by Mladenov as party leader of the BKP and head of state. From then on things improved for the Turks, and on December 29 the Politburo decided, despite substantial protest among a portion of the Bulgarians, to end the assimilation campaign.

As indicated above, the Turks had developed some resistance to the measures of the Bulgarian regime in the second half of the 1980s. Their resistance formed part of the wider resistance in Bulgaria against the rule of the communists. For the Turks one of the main organizations was the Democratic League for the Defence of Human Rights that had been established in November 1988 by ethnic Turks who were kept in the prison on Belene Island. By June 1989 more than 10 thousand Turks had joined, and the number of demonstrations and other forms of protest rose steadily. Not surprisingly, hardly any role was played by the Islamic clergy of the Muslim community in Bulgaria in these protests. Although a few members of the clergy had protested, the *muftis* had already declared during 1985 that there was no problem with the Turks in Bulgaria.[17] Indeed, the new *Grand Mufti* who had been appointed by the regime in 1988 had been the local *mufti* in Kārdžali between 1986 and 1988 and had served the Bulgarian secret police until 1981 (RFE/RL, 25/9/1992; see also Poulton, 1991:129–136; Höpken, 1987b:189). Support did come from the Bulgarian Turkish community in Turkey which had developed strong leverage on the Turkish government and press (Kirisci, 1991:550).

In January 1990 the Democratic League was transformed into the Movement for Rights and Freedom (DPS), which attracted tens of thousands of people as members in a very short timespan; the DPS was under the leadership of a philosopher, Ahmed Dogan (Gehrmann and Naydenov, 1993:16). To the surprise of many, the DPS gained 23 seats in a parliament of 400. The BSP continued to use nationalism as a strategy, presenting itself as the party for 'national unity' and playing on fears of Turkish separatism and foreign intervention (with reference to Cyprus). Although the DPS had already explicitly renounced any desire for territorial autonomy and separatism before the June election, the distrust, also among the SDS, was substantial.[18] Nevertheless, new laws were passed to reverse the name-changing campaign and arrange for the rehabilitation of persecuted individuals (Riedel, 1993:106). Turkish-language education was again allowed in March 1991, although it proved very difficult to implement because of the lack of qualified teachers (who had emigrated to Turkey) and good teaching material.

The new constitution that was negotiated between the BSP and the SDS contained some unfortunate clauses. The preamble of the document defines Bulgaria as a "nationally and politically unified" state of the "Bulgarian people," and article 1 states that autonomous territories are disallowed. The Bulgarian Orthodox Church is the traditional religion (art. 13), and the constitution does not contain rights for ethnic minorities, but only for "citizens for whom the Bulgarian language is not their mother tongue" (art. 36.2). However, they have a right to "learn their language and use it." Organizing a political party on a "ethnic, racial, or religious basis" is not allowed (art. 11.4), and organizations that are directed against the sovereignty, territorial integrity and unity of the nation, and that may increase ethnic, national, or religious hatred are forbidden (art. 44) (Riedel, 1993:107–108; Troebst, 1994:33). The consequences of the new constitution became clear after July 1991, when it was passed amidst great political turmoil (not just because of these clauses, however) (see RFE/RL, 16/8/1991). In subsequent months the BSP tried to have the DPS blocked from participating in the election of October 1991. Initially the Supreme

---

17 Also an illustrative contribution in this respect is the article by the regional mufti Iliev (1989).

18 Thus, when the BSP government under Lukanov fell several months later, the DPS did not participate in the all-party coalition government under Dimittar Popov, because of the latter's anti-Turkish attitude (see RFE/RL, 18/1/1991).

Court ruled the DPS indeed illegal on the basis of the new constitution, and the Central Election Committee only allowed the DPS to participate under heavy pressure from the CSCE conference that took place in Moscow at the same time (RFE/RL, 4/10/1991). As has been said, the DPS succeeded in winning no less than 10% of the 240 seats in the new parliament as well as a wide array of local government offices, such as members of local councils, village mayors and district mayors. They clearly could count on practically all the votes of the Turkish population and on the votes of many Pomaks and Roma as well. The juridical battle was finally decided in April 1992, when the Constitutional Court rejected a new claim by the BSP to ban the DPS and have its parliamentary mandates cancelled.[19]

The election results enabled the DPS to take up a balancing position between the BSP and the SDS, which it used to support the new government under Filip Dimitrov. However, the new government did not succeed in implementing the privatization and decollectivization, and the laws that were passed were not unequivocally favourable for the Turks (Riedel, 1993:115). The mechanism of decollectivization was of course very important in light of the importance of agriculture to the Turkish community. The deterioration of the economic situation, the continuing tension between Turks and Bulgarians at the local level, and high unemployment caused by the dissolution of the collective farms (up to 40% and more in some regions) led to a new wave of unrest and to renewed emigration to Turkey;[20] in September 1992 it was reported that, in the months before, over 70 thousand Turks had left the country for Turkey (RFE/RL, 5/2/1993). When pressure on Dimitrov's government failed to improve the situation, the DPS withdrew its support and, in close cooperation with president Želev and with support of the BSP, formed a care taker government under Lyuben Berov.[21] At that time, the SDS displayed instead an unwillingness to treat the DPS as an equal partner in the negotiations. Perhaps here, aside from frustration over the withdrawal of support by the DPS for the SDS government and the general disdain of the city-based SDS for the agricultural and rural DPS, general antipathy towards minorities also played a role. As Krasteva (1992:18) argues, the fact that the Turkish minority forms an ethnonationally different but still legitimate part of Bulgarian civil society which has the right to represent its interests, no matter how partial, was still hardly recognized among the Bulgarian politicians and population even three years after the changes.

---

19 This was a very close call, as six out of twelve judges were in favour of the claim and five against, with one absentee. The law prescribed a majority of the judges, meaning seven, would be needed to accept a claim (Riedel, 1993:112).

20 A major source of frustration was, for instance, the state monopoly on the buying of tobacco, which meant *de facto* much lower prices than could be obtained on the free market (Troebst, 1994:35).

21 To be sure, the government under Dimitrov mainly fell because of alleged arms-deals with Macedonia, not because of the ethnic issue.

The situation improved somewhat from 1993 onwards, although plenty of problems remain for the Turkish community in Bulgaria. One of the main problems is still the return of goods and houses to the Turks who had left the country but then returned. Nationalist sentiment is also high in the ethnically mixed areas of Bulgaria where extremist nationalist parties have succeeded in gaining three seats in a combined list with the BSP. Most of the cadres from the communist period have remained in place in the countryside, and they resent the loss of their positions of power to local Turks. Moreover, the decollectivization has left the Turks who did not own land before 1958 without a means of economic subsistence; in the present economic circumstances alternatives are almost non-existent. In the political arena, the factionalization of the main Bulgarian political parties has put an end to the balancing position of the DPS. The election results of 18 December 1994, when the DPS only won 15 seats and the BSP achieved the absolute majority with 125 seats, has widely increased the range of possible governments.

Nevertheless, the Turkish problem is certainly not the only nationalist problem to trouble Bulgaria these days. The Pomaks have started to develop their own organizations, and the lack of recognition has led some among them to voice desires for separation and unification with the Pomak areas in Greece (Troebst, 1994:37). The Macedonian question still troubles Sofia, not only because of the instability in the region, but also because of the impossibility of granting any concessions to the people in Pirin-Macedonia without endangering its still existing claims on the Bulgarian nature of the Macedonian nation. In fact, although Bulgaria was the first country to recognize Macedonia on January 16, 1992, it was immediately put forward that this did not imply a recognition of the Macedonian nation (Troebst, 1994:37). In 1994, a major row broke out over the fact that, during a visit of Macedonian president Gligorov, a treaty of cooperation was presented only in Bulgarian, as the Macedonian language was considered to be Bulgarian anyhow.

Despite the present tensions, the international uncertainty over the Balkans, and the enormous costs of the transition, Bulgaria has remained relatively stable since the fall of communism. Moreover, the acceptance of the existence of a loyal ethnic minority seems to have grown among all political parties in the Bulgarian political spectrum since 1992 (apart from the extreme nationalists of course). Until now, only the careful use of the position of the DPS by the Turks as well as the actions of president Želev helped acceptance of the Turkish group as a political and social player in Bulgarian society. However, with the disappearance of the balancing position by the DPS, the improvement of circumstances for the ethnic minorities may rapidly come to a halt. Furthermore, extremist sections of the minorities may gain influence while the poor social and economic circumstances continue, both amongst the Turks and amongst the Macedonians, Pomaks and Roma. This would fuel fears amongst the Bulgarians and could create a devastating spiral of ethnonationalist tension. Indeed, to some extent, chance has played a major role in the stabilization of ethnic relations since 1989 in Bulgaria, but the Turks, and thereby Bulgarian society as a whole, may very well run out of luck either on the national scene or internationally.

4.4 THE BULGARIAN COMMUNIST SYSTEM AND ETHNO-NATIONAL MOBILIZATION

As Schöpflin (1993:24) notes, it is only with the disappearance of communist rule that the shape of the society which it created became visible. The complete transformation of Bulgarian society under communism and the dominant fiction of homogeneousness found their climax in the forced assimilation of Bulgarian Turks between 1984 and 1989. However, these processes began at a much earlier stage: from 1944 onwards the communist regime had set out on its 'historical mission' to modernize their country and develop it along Marxist-Leninist lines. This included an intensive education program for the population as a whole, the development of industry, urbanization, and the collectivization of agriculture. In doing so the communists broke down the old social structures that had been in place since Bulgaria's independence.

Until 1944, the Turks were even more rural and traditional than the rest of the population. They lived concentrated in some specific areas and basically kept to themselves. In dealing with its Turkish minority the communist regime attempted to restructure Turkish life in Bulgarian society, incorporate the Turks into the school system and the political system, and diminish the influence of traditional religious institutions and sentiments. Both economic and cultural policies were used to achieve those goals. Once separate, but socialist, identities had developed, merging into the Socialist Bulgarian Nation would occur. The communists clearly did not succeed in achieving even their first goal of restructuring Turkish life on a socialist basis. The Turks did not join in sufficiently, resisted with vigour some of the changes (such as the collectivization of land), did not join the urbanization process, and continued to differ in their demographic characteristics. When the 'historical logic' did not appear to work on its own, the regime felt obliged to speed up the process. There can be no doubt, given their actions after 1989, that the resolve of the Turks to stick to their own identity has grown as a result of communist policies, in particular after the 1984–1989 campaign. It seems fair to conclude that the modernization process along Marxist-Leninist lines, including the stamping out of diversity and the uniting and homogenization of the various groups within Bulgaria's borders, has in the end only served to strengthen the ethnic solidarity of the Turks. Indeed, it may even have supported the turkification of other Muslims.

Whatever resistance the Turks could provide originated from the fact that they considered the policies an attack on their way of life, and suspected

Bulgarian nationalism as being behind it. The main reason for this was their near complete exclusion from the decision-making process, which was even more crucial given Sofia's complete control over economic and social life in the country. The fact that the Turks did not live in Sofia did not help, of course, as the Turkish community could hardly benefit from the centralization that was undertaken under communist rule. Indeed, in this book there is probably no case in which the distinction between the minority and the state machinery was so clear, and where the capital city was so much regarded as a distant foreign ruler. The Turkish minority was left completely at the mercy of the majority. Moreover, the lack of other forms of opposition (within the Bulgarian majority) that could function as a check and balance on the policies of the regime had disastrous effects as well, because hardly any brakes on the policies were possible. Therefore, even if substantial parts of the Bulgarian population had wanted to resist the assimilationist policies of the regime (which is doubtful, however), they could not voice their concern. In all aspects, from collective farms to local government, the centrality of decision-making eroded any remaining autonomous decision-making. The presence of a few Turkish representatives within the system only served to improve the regime's control over the group, and did not serve as a form of access to the centre. Both newly educated intellectuals and the Muslim clergy were forced to adopt this role, by which the regime not only was able to present its policies as inspired by members of the group itself, but also kept these elites from starting to organize any form of resistance. Indeed, the fact that hardly any open resistance against the worsening circumstances was organized until the excesses of 1984–1985 demonstrates the general pervasiveness of the control.

When the possibility arose, only emigration appeared to be an option. The massive choice of this option shows the lack of other outlets. In a way the border with Turkey was a safety valve, to be opened when the regime considered it necessary. The Turkish elite were generally the first to be expelled. Moreover, the massive out-migration can be seen as the execution of the exit-option by a group without the means to press for secession on a territorial basis. Moreover, the inability to stress this option of course also flowed from the location and split of the Turkish living-areas, and from the difficulty in sharing the experiences as a group and organizing effective resistance on a group basis. In summary, therefore, it is perhaps impossible to speak of a Turkish ethnonational movement under communism, apart from the first decade and the last two years under communist rule. Nevertheless, after the fall of the communist regime, the consequences of its policies have become clear. The long-time docile Turkish minority has reasserted itself and has been able to act in a unified manner. In doing so it has achieved a great deal in terms of reversing the communist policies. However, the balance remains extremely delicate, both in Bulgaria itself and internationally.

5

Czechoslovakia
The Road to Fission

The second case in this book deals with ethnonational movements under a communist and federalized political system. Former Czechoslovakia became a federation on January 1, 1969, and it remained so until its dissolution on January 1, 1993. This chapter will trace the road to the fission of the Czechoslovak Federal Republic and will explore to what extent the dynamics generated under the communist federal political system strengthened Slovak and Czech separateness. Although Czechoslovakia has been plagued by other minority issues, the federation has been organized around the Slovak and Czech ethnic groups, and it is upon their relationship that this chapter will focus. As in the chapter on Bulgaria, although the main emphasis will be on the period for which the case has been selected (stretching from 1969 till 1989), other periods will receive attention as well. Thus, after a short introduction in section 5.1, the ethnic diversity of the state will be discussed in section 5.2. Section 5.3 contains a discussion of Slovak-Czech relations under various political systems, following which section 5.4 contains an evaluation of ethnonational tension under communist federalism.

5.1   INTRODUCTION

5.1.1 The fragile state

The Czecho-Slovak Republic became a state on October 28, 1918, when a group of Czech leaders declared the country's independence in Prague. It emerged out of the ruins of the Habsburg empire, and its borders were highly contested from the start. Slovakia and Ruthenia were only included after heavy fighting during the spring of 1919, and it took until the treaties of St.Germain (September 1919) and Trianon (June 1920) for its borders to gain international acceptance; even then a separate protocol was needed with Poland to arrange for the possession of Teschen/Tešín. The borders of the country delimited over 140 thousand square kilometres and over 14 million inhabitants.

The national character of these inhabitants reflected the multinational nature of the former Monarchy: with large numbers of Germans, Hungarians, Poles, Ruthenians and Jews, besides Czechs and Slovaks, much attention during the interwar years was directed at inter-ethnic relations. Besides the tension between Czechs and Slovaks, which will be discussed below, the main problem revolved around the position of the Germans, the second largest group in the country. Indeed, German deputies who had been elected in Austria in 1911 had proclaimed an independent German-Austrian state on October 21, 1918, and the German deputies in the Czech Lands had declared themselves to be the 'Provisional Provincial Diet' of German Bohemia which was to be an autonomous province within that state (Kalvoda, 1985:111). Czech troops were used to end this resistance. Nevertheless, after initial protests and resistance, most Germans accepted their position in the new state, and several German parties participated in all governments from 1926 onwards; these parties gained between 74% and 83% of German votes in 1920, 1925 and 1929.

The Republic was in fact to become the only country in Eastern Europe that saw its democratic system survive the political turmoil of the interwar period. The constitution of February 1920, in which the country was officially designated as the Czechoslovak Republic (without hyphen) provided for a unitary state in which Bohemia, Moravia-Silesia, Slovakia and Ruthenia had very limited autonomy. Suffrage was universal, equal and compulsory. Under the presidency of the philosopher and humanist Tomáš Masaryk, a political system functioned in which a large number of political parties competed in each election; the fragmented nature of the system was displayed in the need for coalitions that often consisted of five or more parties (Leff, 1988:48–55). Masaryk himself was central to the day-to-day political life of the Republic, and a small group of his trustees in fact made most of the important decisions (known as the Hrad group, after the castle on the Moldau in Prague) (Hoensch, 1991:50).

Over two-thirds of the Monarchy's industrial capacity had been located in the territories of the new state. The Czech Lands in particular were highly industrialized and, in an economic sense, relatively successful. A main part of the industrial capacity was located in German-speaking areas. Therefore, these areas were particularly hard hit by the Depression at the beginning of the 1930s, and around 1933 two-thirds of the country's unemployed were Germans (Hoensch, 1991:56). The unemployment was partly caused by the replacement of Germans in the bureaucracy by Czechs. Already preyed on by its neighbours, the country further destabilized from within: it was the new Sudete Deutsche Partei, led by Konrad Henlein, that gained the Germans' full support in 1935 (it won in fact the most votes of all Czechoslovak parties). Beneš, the successor of Masaryk, who died in 1937, could do nothing to avoid disaster, even though negotiations were started with the Germans over autonomy within the Czechoslovak state (see Yapou 1981). No longer supported by the Western Powers, the First Republic was unable to stop the course of events: in October 1938, the country lost 29% of its territory and 34% of its population (Kalvoda, 1985:119). The remainder was divided into three autonomous regions (Ruthenia, Slovakia and the

Czech Lands). Parts of Slovakia and Ruthenia went to Hungary, while Germany and Poland gained most of the Czech Lands which were seceded. The second Czecho-Slovak Republic (with hyphen) lasted only a couple of months.

On 14 March, 1939, Slovak independence was declared and one day later the Germans overran the Czech parts of the truncated republic; Hungary claimed the rest of Ruthenia. During the war the Protectorate Bohemia and Moravia was occupied by the German army, while the Slovak State, under the presidency of the Catholic priest Josef Tiso, allied itself with the Germans. As will be discussed below, the Slovak State was certainly not unconditionally welcomed by the entire population, and an uprising in 1944, and diplomatic efforts by the Czechoslovak government in exile, succeeded in having the Slovaks accepted as part of the Allies. During the war, almost 100 thousand Slovak Jews died in the Holocaust, and in August 1944 only an estimated 13,500 remained. In the Protectorate, of the 98 thousand who had remained in the area until 1939, only 24 thousand survived, including 8,500 from Ruthenia (Kalvoda, 1985:129–130).

The most important problem at hand after the war was the position of the Germans and Hungarians. President Beneš issued a series of decrees in 1945 and proclaimed the principle of collective guilt. This principle deprived the Hungarians and Germans of Czechoslovak citizenship, and the decrees also called for the subsequent confiscation of their property and their expulsion; only those members of the German and Hungarian minority who had actively resisted the Nazis could be exempted. The Germans started to flee the country immediately after the war, first in a 'wild expulsion' of hundreds of thousands of refugees, and later in a more regulated way when another 2.2 million left the country. Before the war the number of Germans was at least 3.39 million (higher according to German statistics), but in the 1950 census only 165,117 were left (Kalvoda, 1985:123). The transfer of the Hungarian minority proved less attainable because of resistance by the Hungarian government, and when the communists had succeeded in obtaining a dominant position in Hungary itself, Stalin withdrew his support for the transfer (King, 1973:56). Only an exchange of around 70 thousand Slovaks from Hungary against Hungarians from Slovakia took place, while an additional 44 thousand Hungarians from Slovakia were transferred to the deserted Czech borderlands. Moreover, thousands of Hungarians were forced to declare themselves Slovaks, and in the 1950 census only a low 367,733 Hungarians were counted (Kalvoda, 1985:124, King, 1973:53–57). The region of Ruthenia was lost to the Soviet Union.

Of course, the developments during the war had discredited several parties because of their cooperation with – or lack of resistance against – the German occupation and the Slovak clerico-fascist regime. Moreover, the occupation of Czechoslovak territory by the Red Army put the communists in a position to raise their demands and eliminate some of their potential opponents. Thus it was decided in the Košice Programme, negotiated in Moscow and presented in the first major town in Czechoslovak territory that was liberated by the Allied forces, that the Agrarians, the Small Tradesman, the National Democrats (all Czech collaborationist parties), the Hlinka Slovak Populists, and all minority parties would be banned. Only four parties were allowed to participate in each of the two parts of the country, whereby in the Czech Lands three traditional parties became the opponents of the communists, while in Slovakia the opposition consisted of three new political parties. The communists came out as winners, but did not gain an overall majority, and in Slovakia the Protestant-led Democratic Party was the absolute winner with 62% of the votes.[1] Nevertheless, the fact that the Democratic Party did not have a counterpart in the Czech Lands left opposition against the communists highly fragmented. With communist leader Gottwald as premier, and their control over the ministries of Interior, Information, and Agriculture, among others, the communists started to weaken their opponent's position. Thus, in Slovakia they were able to encourage splits in the Democratic Party and initiate Catholic counter-parties (Jelinek, 1983:103). Because of the lack of coherent organization of the Slovak Democrats, and because of lack of support from Czech non-communist parties (who suspected the Slovak nationalist element in the party), the Democrats were successfully outmanoeuvred in the autumn of 1947 (Steiner, 1973:86). In February 1948 the communists took over in Prague, and in June, Klement Gottwald, General Secretary of the Czechoslovak Communist Party since 1928, became the first President of the Czechoslovak Socialist Republic.

5.1.2 Developments in communist Czechoslovakia

The new political system of the Czechoslovak Socialist Republic was reflected in two constitutions, those of 1948 and of 1960. The country was led by the National Front, which was a smoke screen for the Czechoslovak Communist Party (KSČ). However, some parties were allowed to play a small role in the political system, such as the Czechoslovak People's Party (supposedly representing the Christian element in Czech society and with 500 thousand members before 1948), the Socialist Party (with a similar number of members), and two Slovak-based parties, the Freedom Party and the Rebirth Party. By 1968, membership in these parties did not exceed a couple of hundred, however (Ulč, 1974:34). Membership in the Czechoslovak Communist Party was not very elitist; most of the time it stood at around 1.5 million or 10 percent of the population. In May 1949 there were

---

1   The communists had been able to function legally until 1938. They had received barely 10% of the votes in the interwar elections after splitting from the Social Democrats in 1920–21 (see table 5.2).

as many as 2.3 million members, but the Party was immediately purged once the communists had firmly established power. The generally high membership was partly explained by the large number of jobs to which membership provided access (Renner and Závodský, 1991:230–231). Like its sister parties, the KSČ was led by a politburo, and its most important functionary was the General Secretary. This position was subsequently taken by Klement Gottwald (until 1953), Antonín Novotný (1953–1968), Alexander Dubček (1968–1969), Gustáv Husák (1969–1987), and Miloš Jakeš (1987–1989) until the fall of communism. A separate organization remained for the Slovak Communist Party (KSS) which was completely subordinate to the KSČ, although at one stage, in 1968, it was on its way to becoming a part of a federalized KSČ. This plan was soon abolished, however. Membership was slightly lower in Slovakia than in the Czech Lands, and membership recruitment remained somewhat more problematic in Slovakia for reasons to be discussed below.

The organization of the state was completely subordinate to the KSČ, but the pre-war system was nevertheless largely left intact. In fact, the presidency was apparently prestigious enough to be filled by various Secretary-Generals: by Gottwald between 1948 and 1953, by Novotný between 1953 and 1968, and by Husák between 1975 and 1989. Only Dubček and Jakeš did not combine the two functions. The parliament functioned merely as a forum for confirmation of KSČ policies. As Staar notes, "[t]he near perfect attendance record at these sessions [of the National Assembly] before 1968 was surpassed only by the record of unanimity. Between 1948 and 1960 there was not so much as one dissenting vote and no amendment of any type was offered from the floor. Thanks to this harmony, the Assembly enacted legislation with amazing speed. The only incidents that slowed down the proceedings were the "spontaneous outbursts of enthusiasm" and "stormy applause" – carefully graduated according to the speaker's importance – that greeted even such dry reports as the one on the annual budget" (Staar, 1982:66).

In a similar vein the local and regional government was completely subordinated to the central directives of the regime. Between 1949 and 1960 there were 19 regions or provinces, 270 districts, and no less than 14 thousand municipalities. This was reduced to ten provinces (plus a special territorial status for the cities of Prague and Bratislava), around 100 districts, and around 8 thousand municipalities by the end of the 1960s (Dostál and Kára, 1992:19–22; Vidláková and Zářecký, 1989:169–170). The local government was administered by National Committees at each level which worked according to the principle of democratic centralism described in chapter two; thus they were depicted as "bodies representing the socialist state power and state administration in regions, districts, and municipalities" working "under the guidance of the Communist Party of Czechoslovakia" (Dostál and Kára, 1992:24). Moreover, there was an element of asymmetry in the state structure, with a separate Slovak National Council

(SNR) for which no Czech counterpart existed. The SNR continued to have some functions until 1960. After 1968 there was of course a federal structure (see the next section). The point about asymmetry is an important element in the general discussion on Czech-Slovak relations, and there will be further consideration of the changes in regional government below.

Communist control was also extended to other potential sources of opposition, in particular the judiciary, the Church, and the economy. As for the judiciary, their autonomous role was minimized immediately, and their decisions always reflected KSČ desires. Church life was not as easy to curtail; the Catholic Church, Catholicism being the most important religion in the country, in particular continued to form a source of protest against the regime. Nevertheless, relations between Czechoslovakia and the Vatican were severed in 1952, and all activities of the Catholic Church became effectively controlled. Government-controlled alternatives were created for the official Churches, such as Pacem in Terris as a government alternative for Roman Catholic priests and the Christian Peace Conference for the Protestant and Orthodox Church (Staar, 1982:90; see also Kusin, 1978:106–107). The severe restriction on Church life continued until well into the 1980s, with a brief interlude in 1968.

With regard to the economy, the KSČ immediately started to nationalize the means of production, which was made easier in part by the expulsion of the Germans; they formed 22% of the industrial workers in the country (Krejčí, 1990:23). Between 1945 and 1948 there had already been a strong levelling out of income and considerable nationalization: after October 1945 60% of industrial production was nationalized, and after a second wave in 1948, only 5% of industrial production remained in private hands (Staar, 1982:87). The agricultural sector was collectivized slightly later: in 1955 56% of agriculture was still in private hands, but by 1960 this was reduced to 9% (Krejčí, 1990:24%). With near complete control over the economy, the communist strategy could be implemented with full force; this particularly lead to regional equalization between Slovakia and the Czech Lands (Pavlínek 1992).

Politically, the Czechoslovak republic experienced a wave of Stalinization similar to the rest of Eastern Europe after the Tito – Stalin rift, although in the Czechoslovakian case it was particularly severe and prolonged (Rothschild, 1989:133). As Skilling suggests, the comparatively high-handed character of the Stalinist policies may have been directly related to the strength of the democratic forces in earlier times, both during the interwar period and between 1945 and 1948 (Skilling, 1976:825). The result was appalling; in the early 1950s there were 422 jails and concentration camps and an estimated 100 thousand political prisoners (Ulč, 1974:85). Significant victims of the purges were several of the most important Slovak communists (on charges of bourgeois nationalism and Titoism), and Rudolf Slanský, who had been the secretary-general of the Communist Party shortly after the war. Nevertheless, even the death of Stalin did not end the

Stalinist policies, and there was convincing Czechoslovak support, for instance, for ending Hungarian Reforms (the intervention was of course partly justified by referring to the alleged revival of irredentism in Hungary (King, 1973:81)). Only some limited rehabilitations were passed in the wake of the twentieth congress of the Communist Party of the Soviet Union in 1956, and it took until the 1960s for the charges of bourgeois nationalism to be reversed.

Economic growth was partially responsible for this continuing Stalinism, considering that the workers were kept satisfied for a long time by the increase in the standard of living (Rothschild, 1989:167). Indeed, the successful economic transformation meant that a new constitution could be passed in 1960. It recognized the Communist Party and its leading role in society and declared confidently that Czechoslovakia had reached the state of socialism (only the second country to have achieved that status in the world). The preamble announced that the country was "proceeding towards the construction of an advanced socialist society and gathering strength for the transition to communism" (Staar, 1982:63). Nevertheless, despite this declaration, Khrushchev pressured Novotný to review the Stalinist trials; in particular the Slovak communists were rehabilitated. In combination with a severe economic crisis during the first half of the 1960s – between 1962 and 1963 the GNP actually dropped – the need for change became more and more apparent. However, under the very conservative Novotný, economic and political liberalization was delayed time and again, and it was only with his displacement by the Slovak communist leader Dubček as Secretary General in January 1968 (and by Ludvik Svoboda as president in March of the same year) that a complete breakthrough was achieved. During the subsequent Prague Spring an extraordinary experiment was attempted to implement 'socialism with a human face,' which was intended to open up the Party to the developments and ideas within society. The experiment was crushed by Warsaw Pact tanks in August 1968. The issues which arose during the eight months that it lasted will be further discussed in section 5.3.3, as several marked differences arose between the Slovak communists and the Czech communists.

Dubček's replacement by the Slovak Gustáv Husák meant the start of 'normalization,' which was to last for twenty years.[2] The immediate result of normalization was the expulsion or membership-cancellation of 326,817 members, over 21% of the total at the start of the purges, although the fig-

---

2   According to Kusin 'normalization' in Czechoslovakia can best be described as "restoration of authoritarianism in conditions of post-interventionist lack of indigenous legitimacy, carried out under the close supervision of a dominant foreign power which retains the prerogative of supreme arbitration and interpretation but which prefers to work through its domestic agents. It had two principle aims: to remove reformism as a political force, and to legitimate a new regime resting on old pre-reformist principles" (Kusin, 1978:145).

ure was slightly lower for Slovakia (17.5%) than for the Czech Lands
(22%). Moreover, before the purges many members had already given up
their party membership, reducing the total number of members between
January 1, 1968 and the beginning of 1970 by 28%. In fact, by that time
there were more ex-party members than party members (Ulč, 1974:44,74).
In various waves of purges ever stricter criteria were used, and in the whole
process over 5.5 million individuals were screened (Kusin, 1978:80). Naturally, after the purges the composition of the Assembly changed substantially; in the Federal Assembly of 1971, 614 out of 700 had not previously
been elected (Ulč, 1982:122). Normalization certainly had its effect on the
position that elected representatives held in the state organs. As deputy
Božena Machačová commented in 1969: "Never again must parliament be
allowed to degenerate into a political arena" (in Ulč, 1982:123).

As a result, political life in Czechoslovakia under Husák was characterized by low morale, general numbness, and lethargy. The regime that
crushed the Prague Spring succeeded in staying in power until the very end
of communist rule in Eastern Europe; hardly any opposition was to gain a
foothold again, apart from Charter 77. The secret police played a central
role in sustaining the system, as did such institutions as the Central Commission of People's Control. Familiar 'transmission belts' such as the Revolutionary Trade Union Movements, the Czechoslovak Socialist Youth
League, and the Union for Cooperation with the Army assured the implementation of KSČ policies. In the international arena, diversion from Soviet
standpoints was carefully avoided, and during the crisis in Poland in 1980,
Husák was eager to press the Soviet Union into taking a firm position
against the reforms. Only with Gorbachov's rise to power did the position
of the Czechoslovak 'normalization elite' substantially come under threat;
Husák, and after 1987 Jakeš, were clearly much more conservative than
their Soviet counterpart. Moreover, as the economic performance of the
country had been largely disappointing since the mid–1970s, pressure
mounted again for fundamental change. The last defensive action by the
'normalization-elite' in Czechoslovakia, represented in particular by the
Slovak party ideologist Vasíl Bilák, consisted of replacing the aging Secretary-General Husák with the more conservative Miloš Jakeš in December
1987. Jakeš's leadership was to last for barely two years.

5.1.3 Political aspects of the federation

After the events of 1968, the federation was the only reform which was
allowed to proceed by the Soviet regime. It introduced a form of dual
nationality in the state (both of the ČSSR and of the ČSR or SSR), although
this was reversed only two years later. The new constitutional law which
was adopted on 27 October, 1968 brought some fundamental changes into
the organization of the state machinery.

A quite exceptional feature of the federation was that it involved only two constituent parts, the Czech Socialist Republic (ČSR) and the Slovak Socialist Republic (SSR). Therefore, article 1 of the constitutional law declared that the Czechoslovak Socialist Republic (ČSSR) was "a federative State of two equal, fraternal nations, the Czechs and the Slovaks", "founded on the voluntary bond" of those nations, who had, of course, the right to self-determination (Jičinský 1969). In principle the federal level was to be granted jurisdiction only in those areas in which the nations were willing to surrender, whereby the unity of the two nations was based on the following characteristics: 1) a uniform political system, 2) uniform legislation, 3) the implementation of principles furthering economic integration, 4) a uniform foreign policy, and 5) the common defence of the state (Dean, 1973:38). However, whereas the logic of federation would have led to a substantial diversion of political and economic power to the various local centres, the logic of 'normalization' led to the opposite. Even in the initial federal settlement the position of the federal institutions *vis à vis* the national institutions was strong. Between the various levels of the federation, competencies were split in the following manner:

1) to the federal level: foreign policy; defence; federal treasury (currency) and reserves; protection of the federal constitution; implementation of federal laws and control over federal organs.
2) shared by the federal level and the republics: internal security; planning; finance; banking system; price-setting; international trade; industry; agriculture; traffic; post and telegraph; science and technology; work, payment and social politics; press and media; etc.
3) to the republics: everything that has not been appointed to the federal level or to the common responsibility of the federal organs and the republics, such as education; culture; and health.

A constitutional court, in which Slovaks and Czechs were to have equal representation, would protect the arrangements made in the constitution.

The two chambers at the federal level were equal in importance, and the consent of both chambers was needed for passing laws. The Chamber of People was elected state-wide and consisted of 200 deputies (resulting in 137 Czechs and 63 Slovaks). The Chamber of Nations consisted of 75 Slovaks and 75 Czechs who represented their respective constituent republics. The presidium of the National Assembly consisted of 20 deputies from the Chamber of People and 20 deputies from the Chamber of Nations (10 Slovak and 10 Czech). The Chairman of the Assembly and the Vice-Chairman should be of different nations (art.56). At the level of the republic there was only one legislative body. In the Czech Republic this was the Czech National Council, consisting of 200 members, while its Slovak counterpart had 150 deputies. Communist members in both federal and republican assemblies varied between two-thirds and three-quarters of the total, although all were, naturally, nominees of the Party (Ulč, 1982:119). There were communist elections in 1971, 1976, 1981 and 1986.

Arrangements were made to prevent the outvoting of the Slovaks by the Czech deputies. A three-fifths majority of the Slovak deputies and the Czech deputies (voting separately in the Chamber of Nations) and a three-fifths majority of all deputies in the Chamber of People was needed to enable the passing of laws in several cases, such as the enactment of the federal constitution, amendments to the constitution, the election of the President of the ČSSR, and the declaration of war (art.41). A simple majority of Czech deputies and Slovak deputies (separately) was needed in several other cases: laws on citizenship, medium-term economic plans, federal budgets, etc. (art.42). A vote of no-confidence could be passed when either the majority of the Czech deputies or the majority of the Slovak deputies in the Chamber of Nations voted for it (or the majority of all members in the Chamber of People) (art.43). As far as jobs within the state machinery were concerned, it was agreed that each ministry had a State Secretary and that, in the case of a Czech minister, the State Secretary should therefore be Slovak and vice-versa (art.67).

The ultimate arrangements of the federation were the result of a complex process of negotiations between Slovak and Czech leaders. Whereas the federal structure in itself provided improved opportunities for the representation of Slovaks in the centre, the curtailments of republic authority during the first years of normalization reversed some of the deals which had been struck. As will be discussed in section 5.3.4, the federation was certainly not without meaning and consequences, however.

5.1.4 The Velvet Revolution and the Velvet Divorce

The Velvet Revolution ended more than 40 years of communist rule. The changing international environment had eroded the foreign support the regime depended on, and various forms of social protest readily resurfaced, such as petitions, open letters, political demonstrations, open expressions of religious revival, and environmental activism (see Wheaton and Kavan, 1992:24–30). The regime's violent response to the student demonstration on 17 November, 1989, put a definitive end to public compliance with the regime's normalization policies and structures; massive public protests, growing in size as the days went on, erupted in Prague, Brno, Bratislava and other cities. On 18 November, an umbrella organization was created in Prague under the name of Citizens Forum (OF); one of its founding members was Václav Havel, who had also been one of the founding members of Charter 77. Several days later it was followed by a Slovak counterpart, Public against Violence (VPN). The regime was finally buried with the resignation of the government under Miloš Jakeš on 24 November, the erasure of the leading role of the KSČ from the constitution on 29 November, and the resignation of Husák as president on 10 December. On 29 December Havel was elected president by a wide margin, and in the elections that followed in

June 1990 OF and VPN were the greatest winners. Combined, they brought 169 representatives to the National Assembly and together with several other parties formed the first coalition government without communists since 1946.

As Havel declared in his first New Year's speech: "My ... task is to ensure that both nations approach the coming elections as truly self-governing, respecting each other's interests, national identity, religious traditions, and the fundamental symbols of nationhood. As a Czech in the office of president who swore his presidential oath to a famous Slovak and an intimate friend [Dubček], I feel a particular responsibility to ensure that, after the various bitter experiences the Slovaks have had, all the interests of the Slovak nation should be respected and that no offices of the state be closed to its members" (in Wheaton and Kavan, 1992:137). However, whereas during the Velvet Revolution both Czechs and Slovaks had carried slogans like "Strength in Unity", it was not to be that way. In subsequent negotiations over the new political and economic foundations of the state, the relation between Czechs and Slovaks again proved to be a central issue which, after three years of political struggle, led to the dissolution of the common state. More extensive treatment of this period can be found in section 5.3.4.

5.2   THE ETHNIC STRUCTURE OF CZECHOSLOVAKIA

The various constitutions paid substantial attention to the ethnic mixture of the state's territory. The first constitution (1920) of the Czechoslovak Republic guaranteed fundamental civil rights to all citizens, including political freedom, "without consideration of race, language and religion". Nevertheless, as in other Eastern European countries (notably Yugoslavia), various groups were combined to create a single dominant *Staatsvolk*, in this case described by "We, the Czechoslovak nation, ..." by which the constitution opened. In a separate language law submitted with the constitution, the Slovak and Czech languages received a privileged position as official languages which could be used all over the country, while minority languages could only be used in official dealings in each district where more than 20% of the population was of German, Hungarian or Polish origin (Kalvoda, 1985:115). The Ruthenian autonomy that was made possible by the constitution never materialized (Lammich and Schmid, 1979:370). The Socialist constitutions should ideologically have contained full rights for the minorities in Czechoslovak territory. Nevertheless, the 1948 constitution hardly acknowledged minorities, which was not surprising given the events of the preceding decade, but explicitly mentioned Slovaks and Czechs as separate nations. The 1960 constitution acknowledged the existence of the Hungarians, Ukrainians (Ruthenians), and Poles, but the Germans were not mentioned until the 1968 Constitutional Law on Nationalities; Roma have always been ignored. In practice, rights for the Hungarian minority had

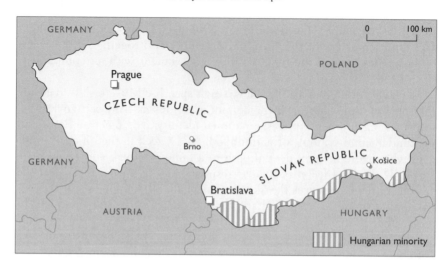

Map 5.1 Czechoslovakia (1969–1992)

already improved during the 1950s, although there was a backlash following the events in Hungary during 1956. As can be seen from map 5.1, the Hungarian minority lives in a concentrated area along the southern border of the Slovak Republic.

The figures in the censuses reflect the political currents the state has experienced in this century (see table 5.1). As has been discussed in the previous section, ethnic plurality in Czechoslovakia diminished substantially during and after World War Two; all minorities together made up 36% of the population before the war, but in 1968 this had fallen to 6%. Of course, the figures in the Czechoslovak censuses were seriously questioned by the Hungarians, who estimated that around 1968 at least 720 thousand Magyars should be living in Czechoslovakia (King, 1973:94). Nevertheless, despite the feasibility of subscribing to a different nationality during some periods in Czechoslovakian history, the Czechoslovak figures belong to the more reliable of those in Eastern Europe. As can further be seen from the table, the share of Slovaks compared to the Czechs has steadily increased during this century, reflecting the somewhat higher birth rates among the Slovaks.

The political structure of the country after 1968 formed the basis for map 5.1. Only limited numbers of Slovaks and Czechs live in the republic of the other group. Before the Second World War, for instance, Czechs constituted 3.7% of the population of the Slovak region. Many of them had come to take up posts in the administration and education (see next section), and they were sent out of the area under the separate Slovak state of the Second World War; in the same period Slovaks in the Czech Lands made up only 0.4% of the regional population. After the war it was the other way around.

Table 5.1 Ethnonational groups in Czechoslovakia (in thousands)

	1930[1]	%	1961[5]	%	1980	%	1991	%
Czech	7,407[2]	51.2	9,060	66.0	9,819	64.1	9,830	63.1
Slovak	2,282	15.8	3,836	27.9	4,665	30.5	4,834	31.0
German	3,232	22.3	140	1.0	62	0.4	54	0.3
Hungarian	692	4.8	534[6]	3.9	580	3.8	587	3.8
Ruthenian[3]	549	3.8	55	0.4	48	0.3	41	0.3
Polish	82	0.6	68	0.5	68	0.4	62	0.4
Other	237[4]	1.6	43	0.3	70	0.5	169	1.1
Total	14,481		13,736		15,312		15,577	

Sources: Kalvoda 1985, Minority Rights Group 1993

General remarks:
- The number of Roma has generally not been given. They have been estimated to number over 300 thousand in 1980 (see Kalibova et al. 1993). Only 109 thousand Roma registered officially in 1991. The Roma are therefore generally divided over the categories Slovak, Hungarian, and others.
- The identity of the Moravians is a matter of dispute. Approximately 3 million people inhabit the region of Moravia and Silesia, and in 1991 approximately 1.4 million opted for a Moravian identity (RFE/RL, 13/12/1991).

Specific remarks:
1   This census is categorized according to national groups. The figures are not comparable with those after the war, since the Ruthenian territories still belonged to Czechoslovakia. The sudden decrease in the number of Ruthenians was therefore due to the secession of part of Czechoslovakia to the Soviet Union in 1945 and Ruthenians and Russians being lumped together. The decrease in the number of Germans, Jews and Hungarians has been discussed in the text.
2   As will be explained in the next section, the figures for the Czechs and Slovaks were initially published in a combined category of 'Czechoslovaks.' The number of Czechs and Slovaks may have been overrated, because of the fact that it was more opportune for people to declare themselves Czechoslovaks than for instance Hungarians.
3   This includes Ukrainians.
4   This includes 187 thousand Jews. The number of people that registered as having a Jewish faith was 356 thousand (Kalvoda, 1985:123).
5   The practical means of measuring an individual's affiliation after the war was by mother tongue, although in the 1961 census a criterion of nationality was used.
6   In the 1950 census only 367 thousand had declared themselves Hungarian, due to the Slovakization campaign that followed the Second World War.

Thus, in 1980, there were over 320 thousand Slovaks in the Czech Lands, making up 3.3% of the population, against 55 thousand Czechs (1.1%) in Slovakia (Kalvoda, 1985:125). By the time of the split these numbers were approximately similar (RFE/RL, 4/6/1993).

5.3   THE TENSION BETWEEN CZECHS AND SLOVAKS

5.3.1   *The interwar period*

As has been explained in section 5.1, the conflict between Czechs and Slovaks was conditioned from the start by the geopolitical situation of the country and by the presence of other minorities in its territory. In fact, the emergence of their common state as such had certainly not been the result of a long-term process of national liberation (even if such a thing would have been possible). At first, until World War One, the small Slovak elite had simply aimed at strengthening its position *vis à vis* the Hungarian majority, and not at gaining independence from the Monarchy (Paul, 1985:120). Neither the Czechs nor the Slovaks had originally contemplated a united state, and it was in fact among the émigrés in the United States that this idea first gained ground (Mamatey, 1979:82). The Slovak and Czech organizations agreed in Cleveland in 1915 to strive for independence, and for a "union of the Czech and Slovak peoples in a federal union of states with full national autonomy for Slovakia." Several years later, on May 30, 1918, the Pittsburgh Agreement again confirmed this intention, this time in the presence of Tomáš G. Masaryk. Masaryk was at the time the Chairman of the Czecho-Slovak National Council in Paris and was later to become the first president of the Czechoslovak Republic (Mamatey, 1979:83). The Martin Declaration, issued by a group of Slovak political leaders two days after the declaration of Czechoslovak independence on October 30, 1918, did not quite take the same approach. It declared that: "The Slovak people are a linguistic and cultural-historical part of a united Czechoslovak nation" and there was no mention of Slovak autonomy (in Steiner, 1973:18). At the Peace Conference there was no urge to challenge this conception, as the Allies saw possibilities for a strong government and a potential new ally (Johnson, 1985:54).

During those years cultural unity of the two groups was also the interpretation of the Slovak leadership. Most important among them was the Defence Minister in the new Czechoslovakian government Milan Štefánik, who, as one of the few Slovaks of world stature and the central figure in the Slovak movement in exile, was perhaps the only Slovak leader who could negotiate on an equal basis with Masaryk and Beneš (Leff, 1988:200). Unfortunately he died in a plane crash in 1919 on his way to Czechoslovakia. Other Slovak leaders were equally inclined to give priority to the common characteristics of the state. Ivan Dérer, for instance, a Slovak Social Democrat, argued that "[t]he Czechs and the Slovaks create a single nation. By Czechoslovak unity I understand such a degree of ethnographic, linguistic, national and cultural affinity of the·Czech and Slovak nations that neither, without the other, can generally or even fully attain its cultural, national and political ideals" (in Johnson, 1985:55). Other Slovak leaders, such as the influential Agrarians Milan Hodža and Vavro Šrobár, were equally firm in the concept of Czechoslovakism, even though they did not want to erase the particularities of the Slovak branche of the nation; they merely wanted to enrich Slovak culture and prevent it from being dominated by conservative Catholic priests.[3] On the Czech side, Czechoslovakism as stressed by Masaryk left no doubt. In an interview with a French journalist in 1921, he declared: "There is no Slovak nation. That is the invention of Magyar propaganda. The Czechs and Slovaks are brothers ... Only cultural level separates them – the Czechs are more developed than the Slovaks, for the Magyars held them in systematic unawareness. We are founding Slovak schools. It is necessary to await the results; in one generation there will be no difference between the two branches of our national family" (in Leff, 1988:138). The consequence of this civilizing mission, in which hardly any Slovak cadre was present, was that over 100 thousand Czech teachers and civil servants poured into the region to man the new Slovak schools, the new university, and the new state institutions (Reban, 1981:233). Seen from this perspective it was no surprise that the name of the country in the constitution of 1920 was spelled without a hyphen.

The philosophy of 'Czechoslovakism' also has to be considered in the context of the geopolitical situation at the time. Indeed, although the Czech leadership and their Slovak supporters considered Czechoslovakism the self-evident will of the population, it also had some practical geopolitical aims: first of all, it enlarged the titular group in the state by 2 million, which lessened the numeric importance of minorities in the new state to one third instead of half of the population; secondly, it avoided the need to grant Slovaks explicit political rights (Steiner, 1973:19). These political rights would set an example for the other minorities, especially the Germans and the Hungarians, for territorial autonomy and, following that, could perhaps lead to external interference and the break-up of the state.[4] Of course, over time the national identity of the Czechs and the Slovaks had developed very much in opposition to the neighbouring cultures – for the Czechs against the Germans, and for the majority of the Slovaks against the Hungarians – and irredenta of these cultures exactly constituted the main minorities on Czechoslovakian soil.

Nevertheless, although in the first census after independence (1921) Slovaks and Czechs were placed together as 'Czechoslovaks', this unity in administrative counting did not quite reflect social reality and history. Indeed, the Czech Lands were already much more industrialized and urbanized than the Slovak region, even though the latter part used to be one of

3   Most Slovaks who stressed Czechoslovakism were Protestants, although Šrobár was a Catholic; he was as anti-clerical as the others, however (Leff, 1988:203–204).

4   This fear was quite understandable, because, as mentioned above, in the Czech Lands the Germans had voiced opposition to the new state, while the Czech leadership and their Slovak supporters considered Hungarian revisionism a real option. A leader of the main Slovak party was later found to have been paid by the Hungarian government.

the most industrialized regions of the Hungarian part of the Dual Monarchy. Some 40.6% of the inhabitants in Bohemia and 37.8% in Moravia were engaged in industry, against 17.5% in Slovakia and 10.4% in Ruthenia (Wolchik, 1991:7). The high level of social and cultural life in the Czech Lands and the existence of a broad cultural, social and political elite was very much lacking in Slovakia in 1918 (Mamatey, 1979:79).[5]

Slovaks and Czechs also held different views on religion (Leff, 1988:20–22). Czechs were, in general, more secular in outlook and, although almost all were Catholics (95.7% in 1910), the historical role of Jan Hus was considered central to the identity of the Czechs as a nation.[6] Moreover, the Habsburg regime had used the Roman Catholic Church as a tool for germanization, which had created considerable resentment, especially among the Czech elite (Skalický, 1989:298). This prompted part of the Catholic clergy to separate themselves from the Roman-Catholic Church at the emergence of an independent Czechoslovakia and to set up their own Czechoslovak Church. On the other hand, fewer Slovaks (69%) were Catholics, but they considered their religion much more central to their identity; they also felt less resentment towards the Catholic Church as they had less experience with magyarization through the channels of the Church. Between the Hungarian Bishop and the Slovak Catholic flock in the agricultural Slovak society there always stood the Slovak parish priest (Skalický, 1989:307).[7] At the same time there existed in Slovakia an influential group of Protestants (18.7% of the population) which used an evangelical liturgy in the Czech language. The Protestants were more inclined to political union with the Czechs and played an important role during the First Republic, taking the lion's share of the new governmental positions for Slovaks (Kirschbaum, 1989:174–177). As an illustration of the difference in importance of religion: the number of Czechs in Bohemia declaring themselves as Catholics had dropped from 95.7% in 1910 to 76.3% in 1921, while the number of Catholic Slovaks even slightly increased during the same period (Leff, 1988:21–22).

Concerning languages, there was a major difference in the timing of their official standardization; following serious conflict between the Catholic and Protestant parts of the Slovak elite, the character of the Slovak language

5   The magyarization policy followed by the Hungarians after their 'Ausgleich' within the Habsburg Empire in 1867 had almost wiped out the Slovak institutions previously existing; social mobilization was, therefore, often accompanied by magyarization or germanization (in the cities), and the sense of Slovakness among the rural nobility had almost disappeared. Only a small group had attempted to resist these pressures (Niederhauser, 1981:224; see Paul 1985).

6   A row emerged between Rome and Prague in 1925 over the 510th anniversary of the death of Jan Hus, when the flag of the republic was replaced by a Hussite banner and the Papal nuncio left in protest. At the occasion the nuncio thanked the Slovak Catholic leader, Andrej Hlinka, for his support on the issue (Skalický, 1989:302).

7   Many among the Catholic clergy had served the state under Hungarian rule and were subsequently distrusted by the new government.

was still very much disputed in the 1840s, when L'udovit Štúr published his works. The question of whether the Slovak language was a mere dialect of the Czech language or a genuine language in itself was even more important. Practically all Czech leaders did not think that the Slovak language was sufficiently different to indicate a clearly separate Slovak nation.[8] However, the introduction of a Czechized Slovak grammar in the 1930s created an uproar nonetheless (Leff, 1988:7). On the whole the balance between Czechs and Slovaks was not only problematic due to the closeness yet distinctness of their cultural characteristics, but also because of the numerical imbalance within the Czechoslovak state. As Leff points out, "Slovakia [was] too small and closely related a nation not to provoke Czech efforts to bring it into line," while it [was] "too large and distinct a nation to suffer such attentions gladly or docilely" (1988:276).

During the First Republic, the influence of the Czechs in the social, cultural and economic life of Slovakia on the one hand improved the level of education of the Slovaks, but, on the other hand, caused the decline of industrial activity in Slovakia (because of strong competition by the Czech industry). The immigration of Czechs and the dominant role of Slovak Protestants caused resentment among the Catholic clergy and the newly educated intellectuals, who both greatly increased in number because of the improved educational facilities. Besides general frustration over lack of opportunities there was also an urge to protect Slovakia from traditional Czech Protestantism (Steiner, 1973:29). Catholic resentment was increased by the anti-clerical attitude of Masaryk, who wanted to restrict Catholic influence in education. As a result the Roman Catholic Church became the breeding ground of Slovak nationalism. For the young intelligentsia the continuing presence of Czechs in the civil service and in the schools decreased their chances of employment, something which became very important during the depression of the 1930s. For example, in 1930, both in the Ministry of Education and in its Slovak department in Bratislava, the Slovaks were outnumbered by Czechs, with respectively 417 Czechs versus 4 Slovaks and 94 Czechs versus 68 Slovaks (Steiner, 1973:30). One of the reasons for this imbalance lay in the fact that appointments in the state administration often depended on affiliation with specific political parties, whose politicians were in (long-term) control of the department. Since the largest Slovak parties did not participate in government for most of the time, their members were excluded from many job opportunities. Interest-

---

8   During the Second World War this attitude was exemplified by the statements of Beneš, the successor of Masaryk as president of the Czechoslovak Republic and leader of the government in exile at the time (1943): "You will never get me to recognize the Slovak nation. That is my conviction, and I am not going to change it. ... I am of firm conviction that the Slovaks are Czechs and the Slovak language is only one of the dialects of the Czech language, like other Czech dialects ... I cannot stop anybody from calling himself a Slovak, but I shall not agree with a declaration that a Slovak nation exists." (in Steiner, 1973:53, see also for instance Lettrich, 1955:26).

ingly enough, although an important result of the First Republic was the improvement of education in Slovakia, in this context it only fuelled Slovak discontent and created an educated elite aware of the inequalities between Czechs and Slovaks (see Johnson 1985, Jelinek 1983).

One of the main reasons for the non-participation of Slovak political parties was the structure of Czechoslovak coalition politics. Whereas the political system in itself was highly permissive and allowed for the expression and articulation of national interest, in practice it was more exclusionary. Governments were generally formed by a coalition of three or more of the following five, all of whom supported the idea of 'Czechoslovakism': the Agrarian Party, the Social Democratic Party, the National Socialists, the Czechoslovak Populist Party, and the National Democrats. In general, bargaining between the coalition partners was already too complicated to allow it to be further confounded by Slovak nationalists (Leff, 1988:74). Slovak members of state-wide parties and the German equivalents of the state-wide parties (in all coalitions from 1926 until 1938) often provided enough support to allow for respectable national governments (see table 5.2 for the election results). The most important party, after the split between the Social Democrats and the Communists in 1920–21, was the Agrarian Party, which provided most of the prime ministers; one of them was Milan Hodža, who was the only Slovak to become prime minister (1935–1938) and minister of foreign affairs during the First Republic. His position illustrates that the contrast between Czechs and Slovaks was certainly not a simple dichotomous one in this period. In Slovakia the class-based Czech party structure was transplanted with small Slovak branches in the major state-wide parties, and in particular there was support among the most important Protestant leaders for the unitarian ideology found among the Czech leaders in Prague. Besides ideological conviction, the 'Czechoslovaks' also supported the unity of the two nations because they could otherwise lose their power to the oppositional leaders in Slovakia (Johnson, 1985:56; Leff, 1988:190–192). As Leff (1988:190–211) describes, as a result the Czech leaders dealt mostly with Slovak leaders who did not fully represent the sentiments of the Slovak constituency.

The other major Slovak voice was the Hlinka Slovak Populist Party (HSLS), which was the largest political party in Slovakia between 1925 and 1938. Andrej Hlinka was a Roman Catholic priest and a Slovak nationalist early on.[9] In 1925, he presented a program for further political autonomy of the Slovaks and a "gradual return of Slovakia to Slovak hands" (in Steiner, 1973:24). This stance, and the fact that the HSLS was less severe with formerly magyarized Slovaks, delivered him one-third of the votes in Slovakia.

---

9   He had already founded a party in 1913 and was thrown in jail in 1920 for travelling to Paris to bring the position of the Slovaks to the attention of the Peace Conference.

The HSLS participated, somewhat reluctantly, in the government of 1927–1929 with two ministers in the cabinet, one of whom (Monseigneur Jozef Tiso) later became the president of the Slovak State. However, in government hardly any of their goals were achieved, for instance with regard to more autonomy; in combination with their apparent moderation towards the 'Czechoslovakists', it cost the HSLS 20% of their voters in the 1929 elec-

Table 5.2 Election results during the interwar period in Czechoslovakia (in percentages)

	1920				1925			
	CS	B	M	S	CS	B	M	S
Agrarians	13.6	12.4	12.9	18.0	13.7	13.2	11.5	17.4
Social Democrats	25.6	22.4	22.0	38.1	8.9	10.4	9.6	4.2
Nat. Socialists	8.1	11.2	6.2	2.2	8.6	11.7	7.0	2.6
Czechosl. Populists	11.3	5.6	18.9	17.5	9.7	8.0	21.3	1.3
Nat. Democrats	6.2	8.8	6.2	–	4.0	5.8	2.5	1.8
Small Tradesmen	2.0	2.4	2.9	–	4.0	5.2	4.6	0.8
Hlinka Sl. Populists	–	–	–	–	6.9	–	–	34.3
Communists	–	–	–	–	13.1	12.6	11.1	13.9
Germ./Mag. Parties	26.8	32.5	21.3	18.5	23.2	27.0	22.7	6.9
Others	6.4	4.7	9.6	5.7	7.9	6.1	9.7	16.8

	1929				1935			
	CS	B	M	S	CS	B	M	S
Agrarians	15.0	13.6	12.3	19.5	14.3	12.7	14.2	17.6
Social Democrats	13.0	13.8	14.8	9.5	12.6	12.9	13.3	11.4
Nat. Socialists	10.4	13.9	9.7	3.0	9.2	11.6	9.8	3.2
Czechosl. Populists	8.4	6.6	17.7	2.6	7.5	6.0	15.6	2.3
Nat. Democrats	4.9	5.2	3.1	3.8	5.6	7.6	3.9	1.6
Small Tradesmen	3.9	4.6	4.3	2.1	5.4	6.4	6.1	2.6
Hlinka Sl. Populists	5.8	–	–	28.3	6.9	–	–	30.1
Communists	10.2	10.3	8.9	10.7	10.3	9.0	8.6	13.0
Germ./Mag. Parties	23.1	26.1	21.8	15.9	24.3	28.7	22.2	14.2
Others	5.3	5.9	7.4	4.6	3.9	5.1	6.3	4.0

Source: Leff, 1988:51–52; Johnson, 1985:64–65.

Remarks:
CS = Czechoslovakia   B = Bohemia
M = Moravia/Silesia   S = Slovakia

tions (Leff, 1988:75 – 84).[10] They only regained their ground in the elections of 1935 when a more radical Slovak nationalism started to gain momentum which proved capable of bridging the distinction between Slovak Catholics and Slovak Protestants; they joined with the National Party of the Slovak Protestant Martin Rázus. Overall, because the HSLS only participated in central government between 1927 and 1929, the majority of the Slovaks voted for opposition parties between 1925 and 1938: 67.6% in 1925, 58.7% in 1929, and 65.5% in 1935 (Leff, 1988:72).

5.3.2 The Slovak State (1939 – 1944)

By the time international tension in Europe reached its zenith there was a large group of frustrated Slovaks, consisting of politicians, clergy, and newly educated intellectuals, which could provide the backbone for the Slovak State. The state was to have a major impact on relations between Czechs and Slovaks after the war. On the one hand it was the culmination of growing nationalism in the interwar years and firmly established the notion of Slovak separateness; on the other hand, although the leaders of the HSLS had always given abundant evidence of their commitment to a common Czech and Slovak state, the fact that the Slovaks capitalized on the international situation in this way caused much resentment among the Czechs (Lettrich, 1955:80 – 1). This did not mean that there was widespread support among the Slovaks themselves for the new state. As Jelinek has argued: "It is legitimate to assume that, in spite of the violent agitation and propaganda, the Ludaks never succeeded in capturing the majority of the Slovak people, and that they probably would not have been able to accomplish this [1938 autonomy] without external developments and foreign support. As it was, the flow of events carried them to the fore – perhaps to their own surprise." The declaration of independence was no less of a surprise for the population (Jelinek, 1976:13,32).

The political character of the state, closely following the German example in many respects, resulted in the imprisonment of numerous political opponents and the expulsion of most of the Czechs (Lettrich, 1955:145). As mentioned above, the fate of the Slovak Jews was even more severe. For the majority of Slovaks, however, the state brought certain improvements, in particular in the economic sphere. In no time enormous German investments were directed towards the Slovak economy, and the Slovak state also

---

10   Hlinka himself did not take a cabinet post, thereby showing the reluctance and perhaps suspicion with which the HSLS joined the coalition. They only gained a little autonomy for Slovakia, but without budgetary powers, and some of the territorial measures taken after the birth of the Republic were reversed. According to one contemporary observer, Slovak territory after independence was divided in such a way as "to dissolve Slovakia 'like sugar in a glass of water'" (in Johnson, 1985:68). The completion of the trial of the HSLS leader Béla Tuka was the immediate cause of their leaving the coalition in 1929.

escaped much of the war damage that neighbouring countries suffered. Various groups benefitted from this development: in particular, "Slovakia's townfolk, semi-intelligentsia, and rich peasantry should be counted as the long-term winners ... They discovered new horizons and acquired incentives to strive for things not known previously. It is a fact that many of the men managing contemporary Slovakia made the greatest jump in the days of the Slovak state, either through themselves or through their parents" (Jelinek, 1976:123). There were also many efforts which helped the process of nation-building: the creation of Slovak institutions manned by Slovaks, the increase in the administrative experience of the Slovak workforce; reforms in education, including the diminution of 'bad' Czech influences (in language, for example); the emphasis on Slovak national myths; etc.[11] There was a major influence of the Church on the society, and state and the Church generally operated in mutual support of one another (although Church officials protested, for instance, the deportations of the Jews) (Skalický 1989).

It is justifiable to conclude that the Slovak state, if only semi-independent under the tutelage of Hitler, was a watershed in the development of Slovak identity and self-awareness. Indeed, "Slovaks had proved something to themselves about their political capacities and their basic identity, to a degree that affected their postwar expectations to a pronounced extent" (Leff, 1988:90–91). In July 1944, a report by Slovak communists, the strongest underground opposition against the Slovak regime, concluded that "[g]enerally speaking after the experience of six years, Slovakia is capable of an independent economic and financial existence. It is in a position to stand on its own feet and has sufficient resources (even technical ones) and production potential to face international competition." The report also stated that "after the war only those prepared to adopt a firm position on this matter can hope to receive support from the population – those who can be relied upon not to take from the Slovaks what they have already achieved, and for which even the Hlinka populists can claim credit. In this respect there is a difference between us and the Czech Lands. The Czechs have lost not only their political freedom but their national freedom as well. The Slovaks are politically worse off than during the Czechoslovak Repub-

---

11   Interesting, for instance, is the credo taught to primary school students: "The solemn and sacred truth of the Slovak nation, in which I do believe, is ... that the Slovaks are an individual nation, different from all others in their blood, language, spirit, culture, and peculiarity of country. The Slovak national roots remained undamaged from alien elements in their blood, spirit and creation. All Slovaks in the whole world create a spiritual community of brothers in blood ... No other nation in the world resembles the Slovaks in honesty of heart, delicacy for understanding of beauty, and creativity of mind. Throughout the whole world a Slovak child has to be educated in the Slovak language. Whoever educates differently is a traitor to the Slovak spirit. Whoever takes the Slovak language from a Slovak child is a murderer" (in Jelinek, 1976:102).

lic, but from the national point of view the Slovaks and Slovakia have gained" (in Steiner, 1973:55).

The Slovak Uprising, organized by the Slovak National Council (SNR) in the autumn of 1944, did much to correct the image that emanated from the Slovak state, and equally did allow the communists to prove their pro-Slovak position after the war (Jelinek 1983). The SNR was established at the end of 1943 by a coalition of communists, Agrarians and members of the Protestant Slovak Nationalist Party, and also found supporters in the ranks of the Slovak army. The goal of the coalition was the toppling of the Slovak regime and the recreation of the Czechoslovak state with a separate constitutional status for Slovakia (Steiner, 1973:58). When the Uprising occurred it was somewhat chaotic and ultimately unsuccessful because of a lack of good planning, lack of external (Soviet) support, and incoming German troops (Jelinek, 1983:69–77). The exact amount of popular support for the uprising (just as the amount of support for the Slovak state itself) is not quite clear, although in the last stages of the war support for the Slovak state was rapidly waning. In any case, it created a framework for post-war Slovak representation in negotiations with the Czechoslovak government in exile, during which the SNR made clear that the constitution of 1920 could not be reinstated after the war, and that other options besides the Czechoslovak state were definitively feasible if no satisfactory agreement could be reached on the relation between Czechs and Slovaks. In October 1944, under pressure of circumstances, the government in exile explicitly recognized the Slovak nation and the SNR as its representative (Steiner, 1973:69–71).

The Košice Programme of April, 1945, which contained the guidelines for the new Czechoslovak government under Prime minister Fierlinger and President Beneš, affirmed this position. It was the result of negotiations between the communist and non-communist resistance from both parts of the country, and from the exile community in both Moscow (Fierlinger) and London (Beneš). Its section on the position of Slovakia recognized the SNR as the basis for the formation of a future Slovak legislative organ, and the broader principle of 'equals with equals' as the guideline of future political negotiations (Leff, 1988:93). Thus, the Programme declared that "the Republic shall be renewed as a common state with equal rights for the two nations – the Czech and the Slovak. This recognition of equality shall find expression in important political state acts. The SNR, founded on the National Committees in villages and counties, shall be not only the legal representative of the independent Slovak Nation, but also the representative of state power in the territory of Slovakia (of legislative, governmental, and executive power) in accordance with the special agreement between the SNR on the one hand and the President of the Republic and the Czechoslovak Government in London on the other" (in Lettrich, 1955:317–18). The Košice Programme nevertheless stopped short of mentioning the word 'federation'.

5.3.3 The post-war Republic and unitary communism in Czechoslovakia (1944–1968)

It has already been noted that the resistance and the exiles decided to have only four parties participate in each of the two parts of the country. Because of the strength of the prewar HSLS, its exclusion meant effectively that the prewar opposition was eliminated in Slovakia (Leff, 1988:95). Nevertheless, the Protestant-led Democratic Party succeeded in winning the overall majority in Slovakia with 62% of the votes, and that fact alone meant that, from the perspective of the communists, the power of the SNR had to be curtailed. Certainly, as had been agreed upon in the Košice Programme, the SNR had become the basis for a legislative organ in Slovakia with a Board of Commissioners as its executive body, but because of the election results the Slovak communists were inclined to cooperate with their Czech counterparts. As a result, when the Czechoslovak National Front in Prague started to limit the powers of the SNR, the Slovak communists agreed (Steiner, 1973:81; see Vnuk 1983). A number of other factors (e.g., trial against and execution of Tiso, the poor harvest) helped to further create an atmosphere of crisis in Slovakia in the autumn of 1947, leading to a reshuffling of the Board of Commissioners, this time with communists in the majority.

When the communists took over in Czechoslovakia they inherited a Czech-Slovak conflict in which Slovak separateness based on initial differences was strengthened by politics during the First Republic and by the impact of the independent Slovak state. However, whereas the constitution clearly acknowledged the existence of separate Czech and Slovak nations, this acknowledgement did not result in a pluralistic political structure. In fact, the Communist Party of Slovakia (KSS) was abolished as an autonomous entity in September of the same year and only remained a branch of the Czechoslovak Communist Party (KSČ), with the Central Committee of the KSS explicitly subordinate to the Central Committee of the KSČ. After 1958 the Slovak congresses always preceded the Czechoslovakian ones, emphasizing their place at the top of the preparatory pyramid of meetings in localities, districts, regions, and Slovakia as a whole (Kusin, 1981:3). Both important jobs in the bureaucracy as well as appointments were controlled by Prague (Leff, 1988:224–226). The membership of the KSS was always lower than in the Czech Lands, in 1948 forming slightly over 10% and, twenty years later, still only 18% of total KSČ membership, much lower than Slovakia's share in the population (Ulč, 1974:29). Nevertheless, many Slovaks were appointed to high positions in the government, in the course of which the Czechs quite logically had a preference for Slovaks who supported the centralist policies. Indeed, the imprisonment of certain Slovak communists (such as Clementis, Novomeský, and Husák) in the beginning of the 1950s on charges of bourgeois nationalism, eliminated the nationalist component in the Slovak leadership and excluded them from positions of power (Leff, 1988:230–235). Naturally, the use of Slovak nationalism had become largely discredited after the Slovak state.

The state structure between 1948 and 1960 was asymmetric since the SNR had no counterpart in the Czech Lands. This frustrated both Slovaks and Czechs; the Slovaks felt that the real decision-making power was located in Prague, and that whatever competencies remained could be withdrawn at any opportune moment without a single Slovak vote (Leff, 1988:101). Czechs could feel frustrated that the Slovaks had somehow obtained an exceptional position. Although in principle the Slovak organs could have been a channel for formulating and pressing nationalist political demands or more general Slovak interests, in practice any dissent of this kind was stamped out. Even the frequency of meetings was reduced – the SNR met fifteen times yearly in 1948 and 1949 but only between zero and four meetings yearly during the 1950s – and the leadership of the organs was hand picked by Prague (Leff, 1988:106–107). Over the years, the remaining powers of SNR and the Board of Commissioners were gradually eroded, and they were turned into organs used simply for implementing state-wide laws and policies (Steiner, 1973:92). In the 1960 constitution the Board of Commissioners was even abolished altogether. Moreover, the 1960 constitution also introduced the partition of Slovak territory into three provinces, which was considered by some to be a deliberate policy to strengthen direct Prague control over the region and circumvent Bratislava in certain fields of policy (Leff, 1988:107–108).[12]

Since the existing Slovak state organs could hardly function as catalysts for nationalist action, the protests increasingly came from outside those institutions. The intelligentsia had gained more breathing space after 1963, when Alexander Dubček, who was a typical career communist at that stage, replaced Czech-born Karol Bacílek as the First Secretary of the KSS. This replacement in itself was against the wishes of Novotný and indicated both Novotný's declining power, as well as, perhaps, a limited degree of autonomy for the KSS (Ulč, 1974:16; Reban, 1981:227). Slovak economists started to voice objections to the current state of affairs in the region (see below), while Slovak journalists at their May 1963 Congress, and in their contributions to the weekly Kulturny Život,[13] voiced strong criticism against the stagnation of Czechoslovak society and intellectual life. Even more important was the fact that by December 1963 an investigative commission decided that the charges of 'bourgeois nationalism' had been incorrect. As a result, important events in Slovak history could be reconsidered

---

12   It has also been suggested that the territorial changes which came with the 1960 constitution created districts with Czech and Slovak majorities, which disabled the Hungarians in exercising their rights; similar gerrymandering was done in the Polish living areas (Ulč, 1974:154; Lammich and Schmid, 1979:372; King, 1973:80–81).

13   As Steiner (1973:121) notes, Kulturny Život was the first Slovak periodical to arouse interest among the Czechs.

and given their place in the country's history. Scientists published on Slovak history, and the historian Gosiorovsky even published his ideas on the creation of the federation (Skilling, 1976:51 – 52). Overall, on the road to the Prague Spring "the Slovak intelligentsia played a key role in articulating Slovak political interests in a system where this prerogative was formally reserved to the Communist Party. It would be difficult to exaggerate the importance of this historic revival. It had a cathartic effect which enabled Slovakia as a whole to recapture a national initiative and spirit which would later find vigorous political expression in the drive for federation and constitutional reform. It also provided the intellectual groundwork for the more autonomous assertion of authority by the Slovak Communist Party" (Dean, 1973:13). For that reason Steiner (1973:112) commented that a 'Slovak Spring' preceded the Prague Spring. Nevertheless, despite the psychological importance of the period, actual progress in terms of political autonomy was by all counts minimal.

5.3.3.1 Economic aspects

The communists did not consider political autonomy a solution for the national question, but instead put their faith in the economic development of Slovakia and more specifically in the industrialization of the region; this could resolve some of the grievances of the Slovaks and perhaps create a work force which could strengthen the base of the communists in Slovakia (Krejčí, 1990:28). Indeed, despite strong growth from 1938 on, mainly during the 'independent' Slovak Republic, the share of Slovak economic production in the total income of Czechoslovakia in 1948 was still clearly lower than that of the Czech Lands. With almost 28% of the population, Slovakia produced 19.2% of national income, although it had been 12.0% in 1937 (with 24.5% of the population) (Capek & Sazama, 1993:216). As a result of this situation and the communist strategy, the whole economic history of Czechoslovakia since the Second World War can be characterized as an attempt at regional equalization (Pavlínek, 1992).

Of course, the disastrous impact of the war and the expulsion of the Germans on the economic structure created the need for a general economic recovery of existing industrial potential, and for widespread industrial development in all regions. In part this spread of industrial development was pursued because of the need to bring jobs to the workers instead of having to arrange for the workers to come to the jobs. This benefitted Slovakia and, for instance, in 1947 and 1948 over 300 companies were moved to that region, creating 30 thousand jobs (Dostál, 1982:334). After the communist takeover in February, 1948, the development of heavy industries was emphasized, and between 1949 and 1953 over two-thirds of investments went to that sector and to mining (Dostál, 1982:334; Pavlínek, 1992:362). The regime used the collectivization of agricultural lands and

121

private industries to (sometimes forcibly) direct large numbers of workers to preferred sectors and locations (Krejčí, 1990:23). After 1953 even more investments were directed at Slovakia; on the one hand, this was because the Czech Lands could hardly provide enough manpower, but on the other hand they were in part a compensation for the curtailment of regional autonomy in the region (Krejčí, 1990:28). The redistribution of income created by these investments amounted to 15% of the produced income in Slovakia in the 1950s, according to some calculations (Capek and Sazama, 1993:216).

Overall, the communist policies led to major economic development in Slovakia. In itself collectivization did not hit the Slovaks remarkably differently from the Czechs.[14] Moreover, the Soviet type model of economic development was more advantageous for an agricultural society like Slovakia than for an industrial society like the Czech Lands. In the period 1948–1953 Slovakia's average yearly growth in the production of capital goods was 22.5% (16.2% in the Czech Lands) and of consumption goods 13.7% (10.1% in the Czech Lands); during the period 1953–1965, with the growth of the economy slower as a whole, it was still 11.2% (7.7%) and 9.4% (6.6%) (Kosta, 1984:124). The percentage of the labour force working in industry increased from 21.3% in 1948 to almost 40% in 1968, while the percentage of workers in agriculture dropped from 59.8% to 23.6% in 1970 (Wolchik, 1991:188–9). Industrialization of Slovakia – and also probably the improved geopolitical position of Slovakia as a result of the geographic shift of the trade towards the Soviet Union and the other Eastern European countries – increased the national income per citizen in the region from 61.2% of the Czech level in 1948 to 74.4% in 1960 (Kosta, 1984:120; Ulč, 1974:47). The rapid industrial growth caused the region to overtake the economic level of certain regions in the Czech Lands (Dostál, 1982:336).

Nevertheless, despite this economic growth the overall economic differences between the Czech Lands and Slovakia remained substantial, while the feeling of domination by Prague had certainly not disappeared. This was also perhaps because of extremely limited access to the central bureaucracy. By 1968 only 3.7% of all employees in the central bureaucracy were Slovaks, although this share rose in the higher ranks, and there were accusations of sloppy implementation of government decisions to the detriment of the Slovak republic (Skilling, 1976:871). This situation prompted Slovak economists, such as Victor Pavlenda, to re-evaluate the highly centralized planning process and the lack of possibilities for Slovak authorities to influence the formation of policies (Dean, 1973:23; Steiner, 1973:131–132). Therefore, while protests of the Slovak economists formed an integral part

---

14   Collectivization worked more to the disadvantage of the Hungarians who had cooperated with the Hungarian regime which had occupied parts of Slovakia during the war.

of a general call for economic reforms in the 1960s which followed the economic stagnation of those years, there was a special Slovak side to the economic problems.[15]

5.3.3.2 Slovakia and the Prague Spring

Protests about the running of the economy were coupled with protests over the lack of Slovak influence in the running of their own political and cultural affairs. This concerned not only the internal situation in the region, but also the lack of autonomy in contacts with foreign countries and with Slovak émigrés (in 1968 only 82 of the 585 diplomats were Slovaks) (Ulč, 1974:15). A row between Novotný and the Slovak communists over the function of the main cultural institute of the Slovaks, the Matica Slovenská, concerned the fact that all contacts with Czechs and Slovaks abroad went through the cultural association in Prague which paid little attention to the Slovak side of Czechoslovak society (Steiner, 1973:152). Novotný, however, was quite notorious for his lack of understanding of Slovak irritation, and apparently succeeded in estranging even the most conservative communists in Slovakia, such as Vasíl Bilák.[16] Nevertheless, even Dubček, when he became the first Slovak to become Secretary-General of the KSČ, did not give the impression that a fundamental rebalancing of Czech-Slovak relations was in the air. Although the status of Bratislava was heightened in February, 1968, it was in fact a Czech who first brought the discussion about the federation into the public debate. Even then, the discussion initially seemed to point to a reorganization and improvement of the asymmetrical arrangements which had existed since 1948, instead of to a full-fledged federation (Skilling, 1976:451–452).

In the course of the Prague Spring – and in particular after a change in position on the subject by Vasíl Bilák, who had become First Secretary of the KSS after Dubček's rise to power in January 1968 – the Slovak communists started to pay less attention to the more general political and philosophical criticism voiced in Prague and focused specifically on the necessity of creating a federation (Steiner, 1973:174; Dean, 1973:35). In 1972, Kusin reiterated, somewhat bitterly, that the "self-evident proposition which the

---

15   Dubček, in his September 1967 speech to the plenum of the Central Committee of the KSČ, put it as follows: "By their design our economic tools must affect not only the needs of the moment but also the scope opened for the development of progressive production, for structural changes and technical advancement. Last but not least, they must promote the implementation of our socioeconomic goals from a territorial viewpoint ... There are new capacities in Slovakia which must be fully developed; their exploitation must be stepped up to open a wider area for employment" (in Remington, 1969:14–15).

16   As Ulč remarks, the only creative idea Novotný was ever able to offer about the national problem was a program for mass intermarriage between Czechs and Slovaks which would obliterate all distinctions between the two groups (Ulč, 1974:16).

majority of the Slovak political presentation failed to accept" was that "[t]he 'reform' (democratisation, renaissance, liberation, progress) was a matter of form and content, while 'federalisation' was by definition a matter of form only. While practically the entire Slovak community, including such political representation as it enjoyed, did not find it at all difficult to rally behind the federative idea, only a few Slovak groups and individuals went on record as saying that the substance of the system required an overhaul. And even many of those professing loyalty to reform, G. Husák being a prominent spokesman of this group, found it easy to switch roles not much later" (Kusin, 1972:143).[17] In his opinion, of the three groups in the reform movement in Slovakia – the communist unitarians (wanting full government in Prague), the reformist federalists (who wanted both democratization and federalization), and the communist federalists – the last one was really the important one. Later it was revealed that the insistence on "Federation First" had been a conscious and purposive policy and an object of dispute among the KSS leadership (Dean, 1973:35). Indeed, Jozef Lenart, who became First Secretary of the KSS some years later, commented in 1971 that in 1968 "it was of the greatest importance that a group of comrades headed by comrade Vasíl Bilák ... gave preference to the solution of the juridical structure of the state on a federal basis ... thus pushing into the background questions which the right-wing opportunists were pressing, particularly the so-called process of democratization" (in Steiner, 1973:179).

A central figure in the Slovak reform movement was Gustáv Husák, who became deputy premier of the Czechoslovak government in April 1968 and later headed the Special Government Commission on the Preparation of a Constitutional Law on Czechoslovak Federation (Dean, 1973:33). His views on the democratization process were reversed once he was in power, and, as he was one of the most important men in Slovakia, he therefore helped to create the impression that Slovakia was less progressive, less revolutionary, than the Czech Lands (Steiner, 1973:169). This impression was partly correct in the sense that the difference between the Czechs and the

---

17   However, Reban (1981:229) quotes Selucký, one of the Czech reformers, who argued that the federation in itself was more than just the solution to the nationality problem: "The setting up of separate Czech and Slovak parliaments and Czech and Slovak governments under a weaker federal parliament and federal government meant the devolution of state power into three centres. The intention was to federalize the Communist Party in the same way as the state, so that there would be a Slovak Communist Party operating in Slovakia and a Communist Party of the Czech Lands in Bohemia, Moravia and Silesia, each with its own Central Committee, Presidium and Secretariat. These national Communist parties would then share political power with the federal Communist Party of Czechoslovakia. This political pluralism within the Communist movement would itself have meant a great step toward the democratization of public life. For the triangular arrangement of both state and Party organs, as well as of other social and special-interest groups, would create a diversity of power centres and control centres in mutual balance. The federalization of the Republic therefore, was intended to play a cardinal role not only in settling the nationality question but also in converting the centralized power into a democratic one."

Slovaks was not entirely confined to the leadership. In one poll, for instance, the Slovak public placed national equality first on the agenda and democratization second, whereas among the Czechs the latter stood first, and national equality in seventh place (Skilling, 1976:243).[18] The Matica Slovenská ('Mother of Slovakia') gained almost 200 thousand new members (Ulč, 1974:16). The Slovaks therefore appeared united about the importance of the national problem, even though some differences existed about its combination with a more democratic socialism.

After some discussion a federal solution was fully endorsed by the new Action Programme of the Czechoslovak Communist Party. In this Action Programme it was noted that "The fundament of Czechoslovak statehood is the voluntary and equal co-existence of Czechs and Slovaks. ... The unity of the Czechs and Slovaks can be strengthened only on the basis of an unhampered development of their national individuality in harmony with progress made in the economy, with objective changes in the social structure of both nations and on the basis of absolute equality and voluntariness" (Action Programme, 1968:5). It also noted that "*there are serious faults and fundamental deformations* in the constitutional arrangement of relations between the Czechs and Slovaks" and that "the asymmetrical arrangement alone was not suitable, by its very character, to express and ensure the relations between two independent nations, as the respective standings of the two nations were necessarily expressed in different ways." As a solution it stated that "It is now essential to respect the advantage of the *socialist federal arrangement* as a recognised and tried state form of the co-existence of two equal nations in a common state" (Action Programme, 1968:10–11). The Czechs, however, understandably remained rather defensive and reluctant, because they did not really have anything to gain from a federation and gave priority to the democratization process as such.

In preparation for the federation, a Czech National Council was created which negotiated with their already existing Slovak counterpart over the new constitutional arrangements. Several issues were severely disputed. First of all, a proposal for a triangular federation with Moravia-Silesia as one of the constituent parts was defeated because of strong Slovak opposition to this diminishing of their power in the new state structure; they insisted on the national element as the organizing principle.[19] A second set of differences concerned regulations to prevent the outvoting of Slovaks by Czechs. Put simply, this concerned two diametrically opposing views: that

18   In fact, a poll among Slovak party functionaries in June, 1968, showed that 89.9% favoured a federation; however, no less than 4.5% of them declared themselves in favour of complete independence, which is quite stunning within the communist context, even in 1968 (Skilling, 1976:523).

19   The Czechs also resented the ethnonational claim of the Moravians. There was even a short-lived plan for a quadripartite federation, with Silesia as a separate part, but it was not seriously considered. Nevertheless, Moraviannationalists obtained a lot of popular support (Skilling, 1976:479; Ulč, 1974:68).

of 'one man, one vote,' and that of 'one nation, one vote.' These opposing views were reflected both in discussions on the mechanisms to be used (e.g., the power between the two chambers of parliament, parity in the executive organs at the federal level), and the subjects for which these arrangements would hold (e.g., constitutional matters, economic plan). A third important difference between the Czech and the Slovak delegations concerned the degree of central organization of the federation, whereby most of the Czechs preferred a much more centralized system than the majority of the Slovaks who wanted to restrict it essentially to general planning and international relations (Skilling, 1976:465–487). However, among the Slovaks themselves there were substantial differences about whether to consider the economy of Slovakia as a separate domain or as part of a single economy within the Czech Lands.

The invasion by the five Warsaw Pact partners, on the night of 20 to 21 August, 1968, indeed made obsolete the plans to hold a Congress of the KSČ that had originally been planned for 9 September. Hastily, a meeting was convened in Prague-Vysočany the next day, during which Gustáv Husák was elected in the Party Presidium under the leadership of Dubček. Husák later refused, however, to accept the legality of the Vysočany Congress and gained the confidence of the Soviets in doing so. During the Congress of the KSS, four days later, he was elected First Secretary, and in that position concentrated on assuring the final implementation of the federal arrangement now that the circumstances had changed so much. Steiner suggests that Husák only could have taken this path with the previous knowledge of Brezhnev, and that he had already secured the federation in exchange for his persuasion of the Slovak people that it was to their advantage to be on good terms with the Soviet ally (Steiner, 1973:196). It is nevertheless unclear to what extent the Slovaks were indeed pacified and lured into cooperation, because the level of public and official resistance against the Warsaw Pact invaders appears to have been no less than that in the Czech part of the country (Skilling, 1976:772–792). On the whole, however, as one observer puts it, Husák's "willingness to use his Slovak base and Slovak nationalism to expedite 'normalization' in the Soviet sense" was a crucial factor in the first months after the intervention (Eidlin, 1980:254). For the Soviets, a choice for Husák meant a choice for someone who was at least popular with part of the population; in March 1969 24% of the Slovaks still trusted Husák, against 2% of the Czechs (Kusin, 1978:46).

Two months later the constitutional law on the federation was proclaimed, and it became effective on 1 January, 1969. Although the negotiations had been completed under Warsaw-Pact occupation, it is unclear whether the Soviets had tried to influence the outcome (Skilling, 1976:868). Of course, the more democratic context in which the federal system was supposed to have operated was gone, leaving "all form" as many had already feared in the month before. All the other changes which had taken place during the Prague Spring were slowly turned back, amidst protests from the population – such as the self-burning of Jan Palach and the celebrations following a Czechoslovakian victory in an ice hockey match against the Soviet Union in March. When Dubček was replaced by Husák on 17 April, 1969, the 'normalization' of Czechoslovakia was already well on its way.

5.3.4 Slovakia and the federation, 1969–1989

The final agreement on the new constitution was a compromise. It was a rather centralised federal system, with controlling powers by Slovaks in the centre itself, such as parity in the ministries. However, the Federal Boards which were created at the same time, and which would coordinate the work of the republic ministries, did not have to follow this provision, while decision-making and implementation of the bureaucracy on the whole took place in the context of the majority principle. Therefore, as Leff remarks, the Slovaks were to be represented on a parity basis only in those organs that tended to be the weakest in communist systems, the constitutional court and the national legislature (Leff, 1988:245). Moreover, the members of the new bicameral parliament were not elected. The old National Assembly became the new Federal Assembly, and its members selected the new Czech National Council. In turn the Czech National Council and the SNR selected the members for the new Chamber of Nations from their own ranks. This guaranteed that the old guard would remain. The political scientist Petr Pithart at the time compared it with an incestuous marriage, "We watch and comment disrespectfully, and therefore we have to be prepared for a couple of slaps because one ought not to peep into the bedroom. Thus we are left only with a platonic worry about the quality of the descendants. Children from incestuous marriages are not likely to be among the most illustrious" (in Ulč, 1974:72). Nevertheless, a short wave of actual parliamentary activism was enacted, before 'normalization' set in.

Not surprisingly, during the first years of the federation, several changes were made which eroded the competencies of the republics (see Dean 1973; Kusin 1978). The first change came in September 1969 when, in a move to integrate the two levels of government, the Czech and Slovak premiers were designated as federal vice-premiers and the presidium of the federal government was empowered to coordinate all state administration. In the beginning of 1970 the state secretaries in the federal ministries were abolished (decided without the constitutionally needed approval of the various three-fifths majorities in the parliament). In the same year the two national citizenships gradually gave way to the common Czechoslovak citizenship, and in the amendments to the constitution of December 1970 it was decided that the federal institutions could overrule the laws passed at the level of the republic. Many shared competencies were transferred to the federal level, not the least among them being the administration of state security. Control over the Slovak police was also transferred to Prague (Ulč, 1974:17). Furthermore, economic functions were centralized (see below) and in a final step the regional national committees were reintroduced even though they had been abolished in Slovakia by the SNR only eighteen months earlier. Indeed, the abolishment of the three regional national committees had been among the very first acts of the Slovak Republic in order to strengthen the direct link between the Slovak districts and Bratislava (Kusin, 1978:120). These regional committees now again were directly linked to the governmental power in Prague, fell under the Ministry of the Interior, and had direct counterparts in the Communist Party. They were granted some powers which previously were the domain of the Slovak republican government. All changes were defended by officials of the KSS by arguing that "[t]he stronger the unity of our nations with regard to the control of the most important affairs of the federation ... the stronger the state, [and] the higher the security of both nations in our federation" (in Dean, 1972:22). In 1979 several other articles in the federal law were struck in favour of stronger centralism.

What remained as the exclusive domain of the republics was education, culture, health, and justice, while the rest was either the exclusive domain of the federal institutions or shared by the two levels. In the case of shared competencies the details of cooperation were not quite worked out until 1971, when three possibilities were given: first of all, if all three governments were in agreement, the problem under discussion would be resolved unanimously; secondly, if one of the national governments disagreed, a compromise would be worked out or the federal government's standpoint would prevail; and thirdly, if both national governments opposed the federal government, either a compromise would be worked out or the federal standpoint would prevail. This arrangement showed the weakness of the national bodies (RFE/RL, 6/12/1972). As the federal institutions also had the power to overrule all decisions made in a republic if it considered it in conflict with the federal regulations, Niznansky and Robinson (1979:6) concluded that "the state administration apparatus has merely the bureaucratic form of a federation, while the real seat of power is once again in Prague." Moreover, the start of federalization enabled the removal of unwanted Czech communists in the State machinery on the basis of the parity argument. This happened with the reformer and Chairman of the National Assembly Smrkovský in 1968, who was replaced by the Slovak Colotka; federalization also enabled the removal of unwanted Slovaks to one of the new, but unimportant functions in the new organs of the national republic (Leff, 1988:244; Reban, 1981:228).

Despite the restrictions, it was nevertheless clear that some of the changes had substantial psychological significance, for instance the naming of the executive officials pointed at equality. But the changes were not just of psychological importance. To start with, the restructuring of the government towards more centralisation was accompanied by an effort to enlarge Slovak representation in the government as some kind of informal application of the parity principle (Leff, 1988:248). The increased Slovak share in top positions was therefore also real: in 1979, four out of eight deputy premiers were Slovaks; eight out of sixteen full ministers; eight out of fifteen first deputy ministers; and some 25% of the 75 deputy ministers (Niznansky and Robinson, 1979:7–8). Also, Slovaks headed some key ministries, such as Defence, Foreign Affairs, and Foreign Trade and, of course, held top positions in the KSČ itself, not the least of which was the position of First Secretary which Husák filled until 1987. Moreover, a sizable proportion of the Slovak intelligentsia could profit from the career opportunities in the newly created institutions, both at the republic and at the federal level. Although it is hard to give precise figures, estimations point to some substantial advantages. Thus, while the number of employees in non-productive sectors in the Czech Lands between 1968 and 1973 increased from 1,054,000 to 1,132,000 (+7.4%), in Slovakia it rose from 386,000 to 468,000 (+21.2%). More specifically, in the administration and the judicial sector, similar figures in the Czech Lands are 80,000 to 96,000 (+20.0%), while in Slovakia it went from 31,000 to 44,000 (+41.9%) (Kusin, 1978:122).

Until then, in line with the economic growth in Slovakia, a rapid urbanization process had taken place in Slovakia after World War Two. As a result the differences in the rate of urbanization between Slovakia and the Czech Lands had decreased tremendously, and Bratislava had already doubled its population from 143 thousand in 1945 to 306 thousand in 1970. Its elevation to political, cultural and economic centre of the federal republic of Slovakia in 1968 and the creation of a large government apparatus guaranteed a large influx of money. Thus, in the five year plan of 1976–1980 nearly 18% of the total investments in Slovakia were spent for this purpose (Niznansky and Robinson, 1979:7). In 1979 Bratislava (373,353 inhabitants as of 1 January, 1980) overtook Brno (372,167) and became the second largest city in Czechoslovakia after Prague (1,192,849)(RFE/RL, 5/3/1980). Other Slovak cities grew as well, however, confirming that the rapid growth was not solely linked to the change in political status.

Naturally, the changes within the KSČ itself were most crucial for the development of the political system in Czechoslovakia. Since one of the most important reasons for the 1968 intervention was the restoration of the Party's exclusive authority in the political system of Czechoslovakia, the split of the KSČ along federal lines now became highly unlikely (Dean, 1973:4). As discussed above, before 1968 the KSS had already been a separate organization in Slovakia during several periods, despite the fact that it was usually completely subordinate to the KSČ directives.[20] Husák, who,

---

20 For instance, when the depression hit Slovakia in 1930 the communists decided to form some sort of regional organization of the Communist Party in order to counter the rise of the right-wing nationalist parties. And immediately following that, during the war itself, difficult contacts with Moscow assured an exceptional independent operation of the KSS (see Jelinek 1983).

after his appointment as First Secretary of the KSČ on 17 April 1969, had at first supported federalization of the Party, reversed this position only a few weeks later. In May he claimed that "the Party is not federalized; on the contrary it is unified, and we (the KSČ Central Committee) are responsible for the work of communists at all levels, federal as well as national" (in Dean, 1972:12). The party also remained organized on a sub-republic level to avoid chances of republic-based activism and strengthen the centralist part of 'democratic centralism'. The control of the KSČ over the KSS was, among other mechanisms, assured by three members of the 11 member presidium of the KSS. They were also full or candidate members of the presidium of the KSČ which served as an interlocking directorate (Staar, 1982:80; Steiner, 1973:215). Despite this increased control, the purges in the KSS were relatively mild; 18% of its members were dismissed, against 28% for the country as a whole. In the end, a Czech Party Bureau which had existed since June, 1968, functioned solely to organize and implement purges during the 'normalization' process, after which it was disbanded in May 1971 (it was simply not mentioned any more in the Party statutes (Dean, 1972:16)).

Overall, the KSS was brought into line with the general KSČ policies, although these were formulated to a much larger extent by Slovak politicians. Kusin therefore concluded in 1981 that the "only difference between the present and pre–1968 times is that a great many Slovak communists (too many, some Czechs would claim) have been co-opted into positions of state-wide authority, not infrequently because of their Slovak background, for the sake of rectifying the anti-Slovak bias of earlier years. They, the 'Slovaks in Prague,' like their comrades in the Slovak CP in Slovakia proper, can, however, exercise the newly acquired authority and influence only within the framework of political unitarism" (Kusin, 1981:4). Therefore the Slovak Communist Party "is now what it in fact claims to be – namely, only a regional organization resting on ethnic principles. By the same token, however, it is not what it has aspired to be at various points in its history; namely, a political representation of the Slovak people. It is a training ground for functionaries. Every five years it assembles to allow about one-quarter of its top caucuses to be replenished with especially meritorious comrades, and to perform a ritual in the mobilization drive which, next to coercion and consumerism, has become the permanent mode of government in Czechoslovakia" (Kusin, 1981:9). According to the Czech historian Vilém Prečan, "the balance of twenty years experience with the Czechoslovak federation shows that federation under socialist conditions does not create conditions for the expression of the Slovak nation's free will for the making of decisions about how the Slovaks want to arrange their political, economic, spiritual, and religious life" (in RFE/RL, 30/3/1989). Moreover, although the position of the Slovaks in the centralized federation was clearly stronger than it was before 1968, it nevertheless remained vulnerable. The Czech historian Milan Hübl warned, for instance, that personnel changes in 1988 had resulted in a decrease in the share of Slovak members in the presidium of the Central Committee of the KSČ from one-third to one-fourth, reducing it "almost to the level where it had stood at the time of former President Antonín Novotný." At the time, only two federal ministers out of thirteen were Slovaks (RFE/RL, 30/3/1989).

Seen from the perspective of the Czechs, however, one could also argue that the Slovaks had some sort of a secure territorial and political base, while at the same time they could still influence events in the Czech Lands through the central organs of the KSČ (Leff, 1988:246). Indeed, the Czechs themselves did not have their own government, only the Czech National Council in the Chamber of Nations. The Czech Rudé Právo thus published a letter in 1989 in which the "flagrant abuse of the federation" by the Slovak side was mentioned, while others argued that there was already a case of 'overbalancing' between the Czech Lands and Slovakia (RFE/RL, 30/3/1989). Both Czechs and Slovaks therefore had reasons to be dissatisfied.

5.3.4.1 Economic developments under the federation

During the Prague Spring and thereafter, the special economic position of Slovakia was acknowledged, and measures were taken to speed up the equalization of the two regions. However, although the Czech and Slovak planners, when preparing the federal system, undertook to rectify the excessive concentration of economic authority, they did so with a view to preserving and extending the economic integration of the country.[21] Nevertheless, less than two years later, at the plenum of the Central Committee in January 1970, the recentralization of economic planning was re-emphasized; Václav Hula (the CC plenum Planning Chief) stated that the role of the republics was "primarily the creation of concepts of the development of individual branches and the preparation of data for the binding decisions of the federal organs" (in Dean, 1973:47). While some of the competencies important for planning and economic development had already been allocated to the federal level, the existing 'federal committees' (in areas such as prices, technical and investment development, industry, and post and communications) now became federal ministries as well, with virtual veto power over their counterparts at the level of the republics (Dean, 1973:48). As mentioned above, the ten provinces were reintroduced in 1970, accom-

---

21 A constitutional law in 1968 had formulated that the Czech and Slovak nations were "economically autonomous," but that at the same time there existed an "integrated Czechoslovak economy." This confusing use of words led to a great deal of discussion over the exact economic goals. In the 1970 amendment to the Czechoslovak constitution therefore the word "uniform" is used to describe the Czechoslovak economy (Niznansky and Robinson, 1979:12).

panied by the regional national committees, and they were given a special role in the law on National Planning which resulted from the 1970 constitution (Dostál, 1982:336).

In the federal period the equalization between the two parts of the country proceeded at a continually high pace. Also equalization within the republics was considered important, and compared to the Czech Lands, the territorial spread of investments in Slovakia covered a greater area and was less likely to create or allow the emergence of differentiation of life chances and welfare. Internal differentiation in the Czech Lands in fact became greater than in Slovakia (Dostál, 1982:337–339). Indeed, although the transfer of resources as a percentage of the National Product in Slovakia went down from 15 in the 1950s to 11 in the 1970s, the continuing high pace of equalization was reflected in the rise in industrial labour in Slovakia. Between 1967 and 1978 the number of industrial jobs in Slovakia increased by 191 thousand compared with only 6 thousand in the Czech Lands (Kopačka, 1994:44–45; Kosta, 1984:121). Further equalization between the Czech Lands and Slovakia showed in the rise of the number of workers in industry and construction from 39.4% in the period 1964–68 to 44.3% in 1987, or 94% of the Czech level, in the increase of the level of income as a percentage of the Czech Lands from 61% in 1955 to 84% in 1983, and in the increase in the level of consumption per inhabitant as a percentage of the Czech Lands from 81% in 1948 to 91.4% in 1980 (Kosta, 1984:120; Krejčí, 1990:27, Wolchik, 1991:188). By 1989, the national income produced in Slovakia as a share of the country as a whole was 30.4%, for 33.7% of the population. Besides the continuing transfer of resources from the Czech Lands to Slovakia, there were other reasons for growth in Slovakia as well. To begin with, as mentioned before, normalization of the economic sector in Slovakia was less severe than in the Czech Lands, leaving more economic experience intact in that republic. Secondly, the industrial capital was younger and therefore more modern. Thirdly, the population increase was bigger, leading to a more rapidly increasing labour force. And fourthly, labour productivity increased more than in the Czech Lands, partially because of a higher level of education at secondary level and university (Niznansky and Robinson, 1979:13–15; see also Capek and Sazama 1993). Efficiency still remained lower in Slovakia than in the Czech Lands, meaning that the emphasis on the industrialisation of Slovakia was not so advantageous for the federation as a whole (Kosta, 1984:125).

After 12 years of federation Gustáv Husák declared that "the task of overcoming historically existing differences [between the Czech Lands and Slovakia] has been essentially fulfilled" (in RFE/RL, 16/3/1983). Equalization had progressed to such an extent that it was almost decided that subsidies could be cut. Total subsidies, however, remained comparatively higher for Slovakia, rising above the share of the region in either population or production (RFE/RL, 16/3/1983). The fact that the cut in subsidies did not occur could either point to the strength of the Slovak communist elite, or be explained by the fact that the country's economic difficulties in the beginning of the 1980s hit the Slovak industry particularly hard.

5.3.4.2 Slovak separateness under the federation

While the process of economic equalization proceeded, the political autonomy remained rather an empty shell. Nevertheless, the creation of the federation was certainly some form of a moral and psychological victory for the Slovaks and provided them with channels to articulate some of their interests, while the recentralization which took place after the first years was not taken to the extreme and was partially rationalized by the economic situation at the time. Even after the centralization, as Skilling pointed out, the national organs of the Slovak Republic remained as "symbols of Slovak statehood and of national equality, and continued to enjoy some degree of administrative autonomy in education, culture and the economy. This, plus the existence of a separate Slovak Party, gave the Slovaks at least an illusion of power and influence, and what is more, opened up career opportunities for thousands in Prague and Bratislava" (Skilling, 1981:56). In an interview two years later Skilling therefore expressed his belief that, "even though the Slovaks have often been disappointed by their co-existence with the Czechs, today if free they would opt for a common state" (in Duchacek, 1988:26–27).

Nevertheless, the federal institutions strengthened the existing differences between the two parts of the country in several ways. Leff, for instance, notes how the existence of separately educated elites, operating in separate political arenas and interpreting events generally from different national viewpoints, led to divergence of the country's elite (Leff, 1988:260). Moreover, this phenomenon was clearest among the younger generations; during the federation the Czech and Slovak elites were increasingly educated at home, after which their career paths also took place inside their own republic. For Czechs an existence in Slovakia was not even considered (96% had their education and careers in the Czech Lands), while the Slovak elite over the years increasingly turned inward (59% stayed solely in Slovakia, even more of the younger generation) (Leff, 1988:292–3). Interestingly, this was not just the case for the communist elite, but also for the opposition where "bipolarity in the counter-elite" had become apparent (Leff, 1988:268). Thus, the most important opposition in Czechoslovakia from outside the system, Charter 77, had surprisingly little support from Slovak personalities. Only a few Slovaks, who permanently lived in Prague, had initially signed the Charter, and later only a couple of Slovaks in Bratislava followed suit. This can indeed reflect a lack of support among the Slovak population for the activities of Charter 77, and perhaps even some satisfaction with the political arrangement at the time and with the mildness of the purges in Slovakia (Skilling, 1981:55; see also Reban, 1981:232; Leff, 1988:264–268).

Differences also showed in cultural life (literature, the arts, and also attitude and behaviour) and were fostered, in part as a result of the fact that the 'normalization' process had been done more sensibly and with less dogmatism. The Slovak artistic unions had retained a far greater number of recognized artists than their Czech counterparts (that is, the artists were not forced to exchange the pen for the pick-axe, but were, in the worst cases, forced to do clerical work); indeed, even the 'normalized' leadership of the Slovak Writer's Union did not regard the members of the Czech Writer's Union as genuine representatives of Czech literature. Cultural contacts lessened, as ousted Czech artists were often checked by state security forces when they had contacts with Slovak artists and vice-versa. Naturally, the pre–1968 differences in the attitudes of the Czech and the Slovak elite (and within the Slovak elite) concerning the federation-democratization debate also continued to affect post–1968 attitudes. The artists who had pressed for 'federalisation first' remained as the most influential after the 'normalization' in Slovakia, and "While the Slovak artists may go through the required motions of 'socialist integration,' they could still balk if the slightest suspicion is aroused that this integration is just another word for Czechoslovakism" (Niznansky and Robinson, 1979:18). With respect to cultural life, in fact, the federation was supposed to foster in both form and substance the independence of the two national cultures in the hope that a status of equality would promote mutual relations. But, as Niznansky and Robinson (1979:16–18) argued in 1979, in practice the two cultures were "drifting apart" with less and less contact between representatives of the respective cultural elites. Among the general public in Slovakia, the hold of religion (both Protestant and Catholic) remained stronger, and by the end of the 1980s most of the protest in Slovakia against the regime concerned religious life (Leff, 1988:265). Moreover, the industrialization of Slovakia had created numerous environmental problems which also prompted new Slovak activism and the defence of specific Slovak interests, both at the regional level itself and at the central level. Overall, as Kusin (1983:2) notes, the separate Slovak approach contained nation-building elements, including the tendency to self-determination, even though the communist ideology claimed that self-determination had successfully been achieved with the federation.

Among the Czechs this separate scene in Slovakia, and this apparent lack of opposition, caused irritation. Not only had the Slovaks secured the federation after the invasion, they had also shown disloyalty to the country while it was being 'normalized.' According to Leff: "The passage of time has consolidated an irritable Czech impression that Slovaks are overrepresented in the state bureaucracy, and that erstwhile nationalist critics have been bought off with access to power, or at least out of loyalty to Husák. Nor was the 'new asymmetry' of Czech and Slovak organizational development within the party appreciated. Even the comparative mildness of the Slovak purges engendered distance and a feeling that Slovaks had sold their reformist birthright for a mess of federalist pottage" (Leff, 1988:270). By the time the rule of communism became untenable, it was clear that the federation had done nothing to bring the two groups closer together in a political and psychological sense, and in many respects had made them drift further apart.

5.3.5 Slovak separateness, the Velvet Revolution and the Velvet Divorce

While many of the developmental differences between Czechs and Slovaks had diminished in the preceding seventy years, they had certainly not been completely erased. For one thing, the developments in the two regions had been largely asynchronous and had occurred at a different pace and with a different impact (Musil 1993). For instance, as discussed, the economic transition of Slovakia from an agricultural to an industrial society followed the Czech Lands by fifty years, and the fact that it occurred under a socialist system had a major impact on the character of the process. On the one hand, this had psychological importance, as for the Czechs the period of relative economic success was the interwar period, while for the Slovaks it was the postwar period. On the other hand, industrialization under socialism had created some structural differences, although these were not as straightforward as the political discussion made them out to be (Capek and Sazama 1993). One of the main bones of contention became, for instance, the arms industry that produced an estimated 5 to 6% of the industrial output in Slovakia, whereas this was only 2% in the Czech Lands (Capek and Sazama, 1993:223; see also RFE/RL, 24/9/1993; Bookman 1994). The new regime's decision to curtail the production of arms was therefore to hit Slovakia much harder. Overall, the economic restructuring of Slovak society that was to follow the fall of the communist system was thought to have had a different and much more severe effect when compared to the Czech Lands. This indeed showed in the rise of unemployment in Slovakia, compared to the Czech Lands, which went from a equal level of approximately 2% at the start of 1991 to over 11% in Slovakia against 2.8% in the Czech Lands in June, 1992. This unemployment rose to even higher levels in the eastern parts of Slovakia (Dostál, 1992:82). More importantly, while in the Czech Lands, two-thirds of the population held the former communist regime responsible for the present unemployment, in Slovakia two-thirds blamed the post-communist regime (Radicova, 1993:52).

Czech and Slovak perceptions of the transformation were also different in other fields. The transformation involved, besides the changing of the economy, the creation of a new constitution, and the re-emergence of a civic society (see Musil 1992). With regard to the latter, the Catholic character of

Slovak society resurfaced, and in 1991 membership of the Catholic Church had risen to 72% (RFE/RL, 6/9/1993). The 'Catholic vote' in Slovakia reappeared likewise (Jehlicka et al., 1993:249). With regard to the constitutional question, many Slovaks were suspicious of Czech intentions. Although they knew what they would lose – a limited but recognizable form of autonomy under the communist federation – the negotiations over a new state structure made it clear that they could not predict what they would gain. In a way this was displayed in the different support for the anti-communist movements in the elections of June 1990: in the Czech Lands Civic Forum (OF) received 53% of the votes, but in Slovakia the Public against Violence (VPN) won only 32.5%, reflecting the competition of, in particular, the Slovak Nationalist Party (SNS) and the Christian Democratic Party.[22] The communists in both parts of the country received around 13.5%. The fear of centralization was displayed in the Slovak reaction to Havel's plans on the new power sharing arrangements in December 1990; his proposals for a strong presidency caused his popularity to plummet in Slovakia (Wolchik, 1991:66–67).

Moreover, the federal structure of the state became highly relevant in the new democratic context. Having been created under a communist setting where the constitutional procedures would never obtain practical meaning, some of these procedures now created frustration, particularly among the Czechs. Due to the nature of the procedures in parliament, which stipulated that three-fifths majorities were needed for the passing of many laws, the suspicion felt by many Slovaks could very effectively be translated into a blocking of important changes (see Illner 1994). In practice therefore, 40% of the Slovak parliamentarians, representing about 12% of the country's population, could obstruct all important legislation. Moreover, the federal system helped in creating a party system that was split between the two republics. Already in the 1990 elections – which functioned as a referendum on the general question of system change involving mainly the communists and their opponents – state-wide parties had received very little support, and for the 1992 elections there therefore remained just a few of those. Even the communists had split up (Olson, 1993:307; Jehlicka et al., 1993:251–252). The post-communist electoral law itself worked in favour of republican parties, among other reasons because of a threshold in each republic (for the National Councils, 5% in the Czech republic and 3% in Slovakia, and for the Chamber of the People 5% in both republics; higher

---

22   Interesting in this respect is the fact that long dormant electoral structures resurfaced. In Eastern Slovakia the support for less nationalist parties was much stronger, reflecting the older desire to stay in political union with the Czech Lands, whereas in the northwestern part of the country, previously a Hlinka stronghold, more extremist nationalist parties were successful (see Jehlicka et al. 1993). As noted in the text, the northwest was, paradoxically, not the area with the highest unemployment. Local parties in Moravia achieved over twenty percent of the votes.

for electoral coalitions). Parties therefore had to appeal to regional preferences in order to stand a chance of being elected to office, and only a few parties sought allies across the republican border. Remainder votes were also reallocated within each republic (Olson, 1993:304). In light of the possibilities for obstruction in the federal parliament, the question about which party system would develop within each republic therefore became of central importance.

The new Slovak political elite which had replaced the communists had to compete hard for the confidence of the Slovak electorate, and they started to demand more autonomy, partly as negotiation tactics (Wheaton & Kavan, 1992:168; Wightman, 1993:57). Many Slovak politicians assessed that the Czech attachment to the state would be so strong that the Slovaks could wrest endless concessions from their counterparts, and in this they were pushed to more extreme positions by the separatist demands of the SNS (14% of the votes in the 1990 elections), and by the increasing nationalist sentiment among the electorate. It was indeed clear that the general political and economic uncertainty in Slovakia was translated into the public support for the more nationalist parties, as they were considered to be the most able to defend Slovak interests in these volatile times.[23] At the same time there was a certain ambiguity about Slovak public opinion: whereas the electorate of all Slovak parties desired a common state with the Czechs (with the exception of the SNS voters), the most nationalistic offspring of the Public against Violence, the Movement for a Democratic Slovakia (HZDS) of Vladimír Mečiar, who was at best unclear about that subject, was the most trusted of all parties (Bútorová, 1993:66).

Overall, however, even when desiring a common state, the general public in Slovakia held a different perspective from the Czech public on how that state should be organized. Thus, in June 1990, only 8% of the people in Slovakia wanted independence (against 5% in the Czech Lands), but 30% wanted a confederation (against 16%) and 41% wanted strong republican governments (against 30%); no less than 42% of the Czechs (against 16% of the Slovaks) wanted a common state with a strong central government (Wolchik, 1991:125). A perhaps equally crucial distinction between the two parts of the country was the difference in views on the importance of economic and constitutional dilemmas. Whereas in the Czech Lands economic reform was considered to have top priority, among the Slovaks it was the constitutional question.

Differences in perception were ultimately reflected in the political arena, and different sets of party systems emerged. In Slovakia, Mečiar became the most popular leader by far and won the elections in June 1992 with a pro-

---

23 This increasing nationalism was partly the response to the re-emergence of older antagonisms between Slovaks and ethnic Hungarians in Slovakia, the latter understandably wanting to keep the common state with the Czechs (see Pufflerová 1994).

gram which promised the Slovak electorate a maximum program of emancipation for Slovakia, even though it stopped short of outright independence and was mainly meant to slow down the process of economic transformation. Other parties which had a strong showing were more to the left side of the political spectrum, while the ambiguousness of Slovak nationalism was reflected in the decline of support for the SNS. In the Czech Lands, on the other hand, the Civic Democratic Party of Václav Klaus won the election with a program that centred on a radical change in the economic system. Overall, the 3% to 5% threshold at the republic level had helped to crush the centre of the political spectrum, previously formed by the Civic Forum and the Public against Violence. The communists remained with 14% in each republic and in Slovakia they were in fact the most pro-federalist party, which naturally did not improve the image of federalism. After the election in June, events proceeded rapidly. On 17 July, 1992, the SNR issued a symbolic declaration of independence, which resulted in the resignation of Havel as president; he chose not to preside over the divorce of his country (RFE/RL, 31/7/1992). And indeed, the two winning parties, which held such vastly different views on the constitutional and economic future of the state, in July agreed to form a coalition with the sole purpose of breaking up the country. The Velvet Divorce became reality on 25 November, 1992, when the Federal Assembly ultimately voted to abolish the Czech and Slovak Federation.

In the end, the combination of societal differences, leading to a fundamentally different opinion on the crucial points in the negotiations, coupled with the competition between politicians in a fast changing political landscape, led to a reordering of priorities for the Czechs and the Slovaks. Clearly the basis for further cooperation was so differently perceived in the two parts of the country that further political cohabitation proved impossible. The Czech leadership wanted the split as much as the Slovak leadership, because Václav Klaus badly wanted his hands freed from Slovak interference so as to get on with economic reforms; the continuing negotiations threatened to destabilize the Czech part of the country too, and to block any progress in the economic and social transition. In contrast to earlier experiences, therefore, the negotiations between Slovaks and Czechs were greatly influenced this time by an assertion of a form of Czech nationalism, based on 23 years of living in a federal state in which the Slovaks were perceived to have gained the most. While the electoral results pointed to the differences between the Slovak and Czech constituencies, it must be said that the population did not have the opportunity to voice its opinion in a referendum on the issue. To what extent the split was in fact supported by the Czech and Slovak peoples can therefore not be established, although the polls systematically pointed to a desire for a common state by the majority in both groups.

Sixteen years before, Skilling (1976:850–851) concluded that the "dialectic of Czechoslovak history" has been a succession of triumphs and disasters, "each triumph seeming to offer a solution to the problem, but each one followed, at ever shorter intervals, by disaster. Discontinuity, rather than continuity, has been the central feature of that history. The liberation of 1918 was followed by partition and German occupation twenty years later. Independence, restored in 1945, lasted only three years until the communist takeover in 1948. The democratization efforts of 1968 ended abruptly, after eight months, with a Soviet occupation." In a way this dynamic came to its ultimate conclusion after the Velvet Revolution; it led to the complete disappearance of the country as such, although lack of violent traumas and a low intermixture of the groups made it disappear peacefully.

5.4   COMMUNIST FEDERALISM AND ETHNONATIONALISM: THE CASE OF CZECHOSLOVAKIA

The communist federation was intended as a political solution for a national problem that had emerged and matured under very different circumstances. The political awareness of Slovak identity had already developed during the permissive system of the interwar years, when it had radicalized under almost continuous exclusion from the political centre in Prague. The separate state, even if under German tutelage, meant a climax in this development and also meant the affirmation of cultural separateness and governmental potential. The Slovak Uprising provided some form of rehabilitation for the character of that state, while the lack of support for the communists confirmed the separate character of Slovakia within the renewed Czechoslovakian polity. This latter point, however, set the stage for curtailment of Slovak nationalism as exemplified in the trials against the Slovak communists, even though Slovak culture had initially been acknowledged by the communists as being separate. Clearly, the substantial economic equalization which was already achieved in that period could not be a replacement for this curtailment. Moreover, the centralized control imposed by Prague backfired: for the Slovaks even beneficial policies continued to originate from a distant centre, and they felt they were left at the mercy of the Czech majority. Indeed, the Slovaks accused Prague of sustaining pro-Czech policies, for instance caused by the fact that official decisions failed to be implemented by the Czech-dominated central bureaucracy in Prague. The territorial division of Slovakia in 1960 was equally felt as an attack on Slovak interests and even Slovak identity. Nevertheless, only during the 'Slovak Spring' and the Prague Spring could the separateness of Slovak life and history re-emerge as central issues in the political debate.

Of course, strictly speaking, the federation did not qualify as a full blown case, because of the lack of democracy and the erosion of *de facto* competencies of the republic. Nevertheless, the politico-territorial affirmation of

Slovak identity – not as a sub-branch of a Czechoslovak nation, but as an equal partner with *de jure* veto rights in the centre – was the first such clear-cut attempt within a common state with the Czechs. Moreover, aside from definitive autonomy in the cultural field, the creation of the federation meant the opening up of substantial job opportunities, both in the bureaucracy of the republic as well as in the political centre. This was of course crucial given the central importance of the state in Czechoslovak economic and social life. It was a major difference from earlier autonomy arrangements, and the combined effect of cultural autonomy and political access to the centre was probably responsible for the relative complacency among the Slovaks under the normalization policies. The central role of Slovaks in these policies, not the least of whom was Husák, naturally created a markedly different image of the centre than had been the case in the pre–1968 period. In comparison with the Czech Lands, in Slovakia the situation seemed by all measures equal or perhaps even slightly better. Separatism therefore remained limited until 1989, although the Slovaks increasingly turned inward.

This changed radically after the fall of communism. The federation provided the framework for reorientation for the new political actors, and the fact that it consisted of only two parts meant that the balance sheet of Czech and Slovak gains and losses was relatively simple to make up. Certainly, as perceived by the Slovaks, the complete economic equalization of the two parts of the country did not affect the balance-sheet positively, because that achievement as well as political equalization now came under threat. Moreover, the consequences of the communist system became only evident with the fall of communism, showing that the differences between the two parts of the country in a cultural, educational, and political sense had grown. Internal differences in Slovakia itself had also become much less important. Furthermore, after the demise of the KSČ the only unifying political force in the country had disappeared, and the reformed communists' support for the federation did not help the image of the federation at all.

The competencies were now completely transferred to the legitimate institutions. The uncertainty of the transformation made the power relations within these institutions extremely relevant. Now, the deliberate over-representation of Slovaks in the Federal Parliament was a serious brake on the negotiations, particularly because of the scramble for electoral support which took place among the new Slovak politicians between 1990 and 1992. In that scramble, the diversity of interests was suppressed in favour of a conception of Slovakia as a single unit. The stress on separateness was a major tool in that fight, and this time Czech interests and frustration were also much more clearly perceived as Czech interests and less as Czechoslovak interests. Therefore, at the state level, the negotiations took place between the republics and hardly between various groupings on both sides of the constitutional divide. Overall, the image of a re-emerging distant political centre – in which Slovak influence was as yet unsure, now that tremendous social changes were to arrive in the near future – was strong enough to be politically exploited by Slovak politicians. With interests in the two parts of the country diverging, there were too few reasons and mechanisms to keep it together.

6

Belgium
The Dynamics of Linguistic Conflict

The third case in this book, Belgium, has experienced substantial linguistic conflict since it became independent in 1830. At first, this conflict entailed the struggle by Dutch-speakers for full linguistic rights in a state where national unity on the basis of the French language was stressed; later the struggle included socio-economic rights and political rights. During the 165 years of the state's existence, its institutional shape slowly adapted to dealing with the ongoing struggle, leading to near complete federalism in recent years. However, since this case was selected for the insights it may provide into the dynamics of ethnonationalism under a federalized system, the last 25 years of the state's political history are the most important ones. As in the chapters on the Eastern European cases, the first section contains a general introduction to the history of the country, after which in section 6.2 I will give a short overview of the ethnonational structure of Belgium. In section 6.3 I will analyze the tension between the two main ethnic groups. This chapter ends with section 6.4, in which I discuss the dynamics of ethnonationalism under a federalized liberal-democratic system.

6.1   GENERAL INTRODUCTION

Belgium became independent in 1830 when an uprising successfully challenged the rule of the Dutch King William I. The basis of the uprising lay in a complex combination of linguistic, religious and socio-economic distinctions that created a temporary cooperation of very diverse groups, all of which deplored the position the southern provinces held under the rule of the northern provinces. It was not a nationalist uprising in any real sense, if understood as a culmination of popular discontent by a unified culture, although it became one as a result of the rather rigid response by the northern provinces (Kossmann, 1976:103, Vos 1993). In fact, identification of the population was mainly at a local level (see De Schrijver 1981, Stengers 1981). The Belgian parliament chose a German Prince, Prince Leopold von Saxe Coburg-Gotha, as the ruler of the new Kingdom, and made French the official language of the country. The language of the elites in the southern provinces was French, and between 1795 and 1814 French rule had in fact reinforced this. Subsequent attempts by King William I to strengthen the position of the Dutch language had therefore been widely rejected, just as his attempts to modernize the educational system had been; this would have eroded the powers of the Catholic Church in that field (De Schrijver, 1981:23–24; see also Lorwin, 1966:149–150).

The constitution of 1831 created a 'unitary and decentralized' Belgian state, with a strong central government, but with considerable competencies and autonomy for the existing 2,500 communes and nine historical provinces. It was widely regarded as one of the most liberal constitutions of Europe, and its character remained fundamentally unchanged until 1970 (Molitor 1981). The constitution established a parliament consisting of two chambers with equal legislative powers: a Chamber of Representatives, elected directly, and a Senate, partially elected directly, partially elected by provincial councils, partially coopted, and with one seat reserved for the Crown Prince. Despite these democratic institutions, political power remained in the hands of the very few. Voting rights were only for those males over 25 who paid a certain amount of taxes. As a result, in 1830 no more than 5% of the male citizens over 25 could vote, and their numbers rose only very slightly in the next 50 years (Mackie and Rose, 1991:39). Substantial changes first occurred in 1893, when universal male suffrage was introduced under the increasing pressure of the Socialist movement. However, a system of plurality voting preserved some differences in electoral power, with extra votes for those who owned a specified amount of property or had received higher education. Of 1,370,000 voters in 1893, 290,000 had two votes and 220,000 had three votes (Mackie and Rose, 1991:39, see Lorwin, 1966:156–157). In 1899 the electoral system was changed from a majority system to a proportional system, in which *arrondissements* were the basic political units. Each *arrondissement* was accorded a certain number of seats, depending upon its population. Due to population growth the total number of seats in the Chamber of Representatives increased from 108 in 1848 to 212 in 1949, after which the number was fixed. In 1919 plurality voting was abolished – after the Socialists had shown their loyalty to the state during World War One – and the voting age was lowered to 21. Universal suffrage only came in 1948, and the voting age was ultimately lowered to 18 in 1979. Voting has remained compulsory till this day.

Economically, Belgium was industrialized early, particularly in the French-speaking regions (Kesteloot et al., 1990:14–23). Indeed, while the existing industries (e.g., textile) in the Flemish provinces slumped, existing coal supplies and large-scale investments in steel industries greatly increased industrial production around Liège and in the Borinage. Furthermore, crop failures and international competition (especially during the last decade of the century) worsened agricultural life in Flanders to such an extent that large scale 'poverty migration' to the southern provinces and Brussels became necessary. By the turn of the century, however, economic fortunes had moved from the older industrial areas to the so-called ABC-axis (Antwerp-Brussels-Charleroi); in the northern Dutch-speaking provinces investors were attracted to the quieter and cheaper labour force and by the possibilities provided by Antwerp's harbour for developing various kinds of light industry. Moreover, coal was found and developed in Limburg, and by 1920 46% of industrial activities already took place in the northern half of the country (Kesteloot et al., 1990:23). Industrialization received a further impetus when, through the personal efforts of King Leopold II, the successor of Leopold I, a large area in the African Congo was colonized which provided natural resources for the Belgian industry. These colonial relations were to last until 1960.

Until World War One Belgian politics were dominated by a religious and a socio-economic cleavage; the two cleavages combined to result in three *familles spirituelles* or *zuilen* (pillars): the Catholics, the Liberals, and the Socialists (see Lorwin 1966, Lijphart 1981, Huyse 1981). During the nineteenth century, the most important division in the Belgian political system concerned religion, most particularly the character and extent of State-Church relations. After strong economic growth, the Liberals came to power during the 1840s, but their attempts to reduce the influence of the Church in education was despised by Catholics. Although a network of state schools was created, control of the Catholic Church over the population was strong enough to keep it within bounds. The Catholics gained political power in the 1870s and 1880s and have remained the central party in Belgian politics ever since. The second cleavage, involving the Socialists, became a major force in political life following the introduction of universal male suffrage in 1893 (see Table 6.1). Indeed, a couple of years later the proportional system was mainly introduced because the Catholics wanted to avoid a two-party confrontation with the Socialists. The Socialists established a broad subculture of cooperatives, unions, and societies, which set a pattern for the other two *familles spirituelles* (Lorwin, 1966:156). Thus, in competition with the rising strength of the Socialist unions, a Christian Labour Union was created in 1912 to limit the rising influence of Socialists in the Catholic-dominated rural areas. In particular, this prevented the northern Belgian provinces from becoming dominated by Socialists, which would become important later on. More on pillarization and on the consociational political system in Belgium will be given below.

Throughout the nineteenth century a slight increase in the level of linguistic tension could be observed, although this did not at all have the same relevance as it has now. For more than a century, the tension was between a frenchified Belgian state and a Flemish Movement which, following an initial emphasis on cultural issues, broadened in its scope and purpose. The first compromise was struck in 1898 when Dutch and French became equal before the law, which made the country *de jure* bilingual; language laws in the 1930s and 1960s further implemented this notion. However, Belgian political development, certainly including its linguistic relations, was highly influenced by the two World Wars. Belgium was occupied by the Germans in both wars; during World War One only a very small corner of Belgium remained on the Allied side of the trenches, in contrast to the entire territory being occupied during World War Two. The diverse perspectives of French-speakers and Dutch-speakers on Flemish collaboration with the Germans have remained a bone of contention to this very day. Belgium's linguistic situation became slightly more complicated after World War One with the inclusion of the German-speaking districts of Eupen and Malmédy.

However, linguistic tension certainly was not always central to Belgian politics, even after World War Two; other issues dominated political life, such as the Royal Question, which concerned the position taken by King Leopold III during the War, and the ideological conflict over state and private education. However, regional differences which came to the fore in these conflicts – in combination with the economic crisis that followed the industrial decline in Wallonia, and unrest over the results of the 1947 census – set the stage for a full-scale conflict over the linguistic question. This time not just a Flemish Movement was involved but an active French-speaking movement as well, particularly in Wallonia. New language laws in the 1960s could not solve the issue, and by the end of the 1960s, since the statewide political parties became ever more divided over the issue (both metaphorically speaking and, ultimately, even literally), it became clear that fundamental changes were needed. These came in the form of the 1970 constitutional reforms (see section 6.1.3).

In the decades that followed, the implementation of the new structure and the solution of the remaining controversies, such as that over Brussels and the question of Voeren, caused the fall of numerous governments. A prolonged impasse was only overcome through a series of bargains struck in the 1980s, ultimately creating the laws which provided the groundwork for a genuine federation. The law on the federation was passed in parliament in July 1993. Since the linguistic question has been inextricably bound up with the course of political events in the last 25 years, more extensive treatment will follow in section 6.3. The next sections, however, will briefly discuss the workings of the consociational system in Belgium and will provide a short overview of the main constitutional changes since 1970.

6.1.1 Consociationalism in Belgium

According to most analysts, the political system of Belgium is best described as a consociational system, meaning one in which cultural diversity within society is prevented from becoming politically divisive by a system of internal autonomy for the groups involved, and by participation of the elites of each group in the state-wide decision-making process. The notion of consociationalism involves different perspectives (McRae 1974, see also McRae 1990, Van Schendelen 1984, Huyse 1970, Huyse 1981).

First of all, as Lijphart (1977b, 1981) has proposed, it may focus on the workings of the political elite in a deeply divided society. Central to a consociational system is the existence of a grand coalition of the leaders of all significant segments of the pluralistic society; in this it differs fundamentally from the more competitive majority government in which minimal majorities will be formed. Three other basic elements include a mutual veto for each segment on issues which are central to its existence, proportionality in political representation and in civil service appointments, and a high degree of autonomy for each segment to run its own internal affairs (Lijphart, 1977b:25–44). As Lijphart sees it, contrasting Belgian patterns of politics with the majoritarian type, Belgium is a more than perfect example of his model in terms of the breadth of its coalitions, minority vetoes, a multi-party system, a commitment to maintaining the system, and so forth. To him, Belgium is the most significant and constructive example of consociational democracy world wide. The leadership in Belgium is trained in consensual politics from the communal level to the national parliament, and at the highest level in particular, the party leaders negotiate complex package deals in which all parties have both gains and losses.

A second perspective concerns the segmented social structure and focuses on the way the *familles spirituelles*, or *zuilen*, have developed and are organized, and how they participate in political life and arrive at consensus (or don't) (see Lorwin 1966). It concentrates on the degree of social separation, the extent to which one can live one's life in one's own type of organization. In Belgium, as already noted, the degree of social separation has been very high, in particular where the three traditional groupings of Socialists, Catholics and Liberals are concerned. Nevertheless, and this brings in the third perspective, the prolonged historical traditions in which the divisions became relevant, dating from before the existence of the Belgian state and certainly from the revolution onwards, have given rise to a political culture in which non-violent accommodation of these types of divisions has been taken as a standard. The country is predisposed to consociationalism, so to speak. Indeed, the 'Unionism,' meaning coalition formation between Liberals and Catholics, started as early as the Belgian state. The very early inclusion of Socialists in Belgian cabinets, immediately following World War One, is also a significant sign of the validity of that perspective. However, McRae (1974:21) considered this historical tradition to be rather ambiguous in the Belgian case. The various aspects of consociationalism and the fragmented society will come forth in the discussion on the historical development of the linguistic conflict.

At this stage it may already be pointed out that Lijphart considers Belgium after 1970 to be "an outstanding example of the non-territorial form of federalism," by which he means the high degree of autonomy in cultural matters which could be exercised by the cultural councils (Lijphart, 1981:8–10). However, by this he was not describing the religious and class cleavages, but the one dividing Flemings from Walloons. Belgium therefore serves as an example for analyzing whether consociationalism can work in a society which is divided by an ethnonational cleavage. The question is how the linguistic issue interacted with the other cleavages which existed in Belgian society, and how the political system which developed to accommodate these cleavages has been used to confront and pacify the linguistic conflict between Dutch-speakers and French-speakers in Belgian society. There was nothing automatic in this process. Indeed, as noted by McRae in the beginning of the 1970s, "[t]here is ... a notable difference in tone between religious-ideological argument and linguistic argument in Belgium. Religious-ideological debate may be sharp, even hostile, but the differences are long established, understood, accepted, and tolerated, if not always treated with respect. Linguistic differences are bitter, intolerant, and reveal little reciprocal understanding" (McRae, 1974:20–21). Moreover, the linguistic segments were not traditional pillars, and their separate clusters of institutions remained limited (McRae, 1986:128). As has been discussed in chapter two, the analysis will be particularly concerned with the effects of the "non-territorial form of federalism," which eventually turned out to be territorial federalization.

6.1.2 Constitutional changes since 1970

The fact that the political system has changed at all may be considered rather remarkable, given the fact that the unitary nature of the Belgian state had not changed since the passing of the constitution in 1831. In fact, it is not easy to alter the constitution in Belgium. Apart from the ever-present need to unravel the existing laws and arrangements, negotiations must result in two-thirds majorities and, since 1970, in majorities in both language groups. Under Belgian rules for constitutional change, first the articles to be amended have to be named, after which the next elected parliament can pass constitutional changes. In this way, many individuals become involved: the presidents of the (future) government parties, the ministers of old and new governments, and the MP's in the two Houses before and after elections. Besides the changes in electoral fortunes, these procedures give the participating parties and individuals more time to rethink their gains and losses, and sometimes lead to withdrawal (McRae, 1986:160; Rudolph, 1989:101, Huyse, 1981:150). Discussion of Belgian developments becomes further complicated because of the need for normal laws as well as special laws to implement the constitutional arrangements. Here again deadlocks may occur, causing the provisions in the constitution to remain dead letters for prolonged periods of time.

Basically, the constitutional changes have followed two lines, simultaneously creating on the one hand cultural communities (Dutch-speakers, French-speakers, and German-speakers) which could wield authority over delimited language areas, and on the other hand economic regions (Flanders, Wallonia, and Brussels). As will be explained during the course of this chapter, these two kinds of territories did not coincide; Brussels, which is a

French-speaking city surrounded by Flemish territory, is the main problem. This rather complicated construction has been implemented in three stages (see Hooghe 1991, Hooghe 1993, Covell 1993, Senelle 1989, Molitor 1981, Berckx 1990).

First of all, in 1970, numerous articles were added to or amended in the constitution to embed linguistic areas and to arrange for the creation of the two types of sub-state units, cultural communities and economic regions. Thus four linguistic territories were created: a Dutch-speaking territory, a French-speaking territory, a German-speaking territory, and the bilingual Brussels Capital. To ensure the stability of the borders of the linguistic territories, it was stipulated that they could only be altered or corrected by special majorities (Senelle, 1989:57). Cultural Councils, consisting of the members of parliament of the various language groups, could pass decrees in specified areas in the cultural field, while on the competencies of the economic regions no consensus could be reached. Parity between the two main language groups was to be created in the central government, while alarm bell procedures were to guarantee that linguistic groups could block the passing of a law which they considered to have a "serious effect on relations between the communities"; the government was then to re-evaluate. In the end, to guarantee the cooperation of all major political parties, it was stipulated that "laws and decrees shall guarantee amongst other things the rights and liberties of ideological and philosophical minorities."[1]

The second stage came in 1980, during which the power of the Cultural Councils was extended with a newly invented phenomenon, called 'personalized matters,' which meant matters in the sphere of health policy, aid to individuals (care for the elderly, family policy, the integration of immigrants), and applied scientific research. The executive powers of the regional authorities were also increased, although overall the 1980 changes only involved about 9% of the state budget (Dewachter, 1992a:18). The Dutch language community and the region of Flanders were from then on governed by a single Flemish Council.[2] Given the problems that might emerge as a result of an increase in regional authority, a Court of Arbitration was to be created.

---

1   Indeed, as will be explained below, the Catholics and Liberals had reason to fear a Socialist-dominated Wallonia, while the Socialists and Liberals were uncomfortable with the prospect of a Catholic-dominated Flanders. As a result, the Cultural Councils only had very limited competencies in education, because of fears on the part of the respective 'cultural minorities' that the balance of the 1958 School Pact (see below) would be disrupted (Van Impe, 1983:185). To take away some of the fears, a 'Cultural Pact' prescribed that public and private cultural organizations had to enjoy equal treatment, and that various opinions had to be represented in accordance with their respective importance in the official cultural institutions. A commission was even created to arrange for this (see Huyse, 1981:145; Dewachter, 1987:334).

2   In Wallonia no such combination was created because of the high number of French-speakers in Brussels (see 6.2). The Brussels problem was temporarily solved by creating a regional executive council for Brussels whose members were part of the central govern-

The third wave came in 1988–1989. Authority allocated to the regions increased substantially, in particular in the field of sectoral economics and infrastructure. The communities now received full powers over education, over the use of language in their linguistic territories, over cultural matters and extended personalized matters, and even over foreign relations in their fields of competence. This transfer of competencies has in fact meant that regional and community laws (decrees) in those fields can now cancel out the state-wide laws. The total budget allotted to the communities and regions increased to 32% of the total state budget, and over 350 thousand persons were employed by them (40% of all persons employed in the civil service) (Dewachter, 1992a:18; Res Publica, 1993:570–2). In subsequent years some further issues were discussed, such as the double (or triple) mandates of the members of parliaments, the role and composition of the new Senate, the fiscal requirements of the constituent parts, the adaptation of the last bilingual province (Brabant) to the language borders, and the direct election of the members of the community councils and regional councils. Ultimately, the federal structure was officially recognized in the constitution by a law passed in parliament on 14 July, 1993. More will be said on the discussion surrounding the implementation of the federal structure in section 6.3.5.2.

In sum, the three stages of constitutional reform have created a federal state composed of both regions and communities. This is certainly a rather unique construction. Moreover, these two sub-state entities have not been combined in the same way in the Dutch-speaking part and the French-speaking parts of the country, mainly because of the awkward position of Brussels (and also for a very small part because of the German-speakers in the country). After the next section has given the basic figures on the eth-nonational diversity in the Belgian population, section 6.3 will discuss various episodes in Belgian history in more detail to analyze the background and effects of this peculiar construction.

6.2   THE ETHNONATIONAL STRUCTURE OF BELGIUM

When Belgium became independent in 1830, a 'language border' ran through the middle of the country, and had done so since roughly the eleventh century. The border separated the Belgian population into Dutch-speakers and French-speakers, although a large number of people spoke French in the Dutch-speaking region, particularly the elite. The border had

---

ment (see 6.3.5.1). It was thus controlled by the national parliament, while at the same time its competencies remained limited (Witte, 1987:62). Three years later, in 1983, the German community received the same powers as the other two in community affairs; regionally it fell under the jurisdiction of the Walloon authorities.

been remarkably stable over the centuries, but it was not completely fixed; also it had no political relevance at the time. Despite the dynamics of the linguistic conflict the language border has not changed very much. Map 6.1 provides an overview of the political situation after the constitutional changes of 1970, with the four separate language territories distinguished.

The reason for using politico-territorial demarcations is that linguistic questions have disappeared from the census since 1947; until then there had been language questions (with the exception of 1856). These posed certain problems, however. The questions made no distinction between dialects and standard languages and they changed over time from "which single language is usually spoken" in 1846 to "which of the three national languages do you understand," with the possibility of giving multiple responses. In the censuses of 1910, 1920, and 1930, a second question was added to clarify which of the languages was used most frequently if multiple responses were given (McRae, 1986:35). There was never a question about the mother tongue of the respondent, which disabled any analysis of the language shift from Dutch to French which was constantly taking place; apparently, the initial intention of the government was to underline their citizens' capacity for speaking or understanding French (McRae, 1986:41). When the language shift became a highly politicized issue, at some locations the census turned into a referendum in which respondents declared their preference for a certain language of administration (notably French). As will be discussed

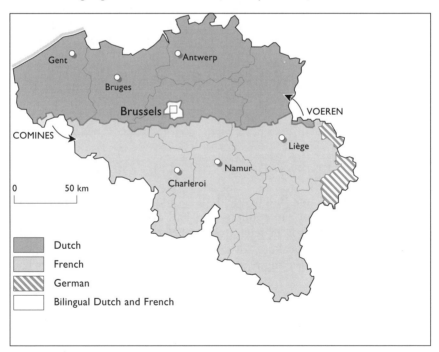

Map 6.1 Language territories in Belgium since 1970

below, the results of the 1947 census became so controversial that no language questions have been asked in the census ever since.

Table 6.1 therefore provides an overview of the numbers of Dutch and French speakers as reported in the census until 1947, following which the territorially based numbers are listed. For the first three years in the table, the "language most spoken" is used. Despite the different basis, the general increase of Dutch-speakers compared to French-speakers is visible; this is to a large extent caused by differences in natural growth (see Hooghe 1993:52). Part of the higher natural growth has in turn been offset for a long time by the frenchification of Dutch-speakers (McRae, 1986:49–53). Part of the reason for the higher number of Dutch-speakers based on territorial criteria is found in the fact that a substantial number of French-speakers have always lived in the northern provinces of Belgium, particularly in the urban centres where they formed an important part of the Belgian elite. Although their precise numbers since 1947 are unknown, in the 1980s they were estimated to form between 2 and 3% of the population in Flanders (McRae, 1986:276–285). The number of Dutch-speakers in Wallonia is much lower. In Brussels, on the other hand, Dutch-speakers form an estimated 10 to 20% of the population, but also in that case the precise numbers are unknown. As has been noted in chapter one (table 1.1) it is in fact very questionable whether the Bruxellois should be treated a separate

Table 6.1   Ethnonational groups in Belgium (in percentages)

	Linguistic[1]			Territorial[2]		
	1846	*1910*	*1947 (ling.)*	*1947 (terr.)*	*1970*	*1991*
Flemings/Dutch	57.0	51.6	52.6	53.3	56.1	57.8
Walloon/French	42.1	42.9	41.9	34.7	32.1	31.9
Bruxellois	–	–	–	11.2	11.1	9.6
German	0.8	1.0	0.9	0.6	0.7	0.7
Others/unknown	–	4.5	4.0	–	–	–
Total	4,337	7,424	8,512	8,512	9,651	9,979

Source: McRae 1986, Hooghe 1993

Remarks:
1 'Non-speakers' and 'unknown' in 1910 and 1947 particularly concern infants under two years of age.
2 The territories have been based on the post–1963 arrangement, and the data for 1947 have therefore been recalculated (see McRae, 1986:47–48).

group. If they are, they are so by default, as a part of the population which is stuck between the clear-cut linguistic-territorial cases. A separate discussion on Brussels can be found in section 6.3.5.1.

6.3 THE DYNAMICS OF LINGUISTIC CONFLICT IN BELGIUM

6.3.1 *Centralized Belgium and Flemish language and culture*

It should immediately be pointed out that the two regions which became central to the linguistic conflict in Belgium, Flanders and Wallonia, were not perceived as distinct entities immediately after independence. Flanders stood for the two historic provinces carrying that name, while the term 'Wallonia' was used to describe the southern French-speaking provinces first mentioned in 1844 (Encyclopedie, 1973:1911)[3]. As mentioned above, national sentiment and national symbols existed predominantly at state level, in combination with a regional identification with the historical provinces of Belgium, and identification at the level of the local communes. As a result, as Murphy (1988a:53 – 55) argues, "the inhabitants of the newly independent Belgian state did not define themselves in terms of language communities, and the linguistic geography of the country was not the basis for conceptual, functional, or formal territorial divisions at the time ... Belgium's subsequent linguistic polarization must ... be understood as a social and territorial development that largely took place after the founding of the Belgian state." Moreover, as will become clear, it was government action in particular which helped politicize and institutionalize the language differences.

Of foremost importance was the fact that French became the only official language throughout Belgium. The choice of French was considered only natural at the time. Although Dutch-speakers had played their role in the chaotic uprising – especially because of unease with the protestant character of the northern parts of the Low Countries, and out of a general awareness of growing differentiation between the two parts of the Low Countries – the main resistance came from the French-speaking elite from all parts of Belgium. Thus, in 1831, the French language was needed to emphasize the separate national identity of the new country from the Netherlands and to strengthen its internal cohesion and unity; this was affirmed in a series of decrees concerning the language in the administration and the military (Murphy, 1988a:59 – 60). The fact that article 23 of the Constitution provided for the freedom of language usage did nothing to change this official government decision. In fact, the linguistic freedom it guaranteed also

---

3   Before that the term 'Walloon provinces' was used, *walloon* being derived from the germanic word for romanized Celts (Murphy, 1988a:51n40).

assured that officials could use the language of their choice regardless of the language of the local population. Following the same logic, the state appointed mainly French-speaking officials (Polasky, 1981:34).

However, it was not simply the unilingual character of the state that raised the question of language rights. In fact, as Van Haegendoren (1962:27–28) has argued, at the time the strength and institutional penetration of the state machinery were still limited. Equally important therefore was the francophone character of important groupings in Belgian society: the higher clergy, the Liberal elite, the 'haute finance,' and so forth. The linguistic border was social as much as territorial: an individual of Dutch-speaking origin had to change languages in order to rise on the social scale. However, frenchification was not considered a problem most of the time; Flemish was not seen as a language but as a dialect, whereas French was a superior cultural language which should, naturally, be preferred over the dialects which were sufficient for use 'around the house'. A similar attitude indeed befell the French dialects in the southern parts of Belgium; any civilized person spoke Parisian French.[4] Moreover, since the existence of two official languages was considered a potential threat to the unity of the new state, Dutch cultural activists were sometimes classified as enemies of the state. The only protests came from writers and publicists who considered the loss of the Dutch language negative for Belgian culture, but who failed to emphasize anything other than linguistic aspects; their political impact was practically nil (Witte and Craeybeckx, 1983:53–55).[5] The elite of the new state – which mostly lived separated from the masses in both a social sense as a result of the language barrier (equally important for Flemish dialects and Walloon dialects), and in a physical sense as a result of housing segregation – was not very interested in these protests (Witte and Craeybeckx, 1983:73).

The social differences between Dutch-speakers and French-speakers were further intensified by the diverging economic fortunes of the different parts of Belgium. As mentioned above the rapid industrialization in the French-speaking areas and the economic decline in the Dutch-speaking regions created large-scale 'poverty migration' to the southern provinces and to Brus-

---

4   The 'mother culture' itself thought so too. Many years later, in 1888, a Paris-based newspaper commented on the decision to use Dutch text on Belgian coins: "Avez-vous remarqué que les pièces belges frappées depuis 1886 ne portent plus l'inscription française: *l'Union fait la force*? A la place on lit: *Eendracht maakt macht* ou quelque chose d'approchant; enfin un micmac, un charabia flamand, qui doit vouloir dire quelque chose: peut-être que l'union fait la force. Enfin on ne sait pas. Il faut être linguiste pour savoir du flamingant pur. De même *Leopold II, roi des Belges*, est remplacé par *Leopold II, koning der Belgen*. Signe du temps! Triomphe des barbares sur la civilisation" (in Van Haegendoren, 1962:134).
5   The most famous are Jan Frans Willems and Hendrik Conscience. In 1838 the latter published 'The Lion of Flanders' which referred to the Battle of the Golden Spurs in 1302.

sels.[6] The overall differences between the two parts of the country – and the migration of 'flamins' to the southern provinces and Brussels – strengthened the image of Dutch as the language of the impoverished and chanceless (Van Haegendoren, 1962:34). However, as Heisler points out, it also meant the co-option and acculturation of many among the Dutch speakers who were more resourceful, ambitious, and intent on integration, thereby increasingly concentrating "a large proportion of those who were less well-off, less mobile, less secularized, and less Belgian" in the northern part of the country (Heisler, 1990:181).

Besides the choice for a French-language state, the political organization of the new state also did not work in favour of the Dutch-speakers in Belgium in other ways. As mentioned above, the electoral arrangement put power in the hands of the very few; these were almost all French-speakers (McRae, 1986:174–178). Furthermore, the clerical/anti-clerical cleavage unmistakably dominated the linguistic issue (where in fact no cleavage was perceived as yet), although the patterns partially overlapped: in some of the Dutch-language provinces of Belgium the influence of the Catholic Church was stronger, while the industrialized southern provinces were more anti-clerical (they for instance had more public education). Indeed, many among the powerful lower clergy in Flanders became active in the Flemish movement through their anger over these 'perceived godless French influences,' which were so clearly symbolized by the public schools and by the French-speaking Liberal elite in Flanders. To these members of the clergy, French "became the enemy language" (Claeys, 1980:174, see also Lorwin, 1966:160). However, the overlap between the clerical/anti-clerical and Flemish/francophone cleavages was not at all straightforward, and Liberals, Catholics and Socialists were found amongst Dutch-speakers as well as French-speakers (see for instance Kesteloot et al., 1990:36, and Murphy, 1988a:84–87). Indeed, one of the results of the partial cross-cutting of different cleavages was indeed that proponents of the Flemish case were themselves split between Liberals and Catholics, and were approached on that basis. For instance, an effort to establish a Flemish party in Antwerp failed as a result of the conflict between Catholics and Liberals within the Flemish ranks, as did an attempt to establish a daily Dutch-language newspaper (Huyse, 1981:121). Also, as will be discussed below, the Catholics opposed the creation of a Dutch-language university in Gent, partly because they feared the competition for the Catholic (French-speaking) university in Leuven (Huyse, 1981:121). In any case, in contrast to a sizeable part of the

6   Nevertheless, although this migration later became important as a symbol of the economic inequality between Flanders and Wallonia, the situation was not a simple north-south divide; some of the northern provinces (mainly East Flanders) also experienced substantial growth in employment during that period, while some of the southern provinces remained essentially rural. Moreover, the various industrial regions within the Walloon provinces were competing more than acting in a unified manner, for instance when attracting capital (Kesteloot et al., 1990:85).

lower clergy in the northern Belgian provinces, the higher clergy was thoroughly French-speaking and unitary, and remained so at least until the Second World War.

In this political climate members of the growing middle class in Flanders in particular became more and more frustrated. They most clearly experienced the effects of, for instance, the state policies to appoint only French-speaking officials in Flanders and the low status of the Flemish dialects among the elite. Their 'flamingantism' was mainly directed against the Liberal regime although they tried to avoid taking sides with the Catholics but as the division between clericals and anti-clericals became sharper, flamingants joined both sides of the divide. Their organizations fell apart under the weight of this schism, creating the impression that a separate Flemish political movement was an unrealistic perspective. The flamingants were nevertheless not entirely without success and, besides the creation of numerous cultural institutions (theatres, opera houses, cultural funds), several language laws were passed during the 1870s and 1880s: on the use of Dutch in the judicial system (1873, after incidents in which Dutch-speakers were unjustly convicted by a solely French-speaking court), on public administration in Flanders (1878), and on courses in secondary public schools (1883). Extension of the latter law to Catholic private education, however, took until 1910, because of prolonged protests by the French-speaking episcopacy (Witte and Craeybeckx, 1983:152). In all, these laws proved mainly symbolic, difficult to implement, and were used more as a friendly gesture, or in the words of Van Haegendoren as simple philanthropy for wretches unaware of the French language (1962:48; see also Witte and Craeybeckx, 1983:102–3). A more important step was the Equalization law of 1898, which put Dutch at the same level as French before the law, and therefore made Belgium *de jure* bilingual. Although it had no real practical consequences in the short term, for Dutch-speakers it was an important law from a psychological point of view. Also interesting was the fact that in 1891 – accompanying the 1889 law on the use of the Dutch language in courts located in Flemish communes – the communes belonging to the Dutch-speaking part of Belgium were listed; for the first time this established a sort of territorial concept of a Dutch-speaking region called Flanders (Murphy, 1988a:73).

The Socialist movement, which established a political party in 1885, was no strong supporter of the Flemish case either. It had a francophone background, since industries were particularly located in francophone regions, while most of its leaders also associated the Flemish dialects with control by conservative local Catholic clergy (Van Istendael, 1989:123–125). Socialist ideas nevertheless became important in making the cultural leadership in Flanders more aware of the socio-economic issues which were at stake in their struggle. They came to realize that to some extent language discrimination was the cause of material differences between Dutch-speakers and French-speakers, and that the development of a strong Dutch-speaking cultural elite of high standards would enable the equalization of Flemish and Walloon living conditions and the disappearance of a French-speaking elite in Flanders (Witte and Craeybeckx, 1983:149). Lodewijk de Raet in particular succeeded in combining the various aspects of the struggle, for instance by arguing that a Flemish university in Gent could function not only as a guardian of Flemish culture but also as a means to strengthen the overall capabilities of the Flemish people through education.

In sum, the first 65 years of the new Belgian state were characterized by its French language character, both in the use of the language itself, and in the staffing and symbols of the new state. Moreover, despite a relatively liberal constitution, the political system did not facilitate the entrance of the language issue into the political arena, as power was in the hands of only a few French-speaking people, who at the same time dominated economic life and, because of the narrow electoral law, political life. The political arena itself was overwhelmingly dominated by disputes over State-Church relations, and later by the socio-economic cleavage following the rise of the Socialist movement. The Flemish Movement, after an initial focus on cultural issues, became more and more middle class with the increasing frustration of these groups under the frenchified state. The inclusion of socio-economic issues in the language struggle appealed not only to the elite, but also to the ordinary Dutch-speaking citizen, who through his voting power became much more important after 1893, even under a system of plural voting. As a result, the Flemish representatives within each party could improve their status, and some laws on language regulation followed, the most important of which was the equalization law. To be sure, the concept of Flanders, and of the Flemish as an ethnonational community, had hardly developed by then, let alone any concept of a Walloon or francophone community. However, the irritation which was caused by the reluctance of the central elite to deal with the linguistic diversity, and the contingencies of the pillarization, process contained the seeds of later community formation.

6.3.2 *Bilingualism and the language laws of the 1930s*

Despite the increasing importance of Dutch-speakers within the parties, the language question did not gain greater importance in terms of separate parties until the second half of the 1930s. Generally, the percentage of votes for the traditional parties surpassed 90% (see table 6.2 for the period until World War 2). Clearly then, the linguistic balance in Belgium received priority neither from the electorate, nor from the political leadership. Indeed, implementation did not immediately follow the laws. The first steps to implement the 1898 law were taken 25 years later, when the government appointed a commission to make official Dutch translations of the constitution, the civil code and the main laws, as well as of jurisprudence before 1898. The official Dutch-language version of the constitution was only ready in 1967 (Dewachter, 1992b:227). Secondly, in practice any tendency towards bilingualism was completely limited to the Flemish provinces itself, although this certainly affected the French-speaking elite in Flanders and even the French-speakers in Brussels. A Walloon movement was virtually non-existent at the time and, at best, French-language activism emerged in the Flemish cities of Antwerp and Gent and in Brussels. The main effort was, moreover, to stress Belgian patriotism and the unity of the Belgian nation. However, Catholic control over government was mainly based on Flemish votes and in the period up to the First World War this Flemish-based Catholic dominance frustrated many Liberal and Socialist Walloon politicians, even though the dominant language continued to be French (Wils, 1993:552; see also Murphy, 1988a:95 – 6). The most important qualifications to the general lack of Walloon activism were the letter by Jules Destrée to the King in 1912[7] and the organization of a congress of Walloon politicians; this congress was organized after another victory of the Catholics in the election of 1912, and even adopted a set of symbols, such as a national holiday and the *coq wallon*.

Table 6.2   Seats in the Chamber of Representatives in Belgium (1848 – 1939)

Year	Catholics	Liberals	Socialists	Communists	Flemish nationalists	Rex	Others	Total
1848	26	82						108
1857	38	70						108
1864	53	63						116
1870	73	51						124
1894	104	20	28					152
1900	86	34	31					151
1904	93	42	29				2	164
1910	86	44	35				1	165
1914	99	45	40				2	184
1919	73	34	70		5		4	186
1921	80	33	68		4		1	186
1925	78	23	78	2	6			187
1929	76	28	70	1	11		1	187
1932	79	24	73	3	8			187
1936	63	23	70	9	16	21		202
1939	73	33	64	9	17	4	2	202

7   "... laissez-moi vous dire la vérité, la grande et horrifiante vérité: il n'y a pas de Belges ... Non Sire, il n'y a pas d'âme belge. La fusion des Flamands et des Wallons n'est pas souhaitable; et la désirât-on, qu'il faut constater encore qu'elle n'est pas possible" (quoted in McRae, 1986:10).

Developments during the First World War strongly affected political life in Belgium, and, in part, this had a regional impact. Two issues came to the fore. Firstly, some of the flamingants (the so-called activists) had collaborated with the Germans, hoping to achieve a stronger position for the Dutch language, and more autonomy or even independence for Flanders. The Germans, in a divide-and-conquer strategy, made use of this by, for instance, separating Flemish and Walloon prisoners of war, and by allowing the creation of a Council of Flanders in 1917 which was supposed to function as a parliament for an autonomous region of Flanders within the German Reich; however, the Germans dissolved it when it declared independence in 1918. The Germans also established a Dutch-language university in Gent (the Von Bissing university, after the German military governor), but it had little or no success (Witte and Craeybeckx, 1983:159). The second issue was the dissatisfaction which had been expressed by Flemish soldiers (in the allied armies along the frontline near the river IJser) with their position in the army and with the position of Flanders in general. With regard to the army, they considered it unacceptable that all officers were French-speaking and that the commands were, as a result, badly understood by the Flemish soldiers. Some of the better-educated soldiers, in what became known as the Front movement, started to voice demands for more autonomy for the Flemish region after the war; they attempted to push their demands by threatening to withhold their support in the fight against the Germans. In the end, whereas these activities by part of the Flemish movement certainly discredited the movement as a whole, the events during the war put territorial arrangements and even secession on the agenda for the first time. Moreover, as Murphy notes, in terms of community formation the war brought boys from different parts of the northern provinces of Belgium together in mutual contact (1988a:105).

After the war, the defence pact with France and the joint occupation of the Ruhr valley with France in 1923 was not to the liking of many in Flanders;[8] neither were the continuing French-language character of the political parties and of major institutions such as the Church. However, the internal divisions within the Flemish Movement itself prevented effective mobilization: there was so-called 'minimalists' who wanted a Dutch-speaking Flanders within a unified Belgium and, for instance, a Dutch-language university in Gent; and there were 'maximalists' (among others a 'Front Party' that was established in 1919) who wanted federalism in Belgium, independence for Flanders, or even unification with the Netherlands. All were aware, however, that the laws that had been passed thus far had done little to stop the frenchification of Flanders and that new laws, better implemented and with some sort of territorial foundation, would be necessary.

---

8   In 1927 Pétain, victor in Verdun, irritated many Dutch-speakers by calling Belgium the outpost of Latin culture *vis à vis* the German culture ('Germanendom') (Witte & Craeybeckx, 1983:195).

Therefore, while the electoral system was expanded step by step, regionalist conceptions now became more common. As Murphy (1988a:113) argues: "Irrespective of one's attitude toward regional linguistic, cultural, administrative, or political autonomy, by the late 1920s virtually every Belgian had been confronted with regional ideas regarding the so-called language question, and the discourse increasingly reflected regional conceptualizations." A turn-around came with the election of a convicted collaborator, August Borms, in 1928. His success, and growing support for Flemish nationalist parties in general, made the government realize the permanence and the political saliency of the linguistic issue.

This awareness led to a series of laws. In 1921, limited action had already been undertaken by the government when it made knowledge of Dutch obligatory for officials at all levels of the administration in Flanders. However, provincial and local administrations could still opt for bilingualism, and community administrations along the border could opt for the other language if the census indicated that the majority of the population spoke a different language from that in the region. The law also called for knowledge of the 'second language' in Brussels, but implementation was hardly attempted. New laws in the 1930s, however, can be considered as a watershed in the change of focus from the personal to the territorial solution of the language conflict in Belgium. They set the stage for territorial unilingualism in the two linguistic regions of Belgium, with bilingualism in Brussels and in some other areas (McRae, 1986:150). The question of the university in Gent was finally solved by a law in 1930,[9] while the use of languages in the judicial system was dealt with in 1935, and the linguistic problems in the army in 1938. Most important, however, were the law on education (1932) and especially the law on administration (1932). The law on education guaranteed unilingual primary and secondary education in Flanders by eliminating the choice of the 'head-of-the-family';[10] up to then parents had often opted for French-language education in the hope of improving the position of their children. In order to allow smooth access for French-speakers into the Dutch-language educational system, temporary classes could be created in French. The law on administration established unilingualism in the public life of Flanders and of Wallonia. The borders of these language areas could change depending on the results of the census. One new feature here was the fact that officials were no longer expected to be bilingual, but were separated according to the language of their entrance

---

9   The solution had been preceded by a combined Dutch- and French-speaking university, called the Nolf-university, after the initiator of the law which was passed in 1923. However, some of the French-language press kept calling it the Von Bissing University (Van Haegendoren, 1962:65).

10 This right of the 'head-of-the-family' was originally intended to protect the religious preferences of the family in their choice of confessional or public education, but it had been extended to include choice on the language of instruction; this possibility was now ruled out (Van Haegendoren, 1962:66).

exam. Municipalities in Brussels were to be bilingual in their contacts with the public, although they could choose the language of communication inside the office (which therefore remained French). Communities along the border were obliged to publish all decisions in both languages if more than 30% percent of the population declared itself as speaking another language than the one mostly spoken in the region. The general rule for national public service was bilingualism, but again, unilingualism served for its officials.

Interestingly, the creation of territorial unilingualism only partly resulted from Flemish pressure. In fact, many Flemish 'minimalist' politicians basically desired bilingualism for the whole country in order to cement its unity. In contrast, however, Walloon representatives, afraid of becoming 'minorized' by 'conquering Flanders' in a bilingual Belgium, rejected the concept of bilingualism and the prospect of French-speakers having to learn Dutch. They were also afraid of the position of the Flemish immigrants in Wallonia ('a fifth column'). To achieve their objective they sacrificed the French-speakers in Flanders who were now forced to live in a unilingual Flanders (Witte, 1993:213; Fonteyn, 1988:95). As will be discussed below, the territorialization of the linguistic question which was implied in the laws of the 1930s laid the basis for later developments; by then the regional compartmentalization of the country on a linguistic basis was increasingly becoming the most relevant and accepted frame of reference.

It is useful at this stage to remember how the traditional pillars were distributed geographically over Belgian territory. Two important facts emerge: these pillars did not coincide with the language regions (as these increasingly became known), and there was extensive organization of the *familles spirituelles* in all regions. Nevertheless, both in social values and in institutional structure there was, and has in fact remained, a predominance of Catholics in Flanders, and of Socialists in Wallonia. This also translated into the political arena: whereas in Flanders the Catholic Party normally received 44% to 50% of the votes in the interwar years, this was 29% to 37% of the votes in Brussels and 27% to 32% of the votes in Wallonia (Witte and Craeybeckx, 1983:178–170).[11] Given the strong support among the Flemings for the Catholics (even more important because of their higher numbers), it is not surprising that Flemish grievances were initially incorporated in the Catholic party (Claeys, 1980:179). This party, which was organized around several *'standen'* ('estates', such as farmers, workers, the middle classes, and the original Catholic elite), reorganized into two regional wings by 1936; moreover, in the local election of 1938 some lists combined Flemish nationalists and Flemish Catholics (the Flemish Concen-

---

11 Exceptions were the elections of 1936 and 1939, when in Flanders the support for the Catholics dropped to 37% and 41%, in Brussels to 23% and 27%, and in Wallonia to a low 20% and 25%, respectively.

tration). At the same time discussion was started over the restructuring of some of the state institutions, such as the Ministry of Education (Lorwin, 1966:162; Van Haegendoren, 1962:77–79; Van Impe, 1983:184).

Among the Flemish nationalists themselves, maximalist right-wing politics gained influence. Since the First World War Flemish nationalist parties had been represented in parliament, first by the Front party and somewhat later by the Flemish National Union (Vlaams Nationaal Verbond/VNV). The real breakthrough, however, came in 1936 when the Flemish National Union, under the name Flemish Bloc (Vlaamsch Blok), gained over 13% of the votes in Flanders and 6% in Brussels (16 seats in parliament). The VNV, under the leadership of former Front party leader Staf de Clerq and with many confirmed anti-semites among its members, wanted a federal Belgium with an autonomous, authoritarian and corporative Flanders. At least from 1938 onwards the party was supported by Germany (Gijsels, 1992:23–27). More extremist pro-German groupings even declared Dutch and Flemish simply German dialects and argued for a 'Dietsland,' or greater Germany, but internal differences and switches of position were substantial (see Witte and Craeybeckx, 1983:232–5). The extreme right was not restricted to Flanders, however. A francophone party called Rex, less regionally based than the VNV, gained almost 16% in Brussels, over 15% in Wallonia, and 7% in Flanders (21 seats). The Rexists, under the leadership of Léon Degrelle, were mainly right-wing Catholics who agitated against the financial and political dealings of the Catholic members of parliament, who they blamed for the economic malaise of the country. Their emblem was a broom which was to be used to make a clean sweep of Belgian politics. However, they lost almost all support in subsequent years, when the effect of their agitation had worn off (Witte and Craeybeckx, 1983:237). Rex and the VNV agreed not to get in each other's way, and Rex was willing to discuss a federal future for the Belgian state.

In sum, the first 30 years of this century showed an increase in and growing diversity of Flemish aspirations. The growing importance of the Flemish voter and changing economic investment patterns worried some francophone leaders, leading to occasional defensive responses which usually stressed Belgian unity on the basis of a French language.[12] Backed up by the acknowledgement of Dutch as an official language in Belgium, but at the same time frustrated by the lack of implementation and by anti-Flemish sentiments following World War One, an increasing part of the Flemish population rallied around issues such as the linguistic character of the University of Gent and the position of collaborators. When it became clear around 1930 that the acknowledgement of Belgium as a bilingual state needed to be followed by further implementation, unilingualism in the two

---

12   ... nicely put in the phrase "La Belgique sera latine ou ne sera pas" by the Flemish francophone Maeterlinck (quoted in Dewachter, 1992a:8).

regions of Belgium, instead of bilingualism in the whole of Belgium, emerged as the preferable arrangement in both linguistic groups. By now it was clear that the creation of a uniform Belgian nation-state had failed and that a new relationship between the cultures in Belgium had to be forged. This decision to use a territorial approach to accommodate the cleavage set the stage for later developments. Shortly before the Second World War the importance of linguistic differences was clearly on the rise.

6.3.3 World War 2 and its aftermath

Again, however, developments were disrupted by external interference, this time during the Second World War. The activities of part of the Flemish movement during the war proved such that the Flemish movement as a whole was severely discredited and mistrusted, and the expression of any Flemish nationalist points of view had to be avoided. These activities had their roots in the pre-war period, when right-wing parties had already gained influence in Flanders.

Collaboration had been for some a logical step. It was made even easier by the relatively tactful behaviour of the Germans during the first period after the capitulation and by the position taken by King Leopold III, who, together with some high officials and most of the economic establishment, continued to function. After the war, over 400 thousand collaboration dossiers were created and people were convicted in all parts of the country: 0.52% of the population in Wallonia, 0.56% in Brussels, and 0.73% in Flanders (Witte and Craeybeckx, 1983:259). However, despite the fact that the proportions of convicted people did not differ very much, the impression nevertheless emerged (especially among the French-speaking elite) that in Flanders collaboration had been the rule. Overall, the manner in which some seized the oppertunity to crack down on the Flemish movement led to the feeling that the collaboration issue was grossly misused to suppress Flanders itself. Immediately, calls came for a general amnesty (Encyclopedie, 1972:94; McRae, 1986:31).[13] Nevertheless, as Claeys rightly argues, the essential difference was that collaboration in Wallonia was not connected to regional nationalism, making collaboration in Flanders more dangerous to the integrity of the state (Claeys, 1980:188n14). This is not to say that regionalism as such did not exist among French-speakers; in fact, in an emotional gesture, in October, 1945, a congress of Walloon activists took a

---

13 How painful this part of Flemish history was is exemplified by the book of Van Haegendoren (1962). He decided that he could not write a chapter on the collaboration issue because not enough information was available yet. Moreover, as Van Haegendoren explained: "A patient who has suffered from serious mental disorders (in this case Flanders with the collaboration and the exaggerated severity and excesses of the repression) does well during his rehabilitation not to ponder too much" (1962:80 (my translation)).

clear anti-unitary stance and in a *vote de coeur* even voted for unification with France (see Fonteyn, 1991:101).

With the Flemish nationalists in the 'catacombs,' the conflict over territorial and linguistic rights was temporarily suspended. Unitarism was again firmly the central ideology of the state, which was still governed mostly by French-speakers (Witte, 1992:96). As mentioned in section 6.1, several other issues dominated political life. The first was the Royal Question, which concerned the position taken by King Leopold III during the war.[14] The Belgian political parties were divided over his actions, with Socialists, Communists and Liberals mostly against his return, Catholics and right-wing Flemish parties mostly in favour. The issue dominated Belgian politics to such an extent that in 1950 a consultative referendum was called to break the deadlock. The referendum showed that in a majority of provinces (seven out of nine) and arrondissements (21 out of 30) the population had voted in favour of the King's return. However, at the same time, some interesting regional differences came to the fore: in Flanders 72% were in favour, while in Brussels 52% were against, and in Wallonia as many as 58% were opposed. On the other hand, further differentiation within each region shows that two provinces in Wallonia voted in favour of the King's return, while Brabant was evenly split (Murphy, 1988a:127). The situation deteriorated when an electoral victory enabled the Catholics to form a one-party government intent on implementing the result of this referendum and arranging for the King's return.[15] Strikes organized by the Socialists and Communists in Liège and Hainaut, however, revealed so much determination in the opposition camp that the King abdicated in favour of his son Boudewijn (Baudouin). This was perceived in Flanders to be the result of extra-parliamentary force used by a minority to overrule the wish of the majority, and, as McRae remarks, it made the Flemish movement aware of the potential of civil strife and extra-parliamentary action (1986:112). It should be noted that the institution of the monarchy as such was not questioned; certainly not in Flanders – where some of the monarchs (though not all) were appreciated for their stance on the equalization of the Belgian languages – and neither amongst the French-speaking population. In the decades which followed the new King turned out to be an influential force

---

14 His decisions were controversial. Firstly, though his ministers had asked him to go into exile in London, he had decided to stay and lead the defence of his country. Secondly, and more importantly, he had surrendered the country to the Germans after their victory, had negotiated over the future of the country with Hitler, and had refrained from actively supporting the resistance or openly condemning the persecution of the Jews (Witte and Craeybeckx, 1983:247). This was regarded as treason by parts of the Belgian government and population. Thirdly, he had remarried without the consent of the government, thereby breaching the Constitution.

15 A very rare event in Belgium in which a parliamentary majority enabled one party to force its will on the others. Even more uncharacteristic for Belgium is the fact that the Catholics in fact tried to do just that, and ignored the existence of a large minority (Van Istendael, 1989:80).

in Belgian politics, and under his rule the monarchy remained one of the important unifying elements in Belgian politics (Lorwin, 1966:177).

However, the Royal Question was not the only issue in Belgian politics. During the years that followed, the Belgian political scene was again dominated by the ideological conflict over education. The three main political parties, some of them in slightly modified form, had succeeded in winning well over 90% of the votes in the elections of 1950, 1954, 1958 and 1961, the only new electoral heavyweight being the Communist Party (see table 6.3). However, a 'social pact' at the end of the war took the edge off the socio-economic conflict (although it was to reappear around 1960). The other cleavage was less easily pacified, and the stakes were high – there was increasing need for large-scale higher education, particularly for the less well-to-do students who needed cheap public education. Until then, the continuing presence of Catholic ministers in the government had limited the possibilities for the expansion of public education, resulting in the fact that, in 1950, 53.5% of the secondary schools were in the hands of the Catholics. Moreover, primary education was almost completely in the hands of the Catholic pillar (Witte, Craeybeckx and Meynen, 1990:258–259). Over a period of eight years, first the Catholics, and then after 1954 a coalition of Socialists and Liberals, tried to gain decisive influence. The struggle led to large-scale demonstrations, particularly after 1954 by Flemish Catholics. After 1958 the parties decided to go for a compromise when the conflict threatened to get out of hand; among other things the School Pact of 1958 increased the subsidies for Catholic education by paying all the salaries of the teachers in the private schools, enhanced the system of public education whereby a choice could be made between religious and non-religious classes on morality, and developed a system of rules for the number of pupils and the curricula.

The realization of the School Pact paved the way for an unequivocal focus on the linguistic cleavage. In a sense, the political system was temporarily freed of ideological strain between the major *spiritual families*; the common base among the Catholics particularly was somewhat weakened. However, this shift in focus did not make the other cleavages disappear, but caused the various conflicts to overlap as the weaker intensity of the traditional cleavages encouraged the main opponents to find a stronger regional base for their views (see below).

Though the linguistic issue had temporarily been suspended in the political climate immediately following the war, the underlying questions had not disappeared. The difference between this and the interwar period, however, was the fact that this time laws were in place to deal with the linguistic differences in the country, and the territorial basis of these differences had also been acknowledged and accounted for. Indeed, expectations had been high, but as in the interwar years, implementation did not follow automatically, and when it followed, new grounds for conflicts emerged. Thus, for instance, the 1932 law on education could not eliminate all problems: firstly, the French classes which were allowed to provide French-speaking children with smooth access to Dutch-language education were misused in certain areas to create a parallel educational system; secondly, Dutch-language education in Brussels did not always materialize to the extent necessary; thirdly, in private education the law was often only reluctantly implemented (Van Haegendoren, 1962:71). Similar situations arose concerning the law on administration; sanctions were not included, and violations became a constant source of irritation, especially in Brussels where often no more than token Dutch was spoken. French, in fact, often remained the initial language if a dossier was started by the administration itself. Likewise, although recruitment measures were included in the implementation of the law, higher officials in the public administration remained for the most part French-speaking. For example, even as late as 1960, officials on the French register still accounted for 56.8 percent of all higher public servants (McRae, 1986:195; Van Haegendoren, 1962:71).

Table 6.3 Seats in the Chamber of Representatives in Belgium (1946–1995)

Year	Cath	Lib	Soc	Com	VU	RW	FDF	Ecolo Agalev	Vlaams Blok	Other	Total
1946	92	17	69	23						1	202
1949	105	29	66	12							212
1950	108	20	77	7							212
1954	95	25	86	4	1					1	212
1958	104	21	84	2	1						212
1961	96	20	84	5	5					2	212
1965	77	48	64	6	12	2	3				212
1968	69	47	59	5	20	7	5				212
1971	67	34	61	5	21	14	10				212
1974	72	30	59	4	22	13	9			3	212
1977	80	31	62	2	20	5	10			2	212
1978	82	36	58	4	14	4	11			3	212
1981	61	52	61	2	20	2	6	4	1	3	212
1985	65	46	67		16		3	9	1	1	212
1987	62	48	72		16		3	9	2		212
1991	57	46	63		10		3	17	12	4	212
1995	41	39[1]	41		5			11	11	2	150

Sources: Witte, Craeybeckx and Meynen 1990; Mackie and Rose, 1991; McRae 1986.

Notes:

1 The FDF joined the Liberals in the 1995 elections.

Moreover, territorial demarcation and the fact that it could be changed brought new issues into the linguistic conflict. As a result, the delayed 1940 census which was finally held in 1947 became very sensitive politically. When finally published in 1954, the census not only shifted the language border to the north by changing the language of administration in several border communes, but also confirmed a marked change in the percentage of French-speakers in the communes around Brussels. In fact, the census also showed the increase of French speakers within the agglomeration of Brussels itself (from 56.3% predominantly French speakers in 1930 to 70.6% in 1947). This 'theft of territory' (as some in Flanders called it, combining it with allegations of fraud) was loudly condemned by the Flemish movement. More pleasant for the Flemish, however, was the changing distribution of the total population, which added three Flemish seats in the House of Representatives and one in the Senate; the Walloon districts lost four seats in the Chamber of Representatives and two in the Senate (Murphy, 1988a:128–129).

Nevertheless, despite continuing frenchification, the laws on education had by now created a Dutch-speaking Flemish society, with an elite which was educated in the Dutch language. Although the Flemish provinces still lagged behind in their level of education as late as the Second World War, the situation rapidly became more balanced between 1961 and 1971 (Frognier et al., 1982:268–9).[16] As the new laws formed a clear and official basis for inter-group relations in Belgium, the new generation held other expectations on the access of Dutch-speakers to centres of power.

6.3.4 The upsurge in ethnonationalism

The laws of the 1930s had thus altered the context of the linguistic conflict. However, in the 1960s and 1970s the conflict was fought with greater intensity than ever before, and this requires some explanation. Several elements can be distinguished.

Firstly, the economic balance between the French-speaking region and the Dutch-speaking region had continued to change to the advantage of Flanders. By the mid–1960s Flanders overtook Wallonia in terms of gross national product per capita (McRae, 1986:79). The need for economic restructuring was felt strongly in the older industrial regions in Wallonia, while new types of industries, often oil-based instead of coal-based, developed mainly in the northern parts of the country. It followed large-scale for-

---

16   In university education, where the total yearly enrolment quadrupled from under 19 thousand in 1948–49 to almost 65 thousand in 1968–69, the percentage of students under the Dutch language regime increased from 33.1% to 45% (McRae, 1986:227–230). Only in 1987 did it reach 57%, which is roughly the share of Dutch-speakers in the total population (Dewachter, 1992a:11).

eign investment which came with the common European Market after 1958 and which had the harbour of Antwerp as the main growth pole (see Frognier et al., 1982:262–265; Kesteloot et al., 1990:93; Heisler, 1990:182–183). Moreover, the independence of the Congo hit the Belgian economy as a whole, but the austerity package (higher taxes and lower incomes for state officials) which was introduced by the Catholic-Liberal government in 1960 was contested much more by Socialist labour unions than by Catholic unions. The general sense of crisis led to a major strike in the winter of 1960–61, which indeed found substantial support mainly (but not solely) in Wallonia. Regional differences in support for the strike created the impression that Flanders benefitted from Wallonia's economic decline.

Economic decline was not the only problem for Wallonia, however. The 1947 census had shown that the share of Wallonia in the total population of Belgium was actually falling. This combination of economic decline and demographic decline gave the impression of minorization and peripherization of Wallonia, and of the Walloons being outvoted and outproduced by the Dutch-speakers in the north. Under these circumstances a substantial mass-based Walloon movement (the Mouvement Populaire Wallon (MPW)) emerged for the first time as a counterpart to Flemish activity; in previous times there had only been Flemish nationalist movements and, at best, a few Walloon activists who received hardly any support from the Walloon population at large (see Fonteyn 1988). Now both groups felt threatened. In 1965 regionalist Walloon parties participated with success for the first time in parliamentary elections, and in 1967 they were succeeded by the even more successful Rassemblement Wallon (RW), which was to gain substantial electoral support in later years.

The regional movement in Flanders, de Vlaamse Volksbeweging (a grassroots organization which had been set up in 1954 to coordinate the activities of the numerous Flemish organizations), reflected the gradual increase in strength and confidence among Flemish nationalists which had been noticeable since the period of suppression immediately following the war. In the same year a political party – the Christelijke Vlaamse Volksunie (Christian Flemish People's Union), later to become the Volksunie (VU) – was founded which gradually won more seats. Economic demands, linguistic parity in central administration, a definite delimitation of the language territories, and decentralisation of cultural affairs were its crucial concerns (Witte, Craeybeckx and Meynen, 1990:329). Cultural demands remained central to the claims of the Flemish Movement. Thus, in 1961 and 1962, an organization called *Vlaams Aktiecomite voor Brussel en de Taalgrens* (Flemish Action Committee for Brussels and the Language Border) organised several marches on Brussels to protest the effects of the 1947 census and the possibility of new language questions, with between 25 thousand and 100 thousand people participating. As Van Haegendoren (1962:95–96) notes, the importance of these demonstrations was, in part, the fact that large-scale demonstrations proved possible without the extreme-right becoming involved; it appealed to the ordinary citizen as a genuinely felt sentiment of injustice. And injustice was indeed widely felt about the reluctant implementation of the 1930 language laws and about the general position of Dutch-speakers in the country.[17]

Therefore, while both movements had their roots in social dissatisfaction, their backgrounds were substantially different. This was certainly linked to the general political balance in the country, both numerically where it concerned the languages, and ideologically where it concerned the *familles spirituelles*. As Claeys puts it: "... in opposition to the Flemish regionalist movement, which essentially [demanded] cultural autonomy in a country where Flemish predominance [was] insured in other spheres by the law of numbers, the Walloon regionalist movement [demanded] economic and political autonomy, the only means of arriving at the transformation of the Walloon society in a direction which [reflected] the Socialist and lay conception of the majority of its population" (Claeys, 1980:175). The political program of the new parties reflected these basic political profiles, and the VU in Flanders was generally much more conservative in socio-economic terms than the MPW (typically initiated by the Labour Union activist André Renard, who had left the Socialists) and the RW.

However, the timing and dynamics of the success of the regionalist parties was not only related to the culmination of previous frustrations and conflicts in recent years, but also to socio-economic changes in society as whole. As Newman (1994) points out, the changes in the economic structure in Belgium altered Belgian society and new socio-economic groups emerged which proved less inclined to support the traditional parties. This disalignment was reflected in increasing support for the regionalist parties from such occupational categories as managers and liberal professionals. Both parties therefore tried to combine the interests of their more traditional constituencies with these new and growing groups, and attempted to become sort of catch-all parties. In a similar vein, a party for the French-speakers in Brussels, the Front Démocratique des Francophones (FDF), would find its support somewhat later equally distributed among all kinds of socio-economic groups (Newman, 1994:42–43; see also McRae, 1986:139–140). As a result, the contrast between the traditional background of the regions and the variety of support for the regionally based ethnonational parties was to cause substantial tension within these parties.

The diverse and complex background of the various movements certainly inhibits their easy classification into categories such as ethnonational

17 Such irritation was, for example, manifested at the 1958 World Exhibition in Brussels, where the organizers failed to take sufficient account of the Flemish part of Belgian culture. Only after much trouble and strong protests (led by the future prime minister Wilfried Martens) was a Flemish day included in the events (Van Haegendoren, 1962:88–89; see also De Ridder, 1991:19–23). For the Flemish this again proved the unwillingness on the part of the French-speakers to accept Flanders and the Dutch language as an equal part of Belgium and Belgian culture.

activism, linguistic activism, or regionalism. As has been indicated, among the Flemish, a sense of community was forged through a century of linguistic frustration, but the new party represented much more than just linguistic demands. Nonetheless, the linguistic struggle was equally fought by politicians stressing the unity of the country in all fields other than language. However, among the French-speakers until then there had existed a confusing mix of linguistic community, Belgian patriotism, Walloon and Brussels regionalism, and linguistic rights for French-speakers in Flanders. This confusion did not disappear with the rise of the new parties, even though the development of separate interest defence on the part of Wallonia was a marked change; among other things it forced the French-speaking inhabitants of Brussels to develop a position of their own. As will become clear, however, this confusion would remain an important complication in the years to come.

In summary, by the beginning of the 1960s, there were not only many grounds for improvement and refinement of the 1930s laws, but also an increased political pressure to implement the changes.[18] After extensive discussion amongst the three main parties – after all, even then political support for the regionalist parties was still very limited (see table 6.3) – new laws were introduced which were to ensure proper implementation of the 1930 laws and to account for some of the gaps which they had left. With one major exception, the laws of 1962 and 1963 were based on the same principles as those of the 1930s, including: a unilingual Flanders and a unilingual Wallonia (and an arrangement for the German-speaking areas); bilingual services by the central government but unilingual officials who were enrolled according to the language of their entrance exam; Brussels as the capital of a bilingual country, (supposedly) serving as the example of peaceful coexistence; and two equal official languages in Belgium. More extensive mechanisms for enforcement were put into place to avoid the mistakes of the past. The single most important difference *vis à vis* the laws of the 1930s, however, was the fixation of the language border (McRae, 1986:150–155, Witte, 1993:213–214).

---

18 Some isolated initiatives had been undertaken earlier to address the issue. Walter Couvreur, who later became president of the Volksunie, and Fernand Schreurs, one of the leading figures in the Walloon Movement, had published a manifest as early as December 3, 1952, which suggested some form of federalism as a solution. In this manifest Brussels was described as historically Flemish territory, a point of view which was later dropped by the Walloon Movement under pressure from the Brussels francophones. The intellectual cooperation was therefore short-lived, since the Walloon leaders decided to support the French-speakers outside Walloon territory (mainly in Brussels and (later) Voeren) (see Fonteyn, 1988:113–115). A second initiative came from the government, who created a commission, the so-called Harmel Centre, in 1948 to study the linguistic difficulties. The commission reported on their work in 1958, and its conclusions contained many of the seeds for later institutional solutions (Senelle, 1989:57; see below).

The law of November 8, 1962, established four language areas in Belgium with strict demarcations: French-speaking Wallonia, Dutch-speaking Flanders, bilingual Brussels, and a German-speaking area. On the basis of the 1947 census 25 communes (est. 87,000 inhabitants) went from Wallonia to Flanders and 24 communes (est. 23,000 inhabitants) the other way round (McRae, 1986:152). However, problems arose over the districts of Voeren, Comines/Mouscron, and Brussels (see map 6.1). While the first two were initially designated to stay in their respective French-speaking and Dutch-speaking regions (to avoid enclaves), Comines/Mouscron was so overwhelmingly French-speaking that the law-makers were compelled to transfer it to the province of Hainaut. As a balance, Voeren, where the majority of the population spoke a Dutch dialect, was transferred from Liège to Limburg, although its population had opted to stay in Liège. Special arrangements were created for minority-language groups in these areas and in some other border communities. One year later a solution was negotiated about Brussels (see 6.3.5.1), concerning stricter implementation of the 1930 educational laws, and the adaptation of judicial districts to the new territorial arrangements. Some fifty decrees were issued in the years which followed to actually implement the laws (McRae, 1986:151). Several suggestions by the Harmel Centre (see note 18) in the cultural field were also implemented, leading to the *dédoublement* of many institutions: the split of television and radio in 1960, the split of the Department of Culture into two language sections in 1962, the creation of two separate ministries of Culture in 1966, and the creation of two separate ministries of Education in 1969. The government of 1968–71 included a Minister of Dutch Culture and a Minister of French Culture for the first time, as well as two ministers of National Education and two ministers with the status of secretaries of state for regional autonomy (Senelle, 1989:58).

One of the most painful problems was the linguistic separation of the Catholic University of Leuven (Louvain). Located on Flemish territory east of Brussels, the university was forced to become a completely Dutch-language institution against the strong opposition from the francophone part of the Belgian elite (many of whom had received their education at the university).[19] For Flemish nationalists, Leuven was too close to Brussels to allow any further frenchification, lest a francophone triangle emerge in the heart of Flemish Brabant. The conflict became even worse when plans were revealed for new investments and increased enrolments for the francophone

---

19 As late as 1966 the episcopacy of Belgium decided that the University of Leuven was unified and was to remain that way (the university was after all a Catholic one). Their opinion was perfectly in line with the bishops' view of a unified Catholic community in Belgium, one not separated by something of lesser importance such as a language border, but in the end it proved a major mistake; some have argued that it alienated a complete generation of young Flemish intellectuals from the Church (Van Istendael, 1989:216).

part of the university (McRae, 1986:115). Under the slogan 'Walen buiten' (Walloons out), demonstrations were organized which ultimately pressured Flemish Catholics to withdraw their support from the government. In ten years time, a whole new university was created south of the language border (Louvain-la-Neuve). In 1969 the university in Brussels was split up in a similar fashion. As will be more extensively discussed below, the conflict over Leuven created a split in the Catholic party, which broke up in the same year; the other parties also experienced severe strains (Murphy, 1990b:238).

The laws of the 1960s again changed the context of the linguistic conflict, and their implementation was accompanied by a tremendous upsurge in support for the various regionalist parties (see table 6.4). The VU had been on the rise since the 1950s, but major progress came in the elections of 1965, 1968 and 1971. In Wallonia after 1968, the RW made its major jump to 21.2% of the votes (14 seats) in 1971. The party for the French-speaking inhabitants of Brussels, the FDF, was founded in 1964. Initially it was closely related to the Walloon Movement, but out of fear of a loss of influence by Brussels in a bipartite Belgium, the FDF soon started to advocate an extensive and autonomous Brussels region; this would be the best way to keep the power in and around the capital in the hands of the French-speakers (Witte, 1992:97). The electoral strength of the FDF – between nine and eleven seats and with no less than 39.6% of the Brussels-vote in 1974 – was sufficient to ensure a strong presence of French-speaking Brussels in the political arena. In 1972, with the foundation of a German-language party (Partei der Deutschsprächigen Belgier), the regionalist political spectrum was complete. However, notwithstanding the German party and the FDF, the major difference between this period and earlier decades was the presence of both a Walloon and a Flemish movement. In fact, as the political scientist Dewachter (1987:289–290) concluded, their parallel existence paved the way for the inclusion of both in the governing coalitions of Belgium.

It is useful to end this section by briefly looking at the more structural consequences of the events of the 1960s. In the first place, the new laws were crucial in setting the stage for the next round in the conflict – the constitutional changes. In fact, whereas these laws had essentially sought to guarantee the solid implementation of the decisions already made in the 1930s, they ultimately strengthened the base for federalization because the appropriate territorial units had now been created and made permanent (Witte, 1993:214). Moreover, by fixing the borders of the language areas and by enforcing the laws within these territories, the ultimate consequences of the language struggle became apparent to everyone, as could be seen in the case of Leuven University.

In the second place, the traditional parties became seriously involved in the conflict. As has been noted above, support for the traditional parties before the war was not evenly distributed, reflecting the diverse social structures of the various regions. After the war, as McRae concludes, Flanders remained preponderantly Catholic and Wallonia and Brussels preponder-

Table 6.4   Regional votes for the Belgian Chamber of Representatives (1946-1995)

Wallonia

Year	Cath	Lib	Soc	Com	RW	Ecolo	UDRT	FN	Other
1946	26.4	9.3	36.7	21.7					5.9
1949	31.2	14.8	39.3	12.7					2.0
1950	32.9	11.5	45.1	7.9					2.5
1954	29.7	11.7	48.2	6.8					3.6
1958	34.2	10.5	46.8	4.5					4.0
1961	30.1	11.8	47.1	6.5					4.5
1965	23.3	25.8	35.7	9.8	3.3				2.1
1968	20.3	26.5	35.1	7.0	10.6				0.5
1971	20.1	17.3	35.0	6.0	21.2				0.4
1974	22.2	15.0	37.4	5.9	18.8				0.7
1977	25.7	19.2	38.7	5.4	9.5	0.7			0.8
1978	26.9	17.5	36.7	5.9	9.2	1.2	1.3		1.3
1981	19.6	21.7	36.2	4.2	5.5	6.2	3.9		2.7
1985	22.6	24.2	39.5	2.5	0.6	6.2	1.6		2.8
1987	23.2	22.2	43.9	1.6	0.8	6.5	0.3		1.5
1991	22.5	19.8	39.2	0.3	0.2	13.5		1.7	2.8
1995	22.5	23.91	33.7	0.3		10.3		5.5	4,0

Flanders

Year	Cath	Lib	Soc	Com	VU	Agalev	Vlaams Blok	Rossem	Other
1946	56.2	7.7	27.4	5.5					3.8
1949	54.4	13.3	24.3	3.6					4.4
1950	60.4	9.4	26.0	2.5					1.7
1954	52.0	10.7	28.7	1.5	3.9				3.2
1958	56.5	9.8	27.8	0.1	3.4				2.4
1961	50.9	11.6	29.7	1.0	6.0				0.8
1965	43.8	16.6	24.7	1.7	11.6				1.6
1968	39.0	16.2	26.0	1.4	16.9				0.5
1971	37.8	16.4	24.4	1.6	18.8				1.0
1974	38.9	17.3	22.5	1.6	16.8				2.9
1977	43.7	14.5	22.3	1.3	16.3	0.1			1.8
1978	43.5	17.4	20.9	1.9	11.5	0.3	2.1		2.4
1981	32.0	21.1	20.6	1.3	16.0	4.0	1.8		3.2
1985	34.6	17.4	23.7	0.5	12.7	6.1	2.2		2.8
1987	31.4	18.5	24.2	0.5	12.9	7.3	3.0		2.2
1991	26.9	19.0	19.4		9.3	7.8	10.3	5.1	2.2
1995	27.6	20.9	20.7		7.3	7.2	12.3		4.0

Table continued on page 173

Brussels

Year	Cath	Lib	Soc	Com	FDF	VU	Agalev Ecolo	RAD UDRT	Vlaams Blok	Rossem	Other
1946	30.2	13.4	35.4	17.4							3.6
1949	31.0	25.0	29.5	9.5							5.0
1950	34.7	18.4	41.4	5.5							0.0
1954	24.6	19.4	45.1	3.7		0.9					6.3
1958	33.5	18.2	43.0	2.7		1.0					1.6
1961	28.0	17.0	41.6	3.6		1.6					8.2
1965	19.5	33.4	26.3	4.1	10.0	2.4					4.4
1968	27.6	26.3	20.0	2.4	18.6	4.3					0.8
1971	20.1	13.5	20.6	2.8	34.5	5.6					3.3
1974	22.7	5.9	20.5	4.0	39.6	5.9					1.4
1977	24.3	11.8	17.1	2.8	34.9	6.2	1.2				1.7
1978	24.1	10.2	16.2	3.0	35.5	3.6	1.8	2.9	1.6		1.1
1981	16.0	21.5	15.8	2.1	22.6	4.4	5.5	8.7	0.7		2.7
1985	18.4	30.6	19.9	1.2	10.9	3.4	6.5	5.0	1.0		3.1
1987	16.5	28.1	25.7	1.0	10.9	3.7	11.3		1.0		1.8
1991	15.5	27.1	18.4		11.9	2.8	11.1		3.9	1.6	7.7
1995[1]	18.5	33.5[2]	18.2			4.3	9.4		7.3		8.8

Sources: 1946–1974: Witte and Craeybeckx, 1983: 269–270
1977–1995: Res Publica, De Standaard

Notes:

1 In 1995 election, the FDF joined the French-language liberals
2 Including Halle-Vilvoorde

antly non-Catholic in every sector (McRae, 1986:65–70). Not surprisingly therefore, political support for the Catholics remained higher in Flanders; until 1981 the Catholics (Christelijke Volks Partij (CVP)) received more than 37% of the votes in all parliamentary elections, with a maximum of over 60% of the votes (see table 6.4). In contrast, its francophone counterpart in Wallonia, the Parti Social Chrétien (PSC), received maximum support of 34.2% of the votes in 1958, but since 1961 has won only between 19% and 27%. The Socialists, on the other hand, have their strongest support in Wallonia with the Parti Socialiste Belge (PSB) winning over 33% in all years since World War Two, while in Flanders the Belgische Socialistische Partij (BSP) has only touched 30% once, and since 1968 scored less than 25%. The more leftist orientation of the population in Wallonia can also be seen in stronger support for the Communists, who in 1978 got almost 6% of the regional votes. The regional stronghold for the Liberals is somewhat less clear, although, apart from the 1970s, their performance in Brussels has always been particularly good.

The electoral shift towards the regionalist parties and the appeal these parties had among a broad range of social groups were therefore a clear signal to the three traditional parties of the political importance of the regionalist sentiment. During the 1960s the parties attempted to arrive at a compromise through classical means of pacification, ranging from putting the issue in cold storage, to introducing some legislation and negotiating agreements between senior leaders (Dewachter, 1987:196–7). However, proposals for reforms agreed upon by the Socialists and Catholics before 1965 (with the Liberals in opposition) failed to make it through parliament mainly due to the intricacies of Belgian constitutional law-making that have been set out in section 6.1.2. In the election of 1965, Catholics and Socialists lost 39 seats and their two-thirds majority in parliament. Prolonged negotiations, this time including the Liberals and a carefully balanced involvement of all languages and parts of the country (but not the regionalist parties), did not result in a final solution as the Leuven crisis broke out and the government fell. During these negotiations, however, the new regional parties already acted as extremist flanks (so-called *zweeppartijen*) for the traditional parties in a way that reflected their regional strongholds: the VU to the Flemish Catholics, the FDF to the francophone Liberals and the RW to the Walloon Socialists (Dewachter, 1987:300). Thus, for instance, when the VU gained electorally on a program of unconditional devolution, a group of younger Flemish Catholics moved, at least partly under pressure of this body of opinion, towards a moderate federal stance and began to put pressure on the party's strong unitarist wing (Witte, 1992:96; see also De Ridder, 1991:49–71). In general, the intensification of the linguistic struggle came at a time when the old group of leaders of the traditional parties, who had negotiated the various post-war crises, were challenged by a new generation of politicians. This new generation, which emerged in both parts of the country, was much less willing to compromise over the linguistic issue than the previous one (Huyse 1982, Covell 1993).

In a crucial turn-around, the main parties decided, under increasing pressure from the regionalist parties which had gained substantially in the elections of 1968, to change their course. Thus, instead of earlier plans which involved cultural autonomy strictly within the context of the national parliament, economic and administrative decentralisation to the provinces and municipalities, and modernisation of the state machinery, it was decided to turn to territory-based regionalism along lines of both cultural and economic autonomy (see Groep Coudenberg, 1991:50–56). Proponents of regionalism along other lines, for instance on the basis of provinces, lacked sufficient support and credibility. The new constitutional proposals which made it through parliament therefore effectively started to fill in the territorial basis which had been laid down with the 1962–63 laws. The resulting complexity of this new reform was, according to one observer, very much in line with the typical Belgian habit of institutional "muddling through" (Molitor, 1981:140). It has been described in section 6.1.3.

6.3.5 *The dynamics of regionalism*

The constitutional revision of 1970 granted some cultural autonomy to the Dutch-, French-, and German-speaking communities and enabled the creation of the regions of Flanders, Wallonia and Brussels-Capital. This in fact meant the explicit recognition of these sub-state territories. Indeed, in the same year, a law on the creation of regional economic councils mentioned the names of Flanders and Wallonia in the text of the laws for the first time (Murphy, 1988a:144). Cultural Councils were created by law in 1971 by splitting up the parliamentarians along linguistic lines, and, in 1973, a special law was passed to create the Cultural Council for German speakers. The precise competencies for the economic regions were left for later since no agreement could be reached.

This decentralisation along two lines was the result of the basic incompatibility of the two positions of the ethnonationalist movements. In general, as has been explained above, Flemish activists sought autonomy chiefly for cultural reasons, while Walloon activists sought regional autonomy to improve their region's economic prospects, and to carry out the economic and social reforms they could not win on a national basis. The conflicting aims and positions collided in particular over the economic competencies for the regions and over the Brussels question. These issues were partly linked. The main problem was the fact that the territorial impact of the two lines of reasoning did not coincide; whereas Walloon regionalism was based more on economic motivations and therefore tri-partite (with Brussels as a full region), Flemish regionalism was based more on cultural grounds and therefore was bi-partite (McRae, 1986:159; see also Lorwin 1966). Flemish nationalists wanted a Brussels with clearly limited authority for fear of being confronted with two French-speaking regions and being outvoted. The hybrid system which was cooked up by the traditional parties therefore satisfied neither position.

As a result, the constitutional revision of 1970 proved unsuccessful as a mechanism for pacification by the major parties. On the basis of the theories of Lijphart, Hooghe (1991:32) argues that several more conditions needed to be fulfilled for a traditional consociational solution to the new linguistic problem to be effective. First of all, the system of highly centralized decision-making in Belgium was not able to cope with the impact and volume of the new demands caused by the cleavage, while no possibilities existed as yet to decentralize the conflict. Secondly, the aforementioned nature of the cleavage itself was not clear, because a francophone-Flemish cultural schism, a Flemish-Walloon-Brussels economic conflict, and even a Flemish/Walloon/Brussels-versus-Belgium conflict could be perceived. This ambiguity and the muddled nature of the new cleavage very much diminished the elite's capacity to come up with satisfactory solutions, even more so because different perspectives needed different kinds of solutions. Thirdly, the internal organization of the 'new' segments was very weak, making the articulation of the wishes of the masses to the elite level more difficult. Indeed, although some elements of 'linguistic pillars' were present, particularly in Flanders, such as employers, organizations and tourist organizations, most organizations were enclosed in the traditional pillars (e.g., the cultural associations). Therefore, the traditional solutions of the consociational decision-making system failed to work properly.

Moreover, the growing strength of the ethnonationalist parties and the increasing divergence of Flemish and Walloon points of view over the future of the Belgian state proved too much for the major parties themselves. They split up under the pressure – the Catholics in 1968–69 immediately following the Leuven crises, the Liberals between 1968 and 1972 and the Socialists in 1978. Even the Communist Party could not escape the trend and followed suit in 1984. The political relevance of the new cleavage made it therefore inevitable that the ban on entering cabinets was lifted for the regionalist parties (see Zolberg 1977). Their inclusion was also needed in creating the parliamentary majorities which could pass and implement further changes. In 1974, the first regional party, the RW, was included in a coalition and the FDF and the VU followed suit in the succeeding cabinets.

Until well into the 1970s, however, the competencies of the newly created sub-state units remained limited. The Cultural Councils were controlled by the centre because they were made up of parliamentarians. By this construction the loyalty of the MP's could not rest solely with their communities, but also had to rest with the national parties and the government coalition. A further limitation of the competencies was the fact that the Councils did not control their own executives or finances. Nevertheless, even within these limits, their impact was widely felt, especially in the case of the Dutch language council. Some decrees issued by them had important consequences: for instance, the decree to enforce the use of Dutch in private firms in the Dutch-speaking region. It was vehemently contested and criticized by French-speakers (see McRae, 1986:264–267). The economic regions hardly functioned at all. Economic devolution was practically non-existent, not only because of the question of Brussels and the different backgrounds of the ethnonational movements, but also because all sorts of regional and provincial economic councils already existed among which the new regions had to be positioned (see McRae, 1986:164–165).

An attempt to resolve the outstanding issues was made in 1976 and 1977. Representatives of all political parties, including the ethnonationalist parties, worked on a new package for dealing with the next steps in the reform. The result came to be known as the Egmont-Stuyvenberg Agreements and even contained solutions for the position of Brussels (see the next section).[20]

---

20 The deal was struck between the Socialists, the Catholics, the VU and the FDF. The Liberals did not agree with the Pact, but did not oppose it seriously, while the RW was in disarray over the direction of its policies.

In the end, however, the implementation of the Agreements failed because of the fundamental opposition by the Flemish movement – through the actions of ad-hoc organizations and with the support of some influential Flemish newspapers – against the concessions made by the Volksunie over Brussels (Dewachter, 1987:352). It led to a schism between the leaders of the Flemish parties and their more extreme rank-and-file members, and to the creation of extremist nationalist Flemish parties (see Gijsels 1992). Indeed, all regional parties found that their participation in coalitions was not completely to their advantage; they were all plagued by internal splits and dissents, and lost in the elections that followed (McRae, 1986:146–147).

6.3.5.1 Intermezzo: the question of Brussels

It is useful at this stage to take a closer look at the issue of Brussels, which can be seen literally as the centre of the linguistic turmoil in Belgium. Being the capital, it has played a central role in the process of frenchification; the mainly Dutch-speaking population of 1830 (ca. 65%) has by now become mainly French-speaking (ca. 80%) (see Van Velthoven 1987).[21] It was in Brussels that the differences between the lower status Dutch-speakers and the higher status French-speakers were most apparent, and where upward social mobility was most connected with the necessity of speaking French. Brussels, as a capital, was to be an example of the unilingual Belgium as it was desired by the elite in the nineteenth century, and considering that much of the employment was found in central government or in the economic institutions which were run by French-speakers, this had substantial effects (Van Velthoven, 1987:26–28). Moreover, because of the importance of Brussels in terms of electoral districts (26 out of 186 in 1912), politicians in Brussels seriously attempted to postpone the effect of the earlier language laws; Flemish activists only succeeded in gaining concessions over Flanders by allowing for a 'status aparte' for Brussels. This situation could continue for a long time since the Flemish movement was fully occupied with the situation in Flanders itself, and even unwittingly strengthened these tendencies by 'forcing' unilingual French-speakers to leave Flanders following the language laws of the 1930s; these officials often received new appointments in the administration in Brussels (Van Velthoven, 1987:32). In Brussels, the rules of the 1930s language laws regarding bilingual Brussels only applied to the communication of state institutions with the population and not to their internal use of language. Civil servants who were bilingual were there-

---

21 The timing of the frenchification is a matter of dispute. Van Istendael (1989:125) holds that frenchification really got under way only after the Second World War, since in 1947 over 60% of the population spoke either Dutch or more than one language, and this latter group consisted in all likelihood of mostly Dutch-speakers as well (see also Van Velthoven, 1987:22).

fore mostly found at the lower ranks (Van Velthoven, 1987:39). The effects of the other laws were also minimal in terms of creating bilingualism or protecting the Dutch language. In this context Brussels became a French-speaking city.

Nevertheless, it was only during the 1960s that the linguistic problems in Brussels started to become a major issue, after the balance in the country as a whole had changed, and as a culture-conscious elite which had been educated completely in Dutch started to rise in state-wide institutions (Witte, 1987:49). By then, moreover, the urban sprawl of Brussels had gained momentum and this 'oil stain'-like feature of Brussels (as Flemish nationalists like to point out) continued in the next decades. Over 175,000 inhabitants of Brussels settled in the urban fringe of the capital between 1974 and 1987, leaving a suburbanization balance of roughly 80 thousand (Kesteloot et al., 1990:166). This resulted in substantial frenchification of Flemish municipalities in the south and southeast of Brussels in particular, although the lack of linguistic data makes definite conclusions difficult (see De Lannoy 1987).

Due to the nature of these processes, the Flemish Movement wanted to secure the territorial limitations of Brussels and to prevent the 'connection' of Brussels with the territory of the French-speaking region (the neck under the head, so to speak; see map 6.1). The Flemish also wanted the adaptation of suburbanizing French-speaking families to their new Dutch-speaking environment, and firm guarantees that any arrangement to facilitate this adaptation would not be misused as it had been in the past. In the context of the 1960 laws a compromise was reached in July, 1963, in the castle of Hertoginnedal/Val-Duchesse; six municipalities bordering Brussels were given special facilities for French-speakers, enabling them to use French in their dealings with the administration while the internal language of the administration remained Dutch (the so-called *faciliteitengemeenten*). Improved facilities were also developed for Dutch-speakers in Brussels, while parity was guaranteed in the executive. To limit the influence of Brussels on its surroundings, the old administrative arrondissement of Brussels was split up into a smaller bilingual arrondissement of Brussels-Capital made up of 19 municipalities, a separate arrondissement containing the *faciliteitengemeenten*, and an unilingual arrondissement of Halle-Vilvoorde, which is the Flemish part of the province of Brabant. Seven years later, the main arrangements were stipulated in the 1970 constitution, which also provided for alarm procedures for the Dutch speakers in the Brussels executive. The arrondissement containing the *faciliteitengemeenten* was incorporated in the Dutch language region.

The constitutional changes of 1970 thus confirmed how the position of Brussels had become stuck between the cultural struggle of the Flemings and the more economically oriented perspective of the Walloon Movement. The discussions over Brussels complicated plans for economic regionalization, but in contrast to earlier periods the strength of the FDF guaranteed

178

that the city developed into a tremendous stumbling block in country-wide negotiations. In particular, limitation to 19 municipalities, what francophones called the 'carcan' (collar) or 'the Yoke,' was deemed unacceptable to French-language activists, in particular the FDF. However, Brussels only allowed an agglomeration council to take care of some of the more technical affairs. The agglomeration council then created cultural committees to be accountable for the affairs decided on by the Cultural Councils for Dutch- and French-speakers. Attempts to give the agglomeration council more competencies met with Flemish resistance. The pivotal position of Brussels was made clear by the fact that both the Flemings and the French-language community designated Brussels as their capital.

The Egmont-Stuyvenberg Agreements of 1977 seemed to put an end to the controversy. This was a fine example of Belgian ingenuity: Brussels was to become a third region, with French-speakers in the dominant position in the council, while French-speakers around Brussels would live in the Dutch-language region but could vote on lists in Brussels, and could receive administrative and judicial services from a commune of their choice in Brussels-Capital where they would have fictitious residence. In return some concessions were given to Dutch-speakers, but in Flanders it was nevertheless widely felt that Brussels had now officially become a French-speaking city; together with the creation of the third economic region this meant defeat for two of the spearheads of the Flemish Movement. In the end, extremists within the Flemish Movement succeeded in blocking the implementation of this compromise. In the 1980 changes, the issue was carefully avoided, and Brussels remained under the direct control of the central government. The situation around Brussels remained complicated for a long time by the fact that the electoral *arrondissement* of Brussels-Halle-Vilvoorde continued to be bounded by the combined pre–1963 boundaries. Although Flemish nationalists attempted to break it up and adapt it to the new administrative districts, thereby hoping to limit the political influence of Brussels and discourage francophone expansion beyond the agglomeration, French-speakers vehemently opposed this split. No substantial new steps were taken until 1988.

6.3.5.2 The road to federalization

Although the question of Brussels remained unresolved, the context of the linguistic conflict as a whole slowly changed. As noted above, participation of the ethnonational parties in the coalitions was not to their advantage. They generally failed to achieve the expected results and lost in subsequent elections. What was more important in the long term, however, was that they were slowly overtaken by the increasingly regionalist stands of the traditional parties. Regional differences in organizational strength of the *zuilen* became very important, since the power of the traditional political parties was not simply the result of electoral support but, to a large extent, also came from their links with the organizational basis of the pillars (Dewachter, 1992b: 284–284; see also Hooghe, 1991:63–64). Therefore, the intersection of the language struggle and the other two cleavages caused their interweaving into a particular form over time. Interesting dilemmas arose. For Flemish Catholics, for instance, the paradox lay in the fact that their control over the political system in Belgium since 1958 had been substantial; Belgium was in fact by some French-speakers called *l'état* CVP. The Catholics were therefore not immediately willing to restrict their position to Flemish points of view. However, during the 1970s, and, in particular in the 1980s, tensions increased between the Flemish CVP and the French-language PSC, the latter party coming under ever more pressure from the successful Socialist bid to defend the Walloon interests (Hooghe, 1991:66–67). For the other parties, similar issues were at hand. It bears witness to the strength of the traditional parties that, over the years, the ethnonational battlefield was turned into an opportunity in which they were able to compete effectively. As Huyse (1981:124) argues, "the federalist idea became more attractive to more people in the 1970s not strictly for linguistic or cultural or ethnic reasons, but because it [bore] the promise of the ultimate achievement of Socialism in Wallonia and a sort of Catholic model of societal harmony in Flanders."

The constitutional impasse was finally overcome through a series of bargains in 1980, in which the Socialist parties agreed to support an austerity program in return for the Liberal party's support of constitutional revision; at the same time the French language Liberal, Socialist, and Catholic parties agreed to leave the question of Brussels alone for the time being in return for their Flemish counterparts', agreement to economic regionalization (Witte, 1992:98–99; Rudolph, 1989:100). As described in section 6.1.3, the 1980 state reform still tended to protect the unitary state from a federal structure, although the Cultural Councils received more powers (and became Community Councils), as did the economic regions for the first time. Several typical federal features were not introduced, however, such as the existence of separately elected parliamentary bodies and clearly separate financial resources and areas of competence. Nevertheless, the reform certainly transferred jobs to the regions. Some of these went to Namur which had been chosen by the Walloon regional council as their capital (McRae, 1986:171–2). The now combined Flemish community and region still retained Brussels for obvious reasons.

By then the national debt of Belgium had grown enormously, and the international recession of the beginning of the 1980s made itself severely felt. This had a great impact on community relations, since the decisions to cut back on state spending were carefully monitored on all sides for a regional bias (which they were to have, almost inevitably). Persistent Flemish attempts to limit financial support for Wallonia's declining economy became especially contested. Thus, for instance, the Eyskens government fell in 1981 because of a Walloon demand for more money for the steel industry in Wallonia. Two years later a compromise on cut-backs in state support for the so-called national sectors (such as steel and the harbour) in 1983 was seen by some in Wallonia as the 'end of national solidarity' (see Gol 1993). However, the need for economic restructuring was widely felt in Belgium and enabled a coalition of the Catholic CVP and PSC with the Liberal PVV (Partij voor Vrijheid en Vooruitgang) and PRL (Parti Réformateur Libéral). Being excluded from the centre-right cabinet, the francophone Socialists were able to cash in on Wallonia's difficulties and the government's policies, and effectively made the shift towards the defence of Walloon regional interests (Hooghe, 1991:59).

It took a major crisis to initiate the next step towards federalism. The crisis over Voeren in 1987 had precisely this function. As has been pointed out, in 1962 a majority of the inhabitants of Voeren had opted for remaining in the province of Liège but had been 'exchanged' for other territories along the border. The central person in the Voeren crisis, José Happart, had succeeded in emerging as *the* symbol of Walloon resistance against the consequences of Flemish territorial policies in the linguistic conflict. He gained great popularity in Wallonia as a whole, and on the Socialist list gained by far the most personal votes of all Walloon politicians. His refusal to speak Dutch in the Dutch-language area of Voeren after having been appointed mayor led to a government crisis, to new elections, and to prolonged coalition discussions. For the Flemish, any concessions were unacceptable, as that would completely undermine the principle of territorially based language arrangements. Moreover, a similar conflict had emerged in Brussels, indicating the possibility of a further spread of such issues. Voeren is therefore a good example of how local linguistic conflicts can paralyse the centre of Belgian politics (see Witte, 1992:100–101).

After the 1987 elections, in which the Walloon Socialists won substantially, a coalition was created consisting of the Catholic parties, the Socialist parties, and the Volksunie (without a Walloon counterpart). The negotiations followed the old pacification pattern, with secret negotiations including the leaders of most of the political parties. The length of the negotiations (105 days) gave the two Catholic parties time to renegotiate their relationship after the Voeren fiasco, and to get used to the Socialists. All parties needed a slow process to smooth over unrest within their own organizations now that a new round of institutional changes was in the making. This time, however, in contrast with the 1970s (at the time of the Egmont Pact in particular), the challenge from outside the traditional parties was not as strong (Hooghe, 1991:84–87). Based on the newly organized linguistic cleavage, the restructured traditional political forces were therefore able to strike a deal using traditional methods.

In the end, the comprehensive new package deal not only dealt with Voeren but also firmly established federalization in Belgium. It was implemented through continuous negotiations in the five years that followed. The package was difficult to implement because some of the Gordian knots which had plagued Belgian politics for 25 years finally had to be cut in order to create a more transparent form of federalism; this included such issues as the final competencies for the constituent units, the question of the status of Brussels, the split of Brabant, and the financial arrangements. The package transferred extended competencies to the regions in town and country planning, the environment, nature conservancy, the economy, energy, public works, transport, local authorities and scientific research. New powers in cultural policies, *personalized matters*, language issues, and, particularly, education were transferred to the Community Councils, giving them full competence in these fields. The regions and the communities were also to have the right to conclude international treaties on matters within their authority. Brussels would be one of the regions, although its 'ordinances' would have slightly less power than the 'decrees' of the other regions. In return, Flemish speakers were to have parity in the Brussels regional executive and more protection through the use of special majorities, while cultural affairs in Brussels remained the authority of each language group through community commissions (Witte, 1992:102; Hooghe, 1991:23). In January 1989, 19 years after it was first mentioned in the Belgian constitution, a special law created the region of Brussels-Capital, with an elected council and an executive. A final important element of the 1988 package was the authority of the Court of Arbitration which could now check on the constitutionality of laws, decrees, and ordinances in their compliance with the constitutional principles of equality, non-discrimination, and freedom and equal rights for education. This was done to ensure the cooperation of all parties in the complete transfer of education to the communities (Hooghe, 1991:25).

The new competencies also implied that new subjects were to be discussed (although old conflicts, such as that over Voeren, also resurfaced again and again). In particular, the devolution of international relations and international trade were contested issues. These discussions reached a climax when a conflict arose over the selling of arms to countries in the Middle East. Seen by the Flemish parties in central government as an explicit case which should be decided by the central authorities, the Walloon regional government, arguing that a great number of Walloon jobs were involved, threatened to export the arms in a one-sided decision (which would be against the constitution). A characteristic Belgian solution – the francophone ministers in the central government would form a separate commission on the issue (thus *de facto* regionalizing the issue) – was ultimately not accepted; this caused the downfall of the government. Subsequent elections showed large-scale protest ballots with losses for all major parties and the breakthrough of the extreme right-wing Vlaams Blok in Flanders (see Swyngedouw 1992).

Following their initial rise, the ethnonational parties to a large extent disappeared or lost their political relevance; from 1974 onwards, the electoral importance of the regional parties fell steadily, from 44 seats in parliament in 1974 to 13 in 1991. The RW no longer participated in the 1985 elections, while the FDF is close to political irrelevance, with 3 seats from 1985 until 1991 (10% of the votes in Brussels). The VU started to lose support later on, particularly from 1987 onwards, and in the 1995 provincial elections they only received 7.3% of the votes in Flanders, against 9.3% in 1991 and 16% at the beginning of the 1980s. Insomuch as their decline has been offset by the success of the right-wing Vlaams Blok, this concerns a different side of the phenomenon of nationalism. Only a very limited part of the electorate votes for the Vlaams Blok because of its stance on Flemish nationalism, and most voters are attracted to their views on migrants, or use it as an expression of general protest (see Swyngedouw 1992). The trend therefore seems to point at a diminishing ethnonational sentiment of the Belgian electorate, with Belgium as the main focus of identity. Indeed, a poll in March-April 1990 showed only 12% of the Belgian population considered Flanders or Wallonia solely as their motherland, with 18% mentioning both Flanders (or Wallonia) and Belgium; 66% considered Belgium solely as their motherland. The same question two years later resulted in 80.3% giving Belgium as the answer, with 3.7% mentioning both, and 11% solely Wallonia or Flanders (Coppé, 1992:98–99). In particular, the situation remains ambiguous in Wallonia, where following initial demonstrations in 1961 and voting for the RW between 1965 and 1974, hardly any more popular actions have occurred (Javeau, 1989:151, see also Dubois 1989). However, as should immediately be pointed out, other indications can be found as well. For instance, some other polls show that in Flanders identification with the region is now higher than it is with Belgium (Dewachter, 1992a:29).

Anyway, there are other reasons as well for the loss of ethnonational momentum as indicated by the demise of the ethnonational parties. Foremost among them is the severe economic climate in Belgium during the 1980s and 1990s which diverted attention to the sobering of state expenses; with a solid 140% of the GNP by 1993, Belgium's foreign debt was the highest of the European community per capita. This may have inclined voters towards the traditional parties, or, on the other hand, towards voting for new ecological parties. Moreover, the internal fragmentation of the ethnonationalist parties is also certainly a reason. Particularly during participation in the national government, when the regionalist parties failed to achieve credible results, not only their support, but also their internal cohesion dwindled. Nevertheless, their final impact was of longer duration because their members, after the party had fallen apart, joined (or returned to) the traditional parties, taking with them the regionalist perspective (see Fonteyn 1988).

This brings us to the traditional parties. A fourth major reason for the decline of the ethnonational parties lies in their adaptation of regionalist standpoints. Needless to say, the combination of regional strongholds for the pillars with linguistic interests of the language groups, in a regionalized and territorially demarcated Belgium, proved a potent mixture, in which almost every issue, regardless of its background, could turn into a point of ethnonational conflict. As the traditional parties experienced the need to reorient themselves under these pressures, differences in support for the pillars between the various regions resulted in Flemish demands gaining more influence in the Catholic party, and Walloon demands being slowly incorporated in the Socialist party. In this way, the whole political spectrum was reorganised along linguistic lines. This is especially crucial in the Belgian context, because of the importance of the political parties in the Belgian political system (for which the term *particratie* is often used (Dewachter, 1992a:16–17)). The consequences of the split of the traditional parties were therefore substantial. To begin with, the traditional parties ceased to be 'national parties,' that is, parties which have a considerable electorate on both sides of the linguistic border (Dewachter, 1987:198). This was unique compared to other cleavages, and it prevented the Belgian population from showing their views on the linguistic conflict. Although they can still choose between more or less regionalist parties, they cannot for the most part choose between opposite points of view (Flemish and Walloon), as in the case of the other cleavages.[22] Moreover, the structural effects of the splits were much stronger, because pacification of conflicting ethnonational standpoints could not be achieved within the parties; more issues turned up in the political arena and more issues took on a regionalist flavour (see Dewachter, 1987:298–299). Nevertheless, if regionalization has been completed to prevent the traditional powers from losing their support, as has been suggested above, this has to a large extent succeeded, albeit at the cost of their own disappearance as state-wide units.

The ultimate fine-tuning of Belgian federalism was completed in an atmosphere of continued and tense debate over the remaining dilemmas, and as discussed, the Belgian general public by now showed clear signs of ethnonational fatigue. The need to wrap up the discussion led to a 'Dialogue of the Communities' which was started in April 1992. Two long and complicated sessions of negotiations in which all political parties (except the Vlaams Blok and the new libertine R.O.S.S.E.M party) were involved resulted in the St.Michaels Agreements of September, 1992. Since the package of 1988, discussions had mainly concerned three dilemmas aside from international affairs: the direct election of the constituent parliaments to put an end to the double (or triple) mandates of MPs; the role and composition of the new Senate; and the fiscal requirements of the constituent parts (Witte, 1992:105–6). Regarding the first, the main proposition was to solve the

---

22   It could therefore also be argued that they now in fact became 'national' parties. In the electoral district of Brussels-Halle-Vilvoorde, however, where this choice did remain available for some time, it was hardly used.

question of the old electoral district of Brussels-Halle-Vilvoorde and the province of Brabant which were to be split up. This would block French-speakers around Brussels-Capital from voting for French language parties in Brussels, but would by the same token limit control of Dutch-speakers in Brussels itself. It was finally decided to keep the electoral district of Halle-Vilvoorde intact for elections at the federal level, but not for elections of the constituent units. The province of Brabant, the only bilingual Belgian province, was also split up along language lines.

The second dilemma concerned the function of the future federal parliament, particularly the Senate, which could either become a full-fledged participant in national law-making and equal to the Chamber of Representatives, or just an arena where representatives from the communities and the regions would gather. This stumbling block had to be resolved to enable the direct election of all councils of the constituent units of Belgium which had, after all, been composed of members of parliament until then. The final decision was to limit the number of Members of Parliament (the Chamber of Representatives to 150 and the Senate to 71) and to have the Senate play a limited role, for instance by lacking in powers to initiate new laws. It will now consist of 40 directly elected Senators (25 Dutch-speakers and 15 French-speakers), 21 Senators as representatives from the communities (10 from the Flemish Council, 10 from the French community council, and 1 from the German-speaking community council), and another 10 Senators who will be co-opted (6 Dutch-speaking and 4 French-speaking).

The third dilemma concerned the financial costs of the new regional and communal competencies. For the Flemish any further transfer of money had to be accompanied by new transfers of competencies, while Wallonia and the French-language Council, whose financial position had been poor from the beginning, basically wanted more money for their present competencies. The crucial financial question of social security – which many Flemish politicians wanted to federalize but which Walloon politicians wanted to keep at the federal level as a mechanism of state-wide solidarity – also played in the background. For the time being social security has been left at the federal level, but, as prime-minister Jean-Luc Dehaene suggested, the agreements of 1992 and 1993 could very well be a mere phase in the Belgian habit of evolving federalism.

Official federalism was written into the Belgian constitution in 1993. What has developed over 30 years of prolonged and often painful negotiations is a system in which different kinds of sub-state units wield authority in different fields and cover different overlapping territories. Decisions made by the various authorities have equal juridical status in the sense that authorities of one kind cannot interfere with the decisions of other authorities; most importantly, central government cannot overrule the decisions of the sub-state units within their authority. However, an extensive set of consultative mechanisms has been put in place, some of them compulsory, to ensure cooperation. The autonomy of the sub-state units and their importance has been enlarged by the fact that they have been given the residual competencies, meaning that the central state can only wield authority over those fields which have specifically been awarded to it in the constitution (Van den Brande, 1993:557–558). The territorial overlap of different authorities, however, virtually ensures ongoing conflicts and negotiations, even though the latest changes have simplified the situation.

The increasing importance of the regions was displayed in the decision of the leader of the francophone Socialists, Guy Spitaels (nicknamed 'Dieu' because of his power), to become the premier of Wallonia instead of minister in the national government in January, 1992. Indeed, as Dewachter (1991) has shown, regional politicians are clearly rising in the pyramid of Belgian positions of power, particularly the ministers of education. Moreover, simplification of institutional arrangements is on its way now that differences between the French-speaking inhabitants of Brussels and Wallonia have become more obvious, and the attempt to equate the francophone language with Walloon and Brussels' interests becomes more and more untenable. Political parties in Wallonia are increasingly unwilling to have the development of their region hampered by links with the francophone community in Brussels, now that substantial autonomy is assured (Witte, 1992:111). It may be conceivable, therefore, that a Walloon Community Council will be created in the near future. Moreover, a combination of regional and community authority would place Wallonia in the same position as its Flemish counterpart, which would ease its position at the negotiation table.

At least two traditionally unifying elements merit some final attention. The first is Brussels itself. As the Flemish capital, the city remains a central concern not just because of the continuing spread of the city to its environment – after all its borders are fixed – but because it is the single factor preventing the Flemish from pressing for straightforward independence. Surrounded by Flemish territory, it can hardly be brushed aside by Flemish separatists, but including it in an independent Flanders means the inclusion of a French-speaking city and a continuation of the linguistic battle. Seen from this perspective it will continue to act as a unifying element as long as the Flemish movement is unwilling to relinquish the city. The developments surrounding Brussels will therefore continue to decide the fate of Belgium.[23] One of the other elements that is traditionally considered as unifying, the monarchy, received a blow following the death of Boudewijn (Baudouin). After 1951 Boudewijn built up a tremendous amount of knowledge regard-

---

23 Even after its upgrading to a region, Brussels' position is hardly enviable; its fiscal base is not sufficient to its tasks as capital of Belgium and of Europe, and the compensation it receives remains too little. Its fiscal base is further eroded by the fact that wealthier inhabitants of Brussels move to the Brabant province which is part of Wallonia and Flanders, and is therefore becoming the richest part of these two regions (Deschouwer, 1994:484).

ing the Belgian political scene and also gained substantial popularity with the population. Particularly after elections, when coalitions had to be constructed, he could wield considerable influence behind the scenes, although the extent of his influence remains unclear. Since it was based on experience and respect and not as much on constitutional powers (which are limited), the new King, Albert II, has to rebuild this influence from the start.

6.4 LIBERAL-DEMOCRACY AND FEDERALISM IN BELGIUM: THE IMPACT ON ETHNONATIONALISM

In this chapter, I have discussed how the ethnonational question in Belgium became topical under the linguistic policies of the new Belgian state in 1830. Due to a very limited electorate, which consisted almost entirely of French-speakers because of the electoral rules, the situation hardly changed for several decades. This led to increasing protests by Flemish activists, who started to have more substantial influence thanks to universal male suffrage in 1893. The 1898 equalization law formally equalized the two languages, but its extremely slow implementation only heightened frustration. In the process, regional conceptions of Flanders and Wallonia slowly came to life. The events which took place during the First World War initially implied a setback for the Flemish Movement, but during the 1930s, amidst increasing activism, new laws were passed. These laws were based on territorial principles, and brought with them a whole new set of problems. Slow implementation, an explicit but shifting language border, and several territorial points of contention (including Brussels) assured the linguistic issue a permanent place in the political agenda. This situation, plus the events concerning, for instance, collaboration, led many Dutch-speakers to conclude that the state still looked after the interests of French-speakers much more than those of Dutch-speakers. This remained important despite the fact that economic development in Flanders proceeded at a rapid pace and was not hampered at all by the linguistic character of the state; in a similar vein, an important field such as education remained firmly Dutch through private local Catholic education in Flanders. Nevertheless disputes over jobs in the state machinery, for instance, combined Flemish economic interests with the question of political status of Flemish culture in the Belgian state.

Until then the conflict was an issue between the state, ruled by an elite which stressed national unity on the basis of the French language, and the Flemish Movement. In fact, a persistent unwillingness to accept bilingualism in the country as a whole, and the territorial solution which was decided upon in the 1930s, may have helped to create a Flemish community where none existed before. Projected Belgian unity therefore ultimately failed, even though two wars interrupted and discredited the Flemish Movement and gave renewed strength to the concept of the Belgian nation-state. In the 1960s the cumulative history of the conflict, demographic differences, economic changes, and pacification of the other lines of conflict combined to create a new political situation in which a Flemish Movement was now matched by a Walloon Movement (and, later, by a party originating in Brussels). Or, to put it differently, the centre was now confronted with different and diverse ethnonationalist or regionalist organizations. The fixation of the language border reflected the changing balance of power in the country, but led to substantial conflicts when it was implemented. This time the social and political context made the depth of the conflict much greater. The first attempt to deal with the issue by the traditional parties resulted in devolution of some competencies to new sub-state units, but negotiations were severely complicated by the fact that the diverse backgrounds of the two movements inhibited simple territorial arrangements. The solution which was selected created new problems, and the ambiguity of the new institutions enabled activists on both sides of the linguistic divide to keep putting the cleavage on the political agenda. The split of all the traditional parties in itself led to new strains in the political system. The succession of "laboriously built-up equilibria," as Witte (1992) has characterized it, resulted in a system which is now extremely opaque for non-specialists, although the recent steps to more traditional and complete forms of federation may herald the beginning of a process of simplification.

It is clear that the possibilities of the political arena have been fully exploited by ethnonational activists, initially only by Flemish activists and, after 1960, also by Walloon activists. The range of actions included demonstrations, public debate, faction formation in parties, special interest pressure groups, and, of course, separate political parties. Interestingly, these parties were very successful in opposition and suffered when they participated in coalitions; then, internal differences within the movements came to the fore. The rise and decline of these parties are an indication of the political relevance of ethnicity as a sentiment, which, according to the decline, was either largely satisfied by the constitutional changes, or was put into the hands of traditional players in the electoral arena once these had split up. It is indeed fascinating to note how these traditional parties adapted to the new situation and used their traditional methods to create comprehensive packages. The result was not really traditional, however. As McRae (1990:98) concluded, the new cleavage led to "the obvious continuation and even reinforcement of consociational political processes, which were implemented, however, through major changes in political institutions," or, as Hooghe has phrased it, through the "territorial translation of a long-standing non-territorial practice" (Hooghe, 1991:102, see also Covell 1985, Hooghe 1993). Of course, such assurances as, for instance, the alarm bell procedure were not really territorial due to the transitional nature of the arrangements, but the impact was the same in terms of veto power.

Indeed, although the separation of the segments in society is an important part of the consociational way of keeping political stability in a divided society, the territorial dimension of the solution adds a new dynamic. Ethnonationalism thrives on territorial symbolism, and the fixation of the territories visualized the conflict and generated new issues. The territorialization of the linguistic conflict therefore assisted in the process of reconfirmation and adaptation of the ethnonational identities, in which internal differences slowly lessened and the regions and communes increasingly started to represent the group on a more uniform basis. Furthermore, even with the decrease in public support for ethnonationalism, the negotiations continued on a Walloon-Flemish basis, which was exemplified by the 'Dialogue of the Communities' in 1992.

In the meantime the social effects of the solution have become increasingly clear, even if support for ethnonationalism as such has become ambiguous. While historical differences in status between the languages seem to have diminished to a minimum, French for Flemish pupils has now become a truly foreign language of, almost, a foreign country (Dewachter, 1992a:11). If a second language is chosen it is often English, except in the Brussels area. The institutional changes have had their impact on the private sector as well – witness the decree of 1973 on language use in the private sector – and even French sermons in the Flemish part of Belgium and Dutch language sermons in the French parts seem largely to have stopped (McRae, 1986:269). There is less migration between the two parts of the country, while, for instance, suburbanisation of French language speakers from Brussels is mainly directed to the *faciliteitengemeenten* (Murphy, 1988a:158–161). Indeed, Flemish control over the implementation of language regulation in the Dutch language area assures that it is extremely difficult for French-speakers to stretch the regulations. In terms of general perspective the publication of continuous comparisons on a regional basis (particularly since 1977 when the yearbook of regional statistics was introduced (McRae,1986:89)) produces endless grounds for discussion which can be used at any suitable moment by interested 'ethnonational entrepreneurs.'

The political elite itself now has to operate in an arena which is composed of various territorial units with different parliaments and different economic, social, political and ideological structures. Although the traditional parties still have a firm grip on Belgian society, they have adapted themselves to the new linguistic issue, two of them successfully attaching to both sides of the linguistic divide; the Liberals are somewhat stronger in Brussels but offer an important alternative in the other regions. There are in fact many indications that not only the parties but the pillars themselves have successfully adapted to the new situation and that their significance to society is still as great as it was (Hooghe, 1991:64; Hellemans and Schepers 1992). The consequences for the political process are important, nevertheless. Many of the compromises, for instance on education, can now be worked out within each part of Belgium, without need for consensus with political players in the other region (although they still need to comply with

the constitutional guarantees of non-discrimination and freedom of education). Therefore, the ministers of education in the communities are among
the highest ranked politicians in the Belgian power structure. As Huyse
(1982:84–86) notes in his analysis of the changes in the political system of
Belgium since 1970, autonomy of the regions and communes enabled the
majorities in both parts to implement decisions which are made less and less
by the combined leadership of several *familles spirituelles*. Moreover, due to
the regulation of competencies in minute detail and the clear demarcation of
'spheres of influence,' many possibilities for give and take across the language border are blocked, making negotiations appear quickly to be a zero-
sum game and leading to stalemates (see also Heisler 1990). It also appears
less likely that new links would be forged across the language border, while
existent links are being slowly unwound. For individuals this of course
implies a limitation of choices, making it for instance impossible for Dutch-
speakers to support a Walloon point of view (unless a Flemish party by
chance holds the same opinion).

By now, a complete generation of politicians has 'grown up' in an atmosphere of communal conflict, to the effect that now almost everything is seen
through 'communal lenses.' As has been discussed, the fact that all political
parties have split up has strengthened this point of view. The point, therefore, is that there are increasingly fewer centripetal forces at work, and
increasingly more centrifugal forces. The separate languages, separate education, separate cultural systems (including the media), separate political
parties, separate international relations, separate economic policies (though
not monetary), and so forth, more or less ensure further diversion of the
values of Flemings and Walloons. The new regulations generate new struggles of competencies, and each conflict only seems to be solved with further
devolution. And, as could be observed in recent years, conflicts are likely to
emerge over foreign policy and trade, where the competencies between the
regions and communities (or with the centre) will frequently collide. Furthermore, after the 'best informed politician' of Belgium, King Boudewijn,
died in the summer of 1993, it remains very questionable whether his successor, King Albert II, will make the monarchy function as a uniting factor.

Most complicated is the position of Brussels. Its situation has certainly
not become less ambivalent, now that it is no longer the sole centre of the
French-speaking part of the Belgian population (because of Namur). The
constitutional specialist Senelle argued, however, that the main mistake in
the original constitutional arrangement concerned the fact that there were
only two actors of importance, which could lead to an endless confrontation between them; according to him, a Swiss model, with, for instance, the
historical provinces as the federal components of the Belgian state, could
provide for much more balanced political development (in Groep Coudenberg, 1991:61). Seen from that perspective, the long-delayed upgrading of
Brussels to a level comparable with the other two regions may add a new
dynamic to the political process, the effect of which is not yet clear.

7

Finland
The Accommodation
of the Swedish-Speakers

Finland emerged as a polity in 1809, when Sweden was forced to transfer the Finnish territories to Russian rule. From then on, the linguistic differences in the country became politically important. Indeed, the conflict between Finnish ethnonational groups is mainly a linguistic one, although some other issues have come to the fore as well. In the context of this study, it is useful to distinguish four periods in Finnish political history, each having a distinctive bearing on the ethnonational question: the Grand Duchy until 1906; a period of transition from 1906 until 1922; a politically unstable period from 1922 until the Second World War; and a period of carefully balanced neutrality from the Second World War onwards. Whereas in the earlier periods the linguistic cleavage was clearly present in the political arena, nowadays the level of tension between the two main groups in Finland[1] is extremely low. The Swedish-speaking population has been assimilated to such an extent that it could even provide one of the two final candidates for the presidency of Finland in 1994. However, as will be discussed in this chapter, it was not inevitable that this tranquillity would prevail.

Similar to the previous chapters I will start with a short introduction of Finnish history in section 7.1.1 and of the Finnish political system in section 7.1.2. Section 7.2 contains an overview of the geographical position of the Swedish-speaking minority in the territory of Finland. In section 7.3, the linguistic question in Finland is discussed, while section 7.4 contains the conclusions.

7.1   INTRODUCTION

From the thirteenth century until 1808, Finland formed part of the Swedish Kingdom. The Finnish regions, demarcated in a treaty between Sweden and the princedom of Novgorod in 1323, were treated as normal parts of Swe-

---

1   The Saami are the third group. They number around 4000.

den; inhabitants of those regions had, for instance, voting rights for the Swedish King. However, for prolonged periods of time the remoteness of large parts of Finland provided local rulers with virtual autonomy from the political centre (Singleton, 1989:29). In the sixteenth and seventeenth century, Swedish rulers forged tighter links between Sweden and the Finnish regions, and they created a separate Duchy of Finland governed by one of the King's sons. The Duchy had the embryonic shape of a later Finland (Singleton, 1989:34). Religious texts were translated into Finnish and, after the Lutheran Church was established as the official Church of Sweden and Finland in 1686, it gained substantial influence through its grip on education and administration. When the Swedish rulers were at the height of their power, centralization of the Swedish state led to increasing importance of the Swedish language in the Duchy of Finland. In grammar schools, Swedish started to replace Finnish, and church officials as well as state officials came more and more from Swedish-language backgrounds. Local rulers in the Finnish-speaking areas actually very rarely encouraged the development of a Finnish culture (Singleton, 1989:44).

The dominance of Sweden in the region was increasingly challenged by Russia, which occupied Finland between 1714 and 1721 (the Great Wrath) and in 1742 and 1743 (the Lesser Wrath); in those periods about a quarter of the Finnish population lost their lives. Although most of the Finnish areas were afterwards returned to Sweden, some areas remained under Russian control; Russia had now clearly emerged as a major power in the Baltic. As far as the Swedish influence in Finland is concerned, the effects of these periods of Russian occupation were mixed. On the one hand, despite the circumstances under Russian rule, the experiences with Russian occupation challenged the naturalness of political control by Sweden. On the other hand, the elite in Finland was forced to flee to Sweden, where they became totally accustomed to speaking Swedish (Allardt and Miemois, 1981:8).

As a result of the growing strength of Russia and changing fortunes on the European battlefields, Finland became a Russian possession. Paradoxically, the Swedish-speaking nobility and the better educated did not protest this development too vigorously, because the continuous war efforts of Swedish rulers (often on Finnish territory and with Finnish conscripts) were detrimental to their economic interests (Singleton, 1989:64). They were right in assessing that their position would in fact be maintained after the transfer of Finland to Russian rule (Allardt and Miemois, 1981:21). In contrast, many among the Finnish peasantry wanted to remain with Sweden and put up resistance against the Russians during the war between Sweden and Russia (Klinge, 1993:320). The Finnish Diet – formerly the Finnish section of the Swedish Diet and consisting of four estates (nobility, bourgeoisie, peasants, and clergy) – formally ratified the transfer in 1809. This was only done after Czar Alexander I had assured local rulers of their right to practice their religion and to preserve their traditional privileges.

Finland (including the Åland archipelago on its southwestern coast) became a Grand Duchy. It had substantial autonomy in religious, political and cultural spheres. The Czar installed an Imperial Senate of Finland, consisting of 14 members (20 from 1820 on) who ruled the country and, since the Swedish language was officially the language of government, its proceedings were in Swedish. Indeed, overall the Swedish system of government and the Swedish legal system were maintained. The Russian Governor General formally acted as the Czar's representative and chaired the Senate, but since he did not speak the Swedish language the vice-chairman of the Imperial Senate *de facto* functioned as a prime minister (Singleton, 1989:67). The Finnish Diet was, after their meeting in 1809, only reconvened in 1863. Helsinki, with only 4000 inhabitants at the time, was made the capital of the country in 1812, after an immense fire had destroyed major parts of Turku, the capital until then. Part of the decision to move the capital was inspired by the identification of Turku with the period of Swedish rule; the location of the city was also considered: Turku directly faces the Åland Islands and Stockholm beyond them, while Helsinki is substantially closer to Saint Petersburg (Singleton, 1989:70).

During the nineteenth century the question of Finnish national identity came more to the fore. With it, the language question became a major issue in the cultural and political life of the country. As Alapuro (1982:117) points out, the autonomous Finnish state was founded some decades before the linguistic differences became important, making the struggle not so much a struggle for independence, but a struggle over the cultural character of the new political unit. Moreover, the links between the various geographical units of Finland were still very weak, and much needed to be done in terms of nation-building (Paasi, 1992:83; Alapuro, 1982:123–126). Initially, autonomy under Russian rule gave Finland ample room to manoeuvre, and it was therefore nearly an independent polity in which this conflict was fought (see section 7.3.1). The struggle over the direction of linguistic life in Finland, and of Finnish nationalism itself, produced language parties, including a Swedish language party which later became the Svenska FolksPartiet (Swedish People's Party or SFP). This party proved capable of articulating the demands and desires of the majority of the Swedish-speakers in Finland. Indeed, only the Swedish language party survived the introduction of mass politics, because the Finnish-speakers would later organize themselves on the basis of other concerns. Some of these concerns stemmed from the russification drive under Czar Nicholas II at the end of the nineteenth century; this drive threatened to erode Finland's autonomy and its basic institutions. How this russification drive interacted with the linguistic cleavage will be discussed below.

The political context changed fundamentally in 1906, when a new electoral law was introduced. The law was a spin-off from the political events in Russia itself, where the Czar had been forced to allow his subjects to have a parliament, and it introduced the Finnish masses into the political arena.

Before this law only one-tenth of the population of Finland had had the right to vote, but now the electorate expanded from 125 thousand voters to 1.3 million voters (Allardt and Pesonen, 1967:327). A single-chamber legislature was introduced, the Eduskunta, for which all inhabitants (male and female (!)) over 24 could vote. A system of proportional representation was used, which had the double function of assuring the continuous presence of Swedish-speakers in the parliament, and guaranteeing a sufficiently broad and diverse opposition to the rising tide of Socialism. In the first election which followed, the Socialists gave a very strong performance and gained no less than 80 out of the total of 200 seats. The reasons for their strong rise were found in the increase in poverty which came with industrialization, and the new distinction between Socialists and non-Socialists was to dominate Finnish politics from then on.[2] However, the language issue did not disappear from the political agenda; in 1906, for instance, under influence of the populist Finnish nationalists, 200 to 300 thousand people (out of 2.5 million) changed their name from a Swedish form to a Finnish form, to show their political and cultural allegiance (Klinge, 1993:329–330).

Nevertheless, by far the most important political development was the rise of the Social Democratic Party (Suomen Sosialidemokraattinen Puolue (SSP)). The SSP increased its electoral support further with every election up to 1917, and in 1916 even gained an absolute majority in the Eduskunta. Overall, Finnish support for the SSP had its base in the rural areas (see Alapuro 1981). The Socialists created an extensive network of local organizations to tap this source, and, by the time of the 1907 elections, were well prepared to benefit from the extension of suffrage.[3] Membership in the SSP increased from 16 thousand in 1904 and 45 thousand in 1905 to a maximum of 107 thousand in 1906 (Alapuro, 1981:288). Finally, a major strike in 1905 (following events in Russia) created enough revolutionary atmosphere to lead to a large Socialist victory in the 1907 elections, and in the

---

2   Finland's industrialization occurred mainly through the development of its timber industry, and the industries were located in the rural areas. While landowning peasants profited from this development through the rising prices of forest land, the position of landless peasants worsened. The latter remained tied to the countryside, however, as industrial development elsewhere only occurred very late and on a limited scale (Alapuro, 1981:281–283). Even as late as 1910, for instance, only 12 percent of the labour force was engaged in industry, and nearly half of them lived in rural areas (Alapuro, 1981:277; Alapuro, 1982:133). Nevertheless, when industrial development in the coastal areas slowly gained momentum, migration to the coastal regions followed, firmly linking the proletariat in the cities with the population in the rural areas. At the turn of the century, for instance, nearly two thirds of the population of Helsinki (100,000 people) had been born elsewhere in the country, and most had been part of the rural proletariat (Alapuro, 1981:278).

3   Previously, resistance against the russification policies had resulted in a spur of activity, including petitions involving no less than 500 thousand signatures. In light of these activities, the Russian government allowed the organization of Socialist activities in Finland, precisely because they considered them less dangerous than the separatist tendencies found among the leading Finnish politicians.

subsequent decade of unrest the Socialists succeeded in slowly increasing their support.

The absolute majority which the SSP won in 1916 did not mean that they became the dominant political force in the country. The parliament held little power, because of the Czar's rights to veto legislation and the parliament's lack of executive powers (the old Senate remained in place as the government of Finland). The Eduskunta was regularly dissolved when the Russian Governor General disagreed with it or with one of its representatives; Pehr Evind Svinhufvud, the speaker of the House from 1907 to 1912, was even exiled to Siberia in 1917. All this meant that any hopes of reforms through parliamentary means soon disappeared, increasing the willingness to resort to extra-parliamentary force. The First World War, into which Finland was drawn by its connection with Russia, further destabilized the country. Finland had no army of its own, but many Finns joined the Russian army or worked for the army, only to become jobless in 1917 when Russian military activity stopped. Economic damage caused by the war was also severe, since the markets for the timber-based industry (Western Europe and Great Britain) were in turmoil. On the other hand, the war provided a market for metal-working industries, and some branches of agriculture fared well. Increasing differences in income fed the unrest among the poor (Singleton, 1989:106–108).

Chaos therefore prevailed, both internally and externally. Internally, law and order were difficult to maintain, and the food supply was frequently insecure. Military bands emerged on both sides of the political spectrum; workers' militias organized themselves into the Red Guards, and right-wing civil guards developed into a Security Corps (Singleton, 1989:108–109). Political control was split as well. On the one hand, the SSP held the majority in parliament, and in March 1917 the Socialist Tokoi even became the first Socialist in the world to lead a coalition government. On the other hand, the Socialists were confronted with strong and anxious opposition from Swedish-speakers, the Agrarians, and Finnish nationalists. However, the rivalry between Socialists and non-Socialists was not reflected in their attitudes towards Russia, since both groups were weary of the political turmoil and of the polarizing effects it had on the situation in Finland. Indeed, revolutionary developments in Russia threatened any arrangements which might materialize in Finland itself. In July, 1917, therefore, the Finnish parliament declared itself sovereign, except for military and foreign affairs which were to remain under the control of the Russian government.

The provisional government in Russia did not agree with this development, and it forced new elections for the Eduskunta in October 1917. This was considered illegal by the SSP, but was supported by many of the non-Socialists who hoped that it would cost the Socialists their majority. When they indeed lost their majority, a proportion of the Socialists resorted to extra-parliamentary action and violence. Events now happened in quick succession. On November 14, a Central Revolutionary Council, consisting of the leaders of the SSP and trade union officials, called a general strike that degenerated into rebellion and chaos. The Eduskunta, which had claimed all state power after the 'power vacuum' following the Russian Revolution, agreed on some measures to accommodate the strikers and voted in a new government under the leadership of the conservative P.E. Svinhufvud. On 6 December, 1917, Svinhufvud presented the Eduskunta with a formal declaration of Finnish Independence. On 3 January, 1918, Lenin agreed.

At that time, some 40 thousand Russian soldiers were still quartered in Finland. These troops, by their presence alone, functioned as a rallying point for non-Socialists, because they personified the threat of both revolutionary action and traditional Russian interference in Finnish politics. Their presence united such diverse groups as the Swedish-speaking upper class, the Finnish-speaking middle class, and the Finnish-speaking farmers (Hämäläinen, 1978:13). General Mannerheim, a man with a Swedish background who had fought under the Czar, was put in charge of a new army set up by the right-wing government. He established his headquarters in Vaasa. By then, however, the termination of Russian authority had resulted in the total disappearance of central control, despite the fact that the government of Svinhufvud was still officially leading the country; Red Guards were in control of virtually the whole of southern Finland.

The Civil War officially began on the night of 27–28 January, 1918. A Red Government was set up in Helsinki, under the leadership of Kullervo Manner, while the Svinhufvud government was backed by the Civil Guards under Mannerheim in Vaasa.[4] During three chaotic months the White army proved better organized. It was assisted by the return of Finnish volunteers to the German army (the Jäger Battalion) on 25 February, and by the landing of regular German troops on the coast of Finland in Hanko on 3 April. The German army marched to Helsinki, which it seized on 13 April. Two other main players in the region were not actively involved; bolshevist Russia supported the Reds, but did not assist them in a practical sense during the Civil War, while Sweden attempted to remain neutral, only allowing some private help to reach the White Army. On 16 May, Mannerheim paraded through the streets of Helsinki. During the Civil War 5,500 men

4   It must be pointed out that the SSP did not wholeheartedly step into the Civil War, but was drawn into it by the increasing levels of frustration, resulting from slow progress in the parliamentary game and growing inequality (Arter, 1987:9–10). Indeed, political practices of the SSP before the elections in 1917 had been more or less reformist; they had even participated in a coalition government and were generally satisfied with their good performance in the elections. Moreover, hardly any contacts were made with the revolutionaries in Russia before 1917, and no serious military plans for the revolution existed (Alapuro, 1982:148). Rural support for the revolution was also divided; the industrial and agrarian workers actively supported it, but crofters remained passive since they had already succeeded in achieving some changes in laws on land use and ownership before 1918. Nevertheless, irritation of the SSP increased when they were pushed aside after the election of October 1917, and they were also under pressure from the radical Red Guards. The SSP ultimately rebelled against the White Government's demand to have the Red Guards surrender themselves.

were killed on each side, while a further 2,000 Reds were killed by Vaasa agents. Immediately afterwards, the Whites imprisoned approximately 90,000 Reds, of whom 9,500 died in the camps (Singleton, 1989:112–114). However, the precise numbers are debatable.

When the situation had calmed, Ståhlberg, president from 1919–25, pardoned many of the convicted Reds. Moreover, the Socialists were immediately allowed, albeit under a new and moderate leadership, to participate in the elections again. This indicated a desire for reconciliation by the political leadership of the country. Although at the outbreak of the Civil War there had only been a single Socialist Party, a separate Communist Party was soon set up in Moscow. However, it was illegal in Finland and operated through various front organizations, such as the Social Workers' Party; this party participated in the elections from 1922 onwards, but was ruled out as illegal in 1930. Both Socialist parties were excluded from coalitions until 1937, but the SSP formed a short-lived minority government in 1926–27. However, despite their absence in coalitions, the SSP's support was often needed for the governments to pass laws. Overall, the single most important political dividing line in Finnish politics until the Second World War indeed continued to be the cleavage between Socialists and non-Socialists.

Connected with this cleavage was Finland's position in the international arena. The hostility against and fear of the Soviet Union was strong, because the new state functioned both as the successor of Russia, remembered through its russification drives, and as a reminder of the Civil War. Between the wars, the Finnish government attempted to steer clear of foreign influence, but the vulnerability of the new state remained a great concern. This increasingly became clear during the 1930s, when international tensions rose and the Soviet Union several times suggested building military bases against the Germans on Finnish territory. Many of the Finnish elite were sympathetic to developments in Germany, however, and the Soviet Union was kept at bay.

During the interwar years, after the emotions of the Civil War and discussion on the constitution had subsided somewhat, attention also turned to other issues. First of all, land was redistributed to the landless peasantry under the Lex Kallio in 1922 and the Lex Pulkkinen in 1924. This policy ran into much resistance from the large landowners, some of whom were Swedish-speakers. This fed the second issue, the linguistic struggle, which will be discussed below. Thirdly, extreme right-wing politics entered the political scene at the end of the 1920s with the rise of the Lapua Movement, which was mainly strongly anti-communist and used terrorist tactics to achieve its objectives. It succeeded in having the Communist Party banned in 1930, but when a similar move was attempted against the SSP, it was rejected by the government. An attempted coup failed and the movement collapsed, only to resurface as the People's Patriotic Movement (Isänmaallinen Kansanliike (IKL)) (Poulsen, 1987:161–163). In general, the political scene was very fragmented, with many short-lived governments. The political situation between the wars can be illustrated by the fact that out of twenty (!) governments between 1919 and 1939, only five were based on a majority in parliament and only a single one (between 1937 and 1939) was backed by more than two-thirds of the Eduskunta (Arter, 1987:53). These governments were therefore politically vulnerable to extremism of the right and of the left. Uncertainty also resulted from the weak organization of the political parties; in fact, the electorate was only mildly involved in politics and electoral turnout for parliamentary elections only approached 55% during the 1920s and 1930s (Mackie and Rose, 1991:109–129). In 1937 the SSP was included for the first time in a coalition in an attempt to create a united political front against international threats. Table 7.1 gives the electoral results between 1919 and 1939.

On 30 November, 1939, the Soviet Union invaded Finland. In the months which followed, strong resistance by the Finns proved insufficient and the Peace of Moscow of 12 March, 1940, transferred 10% of Finland's territory to the Soviet Union. However, the rest of the country was not occupied by the Red Army. In an attempt to regain the lost territories Finland fought a 'Continuation War' on the side of Germany; Finnish troops almost reached Leningrad. When the war developed in favour of the Allied Forces, Finland, again under the leadership of Mannerheim, attempted to withdraw from the war and cut off relations with Germany. Subsequent peace negotiations, however, cost Finland the Petsamo region in the north and all of Karelia. Overall, the war caused 85 thousand deaths in Finland, and over 400 thousand refugees came from Karelia (Singleton, 1989:131,139).

Very much aware of the geopolitical situation position of Finland and of the damage caused by the Second World War, President Paasikivi attempted to limit Soviet involvement from 1946 onwards. To placate the big neighbour, the embargo on the Communists was lifted, and their organization, the Democratic League of the People of Finland (Suomen Kansan Demokraattinen Litto (SKDL)) immediately gained a quarter of the seats in the Eduskunta. In 1948 an 'Agreement of Friendship, Co-operation and Mutual Assistance' was signed with the Soviet Union. In the treaty's preamble Finland's neutrality was guaranteed, but the text itself also mentioned Soviet intervention in Finland's territory in case of mutual agreement (Singleton, 1989:145).[5] After the communist take-over in Prague, and amidst accusations of similar coup intentions of the Finnish Communists, the Communists were banned from government (but not from parliament). Relations with the Soviets continued to dominate Finnish politics. The presidents Paasikivi (1946–1956) and Kekkonen (1956–1981) attempted to remain outside the great power conflict and gained support for this strategy

5   How 'mutual' this would have been in reality is of course debatable.

Table 7.1 Electoral results in Finland during the interwar years

	1919	1922	1924	1927	1929	1930	1933	1936	1939
Social Democratic Party	80	53	60	60	59	66	78	83	85
Agrarian Party	42	45	44	52	60	59	53	53	56
National Coalition Party	28	35	38	34	28	42	18	20	25
Swedish People's Party	22	25	23	24	23	20	21	21	18
National Progress Party	26	15	17	10	7	11	11	7	6
Social Workers Party	–	27	18	20	23	–	–	–	–
Patriotic People's Movement	–	–	–	–	–	–	14	14	8
Others	2	–	–	–	–	2	5	2	2
Total	200	200	200	200	200	200	200	200	200

Source: Mackie and Rose, 1991:109–129

from all the parties in the Finnish political spectrum. Soviet influence in Finnish coalition politics showed on several occasions, with the Soviet Union using the Agrarian Party as their main partner in conversation and blocking them from forming coalitions with the right wing National Coalition Party and with the Social Democrats under Väinö Tanner. Other forms of interference were attempted as well. Recent opening of former Soviet archives has clarified, for instance, that Khrushchev deliberately created a crisis in 1961 to bolster the position of President Kekkonen in the upcoming elections of January 1962 (NRC, 31/10/94). In the end, assurances on the part of subsequent presidents that their policy of strict neutrality would be continued was sufficient to prevent any crisis from getting out of hand (Arter, 1987:177,182–184).

The Socialist/non-Socialist cleavage continued to dominate Finnish politics, and voting in parliament after the war mostly occurred on the basis of this distinction (Allardt and Pesonen, 1967:335). Nevertheless, within the Socialist camp, the positions taken were not uniform. Among the Communists, friction emerged over Soviet interventions in Hungary and Czechoslovakia, and the Social Democrats and the Communists differed substantially in policies. The Social Democrats themselves suffered very much from competition by the Communists and were forced to do a balancing act for a long time between radicalism (to compete with the Communists for votes) and reformism (to cooperate with the bourgeois parties against the Communists) (see discussion in Allardt and Pesonen, 1967:344–348). After 1975, support for the Communists dwindled (see table 7.2).

Overall, the party system of Finland has remained stable since World War Two: the conservative National Coalition Party, the liberal National Progressive Party (the Finnish People's Party since 1951 and the Liberal

Table 7.2   Electoral results in Finland since World War 2

	1945	1948	1951	1954	1958	1962	1966	1970	1972	1975	1979	1983	1987	1991	1995
Social Democratic Party	50	54	53	54	48	38	55	52	55	54	52	57	56	48	63
Agrarians/Centre Party	49	56	51	53	48	53	49	36	35	39	36	38	40	55	44
National Coalition Party	28	33	28	24	29	32	26	37	34	35	47	44	53	40	39
Swedish People's Party	14	14	15	13	14	14	12	12	10	10	9	10	12	11	12
Liberal Party (=NPP)	9	5	10	13	8	13	9	8	7	9	4	–	–	1	–
SDKL/Left Wing Alliance	49	38	43	43	50	47	41	36	37	40	35	26	20	19	22
Finnish Rural Party	–	–	–	–	–	–	1	18	18	2	7	17	9	7	1
Christian League	–	–	–	–	–	–	–	1	4	9	9	3	5	8	7
Green League	–	–	–	–	–	–	–	–	–	–	–	–	4	10	9
Others	1	–	–	–	3	3	7	–	–	2	1	5	1	1	3
Total	200	200	200	200	200	200	200	200	200	200	200	200	200	200	200

Source: Statistical Yearbook of Finland

People's Party since 1966), the Social Democrats, the Agrarians (who were renamed Centre Party in 1965 and Finnish Centre in 1988), and the SFP have constantly been represented in parliament. The SFP included a representative from the Åland Islands from 1948–79; from 1979 onwards this representative is found in the category 'others'. New parties have arrived on the scene since the 1970s; first the Rural Party and the Christian League, and in the 1980s the Greens (Pesonen and Rantala, 1985:212–3). Among the Finnish political parties general consensus exists over foreign policy, the constitution, the economic system, and the political system. Allardt and Pesonen (1967:361–363) describe internal cohesion in Finnish politics as consisting of four factors: independence, friendliness towards the Soviet Union, instrumental patriotism (as a goal to achieve social welfare, for instance), and strong local ties (see also Pesonen and Rantala 1985).

The disastrous economic situation after the war, including the obligation to pay war retributions to the Soviet Union, was partially overcome by the opportunities provided by Finland's neutral political position. The Soviet Union became its main trading partner in 1953, and in 1973 treaties were signed with both the European Economic Community and with Comecon (see Hjeppe 1993). Consensus economics, for which the first government of Agrarians and Social Democrats in 1937 had already provided the basis, characterized the Finnish system from the 1950s onwards. Rapid industrialization of the Finnish economy changed the character of Finnish society, leading to large-scale urbanization and to the development of a welfare state after 1960.

The events of 1989 and thereafter have greatly affected Finland. In the economic sphere, trade with the Soviet Union was greatly disrupted and fell from the average level of 25% during the economic boom years of the 1980s to 3% by 1993. The decline was accompanied by an increase in unemployment (up to 20%), which only began stabilizing in 1994. The central economic and political role of the big neighbour, now again called Russia, was acknowledged by the new president Martti Ahtisaari in 1994; it showed, for instance, in his insistence that the inclusion of the Nordic countries in the European Community should not lead to the isolation of Russia in terms of economic and security cooperation. Overall, consensus on the neutral foreign policy remains very important and continues to prevent too much polarization from occurring; this includes polarization on the linguistic issue.

7.1.1 The political system in Finland

Since the creation of the constitution of 1919, the political system of Finland has undergone only limited changes. The constitution established a republican state system (although a monarchy was seriously considered for a while), with an indirectly elected president with substantial competencies, a uni cameral parliament elected on the basis of the electoral laws of 1906, and with very much the same administrative system as before. The old Senate was abolished. The 'Young Finn' K.J. Ståhlberg, the main architect of the constitution, was elected the first president of the republic. In the period up to the Second World War, he was succeeded by the Agrarian L.K. Relander (1925–1931), the Conservative P.E. Svinhufvud (1931–1937), and the Agrarian K. Kallio (1937–1940). During the Second World War the position was taken by R. Ryti (1940–1944) and c.g. Mannerheim (1944–1946).

The president in Finland enjoys wide powers. He leads the country in the field of foreign affairs, can summon or dissolve the parliament and call for new elections, can veto legislation, is commander-in-chief of the armed forces, and nominates the prime-minister. Until recently he was voted into office for six years by an electoral college of 300 members (or 301, including a seat for the representative from the Åland Islands) which was elected by the population; he is now elected directly. Even though the reason the constitution gave him such a strong position was concern over a renewed Socialist-dominated assembly, the presidency became even more important in practical politics during the 1930s when the extreme right threatened the parliamentary system. Its standing further increased after 1944, when a balancing act was needed to establish friendly relations with the Soviet Union (Arter, 1987:40–41). The presidencies of Juho Paasikivi (1946–1956) and Urho Kekkonen (1956–1982) were followed by those of Mauno Koivisto (1982–1994) and Martti Ahtisaari.

An electoral law was passed in 1928 to improve upon the one from 1906. Members of the unicameral parliament are voted in for four years under a system of universal voting rights. The electoral system is proportional, based on 14 multi-member constituencies, each with between 7 and 27 representatives, and, since 1948, one single-member constituency, the Åland Islands. The choice for a proportional system (already made in 1906) was due partly to the existence and political importance of the Swedish-speaking minority (Thibaut, 1990:57). Alliances are a much used method of obtaining votes, especially among the smaller non-Socialist parties. In principle, the system has advantages for larger parties who have a strong regional backing, such as the Agrarians, who have a stronghold among the farmers of the north of Finland (Arter, 1987:57–59). One would also expect the SFP to benefit as well, but the party has generally not been over-represented in the Eduskunta.[6] The Parliamentary Act of 1928 forces parliament to arrive at a broad-based consensus before a decision can be made; qualified majorities (two-thirds) are needed when it comes to changing the constitution or the constitutional laws, but also, for instance, when taking

---

6   In fact, out of 22 elections between 1919 and 1987, the SFP found itself nine times with a larger share of seats than its share in votes, eleven times with less, and two times with exactly the same share (see Mackie and Rose, 1991:109–129).

emergency measures in the economic field (a protective measure against the Socialist parties).

The constitution declared Finland a bilingual state – article 14 establishes Swedish and Finnish as the languages of the republic (see also section 7.3.2). The constitutional guarantees were worked out in various language laws, of which the one passed on 1 July, 1922, was the most important. Citizens have the right to use both languages in courts and in the administration. An important goal in the constitution was formulated in the principle that the state should meet the cultural and economic needs of both groups on identical grounds. The language regulations were extensive. The municipality was made the basic unit, although language regulations were set not only for local administration but for all other administrative bodies as well. A municipality is bilingual if its linguistic minority makes up 10% or more of its population, for which the census provides the numbers; the cities of Vaasa, Helsinki and Turku are bilingual in any case, since they are capitals of provinces where many Swedes live. The internal administrative language of the community is the majority language of the population. The required share of the minority in the population was later lowered to 8%. A bilingual municipality would keep its status until its minority decreased to less than 8% (later 6%), while a former unilingual municipality would remain so unless the minority had increased to 12% (later 10%). Candidates for civil service posts in unilingual municipalities must have complete command of the official language of the commune and be able to understand the other national language, while all candidates for posts in bilingual municipalities should have complete mastery of the majority language and be able to speak and write the minority language. Candidates for judgeships must have speaking knowledge of both national languages (Hämäläinen, 1966:89–90). Requirements for higher officials are somewhat more severe than for officials in lower posts. Citizens in bilingual municipalities have the right to obtain documents and other services in their mother tongue, although this right is restricted in monolingual municipalities (Liebkind, 1984:95–97). The laws on language usage also made arrangements for the central government, the military, and the railways; a solution was found for Church life as well, for which a separate Swedish-language bishopric was founded.

As makes clear this introduction, Swedish-speakers have always played a central role in Finland. The next section contains information on the geographical distribution of the Swedish-speakers, following which the history of the linguistic struggle in Finland will be discussed in section 7.3.

7.2   THE SWEDISH-SPEAKERS IN FINLAND

Small pockets of Swedish-speakers have been living in Finland since the beginning of the Christian Era. More substantial migration of Swedish-

Map 7.1   Living areas of Swedish-speakers in Finland in 1991

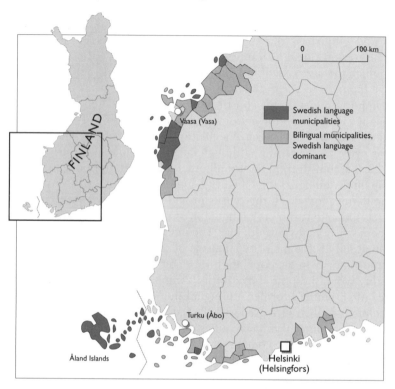

Table 7.3 Number of Swedish-speakers in the Finnish population (1900–1990)

Year	Total population (x1000)	Swedish-speakers (x1000)	Swedish-speakers (%)	voters SFP[1] (%)
1900	2,713	350	12.9	-
1920	3,105	341	11.0	12.2
1930	3,381	343	10.1	10.0
1940	3,696	354	9.6	9.6
1950	4,030	348	8.6	7.7
1960	4,446	331	7.4	6.8
1970	4,598	303	6.6	5.7
1980	4,788	301	6.3	4.2
1990	4,999	297	5.9	5.3

Source: Statistical Yearbook of Finland 1993

Notes:
1   The SFP exists officially since 1907. The percentage of votes indicates the latest results before the year in question.

speakers occurred during the thirteenth century. Swedish nobility successfully attempted to pacify and christianize the Finnish territories, and farmers and fishermen followed in their footsteps (Singleton, 1989:21–22). These settlers mainly colonized the long strip of uninhabited land stretching along the coast of Finland. Over time, the migration of Finnish-speakers from the hinterland reached the coast in the current region of Turku, thus driving a wedge into the settlement area of the Swedish-speakers. From then on, the border between the living areas of the two groups remained remarkably stable over the centuries, although local language shifts often occurred (Allardt and Miemois, 1981:11). The Swede-Finns now live mainly in three separate areas in Finland (see map 7.1): first of all, in the southern province of Uusimaa (Nyland), east and west of Helsinki, and in Helsinki itself; secondly, along the western coast in the province of Vaasa (Vasa), in a region called Ostrobothnia; and thirdly, on the Åland archipelago (Ahvenanmaa in Finnish). According to the 1991 figures, there are now 24 Swedish-speaking municipalities (1 urban against 23 rural) and 41 bilingual municipalities (21 Finnish-dominated, against 20 Swedish-dominated) out of 460 municipalities in all. Of the 24 Swedish-language municipalities, 16 are on the Åland islands where 94.4% of the population (of 25 thousand) is Swedish-speaking, and only eight are found in the rest of the country (of which two are islands adjacent to the Åland Islands). In only two provinces is the proportion of Swedish-speakers over 10% of the population. Just under 50% of the Swedish-speakers still live in Swedish-language or Swedish-dominated municipalities.

As table 7.3 shows, the number of Swedish-speakers has gradually gone down. Until 1940 this decrease was only relative, but since the 1940s the group has also declined in absolute terms; this is reflected in declining support for the SFP. The demographic development will be discussed more extensively in section 7.3.5.

7.3   THE LANGUAGE CLEAVAGE IN FINLAND

For a long time Swedish-speakers in Finland made up the social, economic and political elite in the Finnish territory, the result of six centuries of Swedish domination. Moreover, even under Russian rule, from 1809 until independence in 1917, their position was maintained. Only as late as 1863 was Finnish declared to be an official language in Finland. Nevertheless, notwithstanding this dominant position, the majority of the Swede-Finns made a living as small farmers or fishermen. The two distinct social strata in the Swedish-language community did not have much contact up to the nineteenth century (Allardt and Miemois, 1981:3). Contact came only with the emergence of a strong Swedish-speaking middle class (mainly in the towns of Helsinki (Helsingfors) and Turku (Åbo)) and a Swedish-speaking working class (especially in Helsinki).

Before that, however, during the second half of the eighteenth century, the Swedish language made further headway. Continuing economic and political links with Sweden resulted in a growing command of the Swedish language by the commercial sections of the Finnish populations, by the state officials, and by the nobility. Economic growth stimulated the immigration of traders and burghers from all over the Baltic who used Swedish as their language of communication. Also, most Finns who tried to rise socially adopted the Swedish language, and some even changed their names to Swedish forms (Singleton, 1989:55; Allardt and Miemois, 1981:10). Finnish remained the language of the peasants and the fishermen, and therefore of the mass of people outside the Swedish living areas. As a result, linguistic differences between the elite and the Finnish masses became more accentuated. In the beginning of the nineteenth century, when Russia seized Finland, around 15% of the population spoke Swedish (Singleton, 1989:76; Paasi, 1992:84). As the following sections will show, certainly not all of the developments in Finnish history which were discussed in section 7.1 were experienced in the same way by Finnish-speakers and Swedish-speakers.

7.3.1 The language cleavage under the Grand Duchy

The Finnish situation during the Grand Duchy was beneficial for the Swedish-speakers in the sense that the separate identity of the Duchy consisted not so much in its cultural distinctness, but in its local legal and administrative system; this system remained practically unconnected with the Russian state and was based on the old Swedish institutions (Klinge, 1993:321–322). This is not to say that cultural differences were not relevant. Particularly from the 1840s onwards, a Finnish national movement emerged which published Finnish mythology and history and spread it among the population through plays and books.[7] Surprisingly, however, many nationalist intellectuals, such as J.V. Snellmann, were to a large extent from Swedish homes originally and wrote in Swedish. For Russia, some emphasis on the cultural separateness of Finland from Sweden was politically profitable, and this stimulus produced the interesting effect of slowly creating a Finnish nation under Russian rule, still dominated by a Swedish-speaking elite.

Language, which was potentially very important in distinguishing Finland from Sweden, became more relevant in the middle of the century with large-scale state education and the wider spread of newspapers and books. A new university was set up in Helsinki – the Imperial Alexander University, later University of Helsinki – which became the centre of national culture in Finland (the old university in Turku had burnt down) (Klinge, 1993:324).

7   Most famous in this respect is the national epic Kalevala, compiled by Elias Lönrott.

Students and teachers at the university played a major part in the development of, for instance, a Finnish flag and a Finnish national anthem,
although they were always respectful of the Czar and of Russian rule in general. This development of Finnish separateness in combination with loyalty to
imperial rule was rewarded at the beginning of the 1860s, when Finnish
became the second official language of the Grand Duchy. Parliament was convened, a separate currency was created, and a separate Finnish army was set
up. In 1882 it became obligatory for a public official to use Finnish when a
citizen demanded it (Klinge, 1993:325–326). During the second half of the
nineteenth century all these measures slowly increased the importance of
Finnish in public life.

Nevertheless, the Swedish language was still very much dominant in Finland at the time; in 1870, only 8% of the university students were Finnish-
speakers, and in 1880 less than a third of the grammar schools in Finland
were Finnish-language schools (Singleton, 1989:82). In the same year still
52% of the population of Helsinki (still a small city with 43 thousand
inhabitants) was Swedish-speaking (Allardt and Miemois, 1981:15). This
dominance of the Swedish language did not contradict the development of
Finnish national culture, since much of this culture was based on the traditions and characteristics which had developed under Swedish rule. While
the Finnish language and culture was important in enabling the inclusion
of, for instance, the Finnish peasant in Finnish national culture, the Swedish
language was still the carrier of the older cultural and legal traditions. In
this context, bilingualism often occurred, especially among the clergy
(Klinge, 1993:326–327).

The Finnish nationalist elite slowly changed its language during the last
decades of the nineteenth century, thus extending the language of the common people to the higher culture. The so-called Fennomen, who carried this
change, were convinced that the traditional Swedish-based Finnish culture
could only be maintained in Finland if the Finnish language was used. They
were not intent on creating any social changes; they simply wanted to have
the upper-classes change their language and become linguistically connected
to the majority of the population, not to remove the elite as such (Alapuro,
1982:120). Their promotion of Finnish, however, put an end to the potential Swedinization of Finland (Klinge, 1993:328). Naturally, the Fennomen
encountered resistance. Within the Finnish Diet, some estates favoured a
Swedish-language Finnish culture, while other estates more or less followed
the Fennomen line (Allardt and Pesonen, 1967:327). Thus, the nobility
owed its position to their separate language (from that of the common people), while, in contrast, the peasants wanted promotion of the Finnish language. Less clear was the position of the burghers and of the clergy. The
burghers often depended on the use of Swedish for trade, but the better-educated among them reacted warmly to the finnization movement. The position of members of the fourth estate, the clergy, depended upon whether
their parish was Finnish- or Swedish-speaking; many members of the clergy

were also bilingual (Allardt and Miemois, 1981:24–25). Nevertheless, since most parishes were Finnish-speaking, the majority of the clergy tended to support the Finnish-language movement.

In response to the Fennomen challenge, Swedish-language supporters started to organize themselves. In this way, during the 1860s and 1870s loose groupings developed, making language groups the first party-like organizations to appear in Finland. Swedish-language supporters consisted, on the one hand, of Swedish nationalists who wanted to develop a strong Swedish-language national culture in Finland, but, on the other hand, of Swedish-speaking Liberals, who cared more for the preservation of the political institutions of the Swedish period (Alapuro, 1966:121; Allardt and Pesonen, 1967:121–122). Many among these Liberals also considered Finnish too weak a language for assuring protection against Russian influence. Therefore, as Klinge (1993:329) points out, the majority of the two language-based groupings, the Fennomen and the Svecomen, were not simply opponents, but shared a certain mistrust of Russian rule and a desire to preserve an ethnically, legally and religiously non-Russian Finland.

Differences in strategy became more pronounced, however, with increasing pressure from the Russians. Encroachment on Finnish separateness had already started during the rule of Alexander III (1881–1894), but an especially strong russification drive hit Finland from 1898 onwards, under a new Russian Governor-General Bobrikov. It resulted, among other things, in the service of Finnish conscripts under Russian officers instead of under Finnish officers, and in the abolition of the Finnish autonomy in legislative affairs. Petitions against these measures drew the signatures of over a third of the population of Finland (Singleton, 1989:98). When these Russian policies started to take shape, a new dividing line emerged in the political landscape of Finland (Allardt and Pesonen, 1967:327). On the one side, the so-called Compliers were willing to yield to some of the Russian policies, as long as it did not affect Finland's vital interests; they were afraid of backlashes which might follow strong resistance. A portion of the Fennomen (the so-called Old Finns) held this opinion. On the other side, the Constitutionalists wanted to preserve all rights given to Finland; the Swedish-speaking elite and the other part of the Fennomen (the Young Finns) were found on this side.

Nevertheless, despite these differences, the general character of the elite in Finland remained rather homogeneous during the nineteenth century, even up to independence in 1917. Finland had a special background in the sense that its emergence as a political unit was accompanied by the existence of an elite which was not connected to the dominating political unit, but which had its roots in earlier times. The creation of national unity *vis à vis* Russian encroachment therefore took on a rather unique character. While the Finnish-language supporters sought to strengthen the Finnish character of the territory by means of the development of the majority language, the Swedish-language supporters were attempting to preserve the Finnish character of the territory more by preserving the legal culture and the political institutions which had their origin in the Swedish period. Because the differences in attitude towards the linguistic question were overshadowed by the russification drive and, later, by the increasing importance of the Socialist movement, the Swedish-speaking elite remained an integral part of the Finnish upper class. In the long run, the existence of other issues, and divisions among the Finnish-language supporters themselves, enabled the Swedish-speakers to consolidate their political power. More and more, the Swedish-speaking elite was able to forge closer links between the various social strata of the Swedish-speakers. Their efforts combined rural and urban groups from various social levels, although a main base was found in the growing urban middle class. From 1906 onwards, mass mobilization of Swedish-speakers was to follow.

The last decades of the nineteenth century brought some developments that strengthened the position of Finnish greatly in the national culture and political life of Finland. First of all, the economic advancement of the Finnish-speaking rural population and their increasing political and cultural influence strengthened the finnization movement. Economic development occurred through the development of timber industries in particular, which substantially increased the value of the forest land which was owned by the farmers. Since most farmers were freeholders, this involved large numbers of people who had acquired political influence through the peasant estate in the Diet (Alapuro, 1981:278). Secondly, the establishment of numerous secondary Finnish-language schools created the possibility for educating a new rural strata (Klinge, 1993:328). Interestingly, the energy put out in the fight for secondary schools led to a dense network of schools for both linguistic groups, making Finland one of the best-educated countries of its time and, for instance, greatly stimulating the entrance of women into university education (Allardt and Miemois, 1981:28).[8] Thus, whereas in 1880 only one-third of the 3,500 grammar schools was Finnish-speaking, in 1900 it was already two-thirds of 8,600 schools; similar trends were seen in secondary and university education (Singleton, 1989:82; Paasi, 1992:89).

Most important, however, was the election law of 20 July, 1906. It was a major watershed and completely changed political life in Finland, and thereby the context of linguistic struggles. Not only did it enable the political breakthrough of the Socialist Movement, which in itself was a major change, but it also made the high number of Finnish-speakers on Finnish soil politically relevant. With the law of 1906, therefore, the relative safety of Swedish-speakers came under threat, and tension rose over the new arrangements which had to be created. It became necessary for the Swedish elite to involve all the other groups of Swedish-speakers in the political

8 As Allardt and Miemois argue, it is very hard to avoid the conclusion that the language struggle has had a very stimulating effect on academic life in Finland (Allardt and Miemois, 1981:51). See also further down.

process. After 1906, most Swedish-speakers organized into the SFP, though a minority of Swedish-speakers started to vote for the Socialists.

In the period before 1918, it became clear that Swedish-language support for the Socialists was to remain limited and that the SFP was far more identified with the interests of Swedish-speakers (Allardt and Pesonen, 1981:329). Thus, in 1917, shortly before the outbreak of the Civil War, only 3 out of 24 Swedish-language representatives were Socialists, against 89 out of 176 Finnish representatives (Hämäläinen, 1966:9). The high social status of the Swedish-speaking elite was not the reason for this, because they formed only a small minority of the Swedish-speakers; other differences between Finnish-speakers and Swedish-speakers were much more important (Hämäläinen, 1978:20–28). For instance, when the Civil War broke out, the average Swedish-speaker was slightly better educated than his Finnish counterpart, and even, with the same background, still had somewhat better opportunities. Also, due to a longer tradition, the better-educated Swedish-speakers, who were in any case less prone to accept radical Socialism, wielded more influence among the rest of the Swedish-speakers than did their Finnish counterparts among the ordinary Finns. Moreover, contacts with the Social-Democrats in Sweden had a moderating effect on Swede-Finns who were interested in social changes. A final point is that the relative conservatism of the Swedish-speakers was not unique in the region where many of them lived. Ostrobothnia, the home base of White resistance under Mannerheim, was known to be rather conservative, and its population, Finnish- and Swedish-speaking alike, was focused more on protection of an agrarian way of life than on revolutionary change (Alapuro, 1982:148). They felt compelled to defend the Finnish nation against the threat of bolshevism as embodied by the Russian troops still in the country.

In summary, during the Grand Duchy, the Swedish-language dominance in the upper-classes was slowly eroded, although the Swedish language elite remained an integral part of the Finnish elite. Nationalist ideology convinced parts of the Finnish-speakers that a linguistic linkage between the higher classes and the majority of the population was a necessary condition for the continued existence of Finland as a separate national entity. On the other hand, others put more emphasis on the separate political institutions and legal traditions of which the Swedish language was the carrier. A shared sentiment regarding Finnish national culture and a shared uneasiness with Russian political dominance bridged the linguistic divide, particularly as russification policies were launched. Because of the system of political representation in the Diet, and the fact that the Swedish elite did not belong to the dominating political power but rather represented Finland's separate identity, Swedish language supporters had a considerable influence on political life in Finland. However, with economic growth in the rural areas, increase in education and, especially, the electoral law of 1906, the numerical weight of the ordinary Finnish-speaking population became more and more important. The need for stronger organization of the Swedish-speaking community benefitted the SFP in particular, since this was considered to best reflect Swedish-language interests. Nevertheless, a minority among the Swede-Finns voted for the Socialists.

7.3.2 The Civil War and the linguistic strife

As the Finnish Civil War unfolded, the support from Swedish-speakers for the Red government remained low, which is understandable given their general background.[9] Less obvious was the fact that the Red government developed very moderate policies towards the Swede-Finns, as the Red government and administration therefore was almost completely a Finnish affair; this entailed a complete turn-around of the linguistic character of the administration in Red Finland, both at the 'national' and at the local level (Hämäläinen, 1978:45-53). Nevertheless, even under a Red Government monopolized by Finnish-speakers, such policies as the destruction or dispossession of large manor houses owned by Swede-Finns remained limited. The reason for this moderate behaviour may have been that Swedish-speaking White Guards in the Red areas had been relatively quick to surrender to the Red Army (Hämäläinen, 1978:62). Also, the fact that Sweden had shown its willingness to come to the aid of the Swedish-speakers by intervening on the Åland Islands to restore law and order might have caused the Reds to behave with prudence (Hämäläinen, 1978:69) (see also section 7.3.3.1). Indeed, it is doubtful whether anti-Swedish resentment existed at the popular level in the Red Army at all (Hämäläinen, 1978:107). Overall, this moderateness was important for the Swede-Finns, because, although the White Army had its stronghold in the Swedish-speaking areas in the northwest, at the start of the conflict two-thirds of the Swedish-speakers lived in the regions controlled by the Reds (Hämäläinen, 1978:9).

Since objectively speaking the Reds did not do much to alienate the Swedish-speakers, the relatively large support for the Whites by the Swedish-speakers can therefore be better explained by the psychological effect of the changes which had taken place in the previous decades. For instance, because the Swedish-speaking elite had initially been reluctant to grant the Finnish-speaking masses more political rights, they feared the revenge of these 'angry masses'. Some of them saw the Civil War as a linguistic conflict in disguise, and were certainly not put at ease by the fact that some of the Finnish-speakers, even among the Whites, argued that the privileges of Swedish-speakers were precisely the main cause of the Civil War and of its violent character (Hämäläinen, 1978:93). Indeed, not only the

---

9   The Socialists had not until then countered this limited support among Swedish-speakers with an anti-Swedish attitude. After all, besides ideological motivations, they also needed the Swedish-speakers' votes to arrive at a majority in parliament. There even existed a separate Swedish language section within the party (Hämäläinen, 1978:36).

elite, but Swedish-speakers all over Finland had experienced a shift in position. The increasing importance of Finnish-speakers in the political process, the more virulent nationalism which was sometimes voiced, and uncertainty about the new situation were reasons to intensify organization on the basis of language and opt for a status quo.

As a result, the importance of Swedish-speakers to the Whites was far greater than for the Reds (although the majority of people fighting in the Civil War were Finnish-speaking on both sides). In the White Army there were not sufficient Finnish-speaking officers to lead the troops, since most Finnish-speaking political leaders had been captured by the Reds. Swedish thus became the language of communication at the staff level of the White Army, and General Mannerheim, a Swedish-speaker who only much later was able to command sufficient Finnish to appear as a true national figure, was too successful on the battlefield to be dislodged. There was nevertheless some language-based criticism on the internal situation in the White Army, which Mannerheim tried to counter by formulating language regulations (Hämäläinen, 1978:80). Linguistic tensions among the Whites continued under the surface and grew in intensity as the war drew to a close.

At the end of the day, the fact that the Whites won the Civil War helped to create the linguistic arrangements which were agreed upon in later years. The Swedish-speakers were still among the new Finnish leadership and could influence the new constitution and linguistic rights. This would not have been the case under a Red government. Moreover, the revolutionary challenge to the position of the elite of the country, both Swedish-speaking and Finnish-speaking, definitely strengthened the elite's cohesion, despite any language-based irritation which remained.

7.3.3 Linguistic strife over the constitution

After the Civil War, discussions were started about the constitutional form of the new political entity. Naturally, one of the main concerns was the position of the main languages in the constitution. During the Civil War a basic difference between the Reds and the Whites had already come forward in this respect. The Reds desired guarantees against the oppression of a linguistic minority, but did not mention the Swedish minority in particular, while the preamble of the proposal referred to the fact that 'oppression by half-alien noble lords would no longer be tolerated by the workers of Finland'. The Whites, on the other hand, spoke specifically of the Swedish minority (Hämäläinen, 1978:60–61).

On the Swedish side, concern rose over the influx of Finnish-speakers in Swedish-speaking areas, especially in Uusimaa (Nyland) in the south of the country; despite the official Red policies some Swedish landowners were killed during the Civil War, and their land was to be sold. Swedish leaders were also worried by the low birth rate, which resulted in part from the high percentage of Swede-Finns living in cities.[10] They therefore mainly had defensive demands: protection of the Swedish character of their living areas, continuation of state support for Swedish language schools in Finnish living areas, and creation of Swedish language units in the Finnish army under Swedish-speaking officers. Both Swedish and Finnish should be made the official languages of the republic. However, not all Swede-Finns considered this sufficient. As early as 1917 self-rule of Swedish-language areas was put forward by some Swedish-speakers as a necessary guarantee. These more radical Swedish-speakers were inspired by the events on the Åland Islands, where inhabitants had voiced their desire to secede from Finland and achieve (re)union with Sweden (see below). Differences also emerged between Swedish-speakers in Ostrobothnia, some of whom saw separatism as a means of pressuring the Finns for more concessions, and Swede-Finns in Uusimaa, who did not consider separatism an option at all, given the mixed character of their region (Hämäläinen, 1966:56). Overall, within the SFP separatism gained only limited popularity. Nevertheless, even tentative discussions on self-rule in the Swedish-language provinces of the west were condemned by Finnish-speakers for weakening the country and for being a cover for separatism.

Indeed, irritation mounted on the Finnish side as a result of the argument by the Swedish politicians that they had been responsible for preventing a Red take-over, both before (in parliament) and during the Civil War (in the army). The Finns were also angered by the fact that some Swedish-speakers pointed out that whenever the Finns had to put up resistance or mobilized the population against injustice they were led by Swedish-speakers – be it during the start of the national movement, against russification, or during the fight against Socialism (Hämäläinen, 1966:10–16). In some Finnish parties more outspoken anti-Swedish nationalism mounted.

In June, 1918, a government proposal was issued on the language sections in the new constitution. According to the proposal citizens could use both Finnish and Swedish in dealing with courts and administrative authorities, could get official documents in those languages if it did not cause "great difficulty," and the state would provide for the economic and cultural needs of both groups on the basis of identical principles. The proposal also called for the drawing of administrative borders to separate Finnish-language and Swedish-language areas as much as possible, and for the creation of separate language units in the army (Hämäläinen, 1966:41–42). Finnish nationalists bitterly resisted the proposals, arguing that it would create a Swedish state within a Finnish state. Swedish-speakers on the other hand, although generally satisfied with the proposal, complained that

---

10   In 1910, 32.2% of the Swedish-speakers lived in cities, against 12.2% of the Finnish-speakers (Hämäläinen, 1966:7). Indeed, in 1900 43% of the population of Helsinki was Swedish-speaking, and in 1930 this figure was still 29% (Allardt and Miemois, 1981:15).

Swedish was not made an official language of the state. Moreover, as radical Swede-Finns pointed out, neither did the proposal allow for self-rule in Swedish-speaking administrative areas.

The discussion continued until the election of March, 1919. The election of a large number of Social Democrats, who still held a rather conciliatory attitude towards the language issue, reduced fears among the Swede-Finns. Nevertheless, in May 1919, a Swedish Assembly (the Folkting) was called into life, which functioned outside the SFP and was intended to represent all Swedish-speakers in Finland. Allardt and Miemois (1981:41) note that its success shows that it apparently had broader support and more political skill than the SFP representatives in the Eduskunta. A new government proposal contained further concessions to the Swedish-speakers, by making Swedish a national language, and by providing further guarantees regarding the availability of official documents in the Swedish language. This new proposal may have been inspired by the proven ability of the Swedish-speakers to organize themselves, not only in a political party, but outside the parliament as well. However, also of importance was the need to placate the international powers, in particular the Peace Congress which was to make a decision on the Åland question. Despite the new proposals, representatives of the SFP in the government resigned from office, since they considered the guarantees for self-rule too limited (Hämäläinen, 1966:82–83).

The constitution was passed shortly thereafter, however, and Finland was made a bilingual state. As mentioned in section 7.1.2, both Finnish and Swedish became the languages of the republic, and citizens were to have the right to use both languages in courts and in the administration. An important goal in the constitution was formulated in the principle that the state should meet the cultural and economic needs of both groups on identical grounds (Allardt and Miemois, 1981:48). This point resulted in many differences in interpretation, and the discussion therefore continued because language laws had to be created which would implement the constitutional principles. Moreover, both Swedish-speakers and Finnish nationalists had reasons to be dissatisfied with the way things were developing. The Folkting continued to pressure for more concessions, for instance proposing a federation of four Swedish-speaking provinces ("Swedish-Finland"), including Åland. They also sent representatives to the League of Nations to postpone a decision on the Åland Islands until a satisfactory situation was created on the Finnish mainland, and proposed an 'ombudsman' for Swedish Affairs who would be affiliated with the cabinet (Hämäläinen, 1966:85–87). The Language Law of 1 June, 1922, implemented the constitution in such a way that it satisfied the majority of the Swedish-speakers.

7.3.3.1 The Åland Question

The Åland question interfered with the discussions on the new constitution. With the emergence of Finland as an independent state, the status of the islands became disputed. In 1809, the islands came under the control of Russia, together with the rest of Finland, and in 1856 they were demilitarized following the Crimean War. This situation was challenged around 1907, when the Russian government attempted to put an end to the 'servitude' of the islands and to fortify them. Naturally, these attempts raised suspicion and unrest in Sweden, since the islands offered strategic control over the Baltic (Barros, 1968:12–16). Although a crisis was averted, a similar situation arose shortly before the First World War; this time Russia put a regiment on the islands and built fortifications to counterbalance rising German influence in the region. After this experience, Sweden strongly desired control over the islands.

Their claim was reinforced when an assembly on the Åland Islands expressed its desire for unification with Sweden on 20 August, 1917. It was followed several months later by a plebiscite which generated the same result, and on 2 February, 1918, representatives of the Åland Islands thus offered King Gustav a petition with a request for unification (Barros, 1968:62,69). However, rapid changes in Finland complicated the issue. To begin with, the recognition of Finnish independence by Sweden turned the question into a Swedish-Finnish problem. Secondly, the outbreak of the Civil War caused some clashes on the islands in which the Russian garrison was involved, leading to military intervention on the part of Sweden to pacify the situation and protect the population. The Swedish action raised suspicions both among the Reds and the Whites, who suspected expansionist schemes behind the Kingdom's moves. As noted, Sweden did not support either of the two sides in the Civil War (Barros, 1968:79–84). In the end, with permission of the White government, German troops landed on the islands in March, 1918 (Hämäläinen, 1966:48).

Irritation over Sweden's actions spanned all parties; moreover, all accused the Åland islanders of letting the rest of Finland down at a time of crisis (Barros, 1968:91). For the Swedish-speakers, some additional arguments were important. Swedish leaders (including Mannerheim) worried that the islands' secession would numerically weaken the Swedish element in Finland. The events also put conciliatory leaders in an awkward position, as they were now vulnerable to accusations of separatism. In November, 1918, the SFP leaders thus sent a note to the Åland leaders, asking them to abstain from further attempts at separation (Hämäläinen, 1966:53). Their anger was also directed at Sweden, which they accused of misusing the international situation and the situation in Finland to obtain the islands and satisfy its 'expansionist desires'. The Swedish-speaking leaders saw greater autonomy as the best solution for the islands, with a system of common defence by Sweden and Finland (Hämäläinen, 1966:52–53). This proposal was unacceptable to Sweden, because of its policy of neutrality (Barros, 1968:110). In the end a diplomatic struggle was started which lasted for three years.

In April, 1918, the White government and Sweden reached an agreement on the withdrawal of Swedish troops after fortifications on the islands had been demolished. Sweden wanted the Peace Conference in Paris to decide, on the basis of the principle of self-determination, that the Åland islanders could themselves vote for union with Sweden. The Finnish government, on the other hand, held the opinion that, by recognizing Finland, Sweden had also recognized Finland's territorial demarcations.[11] The Finnish government made clear that the Swedish-speakers in Finland themselves wanted to keep the islands, thus challenging the ethnic argument underlying the principle of self-determination (Barros, 1968:142). The government also argued that they were ready to provide some form of autonomy and that under the circumstances they had not been given a chance to show their good will. Sweden nevertheless appeared to gain the upper-hand in the dispute.

The Åland islanders, who had themselves turned to the Peace Conference in January, 1919, organized another plebiscite in June which showed that 95% of the participants wanted secession and unification with Sweden (only a third of the population voted, however) (Barros, 1968:152). The Peace Conference, after extended deliberations, decided not to make a decision on the issue, but rather forwarded it to the League of Nations. In the same month the Baltic Commission of the League of Nations commenced studying the situation. With the progress of time and the continuation of the deliberations, the position of Finland improved. Its strategic position in the Baltic and its active role as a 'barrier to bolshevism' (compared to Sweden's passive neutrality, even during the Finnish Civil War) was looked upon favourably by the Allies. Finland also countered the claims by offering substantial autonomy for the islands in February, 1920; the offer was rejected by the population on the islands (Barros, 1968:216). Tensions rose when a delegation from the Åland Islands went to the Supreme Council of the League of Nations to press their point in June, 1920; they were arrested upon return to Finland, and a Finnish military unit was dispatched to the islands.

The League of Nations considered itself competent on the issue in the summer of 1920. A separate Åland commission was set up which consisted of a Belgian representative, a Swiss and an American. This composition of the commission proved very much to the advantage of Finland. The first two, because of their country's experiences, were not inclined to follow the principle of self-determination very strictly, while all three members shared an appreciation of Finland as an important barrier to bolshevism (Barros,

11   An interesting complication in this respect was the fact that at the same time Finland attempted to obtain Eastern Karelia, also on the basis of the principle of self-determination.

1968:310–312). Finally, in April 1921, the commission decided to assign the Åland Islands to Finland; they mentioned reasons concerning geography, the political-administrative history, and the small population involved (Barros, 1968:313–318). Autonomy for the islands, however, had to include education at the lower level and at a technical school exclusively in Swedish, the right of pre-emption when buying land, electoral rights only after five years of residency on the islands, and several candidates to choose from when a new governor for the islands was to be appointed. The commission also advised that there should be complete military neutrality for the islands. In June, 1921, a definite agreement was reached, which was grudgingly accepted by Sweden. In the Autonomy Act of 1922, the principles were confirmed, and they were modernized and updated in the later Acts of 1951 and 1991.

The effect of the Åland question on the general relationship between Finnish-speakers and Swedish-speakers in Finland was mixed. As has been said, on the one hand, the Swede-Finns were treated with more suspicion and accused of latent separatism. Indeed, some of the Swedes, especially in Ostrobothnia, were in fact inspired by the actions of the Åland islanders and, to a limited extent, separatism (called *Åland's disease* by some Finnish nationalists) indeed infected parts of Swedish-speaking Finland. At the very least they thought they could use the situation to put pressure on the Finnish government. On the other hand, however, the majority of the Swedish-speakers had themselves been angered by the developments on the Åland Islands and by the actions of Sweden. Most leading Finnish politicians were reassured by this. Ultimately, the Finnish government had to manoeuvre very carefully under all this international attention, especially where the linguistic rights of Swedish-speakers in general were concerned. Therefore, overall, the Åland question stimulated the satisfactory arrangement of both the constitutional question and of linguistic rights.

7.3.3.2 Time of storm: conclusion

Chaos prevailed during the decades leading to Finnish independence. The parliament which had been installed in 1906 clearly showed the political preferences of the population, even though it did not exercise much power at the time. The existence of other sources of authority – the old Senate as the government, and the Russian government as the ultimate authority – created a complex political situation. What was clear was the fact that the increasing strength of the Social Democrats did not come from Swedish-speaking areas, even though the Social Democrats were not hostile to Swedish-speakers or even particularly interested in the linguistic problem. The old Fennomen movement initially (around 1906) succeeded in mobilizing middle-class Finnish-speakers on a nationalistic platform, but their attempts were undermined by the enormous changes in the political landscape and by the social unrest that lay at the base of this. In this turmoil, a Swedish-language party was created which succeeded in mobilizing the Swedish-speaking population at large.

In this period, the relative importance of the three cleavages in Finnish politics were changed. The linguistic struggle between Swedish-speakers and Finnish-speakers lost ground to the struggle for social reform and to the struggle against political and linguistic russification. As a result, the Finnish Party (Old Finns) and the Young Finnish Party became more and more obsolete, and at the end of this period they were succeeded by the conservative National Coalition Party and the centre-based National Progressive Party, respectively. The elite in Finland, still consisting of both Swedish- and Finnish-speakers, initially remained united against Russian policies, because Finnish separateness had Swedish roots as well. Later, they were forced to remain united against the threat of Socialism, of which the Civil War was the ultimate consequence. The fact that the Swedes were most active on the side which won the Civil War guaranteed their continuing influence in the years that followed.

The new electoral laws nevertheless definitely shifted the balance of power to Finnish-speakers. In order to defend their position, the Swede-Finns put much emphasis on the new constitution and on linguistic rights. The international context, which centred on the Åland question, was influential in assuring a decision which satisfied most Swede-Finns. Overall, the chaos during this period caused a strong sense of uncertainty among Swedish-speakers in Finland, which substantiated their complete and thorough mobilization into the SFP.

7.3.4 Linguistic strife in the 1920s and 1930s

The constitution and the language laws had been the result of much deliberation. The arrangements, and the assurances provided by the laws, nevertheless were challenged during the 1920s and 1930s. Increasing tension even led to the exclusion of the SFP from government coalitions between 1924 and 1930.[12] However, the existence of the laws and the difficulties of changing constitutional laws in Finland provided handles for Swedish-speakers to counter these challenges. Although constitutional guarantees and the solution of the Åland question had made the Swede-Finns more confident of their position in the new state, they now changed tactics by focusing more on getting as much as possible out of the existing legislation (Hämäläinen, 1966:95). The legislative arrangements enabled them to set up separate institutions in all fields of life, financed by both private and state funds.

---

12   This did not mean that no Swedish-speakers participated, since they were sometimes appointed on an individual basis by the President, for instance in 1927.

One group among the Finns, the so-called *aitosuomalaisuus*, felt that the constitutional arrangements and the language laws were unduly advantageous to the Swedish-speakers. They deplored what they considered the general weakness of nationalism in Finland (Hämäläinen, 1966:115). Thus, they argued that although Finland was officially considered one nation with two languages, both language groups promoted their own candidates in cases where the mother language was not supposed to matter as long as a candidate could speak the language. In practice, the over-representation of Swedish-speakers in higher positions thus benefitted the Swedish-speakers, for instance at the university of Helsinki (Hämäläinen, 1966:117–118). The nationalist Finns, further wanted to make Swedish a voluntary language at primary schools, thus reducing the number of bilingual people and making the language regulations obsolete and impractical in the long run. They focused on other issues as well: state support for Swedish schools, priority to the education of Finnish speakers, and no Swedish-speakers in the diplomatic service and in the army (Hämäläinen, 1966:121–125). Their ultimate goal was to make Swedish a minority language instead of a national language, and to have the Swedish-speakers be considered as a Swedish minority instead of as a Swedish-speaking part of the Finnish nation, which had been the dominant philosophy until then. An often-used argument by the Finnish nationalists was that they only wanted to limit the privileges of the Swedish-speaking upper class, while the masses could go on and live their life in 'linguistic peace' (Hämäläinen, 1966:261).

Success for the *aitosuomalaisuus* was found especially among students and among people with rural backgrounds who knew little or nothing of the Swedish language. The first group was confronted with a lack of jobs, since most jobs within the new state had been filled immediately after independence; career-opportunities in the Swedish-dominated business sector were limited.[13] This situation was worsened by the economic depression. Through the network of the Academic Karelia Society – a politico-cultural society which wanted unification of Eastern Karelia with Finland and desired a culturally homogeneous Finland to achieve that objective – the *aitosuomalaisuus* gained influence in the official political parties. In this way the language debate was reintroduced in parliament, where the Agrarians and the National Coalition Party were particularly influenced by the nationalists. In response, the SFP attempted to find support among the other parties. Thus, they sided more with the Social Democrats, for instance by supporting their minority government in 1926–1927 (Arter, 1987:15); this indicated a considerable turn in policy for the SFP, as its leaders had generally belonged to the most conservative part of the country. For the same reason, the SFP turned some years later to the Lapua movement and the IKL

---

13 Swedish-speakers, for similar reasons, studied far more business than other disciplines (Hämäläinen, 1966:140).

when need arose. Lapua held a neutral stance on the language issue, and its anti-communism campaign could count on support from numerous Swede-Finns. The parties which were supported by the SFP also had their own objectives. The SSP was interested in cooperation with the SFP, because of the importance of the Social Democrats in Sweden and because of the vulnerable position of the Left in Finland after the Civil War. Lapua needed the support of the SFP to achieve their main objective, the banning of the Communist Party; it indeed received that support in the end. Needless to say, this last switch of the SFP harmed relations with the Social Democrats and resulted in much internal infighting over the political direction of the party (Hämäläinen, 1966:182–184, 214–216). Apparently, most parliamentarians in the SFP during the interwar years put the linguistic position of the Swedes before any other political consideration.

In particular education became a heated issue during the 1920s and 1930s. The Swedish-speakers had gained control over their education through a separate Swedish School Department within the Board of Schools in 1920. The subsequent struggle first of all concerned the University of Helsinki, for which a law was passed in 1923. The law stipulated that the amount of teaching by each department of the state university should correspond to the proportion of Finnish-speaking and Swedish-speaking students in the department during the previous years. There should be instruction in both languages in beginners courses, unless the number of students belonging to one language group was very small, and at least fifteen professors should lecture in Swedish at all times. Students should be examined in their own language. Overall, from the end of the nineteenth century onwards, the number of Finnish-speaking students had grown rapidly and the law on the university therefore was to the disadvantage of Swedish-speakers, who had remained the majority of the teaching corps.

The law and its implementation were very much disputed. Helsinki University was the only state-financed university, and was therefore important as a symbol of the general linguistic situation in the state.[14] Another reason for the tension was the fact many students were active in the Finnish nationalist movement, and were sometimes provoked by certain Swedish teachers who held degrading views of Finns and Finnish culture (Hämäläinen, 1966:229,242). Student bodies, dominated by the Academic Karelia Society, wanted complete finnization of the university and a separate section for the Swedish-speakers. On several occasions riots broke out in the streets of Helsinki, and the students even organized 'citizens meetings' throughout the country to mobilize mass support. The nationalist proposals nevertheless failed to obtain sufficient support in parliament. The stalemate continued until 1937, because government compromises were also rejected.

---

14 Since 1917, there also was a privately financed Swedish-language academy in Turku (Åbo).

A second educational concern was the number and linguistic character of secondary schools. Finnish nationalists pointed to the fact that there were relatively more Swedish-speaking pupils at the schools. Thus, in 1920–21 28.4% of the secondary schools were Swedish-language schools, and in 1930–31 still 20.3%. During the same years, 28% and 18.9% of the pupils in secondary schools were Swede-Finns (Hämäläinen, 1966:120). The number of Swedish-language pupils was thus much higher than the proportion of Swedish-speakers in the country (see table 7.3). There were also arguments that too much state subsidy was pumped into the Swedish schools; as Hämäläinen (1966:288) shows, Swedish pupils at a state secondary school cost, per head, in the period 1920–1938, up to 40% more, while state subsidy for Swedish pupils at private schools could be up to 15% more than for Finnish pupils (Hämäläinen, 1966:195, 233). Furthermore, proposals in parliament and petitions to the government alleged that Finnish schools were not allowed in Swedish-language regions, because, as Finnish nationalists argued, economic pressure was put on Finnish-speakers – by which they meant that Finnish-speakers could lose their job with Swedish-language employers if they pressed the issue. In 1931, they succeeded in passing a law which demanded Finnish schools in Swedish-language areas. A main target of the Finnish nationalists was the Swedish Board of Schools, whose position was under regular attack. In 1929, for instance, this resulted in a substantial reduction of its autonomy (Hämäläinen, 1966:205–207).[15]

Mutual irritation over the linguistic character of the educational system only ended when the influence of the *aitosuomalaisuus* disappeared. The decline of the Finnish nationalist movement particularly resulted from external threats. The felt need for a coalition across the political spectrum materialized in 1937 when a government of Social Democrats and Agrarians was forged. Besides including the left in a coalition for the first time, it also weakened the nationalists among the Agrarians. Several important politicians concluded that the issue had to be resolved in a satisfactory way to enable cooperation with the rest of Scandinavia and thus strengthen the position of Finland in the international arena (Hämäläinen, 1966:298–300). A government proposal was finally agreed upon, in which Helsinki University remained bilingual, with Finnish as its administrative language, 15 professorships for Swedish-speakers, and the right to take examinations in both languages. Despite a final petition against the proposal by 300 thousand Finns, the compromise was passed (Hämäläinen, 1966:304–306; Allardt and Miemois, 1981:51–52). Further settlement and specification were reached after the Second World War.

---

15 A further side argument concerned the cultural and educational position of the Finnish minority in Sweden, which the nationalists said wasn't even half as good as the position of the Swedish minority in Finland.

As pointed out, the interwar years were a tense period for Finland in many respects: narrow-based government coalitions, extremism both on the left and on the right, and an uncertain international position with a particularly tense relation with the Soviet Union. In this political context, linguistic strife was important enough to linger on, but it was never so important as to escalate beyond control. The linguistic arrangements that had been decided upon in the first years after the Civil War proved their worth, even though they came under constant attack by the *aitosuomalaisuus* movement in the fifteen years which followed. This nationalist movement never became enough of a mass movement to achieve all of its objectives, but could still muster enough support to worry the Swedish-speaking leaders. However, the political strategy of the SFP provided the Swedish-speakers with enough support to block most new legislation. In this respect it was crucial that linguistic rights were anchored in the constitution, making special majorities necessary for changing them. In general, the various governments also refrained from pushing nationalist demands, partly because of their need for support from the Swede-Finns, who actually withdrew their support on several occasions when they thought insufficient action was being undertaken to protect their interests. An equally moderate attitude was taken by the various presidents who were concerned with the stability of the political centre in Finland, and who wanted to keep extremists on the Right and the Left at bay.

In the end, settlement was made easier by two structural developments in Finland itself. First of all, the number of Swedish-speakers remained constant between 1900 and 1940, while the number of Finnish-speakers increased by 41.4% (see table 7.3). It greatly decreased the proportion of Swede-Finns and had a clear psychological effect on the Finnish-speakers. Secondly, and partially related to this, the Finnish-language element was now clearly decisive in all aspects of public life in Finland by the 1930s, even though Swedish-speakers still enjoyed relative over-representation in such sectors as business and academic life (Allardt and Miemois, 1981:52). Nevertheless, the slow shift in position pressed the Swede-Finns to organize effectively. Table 7.3 shows that, in contrast to later years, the share of votes for the SFP during this period is larger than, or practically equal to, their share in the population. Given the fact that at least a proportion of Swedish-speakers must have voted for the Social Democrats, this indicates that the Swede-Finns had a stronger voting discipline, probably as a result of the linguistic struggle. Also of importance could have been the fact that there were relatively more Swede-Finns of voting age, due to the demographic composition of the group.

7.3.5 Stability and consensus: the Swedish-speakers after World War 2

The Second World War was a turning point in relations between Finnish-speakers and Swedish-speakers. During the war the loyalty of the Swede-Finns was unequivocally with the Finnish state, and only little friction occurred. For a short period, the immigration of Karelian refugees caused tension in various Swedish communities, and was considered so threatening that after more than 20 years the Swedish Assembly was convened again (Allardt and Miemois, 1981:50). However, after the Continuation War, when immigration restarted, the government made sure that the influx of over 400 thousand refugees from Eastern Karelia did not disturb the local linguistic balances. In 1947, a new law for the university further specified the position of Swedish-language higher education, and President Paasakivi's general conciliatory attitude plus the economic situation made the linguistic struggle disappear into the background. Moreover, the fragile geopolitical situation made Finland look to the rest of Scandinavia even more for closer cooperation (Hämäläinen, 1966:308–309). Overall, therefore, the language conflict practically disappeared with the Winter War.

Swedish-speakers have continued to be represented by the SFP, which has generally received 75 to 80% of the votes of Swedish-speakers; Swedish-speakers make up 85% of the electorate of the SFP, while the remaining 15% come from bilingual or Finnish-speaking homes (Liebkind, 1984:103; Pesonen and Rantala, 1985:221). On the dominant Socialist/non-Socialist divide it has generally been found slightly right of centre and is seen by non-members as conservative (Allardt and Pesonen, 1967:341). Indeed, as Liebkind (1984:113) commented, there emerged an implicit conception that one had to be non-Socialist in order to be a good member of the Swedish-speaking minority. The SFP has been a steady coalition partner: it has participated in 24 of the 40 coalitions between 1945 and 1987, and received 9.3% of ministerial portfolios over the same period (Arter, 1987:69). They therefore have had substantial influence, in particular in fields of policy which are of interest to the Swedish minority: language, education, financial aid, justice, etc. (Pentikaeinen et al., 1985:85). The extent of the political integration of the Swedish-speakers was displayed in the presidential election of 1994, which was decided for the first time by a direct vote of the population. The presidential candidate from the SFP, Elizabeth Rehn (a former Minister of Defence), made it into the final round and was only defeated by a small margin by the candidate from the Social Democrats who won the election, Martti Ahtisaari. This showed her popularity among Finnish-speakers as well as Swedish-speakers, and is a clear indication of the level of integration of the ethnonational group in Finnish society.

Because of the broad political base of the electorate, however, tensions between various social groupings have always been present in the SFP. As Allardt and Pesonen (1967:335) show, between 1948 and 1951, the SFP was (out of the six main parties in the Eduskunta) the party with the least voting discipline, in particular on issues which tended to divide rural and urban representatives and on industrial-agricultural questions. Moreover, a small proportion of the Swedish-speakers has continued to vote for left-wing parties. This has mainly benefitted the SSP, where a separate Swedish federation has been created. Separate Swedish-speaking organizations also exist within the Communist Party and the National Coalition Party (Pentikaeinen et al., 1985:85; Allardt and Miemois, 1981:41). Generally, three to five representatives of the Social Democrats have been Swedish-speakers, while the SDKL has also generally had Swedish representatives (Allardt and Miemois, 1981:42). Indeed, traditionally workers have been the most bilingual group among the Swedish-speakers and have been most vulnerable to assimilation through marriage. This tendency has the interesting effect of underlining the still-existing image of Swedish-speakers as upper-class (Liebkind, 1984:115). Regarding this 'elitist' conception, however, recent research on the elite in Finland shows that Swedish-speakers are at best only marginally over-represented, including the economic elite (Ruostetsaari 1993; Allardt and Miemois, 1981:40 – 42). Overall, their social structure hardly differs from that of the Finnish-speakers.

Autonomy of the Åland Islands was specified in 1951 and again in 1991. Under the Autonomy Act of 1951 the islands were again designated as a province of Finland, with their own parliament of 27 members and with Swedish as the official language. A seven member Provincial Executive Council takes care of the daily government of the province, which has far-reaching powers in education, electoral law, taxation, housing, agriculture and fisheries, commerce and industry, and health care. In education, for instance, it was decided to make the learning of Swedish and English compulsory, and the learning of Finnish voluntary. Symbols of autonomy are many, including a flag, since 1954, and postage stamps, since 1984. Inhabitants of the Åland Islands do not have to serve in the army, except in a civilian capacity (Hannum, 1993:116). However, laws passed by the local parliament must be approved by the Finnish parliament, and Finnish may be used before the courts. The revisions of 1991 have been aimed at transferring additional areas of competence to the islands, and to improve the protection of the linguistic composition of the islands by explicitly making obligatory satisfactory knowledge of Swedish. In the recent discussion on the entrance of the Nordic countries into the European Union, the Åland Islands again took a special position. Whereas a referendum was held on 16 October, 1994, in the remainder of Finland, the one on the islands was held on 20 November, 1994, following the referendum in Sweden; the inhabitants of the islands wanted to include Sweden's outcome in their considerations. As it turned out, both Sweden and Finland voted in favour of entrance into the European Union, and the Åland Islands could therefore follow suit. Further exceptions have been negotiated on the sale of tax-free goods on the boats from Finland to Sweden, which is an important source of income for the islands. Whereas the sale of tax-free goods will be abolished by 1999 in the EU as a whole, the Åland Islands may continue selling after that date (NRC, 21/5/1994).

After the war, the main problem for the Swedish-speakers has been their numerical decline. Table 7.3 shows that their share in the population has been falling steadily since 1900, and that they have been declining in absolute terms since 1940. The table also shows the percentage of votes for the SFP; the decline in their potential electorate is clearly reflected in the decline of their share of the total votes. According to some, the wording in the Finnish census for a long time tended to lower the number of Swedes, because it asked the main language instead of the mother tongue. As a result, bilingual Finns of Swedish origin mostly gave Finnish as their language (Liebkind, 1984:96). Since 1977, however, population statistics do use mother tongue in the question. This has slightly increased the share of Swedish-speakers and seems to have slowed the numerical decline somewhat, but the overall effects are limited.[16]

The decline is also evident in the steady shrinking of territory dominated by Swedish-speakers. In 1960 8.6% of the municipalities were Swedish-speaking communes, in 1970, this declined to 8%, and in 1980 to 5.6%. As pointed out in section 7.2, in 1991 there were only 24 Swedish-speaking municipalities left (1 urban against 23 rural, 5.2% of all municipalities), besides 41 bilingual municipalities (21 Finnish-dominated, against 20 Swedish-dominated), and 395 Finnish-speaking municipalities. Most of the Swedish-language municipalities are located on the Åland Island, and in only two of the remaining provinces is the share of the Swedish-speaking population over 10%. Allardt and Miemois (1981:58) therefore argue that while the language regulations have very well served to protect the rights of the Swedish-speakers, this demographic decline has now made the underlying 'personality principle' more disputable. Indeed, although the territorial demarcations are made to protect the linguistic living-areas of the Swedish-speakers, the method of individual counting makes these territories very vulnerable if the group is demographically weak.

Several reasons have been given to explain the decline (Liebkind, 1984:98 – 100; see also Hämäläinen 1980):
a) emigration to Sweden. It has been estimated that around 300 thousand Finns have gone to Sweden, of which an estimated 20 to 25% were Swedish-speakers. As a result, in 1980, 69% of the Swedish-speakers had at least one relative in Sweden (Pentikaeinen et al., 1985:90). During the 1980s emigration slowed down, and return migration has even

16 The Saami are also counted on the basis of mother language, and their decline has also been a consideration in the changing of the wording of the census question (Pentikaeinen et al., 1985:63 – 66).

caused some optimism regarding the strengthening of Swedish culture in Finland (Arter, 1987:34, Brandt 1992). However, this has not resulted in an increase in the number of Swedish-speakers.

b) lower birth rates, especially during the first decades of this century. Since a higher proportion of Swedish-speakers than of Finnish-speakers used to live in cities this is hardly surprising. As mentioned above, in 1910, 32.2% of the Swedish-speakers were living in cities, against 12.2% of the Finnish-speakers. Nowadays, the figures are almost equal, with 63% of the Swedish-speakers living in urban municipalities, against 64% of the rest of the population (Statistical Yearbook of Finland, 1993: 48–49). The low birthrate (and emigration to Sweden) also had a negative effect on the age structure.

c) mixed marriages. In 1991, 3.8% of the newly wed Finnish or Swedish-speaking husbands had married a spouse from the other language group (Statistical Yearbook of Finland, 1993:94). Some 11.1% of Swedish-speakers live in bilingual families, where children often adopt Finnish as their language. (Marriage across the language border is not condemned or stigmatized.) The linguistic environment outside the family is often decisive in the choice of language; since more and more bilingual families are living in Finnish-language environments, Finnish more often gets to be the choice (Pentikaeinen et al., 1985:91). Just under 50% of the Swedish-speakers are still living in Swedish-language or Swedish-dominated municipalities, but only 50 thousand Swede-Finns live in Swedish-language communes, half of which are on the Åland Islands (Statistical Yearbook of Finland, 1993:70). This means that 250 thousand live in bilingual environments.

d) language shift by individuals. This is mostly the result of labour market processes. Liebkind notes, however, that this process overrates the language shift, because most individuals remain bilingual, which is not a statistical category in Finland. According to Allardt and Miemois (1981:18), bilingualism has rapidly increased since the beginning of this century, in particular among Swedish-speakers.

The decline in numbers has been accompanied by two other developments which have weakened the position of the Swedish-speaking group. First of all, migration processes have further mixed the ethnonational groups; a continuous influx of Finnish-speakers in certain living areas of Swedes has occurred, in particular around Helsinki (Brandt 1992). At the same time Swedish-speakers have continued to move to urban areas. Secondly, a school reform abolished Swedish as the obligatory second language at Finnish-language schools in 1960; nowadays, over 90% of the pupils choose English (Pentikaeinen et al., 1985:74–75). This has strengthened the dominance of the Finnish language especially in 'bilingual situations,' since many Finnish-speakers now have only limited knowledge of the Swedish language; moreover, in these situations Swedish-speakers claim their rights less and less (Hämäläinen, 1980:418). As a result, in Helsinki for instance, just 1% of the Swedish-speakers uses only Swedish in their daily life (Liebkind, 1984:118).

The complete mixture and equal status of both groups implies that assimilation must be relatively easy. This is not reflected in the figures, however. The population growth of the Swedish minority since 1960 has been roughly similar to that of the Finnish-speakers, and this growth has been offset by the assimilation or emigration of about 70 thousand Swede-Finns; the figures mentioned above indicate that emigration has probably accounted for most of this. In the last decades, however, the story is different. Return migration from Sweden is hardly observed in the figures, and therefore must have been offset by assimilation. Furthermore, bilingualism increasingly is the rule, and this might lead to assimilation at a faster pace in the long term.

Despite the decline in numbers and the slow erosion of the position of the Swedish language, the institutional set-up is still complete. Swedish-speakers can go to Swedish-language schools from *kindergarten* to university (for which the bilingual Helsinki University, a bilingual Technical University, the Swedish-language Åbo Academy, or a Swedish language business college is available). There are still Swedish sections in the army, Swedish theatres, a Swedish bishopric, Swedish publishers, Swedish trade unions, and so forth. However, this institutional network does not preclude close contact between Swedish-speakers and Finnish-speakers, particularly in Helsinki.

As mentioned, on the Finnish mainland the Swedish-speakers are distributed over roughly two living areas: the rural areas along the western coast of Finland, where roughly a third of the Swedish-speakers lives, and the urbanized areas of the south, where about half of the total Swedish population lives. These groups have diverging interests. For the latter group, it is most important to create a viable basis for bilingualism and have bilingualism accepted as a philosophy. For the former group, however, it is most important to keep their monolingualism intact; the rural Swedish-speakers consider bilingualism as the gate to finnization and strive for territory-based protection against assimilation which is obviously not the solution for urbanized Swedes (Liebkind, 1984:110–111). Historically, a sense of threat in the regions along the western coast has also been caused by a larger out-migration (both to Sweden and to the urban south) (Pentikaeinen et al., 1985:99). Recently, the regional differences within the Swedish minority have come more to the fore within the SFP.

Nowadays, very close cooperation with Sweden in the political sphere strengthens the importance of the Swedish language and culture. Swedish television can easily be received in Finland, although recently some problems have arisen over the passing on of television signals from Sweden to certain regions of Finland. There have also been discussions on a completely Swedish-language channel in Finland. However, according to the Folkting, these problems have been solved in a satisfactory way (Brandt 1992).

In summary, after the war the most important question in Finland was its relationship with the Soviet Union. The unifying effect of the Winter War and the overwhelming importance of relations with the big neighbour affected the internal political relations and pushed aside all differences which had been relevant before the war. There was no need for the virulent protection of linguistic rights, with all the laws in place and no one to challenge them. Problems have come from another side. An absolute decline in numbers, an increase of Swedish-speakers living in Finnish-language areas, and increasing bilingualism have been the major challenges to the position of the ethnonational group. Linguistic policy in Finland has focused on non-territorial cultural autonomy, and as the populations have increasingly become mixed, bilingualism is on the increase while Swedish-language communes are on the decrease. The Åland Islands, with territorial autonomy, have been the major exception. In this context, the switch from Swedish to Finnish appears to be increasingly opportune.

7.4   STATE AND ETHNONATIONALISM IN FINLAND

When the Finnish polity was established in 1809, this was not the result of the strong nationalism of its inhabitants. Nationalism came only afterwards, in creating the cultural content of the political unit and in preserving its separateness. From the 1840s onwards, a conflict emerged within the Finnish elite over the exact character of this polity, and this elite initially was mainly Swedish-speaking. However, despite divisions among the elite, the threat which russification entailed to the culture of Finland, and, slightly later, the threat which Socialism was to existing stratification in Finland helped to keep the linguistic conflict within limits. After the language question had been central to political life during the Grand Duchy and during the period of transition from 1906 till 1922, the conflict lost its edge. Linguistic rights were only challenged intermittently during the interwar years, but the cleavage was increasingly pushed to the background when these challenges were warded off and when the question of Finland's international vulnerability gained prominence.

The electoral law of 1906, in particular, had a great impact on the character of the ethnonational conflict in Finland. The formation of the modern party system in Finland politicized the already existing language struggle and mobilized practically all the Swedish-speakers into a single party. The choice of proportional representation assured their continued presence in the political arena. Since the beginning of this century, therefore, the SFP has formed a strong linguistic party which has been able to represent the interests of Swede-Finns in parliament and in the majority of the governments. The SFP was the only linguistic party left over from the struggle in the nineteenth century, and in fact the only ethnonational party in Europe which has been present in the political arena from the turn of the century onwards. Their existence has been a major factor in the detailed regulation of linguistic relations in Finland. What was equally important in creating satisfactory arrangements, however, was the threat to existing politico-economic arrangements caused by the increasing power of the Socialists. The White-Red schism in Finnish society, which remained in the form of a Right-Left polarization after the Civil War, overshadowed the linguistic conflict in the elite of Finland itself. The revolution which caused the Civil War originated from outside the combined Swedish-speaking and Finnish-speaking elite in Finland, and therefore did much to strengthen its internal cohesion. The fact that the Swedish-speakers fought on the winning side of the divide assured their continuous presence in the decision-making process.

Generally speaking, the plurality allowed by the liberal-democratic system has benefitted Swedish-speakers to a considerable degree. On the one hand, the continuing Socialist/non-Socialist divide enabled the SFP to switch sides if linguistic issues arose and if support was needed. As a result, nationalist challenges from extremist Finns failed to isolate the Swede-Finns, and proposals which would have eroded linguistic rights could effectively be held off. In that respect, the majority rules in parliament protected the constitution and the language laws sufficiently well, while the influence of the president in the political process has also taken the sting out of some situations. For the Swede-Finns themselves the plurality has implied much diversity in voting on non-linguistic issues over the years, as exemplified by the voting pattern of representatives of the SFP. Swede-Finns also remained influential through their strong position in the economy of Finland, which continued to provide career opportunities and enabled them to continue to set up and finance their institutions; this became increasingly important when state positions were slowly filled up with Finnish-speakers. Also in education, where much of the struggle was fought, the presence of private Swedish-language education guaranteed the continuation of Swedish culture even if the nationalists succeeded, although it did not take away the symbolic and practical importance of the University in Helsinki, for instance. Even without the Finnish nationalists succeeding, moreover, the elaborate educational institutions of the Swede-Finns which could exist in Finland have been an asset to the community.

In terms of territorial arrangements, the Swede-Finns have been in a peculiar situation. While for the great majority the municipality is the central unit of implementation of their linguistic rights, the Åland Islands are a clear and important exception. Moreover, since the birth of the Finnish state, the inhabitants of the islands have not only been an important exception within the Finnish state, but have also formed a separate community from the main body of Swede-Finns. Extensive autonomy arrangements have insured that this has continued up to this day. On the other hand, the concessions granted to the inhabitants of the islands convinced the Swede-Finns, in general, and also the international community, of the willingness of the new Finnish state to develop satisfactory arrangements for the Swedish-speakers. For the remainder of the group, however, the method chosen for implementing the linguistic rights has enabled the shrinking of Swedish-language areas over time. Territorial fixation of Swedish-language areas has at times been promoted by sections of the Swedish-speakers on the mainland, but their proposals have met with resistance from others who lived in bilingual environments. Shortly after independence the calls for regional autonomy were especially loud. Overall, the distribution of the group has hampered successful mobilization on this point; it was, to be sure, very difficult for Swede-Finns in Helsinki to identify with the regional interests of inhabitants of Ostrobothnia or, for that matter, the Åland Islands. Indeed, the importance of a concept of territory for the identity of the Swede-Finns as a group has been very limited, and has at best been played out at the local level.

After the Second World War, linguistic conflict by all accounts disappeared. In causing this decline some other influences on ethnonational relations were important, aside from the internal organization of the state. From the nineteenth century onwards elements of Swedish culture have been central to Finnish national culture, and this served to strengthen the cooperation between the two groups. In other words, Finnish resistance against its overlords, Russia, and later the Soviet Union, did not affect the relationship between Finns and their other previous overlords, the Swedes. Indeed, Finland continued to be preoccupied with its long border with the Soviet Union, and the kind of national identity which prevailed in the country continued to provide ample room for the existence of the Swedish-language group. The importance of the external threat was matched by the importance of the demographic balance, which changed in favour of the Finns and resulted in a new balance in all aspects of social life by the end of the 1930s. Indeed, the major problem for Swede-Finns now is their numerical decline. Although the extent to which it actually occurs is unclear, the solution chosen for linguistic rights clearly does not protect the Swede-Finns from assimilation. Only on the Åland Islands, where strict rules apply for all newcomers, can assimilation be avoided. Since the war, the SFP has remained a completely accepted coalition partner in Finnish politics, and appears very able to defend the interests of its electorate. The party has even been able to present a candidate for the Finnish presidential elections of 1994, who ended only just behind the winning candidate. This shows the extent of integration and the high status of the Swede-Finns.

8

European Ethnonationalism and Political Systems
A Comparative Perspective

In this chapter the cases will be compared along the lines set out in the first three chapters of this book. It was decided in those chapters to focus on how the state generates and moulds ethnonational activism and identity. As pointed out, an emphasis on the state as an autonomous actor provides a shift in perspective which improves our understanding of the interaction between states and ethnonational groups and movements. In order to explore that perspective two dimensions were selected to differentiate between types of states.

In the first section, section 8.1, the ethnonational groups and movements which have been discussed in the previous chapters will be compared. The second section, section 8.2, discusses ethnonationalism under liberal-democratic and communist systems, following which section 8.3 focuses on the differences between unitary and federalized systems. Section 8.4 explores the interaction between the two dimensions in their effect on ethnonational mobilization and identity. Section 8.5 will discuss the broader context by looking at some of the other variables which are important to the analysis of ethnonationalism, such as size, location, economic differences, and the international arena. This enables us in section 8.6 to draw some general conclusions on this powerful phenomenon, and on the role of the state in generating and moulding it.

8.1 ETHNONATIONAL MOVEMENTS

Ethnonationalism was defined in chapter one as the sentiment which sparks off political movements of ethnonational groups within multi-ethnic states for more political autonomy or independence. The four cases studied in this book illustrate the variety in this phenomenon with regard to the intensity of the sentiment as such, and with regard to the dynamics of the movement. Moreover, both the sentiment and the movement remain rather elusive in the sense that their ultimate political relevance does not always correspond with overt support or standard patterns of organization. Nevertheless, the general depth of the ethnonational sentiment and thereby, paradoxically, the real substance of the 'imagined communities' has again become clear in this book. In this section I will discuss the various aspects of ethnonational sentiment and of the ethnonational movements separately. In this comparison I will look most extensively at the movements of the Flemish, Walloons, Slovaks, Turks and Swede-Finns in more recent years, although some of the other groups in the four cases will occasionally be discussed as well (e.g., the Czechs, the Finns, the Pomaks, and so on).

There is hardly any doubt about the existence of the ethnonational communities as such. They became social realities under the pressures of state-building, nation-building and social upheavals which accompanied the modernization process. However, the process of ethnonational group formation has certainly not eradicated within-group differences. At various times, cultural differences between the ethnonational groups have been parallelled by differentiation within groups. This differentiation can have a geographical basis, with regional sentiments creating additional cleavages, but it can also be based on cultural variety. Thus, in Belgium, state-wide loyalties, local loyalties, linguistic loyalties, and ideological loyalties have complicated the building of loyalties at the regional level. Similar complications were found in the other countries as well. In Czechoslovakia between the wars, Slovak separateness was based on peasant culture and Catholic elements, but this was opposed by an influential group of Slovak Protestants who strove for closer connection with the Czech part of the country and felt more strongly for the principle of 'Czechoslovakism.' In Bulgaria, the Pomaks were confronted with pressures to choose between the Turkish-Muslim aspects of their identity and the Bulgarian-linguistic part of their identity. During the interwar years, the Turks experienced differences over the question about to what extent cultural changes in Turkey should be accepted and followed. Swedish-speakers in Finland experienced similar tension between inhabitants of Ostrobothnia and the southern coastal region, in a political sense as well as with respect to the emphasis on monolingualism or bilingualism. The very existence of the autonomy for the Åland Islands, and the irritation by other Swedish-speakers over the actions of the Åland Islanders, underlines the argument that basic cultural characteristics do not necessarily provide the basis of all important lines of distinction. Indeed, the depth of ethnonational sentiment is related to the extent to which this within-group differentiation is relevant. I will return to this point later on.

Extremist expressions of ethnonationalist sentiment remained limited in the cases in this book. Generally speaking, the use of violence by the groups remained low, in particular where interactions between the main groups in each case were concerned. Violence was generally directed at other groups,[1]

---

1   This is not to underestimate the importance of the expulsion of Germans from Czechoslovakia after the Second World War, nor the deportation of the Jews in the Slovak state, nor the sometimes violent relations with the Hungarian minority. Neither do I want to

centred on other issues,² or originated explicitly from the state itself. An evident example of lack of violence is the Czechoslovak state which has completely fallen apart without any clash of arms. Indeed, in the events which preceded the split, hardly any demonstrations occurred which focused on the Czechs or the Slovaks as a group, and the few incidents which did occur were aimed at Czech politicians visiting Slovakia. Public opinion polls in Slovakia didn't show any strong anti-Czech sentiments either, although there was widespread frustration over the political and economic arrangements, great uncertainty about the future, and a very strong desire that Slovakia be protected against the unknown. In Finland, examples of violence between the two main ethnic groups remained limited to the period between the wars and only involved street riots. In that case the threat originating from outside the country certainly forced politicians to manoeuvre carefully and contain the elements of extremism among the Finnish population itself; the wishes of the *aitosuomalaisuus* were partially directed at the Karelian territories in the Soviet Union, all the more reason for the Finnish president and for moderate parties to limit their influence. In Belgium, the use of violence was equally very limited. Apart from rioting and incidents which accompanied some of the mass demonstrations around 1960 and the never-ending events in the Voeren district, the country has not experienced the use of violent force. Finally in Bulgaria, the country where the most violence occurred after World War Two, this violence did not originate from widespread exchanges between ethnic groups, but from the state itself. This would not make much difference if the assimilation drive had been initiated by clear demands among the Bulgarian population for sweeping measures to eradicate Turkish culture on Bulgarian territory. Whereas anti-Turkish sentiments certainly exist among parts of the Bulgarian population, there is little evidence of widespread desire among the Bulgarians to enforce assimilation of the Turks; the drive was straightforward state intervention to suppress ethnic heterogeneity on Bulgarian territory, decided on by a small group among the Bulgarian leadership.

We may nevertheless dwell a little longer on the differences between the two Eastern European and the two Western European cases. In chapter one I mentioned a traditional distinction which was made in the literature between the character of the national sentiment in the two parts of Europe. From the cases it appears that the distinction is still valid, and that, despite the generally low level of violence, there is a difference in terms of the primordial or instrumental character of the ethnonational sentiment. Although

play down the Bulgarian expulsion of Turks immediately after independence, or the pogroms directed at the Greeks, and so forth. They have been crucial elements in the countries' histories.
2   The Finnish Civil War is a case in point. Although the White Army had a Swedish character to a large extent, it was not an ethnonational conflict, as has been discussed in chapter seven.

arguments of this kind can only be tentative, it seems fair to conclude on the basis of the previous chapters that ethnonationalism strikes deeper chords in the Eastern European cases. The primordial dimension of ethnonationalism – characterized by such elements as its emotional character, its non-negotiable nature, its strong sense of 'us' and 'them,' and its emphasis on absolute divisions – seems to carry more weight in Eastern Europe than in Western Europe, where the instrumental dimension of modern ethnonationalism – its changeable character, social function, and the balance that is struck between costs and benefits – weighs more heavily (see also Coakley, 1992b:217–218). In Bulgaria, events since 1989 have demonstrated a high degree of mutual distrust and susceptibility to nationalist rhetoric which is not found in Finland or in Belgium. Czechoslovakia is positioned somewhere in between. The Czech majority appears to resemble the Finns in the sense that overt mobilization along ethnonational lines has hardly been important; this has led some to analyze the Czech case for their lack of overt nationalism (Pithart 1993). Among the Slovaks ethnonationalism has equally remained limited if it is translated into the public desire for a separate state. However, as will be discussed below, in Slovakia, as in Bulgaria, electoral support for extreme nationalist and nationalist-populist parties – in short, support for exclusionary politics – recently has been higher than in the Western European countries. Despite the differences, of course, both the primordial and the instrumental dimensions of ethnonationalism are present in all of the cases. Moreover, it does not allow straightforward conclusions about the permanency or consequence of the sentiment.

In fact, the general lack of extremism itself should not lead one to downplay the basic relevance of ethnonationalism. There is ample reason not to underestimate the strength of the phenomenon. Potential mass support may be far larger than is immediately apparent, but can perhaps only be tapped under very specific circumstances, or "when the chips are down". Former Yugoslavia and in particular the Bosnian Muslims are a case in point; the violent events have forced everybody to take sides where peaceful ethnic cohabitation used to be the rule (see Donia and Fine Jr. 1994). In the cases in this book, the potential for mass support is suggested by sporadic displays such as the Swede-Finn's Folkting and the Flemish demonstrations in Brussels. Even more important is the fact that the lack of public mass support for extremist ethnonationalism does not tell us too much about the ethnonationalist success or likely outcome. If ethnonationalism is seen as a sentiment which may spark off a movement – one which challenges the existing political territorial arrangements and causes the federalization or dissolution of the state – its constant persistence on the political scene and the recent collapse of multi-ethnic states indicate its relevance, even with low levels of overt support. In fact, in Belgium and Czechoslovakia no successful countermovement has emerged to stop the course of events and block further devolution. Apparently, the mass of the population is often unwilling or unable to influence the exact outcome of ethnonational conflict. The lack of a referendum at the time of the split in Czechoslovakia is one of the most pointed examples of this lack of popular control.

Institutions therefore tend to sustain the separate character of the ethnonational group under stable circumstances, and serve as rallying points during more volatile periods. A wide array of organizations is used to that effect, such as cultural organizations (e.g., the Matica Slovenská, the Davidsfonds), educational institutions (e.g., Åbo-Academy, Universities of Gent and Leuven, Turkish teachers' organizations), religious institutions (e.g., Swedish-language bishopric, Islamic structures), grass-roots organizations (e.g., Flemish People's Movement, Democratic League for the Defence of Human Rights), political institutions (e.g., political parties, Swedish Folkting), trade unions and employers' organizations, and so forth. During tense periods, overt support by a large part of the group-members is necessary to enable the successful fulfilment of the demands, but at other times this potential need not be tapped.

The various ethnonational movements were most active at different periods of time. In Bulgaria, Turks generally kept to themselves until 1985, except for some efforts around 1930; certainly from 1989 onwards there has been all sorts of activism. In Czechoslovakia, Slovak activism experienced climaxes during the 1960s and after 1989, although early mobilization was found again during the interwar years and, by definition, during the Slovak state. In Finland, Swedish activism was, apart from the nineteenth century, mostly found between 1900 and 1939 and in particular between 1917 and 1922, after which higher levels of activity were only sporadically observed. In Belgium ethnonationalist mobilization peaked from 1960 onwards, with Flemish activism experiencing some earlier peaks and Bruxellois activism starting somewhat later. The movements, as indicated by the ethnonational parties, had declined in activity by the end of the 1980s, but, as discussed in chapter six, the character of the Belgian movements remains somewhat diffuse. For all the movements it is clear that there has been a fluctuation in the topicality of the sentiment.

Political parties are – apart from demonstrations, political rallies, and petitions – the most obvious elements of movements to reflect the support for ethnonationalist activism in the group. In all of the cases in this book, the ethnic groups have at various points in time (or in some cases continuously) been able to vote for parties of their choice. Nevertheless, Belgium is the only case in this book where explicitly ethnonational parties on both sides of the ethnonational divide have found substantial support in recent years. In line with the argument thus far, extremist parties in terms of demands (separatism) cannot count on massive popular support. The Flemish nationalist parties, for instance, some of whom wanted far-reaching autonomy and even independence at a relatively early stage, gained a maximum of 19% of the Flemish votes. In case of the recent extremist Flemish party, the Vlaams Blok (Flemish Bloc), which can count on support from some 10% of the Flemish population, only a fraction of its voters actually support the party for its separatist programme. Xenophobia, although an element of nationalism in itself, is a far more important reason. A similar situation exists in Wallonia, where at the height of popular support just over 20% voted for an explicitly Walloon party; moreover, the party's programme focused clearly on economic support for the region and on political autonomy. Only in Brussels did the FDF reach as high as 40% at one stage, but its program was equally not secessionist in nature. In Belgium as a whole, the outspoken ethnonationalist parties received a maximum of 45 seats, or slightly over 20% of the seats in parliament.[3] If ethnonational sentiment is measured through support for ethnic-based parties, the sentiment is far more important among Swede-Finns and Bulgarian Turks. In both cases almost the entire group voted for a single party. Perhaps surprisingly, however, these parties have at the same time been very much involved in the government of the respective countries, and have not shown any interest in stressing extremist ethnonational demands. They focus instead on the long term defence of the cultural and socio-economic characteristics of the groups. However, the developments in Bulgaria are very recent and too uncertain to permit hasty conclusions.

The situation in former Czechoslovakia is the least clear, although in the end the consequences of ethnonationalist conflict have been the most severe, namely political dissection of the entire system. Here again, support for extremist ethnic-based political parties is limited. The only party in Slovakia which actually included secession in its program, the Slovak National Party, received a maximum of 14% for the Slovak National Council in the 1990 elections. This is relatively modest since at that time the transition, in economic and political terms, was going through a very rough stage. Support in fact went down in subsequent elections. The decisive party in Slovak politics until independence, Mečiar's HZDS, also received a maximum of 33% of the votes in 1992, at a time when a vote for his party was certainly not a clear vote for independence. To be sure, neither was it a vote in favour of the political arrangement with the Czechs, and as such Mečiar's widespread appeal and his image of being able to "defend the interests of Slovakia" indicate the importance of this general view in Slovakia. It is not an indication of a desire for separation, however. In fact, a similar situation existed before the war, when the Hlinka Populists gained a maximum of 35% of the votes in Slovakia, but their switch in policy towards autonomy and Slovak independence during the last years of the 1930s, resulting in the Slovak state, did not reflect a clear mass desire for secession.

Although public support for extremist solutions has been limited in the cases studied, other demands have certainly received widespread support. The most basic demands concerned dissatisfaction with the possibilities for

---

3   However, at a certain stage the linguistic wings of the two main traditional parties started to incorporate many of the ethnonationalist desires, making straightforward conclusions more difficult.

cultural expression within the borders of the state. Language has been of particular importance. Thus, Swedish-speakers in Finland have protected education in their own language, as well as the opportunity to use their own language in dealings with the state. They have been countered by Finnish-speakers who wanted greater emphasis on the Finnish character of the new state. Flemings strived for acceptance of the Dutch language as one of the official languages of Belgium, and for protection of the Dutch-speaking community against frenchification. Turks in Bulgaria experienced systematic encroachment on their language education, as well as on other cultural elements, after an initial improvement in literacy in their language. In the last case, Czechoslovakia, language has been less important, although Slovaks tried hard, particularly before World War Two, to have their linguistic differences with the Czechs accepted as being substantial enough to merit separate existence as a group on grounds other than the contingencies of history or differences in general outlook by the population. The removal of Czech influences from the Slovak language during the short-lived Slovak state was therefore a logical step in this reasoning.

The importance of religion is somewhat less clear. In the case of the Bulgarian Turks, religion was certainly important, although the tension did not quite point towards an Orthodox attempt at conversion. The Bulgarian regime's overall suppression of religion makes this unlikely. Religion should primarily be seen as an important marker and a publicly visible element of the Turkish identity which had to be eradicated. In the other three cases, the religious make-up of the two main ethnic groups was largely similar, even though the importance attached to religion was dissimilar. This latter qualification has of course played a major role in Czechoslovakia, both before and after the Second World War. Before the war the fear of the Slovak clergy of the Protestant and humanist tendencies among Czech leaders was very important, and at the end of communist rule most demonstrations in Bratislava still rallied around the position of the Catholic Church. Religion is in a similar way more important in Flanders than among the French-speakers. It has been noted that Catholic parties had a stronger support in Dutch-speaking provinces, even though the struggle in Belgium over the State-Church relationship did not coincide with the Flemish-Walloon distinction. Nevertheless, in the cases in this book, the religious cleavage is at best a contributing factor in communal conflict and not the root cause (similar findings emerge in Gurr (1993) and Enloe (1980a)).

Some of the cultural demands clearly have had territorial implications. The most obvious case in point is Belgium, where territorial demarcation of the language border was considered necessary by the Flemings to avoid further frenchification of Flemish populations; for the Walloons it meant the avoidance of a dreaded bilingual Belgium, although at the cost of French-speakers in Flanders. A similar effort has been made in the case of the Swede-Finns, but in Finland, apart from the Åland Islands, the 'ethnic territories' can still come 'under threat' from migration processes (internal and external) and assimilation. The installment of a federation in Czechoslovakia (just as its ultimate demise) was more the result of prolonged dissatisfaction on the part of the Slovak elite with their political status and with the economic situation, than with encroachment on Slovak culture through assimilation in Slovakia. Similarly, in Belgium and Bulgaria frustration over political exclusion and economic deprivation have also been important.

Overall, we can observe some interesting differences between the cases. In terms of sentiment it is puzzling why ethnonationalism, despite the generally low level of extremism, still takes on a more vehement character in Eastern Europe than in Western Europe. In terms of overt support the question is why the Turkish Bulgarians (after 1989) and the Swedish Finns give their votes most systematically to an ethnic-based party, while the other groups only partially do so; in Belgium the explicitly ethnonationalist parties have mostly lost their support, while in Czechoslovakia overt support for the most virulent ethnonationalist parties has remained limited and, among the Czechs, virtually non-existent. Finally, it is striking how the effects of the movements have differed. Looking at it in terms of results, it is clear that the movements in Belgium and Slovakia have been most successful in altering the structure of the state as such. This is not to say that the movements in the other cases have not seen progress. The Turks have recently been able to restore many of their rights, and the satisfactory position of the Swedish-speakers at an early stage already led them to simply play a guardian role. This in itself deserves explanation, indeed.

As has been argued in chapter two, it was expected that the emergence and dynamics of the ethnonational movements would be related to the type of state in which they are found. At this stage we should therefore focus on the differences in political systems. The history of the movements as described in the previous chapters illustrates most clearly that the need for raising demands is usually very much dependent on the action the state takes towards the ethnic group. This is not so surprising since nationalism in general, and therefore ethnonationalism as well, is ultimately an attempt to wrestle from the state certain concessions on how life should be arranged within the borders of the state. How the state may deal with ethnonational demands has been the subject of much study, with options ranging from the granting of autonomy, to the use of state violence, and so forth. In this book, however, the perspective is the other way around: the focus is to what extent the state itself, through its institutions and the activities of its functionaries, generates and moulds ethnonational activism, and how that differs between various types of states. The next three sections will further explore this perspective.

8.2   COMMUNIST AND LIBERAL-DEMOCRATIC SYSTEMS

In chapter two the distinction between communist and liberal-democratic systems was based on a different perspective on state-society relations; the different philosophies of transcendentalism and instrumentalism would result in the political practice of society-led states on the one hand and state-led societies on the other hand. However, both Liberalism and Marxist-Leninism lack room for the phenomenon of ethnonationalism, and in fact, expect it to wither away: Liberalism, because it considers individual action to be central to political life, and Marxist-Leninism, because it considers economic classes to be the central form of group-formation and political life. Theory notwithstanding, practical politics have forced the states based on these principles to take ethnonationalism into account. The effects of the differences in treatment have become particularly apparent after 1989.

The discussion in chapter two resulted in various propositions on how ethnonationalism may be influenced by the differences between states which are related to this dimension. I will discuss these propositions in turn.

8.2.1   General policies and implementation

First of all, I assumed that in communist political systems the efforts of the state to structure society will lead to a wider set of policies by the state toward society as a whole, and towards the ethnonationalist groups in particular. These policies would also be implemented more powerfully under communism, while under liberal-democratic systems the multiple checks and balances would diffuse many of the efforts. It was considered particularly useful to focus on two fields of policy: economic policy and cultural policy. Both aspects are related and further connected to the system of political control which will be discussed in the next section.

Overall, as will be seen in this section, the cases demonstrated that the differences between the two systems are reflected in various policy categories that are relevant to the development and character of the ethnonational movements. Under communism the eradication of alternatives leaves the minority at the mercy of the majority, while the emphasis on homogenization assures, paradoxically, that the ethnonational categories have to be addressed. The ultimate effect of these policies has been to strengthen the sense of community and to generate resentment among the ethnonational groups targeted. In the liberal-democratic states, in contrast, there was less explicit targeting in the field of cultural and economic policy, and there were more alternatives. Despite the general picture, however, these distinctions are not ideally reflected in the cases. Thus, whereas in terms of economic policy the eradication of independent economic life and the explicit attempt at equalization have been central in both communist cases, some aspects in this field are important in a similar way in the liberal-democratic states, in particular the issue of jobs in the public service. With regard to the cultural policies, the most important distinctions between the two systems were the desire for homogenization in communist systems, although this may be attempted in highly contrasting ways, and the complete dependence of the minority on the policies generated by the majority, due to the absence of alternatives. There was, of course, a clear difference between the two communist cases in the degree to which the ethnonational minority was subjected to cultural homogenization. What remains true, nevertheless, is that it is highly unlikely that this kind of society structuring along economic and cultural lines could be undertaken to the same extent in the liberal-democratic states, if for no other reasons than that of the checks and balances which are included in their political system.

One of the most pointed distinctions between the two systems concerns the existence of economic life separate from state planning. Generally speaking, under communism, economic equalization was considered a necessary condition for the successful development of a communist society; it attempted to prove that the economic base mattered politically by restructuring it. Besides the general effect this had on the lives of individuals belonging to the ethnonational group, this policy of equalization was further considered to have an impact on ethnonational life itself: economic equalization would lead to the disappearance of national differences and to the cooperation of the working class across nations; ultimately national differences would become obsolete and wither away. This line of reasoning was put into practice in both communist cases. Most of the economic history of Czechoslovakian communism can be characterized as a policy of regional equalization, while in the Bulgarian case collectivization was thought to uproot the Turkish farmers and bring them into contact with the Bulgarian nation. As noted in the chapters on Bulgaria and Czechoslovakia, these policies did not have the intended results. In Czechoslovakia, economic equalization was accompanied by higher levels of activism by the Slovaks, while in Bulgaria, resistance among the Turks was substantial and economic policies could not make more explicitly cultural policies superfluous.

Economic policies were often not completely free of ethnic undertones, or had at least differential effects on the various ethnonational communities. Thus, in Bulgaria collectivization often resulted in Turks working in lower status jobs in the collective farms; moreover, the collectivization of all means of production was experienced as an attack on the way of life of the group as such. This was all the more important, since no alternative was available. In Slovakia, industrialization clearly benefitted Slovakia, but it was led from and implemented by Prague at least until the creation of the federation. This was made even more explicit by the territorial subdivision of Slovakia's territory, and centralized decision-making was indeed openly challenged during the 'Slovak Spring' of the 1960s and during the Prague Spring of 1968. Related to this is the allocation of state employment itself, which, in the communist cases, was crucial. Slovaks initially felt they did not benefit sufficiently from the rise in central state employment; it was pointed out at the time of the Prague Spring that less than 4% of jobs in central bureaucracy in Prague were taken by Slovaks. Although no figures are available for the Turks, the unchallenged primacy of Sofia and the small number of Turks living in the capital not only affected the political decision-making powers of the Turks but certainly their economic gains flowing from employment in the central bureaucracy as well. These issues are also relevant to a large extent in liberal-democratic countries, where central government is blamed for economic depression, and where economic decision-making may spark off ethnonational protests (see e.g., Newman 1994). This is particularly true for the allocation of state jobs. Belgium and Finland demonstrated how the allocation of positions could become central to the discussion on ethnonational relations.

Nevertheless, despite the fact that similar tensions can be observed under liberal-democratic systems, the explicit claims of economic equality and continuous state intervention by communist regimes are prone to backfire. A combination of economic downturn and centralized rule creates the perception of 'internal-colonialism' which may easily be combined with regionally based ethnic differences. Moreover, the blame is easier to place, even where actual inequality is perhaps less. Thus, in Czechoslovakia, the Soviet-type economic system was in fact far less suited to the more industrialized Czech lands than to less developed Slovakia, but the fact that, before 1968, economic decisions were taken in Prague fuelled perceptions of Czech dominance. Moreover, in liberal-democratic systems there is an alternative. Among the Swede-Finns, for instance, their position in the economic sphere enabled them to uphold an extensive network of cultural organizations.

It was noted that under communism the economic sphere was closely related to the cultural sphere, and that cultural policies have accompanied economic policies in achieving the same goal, namely the creation of a homogeneous society. In the cases, paradoxically, both the suppression of differences and the development of separate cultures were attempted to achieve this goal. From the perspective of the minority the desire for homogenization under communism could therefore be beneficial as well as detrimental to their cultural life. Nevertheless, similarly to economic life, the lack of societal alternatives made minorities ultimately dependent upon the majority, and increasingly vulnerable because communist regimes gain their legitimacy by emphasizing the homogeneity of the population. Thus, in Bulgaria, support for education in the Turkish language was reversed two decades later when spontaneous merger did not occur. The Czechoslovak case is less clear in this respect, however, as the official recognition of Slovak culture (although accompanied by the downgrading views of Slovak culture by some Czech communists such as Novotný) was continued after 1968 (see below). Nevertheless, in Belgium and Finland private education continued to exist alongside public education (sometimes sponsored by the state), and may have helped to sustain ethnonational differences. In fact, in 1968 the European Court of Human Rights decided, after a complaint by French-speakers in Flanders, that the territorial basis of the language law on education did not run counter to the principles of human rights primarily because it covered only public and publicly subsidized education, and did not forbid private francophone schools in the Dutch-language region (McRae, 1986:222). Control over cultural diversity can also be seen in the complete disappearance or extreme reduction of ethnonational categories, as in the Bulgarian case with Macedonians, Pomaks, and Gypsies, and, in the Czechoslovak case, with the Hungarians shortly after the Second World War. Thus, although census-taking can be disputed in liberal-democratic environments as well (e.g., Belgium), this is clearly not the same thing. The occasional vehemence of cultural policies in communist systems, as exemplified by the Bulgarian assimilation drive, is partly caused by the lack of checks and balances.[4]

In summary, the theoretical assumptions behind the communist political system necessitate the contriving and implementation of a wide array of policies both in the economic and in the cultural field. The respective minorities in the communist countries have indeed been profoundly affected and targeted, and although the effects have not all been negative there is a clear element of arbitrariness in the direction of the policies, and a high dependency of the minority on the majority. Although the ultimate effect on ethnonational sentiment and mobilization can only be discussed jointly with the aspects treated in the next sections, the policies have definitely not eradicated any differences. Indeed, the cultural policies towards the Turks in Bulgaria have helped to strengthen their coherence, while for the Slovaks the pretence of equalization has led to careful scrutiny of their situation. However, it was noted that, particularly in the economic field, state policies have been important in the discussion on ethnonational relations in Belgium, while in the cultural field the situation in Bulgaria and Czechoslovakia diverged after the 1960s.

8.2.2 *Parties, bureaucracies, and political uniformity*

As a second proposition, I put forward that in communist political systems the ethnic group will be able to keep threatening policies by the state at bay only if part of the important state organs work towards it, specifically part of the Communist Party or part of the bureaucracy. Furthermore, the stakes in communist systems are higher. In liberal-democratic systems the effective defence of ethnic interests against detrimental state policies will depend on

---

4   Compare, for instance, Greece, which cannot really be considered to favour its Turkish minority, but where the anti-Turkish measures are mild compared to communist Bulgaria (see e.g., Jong 1980; Meinardus 1985, Roessingh and Sytsema 1993).

the level of group organization an ethnic group can accomplish, and on the way in which it can keep ethnic issues on the public agenda. Liberal-democratic systems are also more open to various forms of activism.

Overall, it can indeed be concluded from the cases that control over political decision-making is more crucial for ethnonational groups under a communist system than under a liberal-democratic system. There are no alternative forms of organization, and the stakes indeed become higher. The importance of bureaucracy, however, is too unclear for us to draw conclusions. In attempting to participate in the centre, the Slovaks have succeeded far better than the Turks, not only through the creation of a federation, but also in the Communist Party itself. Although in liberal-democratic systems there is a similar need for participation in the government, there are other ways to influence decision-making which may also be effective, including opposition. In Belgium, for instance, the ethnonational parties were very effective in stressing their point outside the government, and got into trouble when they participated in the government itself. This leads to a second main point, namely the extent to which internal political divisions within the group can become relevant. Under communism, the single-party system and the stress on political uniformity, in particular, are important in the way they affect the ethnonational sentiment and movement in this respect. The impact is difficult to assess, however, as the communist system precludes overt expression of opposition. Nevertheless, experiences after 1989 indicate that under communism the forced uniformity in politics disabled the use of cross-cutting cleavages in political practice, and inhibited the diffusion of tensions by simultaneous attachment to multiple forms of identity. In practice, therefore, this has resulted in a strengthening of ethnic identity as one of the most vulnerable to notions of uniformity, most likely to come under attack from the communist regime, but, apparently, most easily connected to and identified with. Whereas in liberal-democratic systems political control also remains important from the perspective of the ethnic group, the existence of, and public debate surrounding, other cleavages and forms of identification increases the options for satisfactory defence of interest at the level of the individual. This may result in a cyclical support for ethnonational movements, which indeed often demonstrates wave-like levels of activism and of connection between individuals and ethnonational leaders (see Hooghe 1992).

The single most important difference between communist and liberal-democratic systems is that only one party wields power under communism. The road to political control runs through that party; nationalism has crept into all communist parties in Eastern Europe, which involved both the dominant group and the minority groups in sections set apart for them. As Connor (1984:564) puts it: "... the true internationalist, whose vision transcends the interest of his nation and state, has been a rarity indeed in the vanguard of the international proletariat." Whereas this may be true in general, there are some differences between the two communist cases in this respect. For the Turkish minority their inclusion into the BKP was of no avail. It was only meant to improve control over the group by the regime, and to present state policies as if they were originating from members of the group itself. Moreover, in the Bulgarian case there are signs that the inclusion of Turks in the BKP, as well as emigration, was used to rid the group of its potential leaders. The inclusion of Turks was certainly not accompanied by any possibility for separate interest defence. Somewhat different was the situation in Czechoslovakia. Indeed, although in Slovakia the level of party membership remained lower than in the Czech lands and the autonomy of the separate KSS was minimal, the cracks in the supposedly unified KSČ occasionally appeared, for instance during the 1960s. In that sense the KSS remained, though it was curtailed, an ever-present arena for the mobilization of Slovak interest whenever the political atmosphere allowed it. After 1968 the situation became less clear because of the creation of a federation (see below). Although federalization of the state was not followed by federalization of the KSČ, the party was now headed by a Slovak, and Slovak influence was considerable both in the state machinery and in the machinery of the party.

As mentioned, it is difficult to draw conclusions with regard to the importance of the bureaucracy. The cases show mixed evidence. It was clear that the perceptions among the Slovaks of the effects of a Czech-dominated bureaucracy were important before 1968. Although it remains hard to verify, in the Bulgarian case the role of the bureaucracy showed in the topicality of allegations that Turks in the BKP were much more prone to keep close contact with their kin than members of Pomak origin. Nevertheless, in liberal-democratic countries irritation rose as well if the situation was felt to be unbalanced. The importance of this can be seen in Belgium, where a commission controls whether appointments cater sufficiently to all groups; not only linguistic groups, but also the three 'political families'.

Ethnonational interest defence within a communist party is by definition hard to observe, since a unified facade is kept up and the range of political options is not discussed in public. This is, however, precisely part of the problem. By uniting the entire population behind a single party, the other cleavages in society are suppressed and denied. The unidirectional nature of communist politics de-emphasizes other issues which tend to dominate political life in liberal-democratic countries, such as economic differences (since 85% of the population is of a single class) or religious differences. The dominance of these cleavages in Belgium (religious, economic) and Finland (economic) was so overwhelming that it tended to push the ethnonational question into the background for long periods of time. Communist politics blocked these kinds of switches in emphasis. In the two cases studied these certainly could have been possible. For instance, after the Second World War, the formerly important distinction between Protestant and Catholic Slovaks tended to diffuse in favour of a more uniform Slovak ethnonational interest. Divisions in the Bulgarian Muslim population between

Pomaks and Turks (and to some extent also Roma) became more and more irrelevant as anti-religious policies progressed. Of course the regime may attempt to emphasize cleavages, as the Bulgarian regime did by creating separate Islamic institutions for Turks and Pomaks, but it conflicts with the central assumption of homogeneity by stressing diversity too strongly and therefore can hardly be upheld in the long term.

Moreover, in terms of circumstances favourable to the position of ethnonational minorities, the lack of diversity within the majority is equally detrimental. Plurality enlarges possibilities for coalition formation between the minority and sections of the ethnonational majority. Many examples can be found in the two liberal-democratic examples, but even in Bulgaria after 1989 – where the two main parties on the Bulgarian political scene were, at times, hostile towards the new Turkish party – the competition for power forced them to cooperate with the Turkish minority. The possibilities for coalition formation pose problems of their own, of course, and political infighting is central to any ethnonational movement in liberal-democratic countries. In particular, this concerns the overwhelming array of choices which ethnonational movements face regarding the scope and character of autonomy demands, the socio-economic program of the movement, and the dilemma between confronting central government or participating in it, as is seen most vividly in the Belgian case. Under communism this kind of diversity and debate was not allowed to surface and gain political relevance. The Prague Spring was an important and illuminating exception in this respect, precisely because it displayed the diversity which had remained under the previous layer of uniformism. Diversity became apparent not only in an ethnic or cultural sense, but also in a political sense, amongst liberals, Stalinists, main stream communists, and so on. Open debate and negotiations were completely atypical, considering that internal differences were normally not spelled out in front of the general public; they could not obtain political relevance at the level of the masses, and therefore failed to diffuse some of the us-them notions and also failed to create more varied conceptions of self-identity. Indeed, in most instrumentalist theories the observation that different identities, including ethnic ones, are used in different circumstances, becomes to a large extent irrelevant in the communist case since diverse options are either unknown or impossible to implement. The repression of other forms of political organization outside the control of the party therefore leaves individuals without much choice but to see society along ethnic lines, particularly if the identities stressed by the regime are found wanting.[5] In liberal-democratic countries, once concessions are granted (or sometimes if none are granted), public interest may focus on

5   Interesting in this respect is the fact that at a certain stage the regime allowed environmental issues to become the focus of protest to replace more dangerous varieties of protests, including ethnonational ones; however, in several Eastern European countries these environmental issues still developed into general attacks against the regime as such.

other issues, thus defusing tension and creating fluctuations in the political relevance of ethnonational sentiment. However, in the Belgian case, institutional changes have assured the long-term effects of concessions, and several possibilities for a refocus are disabled (see below).

In summary, the struggle for political control is more important in communist cases and more focused on the single party; with regard to the bureaucracy, the difference is less clear. However, even more important is the inability of communist systems to allow for diversity within the ethnonational minorities and majorities.

8.2.3 Central state image and separatism

The third proposition suggested that in communist political systems, sooner than in liberal-democratic countries, unintended negative effects of state policies will lead to resistance specifically directed against the state; the state is held responsible for the development of society. Ethnic nationalism by the group directed at obtaining a state will therefore develop sooner, even if it does not have a chance to be realized.

It can be concluded that the proposition can only be partly accepted. As has been discussed in the two preceding sections, the claims made by the state under communism are more extensive, and failures which accompany its policies are therefore considered more consequential. Nevertheless, though perhaps to a lesser degree, the two liberal-democratic cases show similar mechanisms. Regarding the resulting extremism of demands, it may tentatively be concluded that the desire to separate from the state was somewhat stronger under communism. In Bulgaria this clearly showed in the use of the exit option, through mass emigration. In Slovakia, although during the Prague Spring some elements of separatism were voiced even amongst party officials, the concessions made by the state meant that hardly any separatism developed until 1989. After the Iron Curtain had crumbled, however, the call for separatism became louder, although it did not reach a level which made the execution of this sentiment inevitable. Calls for separatism were also observed in Belgium (to a limited degree), while in Finland separatism has only been found among the Åland Islanders. The evidence is therefore not conclusive, although the basic difference between the communist and liberal-democratic cases appears to stand.

Nevertheless, despite this non-conclusive evidence, the point is still of interest. Because ethnonationalism revolves around the perception of kinship and around the idea that membership in a certain group has immediate bearing on an individual's position in society, the image of the central state and its interventions remains crucially important. This was even more true in the communist cases, where the attempt to completely control society, including the economy, left the minorities at the mercy of the Communist Party and of the groups which were perceived, rightly or wrongly, to control the state's machinery. Indeed, the claim by the Communist Party that it forms a non-national element for integrating the social forces in the state's territory gives it an obligation to act up to this image. Moreover, it is generally the only unifying element allowed to fulfill a public role in the state. If the Party fails, or if the communist system fails for any other reason, the single unifying force in the country is discredited. Religious identities or regionally based ethnic identities are readily found to be alternatives. In this respect the experiences in Czechoslovakia have been most illuminating, not only before but also after 1989: the fact that the reformed Slovak communists supported the federation did not benefit the image of the federation at all. The situation was similar in former Yugoslavia, where the Communist Party used to be the only party to transcend ethnic boundaries. Its demise was not accompanied by the rise of a new state-wide organization, even though some 7% of the population claimed a Yugoslav identity when the state still existed.[6]

Once the communist system collapsed and a party system had to be created, the phasing of the electoral process became important. The absolute centrality of this point is demonstrated in a stimulating analysis by Linz and Stepan (1992), who compared the transitions from authoritarian to democratic rule in Spain, Yugoslavia and the Soviet Union. They concluded that the organization of all-union elections, in contrast to regionally based elections, as the first elections after transition are crucial in creating a state-wide frame of reference for the population. They seem perfectly correct in concluding that "elections can create agendas, can create actors, can reconstruct identities, help legitimate and delegitimate claims to obedience, and create power" (Linz and Stepan, 1992:133). Each liberal-democratic system nevertheless remains vulnerable as regards the tension between regional and state-wide frames of reference. In Belgium the linguistic division of the main political parties has in fact created completely separate arenas of political competition, in which arguments based on state-wide interest may fail to emerge. This withholds from the population the opportunity to consider and support discourse which transcends the interests of the ethnonational groups. If this situation continues for prolonged periods of time, the idea that the central state is superfluous is likely to grow stronger among the members of the group. I will return to this point in section 8.3.

---

6   Indeed, as early as 1975 Klein concluded that "[b]ourgeois democracy has not established an enviable record in the Balkans, and it is not a foregone conclusion that the alternative to the Communist Party is some form of Western liberal democracy. The splintering of Yugoslavia into intensely nationalistic petty states would be a far more likely outcome" (Klein, 1975:362). Klein was not correct, however, in expecting Czechs and Slovaks to come to an agreement after the disappearance of external pressure. In the same article he stated that "[d]uring the Prague Spring, the differences between the Slovaks and the Czechs were worked out on a mutually satisfactory basis. There is little reason to believe that this could not be accomplished again if all outside pressures were removed" (Klein, 1975:363). Unless of course the split is perceived as an accomplishment.

Overall, whereas frustration over exclusion from the central state may be found in liberal-democratic systems as well, this will be much more strongly felt under communist systems as a result of the lack of political participation in the single party on the basis of ethnic interests (leaving aside special cases like Yugoslavia). This exclusion certainly has a physical dimension in the sense that the central role of the capital city, in terms of decision-making powers, takes on extra depth. Thus, the concept of Prague and Sofia as metaphors for distant rulers was particularly apt for the minorities in the case of Bulgaria and in the case of Slovakia before 1968 (and even after). The intention to break away from that centre, where directives and failures are conceived, may thus gain a more geographical significance. One can partially explain the reinforcement of Slovak separatism after 1989 by the psychological return of this image of a distant centre.

8.2.4 Conclusion

The distinction between communist and liberal-democratic states is important for understanding the dynamics of ethnonationalism, and the differences between the systems are highly relevant despite the fact that both types occasionally displayed similar mechanisms. Whereas ethnonationalist sentiment has been continuously present, the consequences of communist rule became particularly apparent after 1989. Overall, as Brzezinski pointed out, communist policies eased the transition to virulent nationalism: "though [communism] proclaimed itself to be the doctrine of internationalism, [it] in fact intensified popular nationalist passions. It produced a political culture imbued with intolerance, self-righteousness, rejection of social compromise, and a massive inclination toward self-glorifying oversimplification. On the level of beliefs, dogmatic communism fused with and even reinforced intolerant nationalism; on the level of practice, the destruction of such relatively internationalist social classes as the aristocracy or the business elite further reinforced the populist inclination towards nationalist chauvinism. Nationalism was thereby nurtured, rather than diluted, in the communist experience" (Brzezinski, 1989:2). Thus, although an upsurge in ethnonationalism was observed in liberal-democratic systems, in the two communist cases ethnonationalism has been more pervasive and consequential.

It could of course be argued that historical variety in the character of the nationalism, as discussed in chapter one, or the shock of transition after the collapse of communism could be responsible for this difference. The first alternative explanation is most intractable, although it certainly cannot be completely excluded: popular sentiment in Eastern Europe more often holds that ethnic characteristics are the basis for political formation. However, the relative calm, in terms of violent extremism, which Western Europe has experienced since World War Two – with only a few violent trouble spots that are explicitly being recognized as exceptions (Basque country, Northern Ireland) – is caused by a nationalism which differs specifically in means and character, not in spread and permanency. Therefore, the difference between Eastern Europe and Western Europe leaves much to be explained about the channelling of popular sentiments in the period since the Second World War; this cannot be explained by historical contingencies.

The impact of the shock of the transition has of course hit the population in all fields of life, including the economical, political, social and, indeed, psychological field. However, this second alternative underestimates the extent to which ethnonational sentiment has remained strong under communism: no Socialist union of ethnonational groups has occurred. Ethnonationalism was not just relevant after the fall of communism, or even just shortly before the transition, but has been present ever since the creation of communist regimes; it has even assisted in the demise of the centralized communist power itself. Communism itself therefore substantially assisted in the upsurge of ethnonationalist sentiment in Eastern Europe.

Indeed, the cases of Bulgaria and Czechoslovakia have illustrated how the communist structure has affected ethnic relations in Eastern Europe. Clearly, the centrality of decision-making and the lack of societal autonomy makes the centre very vulnerable to ethnic-based criticism, as it makes ethnic groups very vulnerable to centre-based policies. To the extent that the centre is thought to represent one group more than the other, if only because the experiences of the other group are not made public, the increase in frustration may lash out when guards are lowered. However, the final impact on ethnonational groups may be very complex. In the case of Czechoslovakia, for instance, many Slovaks felt themselves victim of a regime which was located in Prague and which was considered to represent Czechs more than Slovaks. They were strengthened in their beliefs by the pre-war elections during which communist support was much stronger in the Czech Lands than in Slovakia. On the other hand, many Czechs argued that the Slovaks profited most from the regime's policies on the federation, economic equalization, and influence in the party. In Bulgaria, the focus of Turkish ethnonational mobilization was clearer. It remains doubtful whether the regime's extreme policies towards ethnic Turks did indeed reflect the sentiments of the Bulgarian part of the population, and were intended to increase the regime's popularity among the population. In any case, the system enabled the regime to implement its policies without being checked. The opposite perspective is more important; the regime's character certainly gave the Turks the impression that the Bulgarian national character was the backdrop of communist policies. The Turks were completely excluded from decision-making, and Sofia's policies certainly appeared to them to be nationalist in content. Thus, although a long history of ethnonational conflict in the region preceded communist rule (and accompanied its rise to power), ultimately communist rule did nothing to ameliorate historical traumas, and in contrast provided the structures, the mentality, and to a large extent the reason for people to focus on their ethnonational identity.

In both liberal-democratic states overt public participation in ethnonational politics was very much higher and has helped to initiate changes in the relationship between the groups. The fact that both liberal-democratic cases have a tradition of consensus-type government instead of majority rule has helped to absorb ethnonational conflict and implement solutions through constitutional arrangements; after agreement was reached, there was, by and large, the certainty of implementation and irreversibility. Moreover, in contrast to communist systems, experience with other types of schisms prevented ethnonational tension from becoming the prime reason for political action. The consensus-type of government encouraged the elite to handle tension carefully, because current opponents may be needed for later coalitions.

This is not to say that the two liberal-democratic states are completely similar, of course. In terms of its ultimate consequences, when it comes to changing the state system, the impact of ethnonationalism has been much more pronounced in Belgium. This is also true for Czechoslovakia in the case of the two communist countries, but particularly in the Belgian case we would expect to find diminishing ethnonational tensions, given the basic flexibility of the political arena under liberal-democracy. In Belgium, the push for constitutional reform seems to be a continuing one, and the reason for the prolonged impact of ethnonationalism therefore needs extra attention. As will be discussed in the next section, of particular importance is the territorial nature of the political solution that was sought.

8.3 UNITARY AND FEDERALIZED ARRANGEMENTS

In chapter two I argued that a federal system based on ethnic territories could fundamentally differ from a unitary system in three ways: the territorial demarcation could reinforce the identity of the group; the republic could provide institutionalized political access to the centre; and the political institutionalization could provide the group with the means to protect and strengthen their ethnic characteristics. Despite the fact that the four cases under study are not as sharply defined as may be desirable, it is still quite possible to explore to what extent this dimension adds to our insights into ethnonationalism.

8.3.1 Identity

First of all, I suggested in chapter two that the chances for strong ethnonationalism might be higher with the creation of a federal republic, as a result of the importance of the republican territory for the identity of the group.

Furthermore, I proposed that in unitary systems both the state policies and the lack of an institutionalized territorial basis could hamper the development of ethnic identity and ethnonational activism. In a federalized state, on the other hand, the institutionalized territorial basis could encourage the development of ethnonational sentiment, and lead to severe challenges to the *raison d'être* of the system as a whole.

The cases confirm the importance of this aspect. In the two federalized systems the ultimate impact has been much more severe in terms of challenges to the system than in the two unitary systems; this is connected, in part, to the institutionalization of the territory as such. Connor is right to point out that administrative demarcation gives geographic precision to the 'shadowy notion of homeland' (Connor, 1984:497). After demarcation is achieved, territorial changes become immediate attacks on the core of the group's identity. Thus, in Belgium, after the language laws of the 1930s had delimited the language areas, the linguistic shift was experienced by the Flemish as a dismal development. Once the relevant territory had been established, it was only logical that areas in which the population opted to speak French were perceived as 'lost territories' in the continuous battle against the higher status of the French language and the French-language speakers. The 1960s fixation provided security, although the situation around Brussels and in Voeren continues to present challenges to the arrangement.[7] In Czechoslovakia, the historical borders of the Slovak provinces were used; its unity has not really been questioned, except in the 1960s when the regime created three sub-units that were directly subordinate to Prague. This was indeed considered by many Slovaks to be an attempt to weaken Slovak power and unity.

The situation was different in the two unitary cases. In Finland, specific monolingual and bilingual municipalities were defined, and the decline in the number of those municipalities has indeed worried Swedish-speakers. Nevertheless, from the start of the Finnish state the living area of the Swedish-speakers was not considered a single unit, and losses have mainly been felt at the level of the municipality. Moreover, the connection between territory and identity has been blurred by the differences between the Swede-Finns on the southern coast and Swede-Finns on the western coast; each group attaches different importance to the linguistic status of their living areas. A similar situation exists in Bulgaria for the Turks. Compared to Bulgaria and Finland, therefore, territory in Czechoslovakia and Belgium has become of more explicit importance to their identification as a group.

7   It is of course true that this aspect of identity formation in fact preceded federalization in Belgium in the 1970's and 1980's. It is interesting in itself to note, as discussed in chapter six, that this basic element in Flemish and Walloon identity to a large extent resulted from solutions designed by Dutch-speakers and French-speakers over the years. It should also be noted that in the context of this comparison the word 'republic' is used to denote both the sub-state territories in Belgium and those in Czechoslovakia. This improves the clarity of the argument, but is strictly speaking not correct.

As a result, more than in the two unitary cases, in Belgium and Czechoslovakia there has been a tendency to see ethnonational conflict in terms of these territories. Access is arranged at the level of the republic, and internal political and social differences are played down; inter-republic differences are emphasized. Economic issues are particularly vulnerable to falling prey to the territorialization of political life. As Bookman (1994:185) concludes "Since ethnicity is usually related to regional boundaries, economic injustice becames transformed into ethnic injustice, which is vented by political parties in an era of multi-party power during the period of re-evaluation." The continuous production of statistics on a regional basis tends to stress the distinction between republics. The difference between Switzerland and Belgium is interesting in this respect; McRae (1986:89) concludes that "comparisons between French and German Switzerland typically involved tedious statistical calculations for twenty-six cantonal units, and even then produced only crude approximations of the language boundaries. The two cases suggest some reciprocal relationship between the form in which data are recorded and public perceptions of the structure of the cleavages." In federations based on ethnic homelands, the connection may be very strong, particularly during election time. Then, incentives increase to emphasize regional unities and to stress precisely those characteristics of the ethnic group and region which differentiate them from the larger unit (see Olson 1993). It is for this reason that the breakup of the state-wide parties in Belgium may have such severe effects in the long term. It might be added that every corner of the state's territory is subjected to this territorialization of identity. This could be seen in the case of Brussels, which did not fit neatly into the cultural dichotomy, and where the FDF developed in response; it even created the notion of the 'Bruxellois'.

The effect of the territorialization of ethnic differences becomes acute when the system as such falls into crisis. When full-scale political rearrangement is needed, the existence of demarcated territories enables a wider range of options, including independence. The homogeneity of the republic is put forward in all kinds of ways in times of great transformations, for instance when the economic balance is drawn up. This also concerns the political views in the republic; in the negotiation process in Czechoslovakia, for instance, many territorial nuances in political support for separation tended to be suppressed by the overwhelming force of the territorial dichotomy. Judicial permanency also appeals to the outside world if the system falls into a state of crisis, and it eases the road to international recognition. This certainly operated in Yugoslavia, where the internal boundaries of the old state were used as external borders for the new states.

8.3.2 Access

The second line of thought concerned access to the centre. I suggested that in unitary political systems, ethnonational groups can only develop movements which basically organize themselves on a non-territorial basis, and thus resemble other types of interest groups. Furthermore, they lack an institutionalized and separate political channel to the political centre, an item which could seriously hamper the successful development of a movement. I assumed that in federalized political systems the organization of ethnic interest will occur on a territorial basis, and that the existence of a federal republic provides the ethnic group with their own permanent channel of interest articulation towards the centre; this may increase the possibilities for successful ethnonational activism *vis à vis* the centre.

Overall, the four cases do not quite display the pattern which was expected; both between the two unitary systems and between the two federalized systems there are some important differences. However, several basic points indeed come to the fore. Whereas in the unitary systems, though access is possible, it is not guaranteed and is at times denied, the arrangements under federal systems are constitutionally guaranteed and do provide a high degree of certainty. Despite differences between the federal systems in this respect, Belgium and Czechoslovakia therefore differ from both unitary states in certainty of access. Even the Swede-Finns, although their access and participation has been exceptionally high, were not let in during the 1920s. The fate of the Turks, even after 1989, is even more pronounced in this respect. It is only because of their comfortable position of balance that they could have such influence, and, after the elections in December 1994, this situation ended.

In the two federalized systems, the importance of a separate territory for continuous access to the centre and control over decision-making was not the same. Thus, in Czechoslovakia, aside from the communist party, control was arranged very well through the Chamber of Nations and with special majorities in many fields; in Belgium the alarm bell procedure provided the guarantee. This latter arrangement was not a territorial arrangement because representatives of the communities could set it off. The access of the group on a territorial basis was not made explicit. The rules used by special majorities to change the constitution were similarly constructed on a non-territorial basis, although these effectively blocked any possibility to ignore the other group and change the system unilaterally. The character of safeguards was mainly accounted for by the transitional nature of the Belgian system, and a more traditional system is now being implemented in Belgium. Despite the precise form of arrangements, it nevertheless has the same result in terms of guaranteed access.

A further important distinction between the two federalized systems and the unitary systems is that, once the territories are installed, who represents the group is no longer a question. The mere fact that one is a representative from one of the federal republics implies representation on an ethnic basis, whereas in a unitary structure political parties need to gain large numbers of votes to successfully claim to represent the group on an ethnonational basis. In a federation the group tends to speak with one voice in external contacts. The need for clear representation in all likelihood accounts for the extremely high support of their ethnonational party by the Swede-Finns and the Turks. In Belgium, all parties competed over the Flemish votes initially, but the recent use of terminology like the 'dialogue of the communities' shows the change in emphasis over time. Indeed, the fragmentation and within-group political competition which may become relevant in a unitary context does not have the same political relevance in a federal context at the state-wide level. The group is represented by a single political voice in the debate; it is the republican government which represents the group.

In the cases in this book access to the state was not only achieved through political mechanisms but also through the bureaucracy. When the bureaucracy is included, the access to decision-making not only involves the leadership but also the larger mass of people, both through employment and through their daily contacts with the government. In this respect the two federalized systems demonstrate a similar advantage for the ethnonational group in the sense that they improve the chances for proportionality in the state administration. This in itself increases the legitimacy of the political unit, while at the same time the sense of insecurity and fear for possible reversals is removed. In unitary situations, agreements on positive action are more likely to be undercut at the local level by unwillingness on the part of the dominant group, such as the case of the francophone administration in Brussels until the 1960s. For the same reason the central institutions of the federation remain a clear bone of contention, particularly if the capital is located in one of the other republics, such as Prague from the perspective of Slovakia (see below).

Belgium and Czechoslovakia were once unitary states. Their experience shows the difficulties of groups with a subordinate status in achieving proportionality under unitary arrangements. In Czechoslovakia, before the war Slovaks' access to political power was almost totally blocked by the peculiarities of the Czechoslovak party system and by the then prevailing system of coalition politics. Being opposition, Hlinka and his Slovak electorate were unable to benefit from the patronizing system and enlarge their share in the bureaucracy. In particular, newly educated Slovaks were deprived of job opportunities. Their low representation in Czechoslovak bureaucracy under unitary communism was also one of the reasons behind their protests in the years before the Prague Spring. In Belgium, although politicians from Flanders participated in government and in bureaucracy from the start of the new state, the language of government and the higher levels of bureaucracy remained predominantly French until well into the 1950s, while the under-representation of Flemish speakers was substantial. The exclusion of Turkish-speakers was very clear, and it is uncertain whether this will change even under the new regime. Only Swedish-speakers in Finland enjoy near-perfect proportionality in all aspects and even over-representation in some fields (e.g., in higher education). Therefore, despite a higher probability of difficulties, access can certainly be satisfactory under a unitary system, but continued interest defence on an ethnonational basis requires convincing organization at group level.

Three final comments should be made. The first is that political mobilization generally has a geographical component. Not only is support usually distributed unevenly, but notions of territory and regional interest may be found in most kinds of political activism. For instance, even such basically non-territorial elements as the Dutch pillars clearly had a component of territorial control, which may have been a central element in their creation and functioning (see Toonen 1993). Secondly, specific autonomy arrangements may have similar effects in terms of access. Nevertheless, the basic difference between autonomy and a federal arrangement is the latter's irreversible character resulting from republican control over the centre. Thirdly, in terms of political options, a federalized system may in principle improve access at group level, but at the same time diminish political options for the individual since two separate political arenas may be developed without overlap and possibilities for switching; this was discussed in the context of Belgium and Czechoslovakia. I will return to this point in section 8.3.4.

8.3.3 Self-strengthening policies

As a third aspect I proposed that there could be a major difference in the way and the extent to which the ethnic groups are capable of protecting their culture and internal cohesion against external encroachment. I suggested that in unitary states it is less likely that special policies will be developed which institutionalize the ethnic differences in society. Moreover, even if developed, these policies will not create territorially based institutions; this diminishes the importance of territory for the development of ethnonationalism as discussed above. In federalized states, special policies to institutionalize ethnic differences can indeed be formulated (both by the central and the republican government), and if so, they would further stress the ethnic characteristics of the groups.

The comparison between the two systems demonstrates the importance of the federal structure in this respect. The difference, however, is found not so much in the development of policies as in the compulsory nature of these policies for specified territories. An important example is education, and in Belgium its devolution to the communities was considered of central importance to the political debate. Two linguistic sections of the traditional parties, the Flemish Catholics and the Walloon Socialists, were considered to have received their 'own garden to play in' when the territories were established and the competencies were assigned. The Belgian political tradition

255

of plurality implied explicit acknowledgement of this, which led to the creation of the Cultural Pact. Competencies in education have consequences not only for such things as the ethnocentric content of schoolbooks, but also for the separation of the educational careers of the future elite, as was discussed in the case of Czechoslovakia. In the long run important changes can occur (or at least social changes will not be halted), such as the choice of English instead of French as the second language of the future elite in Flanders.

Moreover, not only control over the population, to put it bluntly, but also control over the natural, infrastructural, and productive resources within the borders of the republics may be channelled to serve the interests of the group. The inclusion of competencies in foreign affairs will only emphasize this. Overall, the chances for cultural exchanges between the groups will diminish with territorial fixation. Depending partly on how much the federal republics are able to stress the cultural uniqueness of the territory, migration to other republics will soon be followed by cultural assimilation. Indeed, parallel cultural circuits (schools, theatres, newspapers) will perhaps be erected within each republic, but only to the extent to which it does not affect the general cultural character of that republic.

The Åland Islands show how this may work through an autonomy arrangement as well. Apart from that exception, however, the two unitary systems display how the population can mix more easily. In Finland, the incidence of bilingual environments is on the rise compared with Swedish-language environments, and despite the creation of an extensive network of institutions this 'erosion' is very difficult to stop. Only if Finnish-speakers in Swedish-language areas had no other option but to speak Swedish, could this tendency be offset. It is precisely for this reason that the territorial option was preferred by the Flemish in Belgium, and the consequences have been clear. Thus whereas in unitary systems the ethnic group may be allowed to continue to speak its own language, and even have the government approach it in its own language, there is a tendency for bi-cultural environments to emerge in the long run. This is detrimental to the group with lower social or demographic status. Czechoslovakia is less clear in this respect, partly because the languages are so similar; nevertheless, before the war the immigration of many Czechs and the introduction of a more Czech-like Slovak grammar necessitated a 'purification' in the eyes of Slovak nationalists following only twenty years of unitary rule.

A final point is that with territorial demarcation the circulation of the elite will also be contained within the territory. Not only are its members likely to receive an education exclusively within their own republic, but they will also have their political careers within it, up to the stage at which they represent the republic at the level of the federation. As a result, they are likely to see everything through the eyes of the republic. This is valid for the ruling parties as well as for the opposition. Indeed, as noted in the chapter on Belgium, the desire by the state elite to uphold the level of centralized power was slowly eroded by the arrival of new elites: in Flanders, at first elites who had been educated solely in their own language for the first time; then young politicians who did not feel the need to keep the state completely centralized; and then, a new generation which had been weathered politically in the context of communal strife. Even the opposition can become divided, as seen in Czechoslovakia in the case of Charter 77, and in Belgium in the split of all the political parties, including the Communist Party. Despite the fact that the political elite of ethnonational groups in unitary systems will mainly be contained within the group, it is less explicitly connected with the group's territory.

In summary, through a federal structure and on an ethnic basis, separate living units may unwillingly be created up to a point where the daily interaction between the various cultures within the state is minimized in most aspects of life. This minimization may also be underlined by specific policies. The installation of a federation has therefore led to a deepening of the differences within a society in both federalized cases. The degree of autonomy in all fields of life, and the political control over resources which may support these policies, is generally not available in unitary countries, where state-wide preferences may more easily overrule local and ethnonational interests.

8.3.4 Conclusion

The three elements generally work in combination. Despite the fact that the cases show some variations, the basic proposition holds: that the federal structure is a type of political system which, in cases where ethnic territories coincide with demarcations of federal republics, in itself influences and strengthens ethnic characteristics. In contrast, a unitary system does not promote mobilization on a territorial basis; this affects the form of representation as well as the possibilities for identity formation and identity protection. It does not necessarily have to weaken ethnonationalism for the group as such, however, as in the unitary system, some aspects were found which helped to reinforce the movement of the group and the implementation of its demands. But certainly, although similar mechanisms may sometimes operate in unitary systems, the implementation of regionalist and federalized systems provides a wide range of mechanisms for further exchange which may be more and more exclusionary. Therefore, whereas federalism is very often developed with cultural diversity in mind, it provides the framework in which separate identities can be fostered and strengthened.

The question, moreover, is not just what mechanisms are at work, but also what are the ultimate consequences. As has been argued in chapter two, the importance of state institutions also concerns their persistence over time. Thus, whereas the discussion in section 8.1 has pointed to the fluctuation of politicized ethnonational sentiment, the implementation of a federalized solution creates a mould in which renewed popular discontent, in whatever form, may be channelled. It differs from federalism in countries like the U.S.A. or Australia mainly in that the cultural diversity which is at the base of the two federalized systems discussed in this book tends to be widened, with each crisis and expression of popular discontent followed by new devolution; in the process, the desire to maintain the political system as a whole gradually weakens. The sub-state political units are slowly filled up with stateness and national identity, so to speak, until a very fundamental crisis (as seen in Eastern Europe) initiates the final thrust.

A question which remains is whether the breaking away of the new states would have occurred if they had been part of unitary states, for instance in the case of Czechoslovakia. This section indicates that under those circumstances the psychological make-up, perceived politico-cultural bonds, and internal and external recognition would probably not have allowed such a drastic step to be taken. In a way, therefore, the federalization of a state may be a phase in between ethnonational assertion and independence, during which the process of internal nation-building and external acceptance (which is crucial when the moment arrives) is being strengthened. It is not predetermined, however; whether new balances can be struck after each crisis still depends on negotiations at the central level.

Some additional comments should be made on the character of the cases. The situation in Bulgaria is the most straightforward; the unitary structure of the state is crystal clear. The second unitary state, Finland, contains an autonomous region which caters precisely for the Swedish-speaking minority of the country. As has been discussed in chapter seven, this is important because the autonomy on the islands provided a clear message that a satisfactory arrangement was sought by the new Finnish state. Nevertheless, the majority lives on the mainland, and it is their fate which has been discussed above. The federal character of Czechoslovakia after 1968 was written into the constitution, but in practice it has been undercut by the existence of a state-wide Communist Party, the erosion of the competencies of the republics by the centre, and the non-development of its Czech counterpart. This aspect will be discussed in the next section. Belgium is the most problematic case, since its federal structure was only devised in 1988 and implemented in the years which followed. Nevertheless, the constitutional changes which were initiated in 1970 – providing the linguistic communities with autonomy and representation in the centre, and initiating (though not yet implementing) the regions – were of such a fundamental nature that the case could clearly illuminate the processes which are at work under federalized systems. Overall, the difficulties do not detract from the usefulness of the cases in analyzing the diverse impact of political systems on ethnonationalism.

It should further be pointed out that the federations treated in this book are somewhat peculiar in the sense that only two groups are involved. In Belgium, the Flemish have opposed a significant role for a separate Brussels region for a long time, for fear of being outvoted by two French-speaking regions in a triple federation. In Czechoslovakia, the Slovaks as well as the Czechs were unwilling to have Moravia become a third republic, and, for the Slovaks at least, because of similar reasons as in Belgium.[8] The importance of this bipartite structure is difficult to assess. The two cases in this book indicate that in an dyadic federation (temporary) coalitions are impossible and deadlocks are likely to happen, the two combatants eying each other with suspicion across the 'front line' in their continuing 'trench war'. It is perceived that gains can only be made at the expense of the other (who has to be compensated), while losses are clearly identifiable by both partners. This is at least partly the reason for the prolonged nature of the discussion in Belgium, and for the final impossibility of finding a satisfactory solution in the Czechoslovak case. It is therefore interesting to hypothesize what would have happened if nine republics had been created in Belgium, and if a separate Silesia/Moravia had been combined with, for instance, three Slovak republics and six Czech republics in Czechoslovakia. Experiences in countries like Switzerland and Nigeria indicate that the high level of fragmentation and an inability to equalize territorial differences with ethnic distinctiveness at the republic level may seriously limit the tension which is now being generated and moulded to more destructive levels (not necessarily violent, but destructive for the state as a political unit) (see e.g., Horowitz, 1985:635–638). From that perspective, the plan which Vance and Owen launched for Bosnia-Hercegovina was well-conceived. Their plan entailed the creation of ten regions (besides other things): three regions for each group plus multi-ethnic Sarajevo. Similarly, the introduction of a third republic in Belgium may alter the current dynamics of the process.

8.4   THE INTERACTION OF THE TWO DIMENSIONS

It has become clear from the analysis of the cases that the two dimensions of the typology interact in their effects on ethnonational sentiment and mobilization. One of the main questions is whether it is a coincidence that the three communist federations in Europe have collapsed in the last years, or, to put it differently, failed to make a successful transition to a liberal-democratic and capitalistic system. However, before the interaction is analyzed it should be noted that the two elements of the communist federations – a communist political system and a federal political system – represent two different approaches in state-society relations. The communist side of the

---

8   Important in this context is also the fact that a Hungarian republic has never been an option in Czechoslovakia, nor is it in Slovakia at this moment; in contrast a German-speaking region has now been created in Belgium and the German community has become an official sub-state unit of the Belgian Kingdom. The reason for this difference is partly numerical: German-speakers are a small group and do not wield much influence in decision-making, but this could be a different situation for the Hungarians.

politico-economic dimension is a suppressive side, playing down diversity in society, and stressing the homogeneity of the countries' population and its unified support for the leading party. The federal side of the territorial dimension, on the other hand, is a facilitating aspect, enabling and even underlining diversity. The dialectical relationship between the two dimensions in their effect on ethnonationalism is therefore illustrative of the complexity of the ethnonational phenomenon.

First of all, the combined effects of the image of the central state under communism and separate identity formation under federalism work in concert to cement ethnonational differences. Clearly, the unifying force of the Communist Party failed to prevent differentiation from being sustained and reinforced, as the failures of the communist system destroyed the trust in the political centre. The centre proved unable to lead the way to a renewed political system during times of transition, when an immense uncertainty increased the popular need for fast and easy solutions. This process is reinforced by, in the second place, the centralized nature of politics under communism both in the cultural and in the economic field. The emphasis on equalization in all spheres of life and the arbitrariness of the centre's policies towards ethnonational groups which form a minority, which are often perceived to be ethnically biased, create a backlash and lead to an emphasis on diversity and differences when the opportunity presents itself. The institutionalization of these differences needs only to be moulded into the already existing federal structure. In fact, communist centralism played out at the level of the republic as well, where the legitimacy of local communists could only be upheld by stressing and intensifying inter-republic differences and intra-republic homogeneity. Indeed, in the third place, the suppression of cross-cutting cleavages under communism is reinforced by the creation of internal borders, in which the Communist Party is the only overarching element. With the demise of the Communist Party, there is no possibility left for channelling the urge for diversity into state-wide alternatives of a non-ethnic kind, and competition between alternatives will only take place at the republic level.

It should be clear that the latter process works in a similar, though less extreme, way in liberal-democratic federations. In fact, there is some tension between a liberal-democratic system and a federal system, in the sense that it appears increasingly difficult to develop fruitful cooperation on non-ethnic issues across the borders of the republics in a federation which is based on ethnic territories. As a result, despite its importance to stable democracy, as was stressed by Lijphart, it is difficult to secure political cooperation between the social segments. Political elites monopolize the process of mediation between groups for themselves, reducing the possibilities of 'cross-cutting' in order to increase their own power. Indeed, paradoxically, while elites support heterogeneity in society as a whole, they act very energetically to impose homogeneity on the groups under their control, and to achieve ideological, religious, or ethnic 'purity' (Stanovčić 1992). Certainly, compared to the communist federal system, where other cleavages are suppressed and regionalized, cross-cutting cleavages are only regionalized under liberal-democracy. Nevertheless, cantonization would seem to create more possibilities for intergroup cooperation and multi-identity formation, since 'border-crossings' become more necessary and common.

Therefore, the theory on consociational democracy underestimates to what extent territorially based ethnic group formation in a consociational system may become a challenge to the state system as such. In contrast to other forms of segmentation, such as ones based on economic or religious characteristics, the promotion of autonomy in these circumstances will fundamentally alter the dynamics of elite interaction and societal differentiation. One can envisage that the dissolution of society into separate territorial segments will have extra impetus; federalization is the physical expression and the context in which the process may proceed unhindered. Thus, whereas under these circumstances consociationalism may prevent plural societies from sliding down the path to violent conflict, the long-term result may very well be the peaceful dissolution of the system itself for lack of reasons for staying together. It can, however, certainly be envisaged that some sort of fundamental crisis must occur before the qualities and the necessity of the common state will be assessed by all sides involved. In that respect, however, the institutional permanency of the state assures a proper context whenever that moment arrives. For instance, the referenda on the position of Quebec are an example of this situation: a single successful attempt will break up the state, but a failed attempt will not lead to a decline in the republic's competencies so that the permanency of the republic's institutions are guaranteed.

Having said this, it nevertheless remains clear that the incentive for extreme ethnic demands to occur (not for mobilization as such) seems weaker under liberal-democratic systems. Of course, this is not immediately observed in Bulgaria and Czechoslovakia, where the impact of communism has yet to wear off. Indeed, the heritage of the communist system – in terms of political system, in terms of economic structure, and in terms of mutual suspicion – has dominated post-communist negotiations and frustrated attempts to find a solution within the existing state system in Czechoslovakia. In Bulgaria, more favourable circumstances are to a large extent due to the tombola of elections, which presented the DPS with a balancing position between the two main parties until the end of 1994. It nevertheless seems to be a *sine qua non* for harmonious ethnic relations that they take place within a liberal-democratic context. The possibility to renegotiate the situation, when circumstances have changed, in a satisfactory way and a subsequent flexible return to other issues in political life are clearly too important.

It is obvious that the political system of the state is not always designed as a solution for ethnonational diversity. It nevertheless influences ethnic inter-action and structures it in various ways. A most obvious case in point is Bel-gium, where consociational decision-making was used to enable the peace-ful coexistence of the various ideological families, but where the inclusion of the linguistic issue has produced unexpected results. In a similar vein, the proportional system in Finland was basically designed to deal with the strong socialist movement (although the consequence of the system that Swedish-speakers would always be represented in parliament was clearly foreseen); the strong presidency was introduced for the same reason, but ensured a presidential grip on decision-making in parliament and on the nomination of ministers which was sometimes used to influence the debate on ethnonational relations. The argument is even more obvious for the communist systems in former Czechoslovakia and Bulgaria.

8.5   OTHER VARIABLES IN THE CASES

The impact of the political system on ethnonationalism takes place in the context of, and in combination with, other influences. Several of these other influences will be discussed in this section. It is useful to begin with a sub-ject which is always high on the agenda of ethnonationalist activists them-selves – the numeric and geographical situation of the groups. Keeping in mind the problems involved with census data, it can be observed that of the four cases, Czechoslovakia is the only country where the share of the minor-ity has clearly increased since the interwar years; however, this has at least partially been the result of the expulsion of other minorities. In Bulgaria and in Finland the share went down slightly; Belgium is of course somewhat of a peculiar case in regard to which group actually constitutes the minority; Dutch-speakers have always remained the numeric majority in the country and increased their share slightly over time. Both in Finland and in Bulgaria, the decline in numbers has mainly been the result of emigration, although in the case of Finland assimilation in later decades has also played a role.

Generally speaking, numbers count, certainly in the long term. In cases where the numerically inferior group possessed political dominance, such as in Belgium and in Finland, the tables turned with the introduction of mass voting; slowly in the case of Belgium, and quickly in the case of Finland. In Czechoslovakia, where the expulsion of Germans and, in part, Hungarians fundamentally altered the ethnic make-up of the country, the relative increase in the share of Slovaks rendered the renewed implementation of the notion of 'Czechoslovakism' far more difficult (if the communists had wanted it). Numbers also count in the perception that groups have of each other. Smallness invites feelings of vulnerability, certainly if it is accompa-nied by demographic decline, and it may form one of the other reasons for the continuing high level of support for the SFP and the DPS. The question remains, however, as to what extent the differences in size hamper the comparison. The differences certainly are a complication, because they alter the general political balance and thereby the context for inter-ethnic conflict and state-ethnonational interaction. However, the relation is not straightforward. On the one hand it is conceivable to argue that Finnish concessions to the Swede-Finns were possible precisely because they would not be a threat to the general character of the state. A similar situation exists for the German-speakers in the East Cantons of Belgium. On the other hand, the treatment of equal-sized minorities in other countries reveals less benign attitudes, such as for the Pomaks in Bulgaria, the Turks in Greece, or even the Hungarians in former Czechoslovakia. Political concessions therefore hinge on other variables as well. Swedish-speakers received concessions precisely because they were very much part of the political elite at the time, whereas they knew that their influence would deteriorate in the near future.

A second question concerns the importance of whether the group stands alone or whether it is part of a larger group; in other words, as some would call it, whether it is a nation(ality) or a minority ethnic group. It has been argued in chapter one that it is extremely difficult to draw a line between the two, because the links between the minorities and the mother culture are often not as close as they appear at first glance. In fact, minorities may develop a separate identity, as demonstrated by the Flemings and Walloons, the Moldavians, the Bosnian Serbs perhaps, and the Swede-Finns. Therefore, if the minority has no inclination towards secession or unification with the 'mother culture', most of the processes at work are similar as long as all involved remain convinced of that. Moreover, on the one hand it has become clear in the cases that an irredenta situation may entail the out-migration of many of the most active and capable, while the mother culture may on the other hand support the group financially and institutionally; this makes it difficult to judge the overall effect. In a broader sense, the international context of course has been central in the cases in this book, and I will return to it below.

Similar considerations relate to the spatial distribution of ethnonational groups within the state, which is also very dissimilar in the cases. Both in Finland and in Bulgaria the minority groups combine a living area where they are the dominating group with an area where they are living mixed with the majority group. However, in Finland it is in the core area of the country where majority and minority live side by side, whereas in Bulgaria it is a more peripheral area; moreover, the degree of mixing at the local level is not as high. Both in Finland and Bulgaria the main concentration of the minority is located at the edge of the country, near the country which forms the 'mother culture,' though not quite bordering it. In Belgium (besides Brussels) and Czechoslovakia, the two groups by and large live separated from each other, although the groups have at different periods during this century lived in small numbers in the other region. Both in Czechoslovakia and in Belgium the irredentas are formed by third groups in the peripheries of the countries, although compared to Belgium their share in the population of Czechoslovakia has always been much more substantial.

The locational aspects are important, and generally much weight is given to them. Secessionist movements can exist where a group has been defined as separate from the rest of the country's inhabitants, inequality is perceived in their position, and, most important here, their living areas are territorially contiguous and at the border of the state (see Heraclides 1991). Both in Finland and in Bulgaria the minorities have therefore been seriously hampered by their split location in the country. In particular in Finland shortly after the First World War, partly under the inspiration of the debate over the Åland Islands, prolonged discussions took place concerning a possible federation with Swedish-language republics. The Swedish-speakers in Helsinki and surroundings, in particular, opposed this, opting for a bilingual Finland instead; the Åland Islands remained the exception. In Bulgaria demands from the Turks for a territorially based autonomy have seldom been heard, although calls for secession have; apart from other considerations, the lack of a contiguous living space is a reason for this.

The question is also to what extent locational aspects have influenced the interaction between states and minorities. An ethnic mix constitutes a clear, though not impossible, problem in terms of solutions and, for instance, the complicating factor of Brussels prevents easy solutions in the Belgian case. Indeed, if the splits in Yugoslavia and Czechoslovakia are compared, in the first case the ethnic mosaic prevented clear territorial demarcations along ethnic lines, even if the borders of the republics had been adapted before independence and had been accepted by the international community. Ethnic mixture clearly increases the likelihood of violence, when attempts are made to force the issue; "cleanse or be cleansed" is the main result of this. It should be pointed out, however crude the realization, that a certain process of 'ethnic cleansing' had already been completed in Central Europe some fifty years ago, involving, among others, Jews, Czechs in Slovakia, Slovaks in the Czech Lands and in Hungary, and of course the Germans, Hungarians, and Ruthenians in Czechoslovakia as a whole (under very diverse circumstances of course), and that the ethnic 'unmixing' of that period at least partly allowed for the lack of violence during the Velvet Divorce.

While the question of ethnic distribution makes each case quite unique to a certain extent, it should be clear that it is at the same time only part of a complex of conditions which influences the interaction between states and ethnonational groups. However, certainly when it comes to state responses, it is clear that the ethnic distribution conditions the possibility of certain solutions, in particular ones with a territorial base. As has been said in chapter one, for that reason alone it is not automatically clear whether immigrant groups and territorially based ethnic groups are comparable, although it can be assumed that certain elements in the interaction process are similar.

264

The location of the capital is also of interest. In fact, in Czechoslovakia the perceived cultural and political dominance of the centre found its geographical image in the capital's location in a distant part of the country (from the Slovak point of view). Cultural and political differences thus become emphasised by geography, and under communism this image of a 'foreign' centre was further reinforced. In the case of Belgium, the location of Brussels close to the language border creates a very different image of the centre than is the case with Prague; the capital is located in the area of what used to be the main dissatisfied group, the Flemish. Nevertheless, this does not diminish its importance, as the position of Brussels in a mainly Dutch-speaking area has been politically crucial ever since its frenchification gained momentum. Its spread into the Flemish hinterland compares psychologically with the notions of vulnerability in a country's 'soft belly,' such as formerly with West Berlin in East Germany, or with a Greek-dominated Cyprus seen from the perspective of Turkey. Indeed, such notions were central to the geopolitical mapping of Czechoslovakia's position *vis à vis* Germany before World War Two by German geopoliticians such as Haushofer. The psychological uses and impact of these political geographical notions should not be underestimated. The difference between the cases of Sofia and Helsinki, both at the edge of the country, is that the Turks have never lived in large numbers in Sofia since 1878, while the Swedes in fact dominated life in Helsinki until the twentieth century. For the Turks this only underlined their peripheral status.

The presence of major cities in the territory of the group indeed seems to be a prerequisite for successful ethnonationalist action (see Murphy 1990a). It may be envisaged that the heightening of the status of cities, such as the designation of Bratislava as the capital of the Slovak Republic, creates a centre which attracts more money, jobs and attention. It may provide the central focus of the group's right to self-fulfilment and equal status in the family of nations. Belgium is again somewhat of a peculiar case, in the sense that the biggest French-speaking town is the regional capital of the Dutch-speaking region, whereas it is not the capital for the French-speaking region. The lack of a clear Dutch-speaking regional centre, the result of a deliberate choice of the Flemish Movement, now dampens desires for complete secession. An interesting development in the Belgian case is therefore the choice of Namur as the centre of the Walloon region; it may in the long term reinforce differentiation between Brussels' French-speakers and the population of Wallonia.

The focus on the different impact of various political systems makes it necessary to stress the inner workings of the state. Certainly, however, the international context should not be neglected. To begin with, the four cases are themselves each located in different regions of Europe, and, as mentioned above, this touches directly upon the character of the nationalism involved. Indeed, the assumption that certain nationality problems have deeper importance than others is an implicit assumption in many studies on ethnic conflict. With regard to the volatility and viciousness of ethnonation-alism in Eastern Europe, which was to a certain degree affirmed in the first section of this chapter, the cases in this book compare favourably with some neighbouring countries. In the last couple of years, indeed, Bulgaria has been a surprising island of stability compared with some of its neighbours, but its own internal tensions, and the wealth of historical claims in the region, create the constant danger of ethnic flames burning the country. Czechoslovakia was truncated at various times during its history and its minority questions have always been central to its existence and very much related to its geopolitical situation. Moreover, these questions have been strongly connected to the policies of its neighbours, in particular Germany and Hungary, but also Poland and the former Soviet Union. Finland also borders the former Soviet Union, and, until 1991, remained the only suc-cessful secession from that country; its relation to that power has been cen-tral to its national identity. Historically dominant Sweden is located on its opposite border, and is the mother culture of its main minority.

In a way these countries differ from the fourth case, Belgium, because of the timing of their creation. It can justifiably be said that whereas in Bel-gium state formation more or less preceded national sentiment at the mass level, it was much more the other way around in the other countries. Bel-gium borders two of the oldest modern states of the world and has been a buffer between the major powers of Europe. Although it has been part of the Netherlands and France during some periods in its history, it has not been subject to continuous territorial claims on their part since 1839. The concept of the historical enemy is therefore almost completely missing in the perception of both the Flemish and the Walloons. In fact, the political sys-tems in themselves reflect the geopolitical division running through the European continent, with Czechoslovakia and Bulgaria on one side, Bel-gium on the other, and Finland somewhere on the edge. It is clearly impos-sible to see the countries apart from their geopolitical context. Nevertheless, whereas their particular location on the European continent is crucial to understanding the political histories of the countries, including the ethnona-tional question, this in itself does not render the subsequent influence of the political system on ethnonational sentiment and activism irrelevant. Put simply, whereas the political system is to a large extent conditioned by the geopolitical situation, the system itself may generate and mould ethnona-tionalism.

Somewhat more complicated are the 'national' identities themselves, each of which has grown in adversity to other cultures and former political influ-ence. Therefore, each case has its particularity in national culture which results from the logic of its original creation, and political leaders will attempt to placate the population by filling in the nationalist content of the state and using symbols to confirm the state's heroic past. Thus, for instance, Finland's national identity emerged in particular in its struggle with Russia and evolved around keeping intact its separate institutions and culture (which were mainly of Swedish origin). This was profitable to the position of the prominent Swedish speakers, who themselves were the first to care about the Finnish national characteristics. In contrast, Bulgaria emerged from the remnants of the Ottoman Empire, and found its identity in its adversity to Islam and to Turkish rule, creating a completely different context for the subsequent Bulgarian-Turkish relation in the new country. However, as seen in chapter four, this was not unidirectional, since, for instance, separateness from Greek influence was also important, giving the Turks some room to manoeuvre. In a similar vein, although perhaps less pronounced, francophone resistance to Dutch rule in Belgium played a main part in the struggle for independence on the part of the Belgian elite, and the French language was considered a necessary prerequisite for the continuing independence and unity of the country. Indeed, secession of Flanders and Germanic irredentism were always suspected behind Flemish attempts to strengthen their culture and power (although the German-speakers themselves have been treated surprisingly well, even after two occupations of Belgium by Germany). National symbols can in fact be diffi-cult to change, therefore, as exemplified by the fact that it took more than a century for a Dutch-language section to be added to the national anthem of Belgium. The vulnerability of Czechoslovakia was so apparent to its leaders that they thought it necessary to stress the commonality of Slovaks and Czechs and play down differences which had grown as a result of their sep-arate histories and socio-economic contexts. Complicating the relations between the two groups was also the fact that their national identity was partially forged in opposition to different outside powers, the Czechs in opposition to the Austrians and Germans, and the Slovaks in opposition to the Hungarians. These central elements in the state's emergence subse-quently became the background for the protracted ethnonational conflict in the country.

A more general treatment of the international environment is therefore very important. The links are numerous, as appeared in the cases studied. This not only concerns relations with neighbours, in particular in the case of irredentas and in the development of national identity, but also major international events and storms such as the World Wars, the raising of the Iron Curtain, or the unification of Europe; these provide the context in which ethnonational tension shifts in importance. A broader perspective, for instance, is taken by Wallerstein (1991) who points at the links between the dynamics of the international economic system and the rise and fall of protest movements such as ethnonational movements. Therefore, these kinds of links deserve much more systematic treatment than can be given in the context of this book (see e.g., Ryan 1990, Heraclides 1991, Carment 1993).

A final point of importance is the difference in economic power of the groups discussed in the cases. In particular the historical economic relation was important. For instance, a dominant economic position was found for the Swede-Finns at the turn of the century, for the Czechs at independence, and for the French speakers in the first century of the Belgian state. It is clear that this influenced the starting position of the ethnonational relations at the mass level, although it must be pointed out as well that this economic position can certainly be influenced by the political decision-makers. Communist-style economic equalization is the most pointed example of this. What is certainly true is that economic downturn is not the only reason for ethnonational activism, considering that both the Flemings and the Slovaks demonstrated increasing levels of activism by the time their economic position had equalized, and Swedish-language activism occurred at the time their economic position was still extremely strong. In the cases in this book, economic factors appear only secondary to political and psychological ones in explaining the dynamics of ethnonationalism.

In summary, it is clear that the impact of political systems on the development of ethnonationalism is conditioned by other factors. However, on the other hand, it is equally clear that the phenomenon as such is relevant under widely different circumstances; it would therefore be incorrect to connect ethnonational conflict solely with historical and geographical contingencies. The purpose of analyzing specific variables comparatively is not to play down the importance of the other factors as such, but to focus on one of the influences and analyze whether it enhances our understanding of the phenomenon under study. That the autonomous role of the state deserves separate attention in its effect on ethnonationalist sentiment – and on the translation of this sentiment into a political movement with goals, means, and support – is the backdrop of this book.

8.6   CONCLUSION: STATES AND ETHNONATIONAL CONFLICT

In this book I have focused on the autonomous role of the state in generating and moulding ethnonational sentiment in Europe. I argued that this perspective improves our understanding of the phenomenon. By using two dimensions which were considered relevant in the European context I explored to what extent interesting differences emerged in the impact of state systems on ethnonationalism. This type of dimension, though slightly different, can equally be selected for other regions in the world. The perspective of this study was formulated to contrast the approach which sees the state as only responsive to ethnonational demands, or which considers the state to be just an arena where ethnic groups fight out their conflict. The conclusion is that among the factors which influence ethnonationalist sentiment and activism, the political system is a crucial one. The central role of the state rests not only on its effects on the group as a whole and on its leaders, but also on the state's effect on the interaction between the ethnonations and their leaders. Different states have diverse impacts in that respect. They allow or even promote, to a different extent, the connection between ethnonational masses and interested leaders, and direct peaceful or more confrontational ways of interaction between various ethnonational groups. Clearly ethnonationalism is highly relevant, at times dangerous, and in need of timely defusion to avoid its darker sides. The differences between political systems are central in explaining why it is defused in some cases and not in others. As Horowitz (1985) notes, the key is to find the institutional arrangements which provide the political incentives for accommodation and which penalize extremism.

Clearly communism was not among those arrangements, as it estranged the population from political decision-making, suppressed most cleavages and elements of civil life, and destroyed trust in the political centre. In some cases, by building separate ethnic cultures in the misplaced hope of creating Socialist Man, communism left the population with only populist-nationalist appeals as the most probable alternative following communism's own failure and collapse. Similar mechanisms will probably be found under other forms of authoritarian rule. Equally, federalism on an ethnic basis helps to foster ethnic sentiment, by creating the institutional structure in which identities can be mustered; not only because of the demarcation of clear territories itself, but also because of internal nation-building and slow erosion of a sense of state-wide common purpose. Although this in itself may not provide sufficient momentum, the institutional structure is there to be expanded with any new crisis. Certainly under liberal-democratic circumstances, devolution of powers in a federation on an ethnonational basis is hard to reverse.

Of course, the question is whether the results of these processes are to be regretted. The usual view is that the breaking-up of states is to be avoided, certainly as long as the mechanisms for interstate cooperation proceed at such a slow pace. However, there seems to be a wave-like character to the acceptance of increases and decreases in the scale of political-territorial units (Knight 1982). At this point in time, we can observe an increasing acceptance of fragmentation, and of the allowance of 'liberal nationalisms' in cases where the split of states into various sub-nations is not confronted by obstacles such as new minority groups or neighbouring expansionist desires (e.g., Lind 1994). Of course, these cases are hard to find. The problem is what to do in cases where these obstacles are found, and where none of the parties involved has any intention of withdrawing its claims. The frequent occurrence of the mixing of several ethnonational groups makes other solutions necessary.

In light of the discussion in this chapter, it would appear remedial if the concepts of state and nation could be disengaged and if both of them were allowed a status in the international arena (see Gottlieb 1993). This would take away much of the incentive to stress the desire for a separate state as the only complete fulfilment of the nation's purpose. It would create a position of status, where the unsatisfactory fulfillment of the individual through the low status of the group is an important backdrop to ethnonational conflict. It would also enable the overlap of territories in which distinct authorities exercise power over different and territorially fragmented fields of policy. In many ways, therefore, it resembles the Belgian solution, and elements of this type of solution can also be found in Irish-British proposals on Northern Ireland. Unfortunately, as the case of Belgium has also shown, the centrality and exclusionary use of territory for both concepts of 'state' and 'nation' makes it extremely difficult to implement. An alternative which follows the same line of thought might therefore be the cantonization of ethnonational territories within states, in order to create a similar diffusion of political authority and identity. This may be an unavoidable option if the continuing state of tension between ethnonational sentiment and existing political-territorial arrangements threatens to degenerate into protracted ethnonational conflict. Clearly, however, any solution to the tension between stateless ethno-nations and multi-nation states depends on the political will to negotiate.

Epilogue

Ethnonational diversity is common to most states, as I noted in the beginning of this book. Less than ten percent of the world's countries appear to be ethnically homogenous, and even in those cases there are usually significant groups of the citizens who do not consider themselves to be part of the dominant nation. Each day, the consequences of this ethnic diversity hit the front-pages of our newspapers: a seemingly endless list of conflict, death and destruction, caused by traumas and an astonishing level of hatred. In Chechenya, Rwanda, Burundi, Liberia, Kwazulu-Natal, Turkey, Kashmir, Irian Jaya, former Yugoslavia, to name but a few examples, groups violently confront each other or their governments, and assert the cultural uniqueness of their kind. Usually they put forward political demands that are inherent in that assertion: independence, full political control over the existing state machinery, or at the very least substantial political autonomy. Despite the rhetoric, the words of US President Wilson, shortly after World War One, have clearly not lost any of their importance : "Self-determination is not a mere phrase. It is an imperative principle for action, which statesmen will henceforth ignore at their peril."

In this book, to some extent the theoretical need to focus on particular cases has obstructed the view of the wider picture, certainly for the world as a whole, but even for Europe itself. And there are many reasons to worry about the course of events since the collapse of the Berlin Wall in 1989, as the international community has not yet found a way to deal successfully with the upsurge in ethnonational activism. In particular, the rather inconsistent implementation of the principle of self-determination bodes ill for future ethnonational conflicts.

Although arbitrariness is nothing new in this subject – take for instance the case of the Åland Islands discussed in this book – the wrestling of the international community with ethnonationalism has certainly been obvious in former Yugoslavia. Thus, the independence of Croatia, Slovenia, and Bosnia-Hercegovina was allowed, albeit reluctantly, without enforcing extensive and internationally controlled minority rights to protect the large Serb populations in Croatia and Bosnia, or, for that matter, the Albanians in Kosovo. Thorough autonomy arrangements should have been the prerequisite for international recognition. Moreover, the possibility of border changes, or the enforcement of a federalised type of government, was not even considered, although implementation of such a scheme would, of course, have been extremely difficult in former Yugoslavia, because of the ethnic intermingling. As it happened, however, the sanctity of the borders of the former federal republics, without extensive protection for the minorities in the new states, certainly set the stage for a horrifying civil war.

To be sure, the violence had its roots in the traumas that have plagued the Balkans this century, and in the political manoeuvring during the communist period, when the tension between Belgrade and the Croat communist party was particularly important. Against that background, cunning ethnic entrepreneurs could reintroduce the bipolar vision of Chetniks versus Ustashas, and could suggest that past wrongs could be put right. Nevertheless, the international community failed to contain the impact of these shrewd politicians, particularly when they brought their nationalist schemes to Bosnia. Thus, even after recognising Bosnia's independence and stressing its territorial unity, the international community did not allow the government in Sarajevo to buy the weapons with which it could defend that territorial unity. But neither was the other option enforced, namely to allow the Bosnian Serbs to govern their own political entity. In the end, years of muddling through left approximately 200,000 people dead and led to extensive 'ethnic cleansing' after all.

In the summer of 1995, the lack of resolve on the part of the international community showed especially with regard to the 'safe havens' of Srebrenica and Žepa, where the Bosnian Serbs deported and massacred thousands of Muslims, and to the Krajina, which the Croat army completely 'cleansed' of ethnic Serbs. Nevertheless, within a month after these war crimes, the Bosnian Serbs were forced to the negotiating table. It is perhaps no surprise to hear accusations that the international community deliberately allowed these war crimes to happen, in order to create a more straightforward ethnic map of Yugoslavia.

The main problem is of course that the muddling through in Yugoslavia did not stop with the cease-fire enforced in Dayton. Most worrying is the complete failure, even after nine months of peace, to allow refugees to return to their homes: Muslims to the Republic of Srpska, Serbs to Sarajevo and the Krajina, Croats to Slavonija, etc. This means the *de facto* political perpetuation of the military situation at the time of the Dayton agreements. While a necessity in the short term – the need to stop the killing was obvious – the long-term impact of this can only be negative. For several generations, people will remember their own experience or that of their parents, and use it as a base for renewed mobilisation in the name of their Croat, Serb, or Muslim brethren. If one compares the situation in former Yugoslavia with the deep-seated hatred which the Greeks hold against the Turks and vice versa, where references to the injustice of the 1923 Treaty of Lausanne are common, one can safely assume that another two to three generations of outright hatred have been created in the Balkans. The paradox is an alarming one: while within the European Union borders are opened under the Schengen agreement, its neighbours build new, impenetrable walls.

Unfortunately, the inability and unwillingness of the international community to deal with the continuing tension between territorial unity and political self-determination is not restricted to former Yugoslavia. Indeed, while the international community in Bosnia attempts to enforce freedom of movement, willing now declared enemies to live together, at the same time it allows the Chechens to be carpet-bombed by Russian fighter jets, and allows Russia to join the Council of Europe. In Turkey, the Kurds are systematically denied their rights at cultural expression, but that does not prevent the European Union from signing extensive economic agreements with Turkey. There are many similar examples.

To be sure, ethnonational conflict need not necessarily be violent to have a fundamental impact. In October 1995, for instance, French-language separatists in the Canadian province of Quebec failed only by a whisker to gain independence for their homeland. In an attempt to act on this turn of events, the central government in Toronto nevertheless felt obliged to offer a package to the French-language politicians in Montréal which included further devolution. Interestingly, and similar to the situation in former Yugoslavia, the English-speaking minority in Quebec did not hesitate to stress that the principle of self-determination need not necessarily stop at the borders of the French-language province, but was just as valid within those borders.

Separatist vocabulary is also heard across Western Europe. In the spring of 1996, Catalonia succeeded in wrestling substantial concessions from the new Spanish Prime Minister José María Aznar, who depended on the support from Jordi Pujols Convergéncia i Unió to be able to form a government at all. In the same period, a group of Catalan intellectuals presented detailed proposals on (con)federalising Spain. Perhaps most striking is that all this happened under the leadership of Aznar and his Partido Popular, probably Spain's most unitarian party which for years on end had accused the Catalans of being blackmailers and bribers.

Similar to Spain, Belgium has taken further steps along the road to separation. The Netherlands these days negotiate with the government of Flanders over the co-ordination of large projects in infrastructure – like the bullet-train or the accessibility of coastal waters and harbours – while it deals with Wallonia over measures to prevent the flooding of the Meuse. In July 1996, French-language politicians, in response to continuing Flemish demands for more devolution of powers, for the first time in the Belgian parliament angrily suggested they might attach Wallonia to France. In Italy Umberto Bossi's Lega Nord stubbornly repeats the message of autonomy for the northern part of Italy – a region he calls 'Padania'. And in the absolute monument of unitary rule, France, Corsican autonomy for many does not go far enough, and French economic and political interests on the island continue to be attacked. Even in the Savois region, an official declaration of independence from France has been issued by a group of notables too important to be qualified as completely ridiculous.

There is now, of course, a growing awareness that the tension between territorial integrity of states and the right of peoples to self-determination will continue to haunt the international community. Courageous attempts to deal with this tension are, for instance, the unrelenting efforts by the High Commissioner on National Minorities of the Organisation for Security and Co-operation in Europe, Max van der Stoel, and by the UN representative on Human Rights in former Yugoslavia, Elizabeth Rehn. It is of course doubtful whether their efforts will yield much. As is all too clear, the possibilities for the international community to influence the position of minorities in many countries are very limited, even when the political will to get involved is present.

Nevertheless, the careful analysis of various political arrangements is much needed to help prevent cultural diversity from degenerating into violence. Although it can be bizarre to do an academic study on ethnonationalism amidst these outbursts of violence and atrocities where thousands of innocent civilians are slaughtered in the name of cultural unity, the endurance and geographical spread of ethnonational conflict necessitates the continuing study of this subject. And not only the failures need to be analysed, but also the successful arrangements. The latter show that full independence and the violent break-up of states need not always be the only option to achieve ethnonational self-determination, and that states can find strength, and not weakness, in their cultural diversity.

Bibliography

Action Programme of the Czechoslovak Communist Party (1968), Spokesman Pamphlet no.8, The Betrand Russell Peace Foundation Ltd., Nottingham.

Agnew, J.A. (1981), Structural and Dialectical Theories of Political Regionalism, in: Burnett, A.D. and Taylor, P.J. (eds.), *Political Studies from Spatial Perspectives*, pp.275–289, John Wiley & Sons Ltd., London.

Alapuro, R. (1981), Origins of Agrarian Socialism in Finland, in: Torsvik, P. (ed.), *Mobilization, Center-Periphery Structures, and Nation-Building*, pp.274–295, Universitetsforlaget, Bergen / Oslo / Tromsø.

Alapuro, R. (1982), Finland: an interface periphery, in: Rokkan, S. and Urwin, D. (eds.), *The Politics of Territorial Identity*, pp.113–164, Sage Publications, London / Beverly Hills / New Delhi.

Allardt, E. and Miemois, K.J. (1981), *The Swedish Speaking Minority in Finland*, Research Report no. 24 (2nd revised edition), Research Group for Comparative Sociology, University of Helsinki, Helsinki.

Allardt, E. and Pesonen, P. (1967), Cleavages in Finnish Politics, in: Lipset, S.M. and Rokkan, S. (eds.), *Party Systems and Voter Alignments: cross-national perspectives*, pp.325–366, The Free Press, New York.

Amersfoort, H. van (1991), Nationalities, Citizens and Ethnic Conflicts: towards a theory of ethnicity in the modern state, in: Amersfoort, H. van, and Knippenberg, H. (eds.), *States and Nations: the rebirth of the 'nationalities question' in Europe*, pp.12–29, Koninklijk Nederlands Aardrijkskundig Genootschap, Amsterdam.

Amersfoort, H. van (1993), *Institutional Plurality: problem or solution for the multiethnic state?*, paper presented at the conference on 'Ethnicity, Nationalism, and Culture in Western Europe', 24–27 February, Amsterdam.

Amersfoort, H. van, and Wusten, H.H. van der (1981), Democratic Stability and Ethnic Parties, in: *Ethnic and Racial Studies*, v.4, pp.476–485.

Amnesty International (1986), *Bulgaria: imprisonment of ethnic Turks*, London.

Amnesty International (1987), *Bulgaria: continuing human rights abuses against ethnic Turks*, London.

Anderson, A.B. (1989), The Changing Situation of Ethnolinguistic Minorities along the Yugoslavian Frontier, in: *Canadian Review of Studies on Nationalism*, v.16, pp.263–275.

Anderson, A.B. (1990), Ethno-Nationalism and Regional Autonomy in Canada and Western Europe, in: Premdas, R.R., Samarsinghe, S.W.R.de A., and Anderson, A.B. (eds.), *Secessionist Movements in Comparative Perspective*, pp.168–180, Pinter Publishers, London.

Anderson, B. (1983), *Imagined Communities: reflections on the origin and spread of nationalism*, Verso, London.

Anderson, J. (1986), Nationalism and Geography, in: Anderson, J. (ed.), *The Rise of the Modern State*, pp.115–142, Wheatsheaf Books Ltd., Brighton.

Anderson, J. (1988), Nationalist Ideology and Territory, in: Johnston, R.J., Knight, D.B. and Kofman, E. (eds.), *Nationalism, Self-Determination and Political Geography*, pp.18–39, Croom Helm, London.

Arter, D. (1987), *Politics and Policy-Making in Finland*, Wheatsheaf Books, Brighton.

Bachmaier, P. (1990), Schulsystem, in: Grothusen, K.-D. (hrsg.), *Bulgarien* (Südosteuropa-Handbuch Band VI), pp.490–517, Vandenhoeck & Ruprecht, Göttingen.

Badie, B. and Birnbaum, P. (1983), *The Sociology of the State*, The University of Chicago Press, Chicago / London.

Balic, S. (1985), Muslims in Eastern and Southeastern Europe, in: *Journal Institute of Muslim Minority Affairs*, v.6, pp.361–374.

Banac, I. (1984), *The National Question in Yugoslavia*, Cornell University Press, Ithaca / London.

Banac, I. (1990), Political Change and National Diversity, in: *Daedalus*, v.119, pp.141–159.

Barros, J. (1968), *The Åland-Islands Question: its settlement by the League of Nations*, Yale University Press, New Haven / London.

Barth, F. (ed.) (1969), *Ethnic Groups and Boudaries*, Allen and Unwin, London.

Bauman, Z. (1989), *Modernity and the Holocaust*, Polity Press, Cambridge.

Bell, J.D. (1986), *The Bulgarian Communist Party from Blagoev to Zhivkov*, Hoover Institution Press, Stanford.

Bell, J.D. (1990), Domestic Politics, in: Grothusen, K.-D. (hrsg.), *Bulgarien*, (Südosteuropa-Handbuch Band VI), pp.56–83, Vandenhoeck & Ruprecht, Göttingen.

Bell, J.D. (1993), Bulgaria, in: White, S., Batt, J. and Lewis, P.G. (eds.), *Developments in East European Politics*, pp.83–96, MacMillan, London.

Bennett, R. (1989), European Economy, Society, Politics, and Administration: symmetry and disjuncture, in: Bennett, R. (ed.), *Territory and Administration in Europe*, pp.8–31, Pinter Publishers, London.

Berckx, P. (1990), *150 Jaar Institutionele Hervormingen in België; door ruime federale macht naar een nieuwe Belgische eendracht*, Kluwer Rechtswetenschappen, Antwerpen.

Berki, R.N. (1979), Introduction: state and society, an anti-thesis of modern political thought, in: Hayward, J.E.S. and Berki, R.N. (eds.), *State and Society in Contemporary Europe*, Martin Robertson, Oxford.

Bernhardt, R. (1981), Federalism and Autonomy, in: Dinstein, Y. (ed.), *Models of Autonomy*, pp.23–28, Transaction Books, New Brunswick / London.

Bookman, M.Z. (1994), War and Peace: the divergent breakups of Yugoslavia and Czechoslovakia, in: *Journal of Peace Research*, v.31, pp.175–187.

Brandt, C. (1992), *The Swedish-Speaking Finns (The Finland-Swedes)*, paper presented at "Democracy and Collective Rights – an international symposium", March 27–29, Timosoara.

Brass, P. (1985), Ethnic Groups and the State, in: Brass, P. (ed.), *Ethnic Groups and the State*, pp.1–56, Croom Helm, London / Sydney.

Breuilly, J. (1982), *Nationalism and the State*, Manchester University Press, Manchester.

Brzezinski, Z. (1989), Post-Communist Nationalism, in: *Foreign Affairs*, v.68, pp.1–25.

Bútorová, Z. (1993), A Deliberate 'Yes' to the Dissolution of the ČSFR?, in: *Czech Sociological Review*, v.1, pp.58–72.

Capek, A. and Sazama, G.W. (1993), Czech and Slovak Economic Relations, *Europa-Asia Studies*, v.45, pp.211–235.

Caporaso, J.A. (ed.) (1989), *The Elusive State: international and comparative perspectives*, Sage Publications, Newbury Park / London / New Delhi.

Carment, D. (1993), The International Dimensions of Ethnic Conflict: concepts, indicators, and theory, in: *Journal of Peace Research*, v.30, pp.137–150.

Carter, F.W. (1994), *National Minorities / Ethnic Groups in Bulgaria: regional distribution and cross-border links*, paper presented at 'The International Conference on Political Geography', 28–30 September, Opole, Poland.

Claeys, P.-H. (1980), Political Pluralism and Linguistic Cleavage: the Belgian case, in: Ehrlich, S. and Wootton, G. (eds.), *The Three Faces of Pluralism: political, ethnic, and religious*, pp.169–189, Gower Publishing Company Ltd., Farnborough.

Clark, G. and Dear, M. (1984), *State Apparatus: the structure and language of legitimacy*, Allen and Unwin, Boston.

Coakley, J. (1992a), Conclusion: Nationalist Movement and Society in Contemporary Western Europe, in: Coakley, J. (ed.), *The Social Origins of Nationalist Movements: the contemporary Western European Experience*, pp.212–230, Sage Publications, Newbury Park / London / New Delhi.

Coakley, J. (1992b), The Resolution of Ethnic Conflict: towards a typology, in: *International Political Science Review*, v.13, pp.343–358.

Connor, W. (1972), Nation-Building or Nation-Destroying?, in: *World Politics*, v.24, pp.319–355.

Connor, W. (1978), A Nation is a Nation, is a State, is an Ethnic Group, is a ....., in: *Ethnic and Racial Studies*, v.1, pp.377–400.

Connor, W. (1980), The Ethnopolitical Challenge and Governmental Response, in: Sugar, P.F. (ed.), *Ethnic Diversity and Conflict in Eastern Europe*, pp.147–184, ABC-Clio, Santa Barbara / Oxford.

Connor, W. (1984), *The National Question in Marxist-Leninist Theory and Strategy*, Princeton University Press, Princeton.

Connor, W. (1994), *Ethnonationalism: the quest for understanding*, Princeton University Press, Princeton.

Coppé, A. (1992), *Polemiek rond België*, Acco, Leuven / Amersfoort.

Covell, M. (1985), Ethnic Conflict, Representation and the State in Belgium, in: Brass, P. (ed.), *Ethnic Groups and the State*, pp.228–261, Croom Helm, London / Sydney.

Covell, M. (1993), Belgium: the variability of ethnic relations, in: McGarry, J. and O'Leary, B. (eds.), *The Politics of Ethnic Conflict Regulation*, pp.275–295, Routledge, London / New York.

Crampton, R.J. (1987), *A Short History of Modern Bulgaria*, Cambridge University Press, Cambridge.

Crampton, R.J. (1990), The Turks in Bulgaria, 1878–1944, in: Karpat, K. (ed.), *The Turks of Bulgaria: the history, culture, and fate of a minority*, pp.43–82, The Isis Press, Istanbul.

Creed, G.W. (1993), Rural – Urban Oppositions in the Bulgarian Political Transition, in: *Südosteuropa*, v.42, pp.369–382.

Dean, R.W. (1972), *Three Years of Czechoslovak Federation*, Radio Free Europe Research Background Report, 1 March.

Dean, R.W. (1973), *Nationalism and Political Change in Eastern Europe: the Slovak question and the Czechoslovak reform movement*, University of Denver, Denver.

De Lannoy, W. (1987), The Brussels Urban Region in the 20th Century: a socio-geographical analysis, in: Witte, E. and Baetens Beardsmore, H. (eds.), *The Interdisciplinary Study of Urban Bilingualism in Brussels*, pp.167–194, Multilingual Matters Ltd., Clevedon.

De Ridder, H. (1991), *Omtrent Wilfried Martens*, Lannoo, Tielt.

Deschouwer, K. (1994), Haalt Brussel de Volgende Eeuw?, in: *Internationale Spectator*, v.48, pp.483–486.

De Schrijver, R. (1981), The Belgian Revolution and the Emergence of Belgium's Biculturalism, in: Lijphart, A. (ed.), *Conflict and Coexistence in Belgium: the dynamics of a culturally divided society*, pp.13–33, Research Series no.46, Institute of International Studies, University of California, Berkeley.

Deutsch, K.W. (1966), *Nationalism and Social Communication: an inquiry into the foundations of nationality (2nd ed.)*, MIT Press, Cambridge / London.

Dewachter, W.F.J. (1987), Changes in a Particratie: the Belgian party system from 1944 to 1986, in: Daalder, H. (ed.), *Party Systems in Denmark, Austria, Switzerland, the Netherlands and Belgium*, pp.285–364, Francis Pinter Publishers, London.

Dewachter, W.F.J. (1991), *Politiek in België: geprofileerde machtsverhoudingen*, Acco, Leuven / Amersfoort.

Dewachter, W.F.J. (1992a), *De Dualistische Identiteit van de Belgische Maatschappij*, Koninklijke Akademie van Wetenschappen, Noord-Hollandsche, Amsterdam.

Dewachter, W.F.J. (1992b), *Besluitvorming in Politiek België*, Acco, Leuven / Amersfoort.

Dinstein, Y. (1981), Autonomy, in: Dinstein, Y. (ed.), *Models of Autonomy*, pp.291–303, Transaction Books, New Brunswick / London.

Dobrizheva, L.M. (1991), The Role of the Intelligentsia in Developing National Consciousness among the Peoples of the USSR under Perestroika, in: *Ethnic and Racial Studies*, v.14, pp.87–99.

Donia, R.J. and Fine Jr, J.V.A. (1994), *Bosnia and Hercegovina: a tradition betrayed*, Columbia University Press, New York.

Dostál, P. (1982), Geleide Agglomeratietendensen in Tsjechoslowakije: een institutioneel-geografische benadering, in: *KNAG Geografisch Tijdschrift*, v.16, pp.328–341.

Dostál, P. (1991), Accommodating Post-Communist National Aspirations: secession or (con)federation?, in: Amersfoort, H. van, and Knippenberg, H. (eds.), *States and Nations: the rebirth of the 'nationalities question' in Europe*, pp.100–129, Koninklijk Nederlands Aardrijkskundig Genootschap, Amsterdam.

Dostál, P. (1992), Transition: regional socio-economic response, unemployment and intermunicipal cooperation, in: Dostál, P., Illner, M., Kára, J. and Barlow, M. (eds.), *Changing Territorial Administration in Czechoslovakia*, pp.71–88, Instituut voor Sociale Geografie, Universiteit van Amsterdam, Amsterdam.

Dostál, P. and Kára, J. (1992), Territorial Administration in Czechoslovakia: an overview, in: Dostál, P., Illner, M., Kára, J. and Barlow, M. (eds.), *Changing Territorial Administration in Czechoslovakia*, pp.17–32, Instituut voor Sociale Geografie, Universiteit van Amsterdam, Amsterdam.

Dostál, P. and Knippenberg, H. (1992), Russification of Soviet Nationalities: the importance of territorial autonomy, in: *History of European Ideas*, v.15, pp.631–638.

Douglas, W.A. (1988), A Critique of Recent Trends in the Analysis of Ethnonationalism, in: *Ethnic and Racial Studies*, v.11, pp.192–206.

Dovring, F. (1965), *Land and Labour in Europe in the Twentieth Century*, Martinus Nijhoff, The Hague.

Dubois, J. (1989), Une Régionalisme Autre, in: Dumont, H. et al. (éd.), *Belgitude et Crise de l'État Belge*, pp.157–161, Publications des facultés universitaires Saint-Louis no.48, Bruxelles.

Duchacek, I. (1973), *Power Maps: comparative politics of constitutions*, ABC-Clio, Santa Barbara.

Duchacek, I. (1986), *The Territorial Dimension of Politics*, Westview Press, Boulder / London.

Duchacek, I. (1988), Dyadic Federations and Confederations, in: *Publius: the journal of federalism*, v.18, pp.5–31.

Duverger, M. (1973), *De Overheden: panorama der politieke stelsels*, Boom, Meppel.

Eidlin, F.H. (1980), *The Logic of 'Normalization': the Soviet intervention in Czechoslovakia of 21 August 1968 and the Czechoslovak response*, East European Monographs no.74, Boulder.

Elazar, D.J. (ed.) (1991), *Federal Systems of the World: a handbook of federal, confederal and autonomy arrangements*, Longman, Harlow.

Emerson, R. (1960), *From Empire to Nation: the rise of self-assertion of Asian and African peoples*, Harvard University Press, Cambridge.

Eminov, A. (1983), The education of Turkish speakers in Bulgaria, in: *Ethnic Groups*, v.5, pp.129–149.

Eminov, A. (1986), Are Turkish-speakers in Bulgaria of Ethnic Bulgarian Origin?; in: *Journal Institute of Muslim Minority Affairs*, v.7, pp.503–518.

Eminov. A. (1987), The status of Islam in Bulgaria; in: *Journal Institute of Muslim Minority Affairs*, v.8, pp.278–301.

Eminov, A. (1990), There are no Turks in Bulgaria: rewriting history by administrative fiat, in: Karpat, K. (ed.), *The Turks of Bulgaria: the history, culture, and fate of a minority*, pp.203–222, The Isis Press, Istanbul.

Encyclopedie van de Vlaamse Beweging (1973), Lannoo, Tielt / Utrecht.

Enloe, C. (1980a), Religion and Ethnicity: some general considerations, in: Sugar, P. (ed.), *Ethnic Diversity and Conflict in Eastern Europe*, pp.347–372, ABC-Clio, Santa Barbara / Oxford.

Enloe, C. (1980b), *Ethnic Soldiers: state security in divided societies*, Penguin Books, Harmondsworth.

Esman, M. (1977), Perspectives on Ethnic Conflict in Industrialized Societies, in: Esman, M. (ed.), *Ethnic Conflict in the Western World*, pp.371–390, Cornell University Press, Ithaca / London.

Esman, M. (1985), Two Dimensions of Ethnic Politics: defense of homelands, immigrant rights, in: *Ethnic and Racial Studies*, v.8, pp.438–440.

Esman, M. (1992), The State and Language Policy, in: *International Political Science Review*, v.13, pp.381–396.

Finer, S.E. (1975), State and Nation-Building in Europe: the role of the military, in: Tilly, C. (ed.), *The Formation of National States in Western Europe*, Princeton University Press, Princeton.

Fonteyn, G. (1988), *De Nieuwe Walen*, Lannoo, Tielt

Franz, E. (1991), The Exodus of Turks from Bulgaria (1989), in: *Asian and African Studies*, v.25, pp.81–97.

Frognier, A.P., Quévit, M. and Steinbock, M. (1982), Regional Imbalances and Centre-Periphery Relationships in Belgium, in: Rokkan, S. and Urwin, D. (eds.), *The Politics of Territorial Identity*, pp.251–278, Sage Publications, London / Beverly Hills / New Delhi.

Geertz, C.M. (1963), The Integrative Revolution: primordial sentiments and civil politics in new states, in: Geertz, C.M. (ed.), *Old Societies and New States*, Free Press, Glencoe.

Gehrmann, U. and Naydenov, T. (1993), *Bulgariens Weg zur neuen Identität: Rückblicke und Aussichten einer unvollendeten 'Preustrojstvo' auf dem Balkan*; Berichte des Bundesinstituts für ostwissenschaftliche internationale Studien nr. 16/1993, Köln.

Gellner, E. (1980), Ethnicity between Culture, Class and Power, in: Sugar, P. (ed.), *Ethnic Diversity and Conflict in Eastern Europe*, pp.237–278, ABC-Clio, Santa Barbara / Oxford.

Gellner, E. (1983), *Nations and Nationalism*, Basil Blackwell, Oxford.

Gellner, E. (1990), Ethnicity and Faith in Eastern Europe, in: *Daedalus*, v.119, pp.279–294.

Georgeoff, J.P. (1981), Ethnic Minorities in the People's Republic of Bulgaria, in: Klein, G. and Reban, M.J. (eds.), *The Politics of Ethnicity in Eastern Europe*, pp.49–84, East European Monographs no.93, Columbia University Press, New York.

Georgeoff, J.P. (1985), National Minorities in Bulgaria 1919–1980, in: Horak, S.M. (ed.), *Eastern European Minorities 1919–1980: a handbook*, pp.274–308, Libraries Unlimited Ltd., Littleton.

Giddens, A. (1987), *The Nation-State and Violence: vol.2 of a contemporary critique of historical materialism*, University of California Press, Berkeley / Los Angeles.

Gijsels, H. (1992), *Het Vlaams Blok*, Kritak, Leuven.

Gjuzelev, B. (1992), Bulgarien zwischen den Parlements- und Präsidentenwahlen (Oktober 1991 – Februar 1992), in: *Südosteuropa*, v.41, pp.613–632.

Glazer, N. and Moynihan, D.P. (eds.) (1975a), *Ethnicity: theory and experience*, Harvard University Press, Cambridge.

Glazer, N. and Moynihan, D.P. (1975b), Introduction, in: Glazer, N. and Moynihan, D.P. (eds.), *Ethnicity: theory and experience*, pp.1–28, Harvard University Press, Cambridge.

Gleason, G. (1990), *Federalism and Nationalism: the struggle for republican rights in the USSR*, Westview Press, Boulder.

Glenny, M. (1992), *The Fall of Yugoslavia: the third Balkan war*, Penguin Books, London.

Gol, J. (1993), Waar gaat het met België heen? De visie van een Franstalige, in: Van Istendael, G. (ed.), *Het nut van België*, pp.25–60, Atlas, Amsterdam / Antwerpen.

Gottlieb, G. (1993), *Nation against State: a new approach to ethnic conflicts and the decline of sovereignty*, Council of Foreign Relations Press, New York.

Greenwood, D.J. (1985), Castillians, Basques, and Andalusians: an historical comparison of nationalism, 'true' identity and 'false' identity, in: Brass, P. (ed.), *Ethnic Groups and the State*, pp.204–227, Croom Helm, London / Sydney.

Grillo, R.D. (1980), Introduction, in: Grillo, R.D. (ed.), *'Nation' and 'State' in Europe*, pp.1–30, Academic Press, London.

Groep Coudenberg (1991), *In Naam van de Democratie*, Roularta, Zellik.

Grosser, I. (1990), Land- und Forstwirtschaft; in: Grothusen, K.-D. (hrsg.), *Bulgarien* (Südosteuropa-Handbuch Band VI), pp.333–354, Vandenhoeck & Ruprecht, Göttingen.

Gurr, T.R. (1993), *Minorities at Risk: a global view of ethnopolitical conflicts*, United States Institute of Peace Press, Washington DC.

Hajda, L. and Beissinger, M. (eds.) (1990), *The Nationalities Factor in Soviet Politics and Society*, Westview Press, Boulder / San Fransisco / Oxford.

Hall, R.L. (1979), *Ethnic Autonomy: comparative dynamics in the Americas, Europe, and the developing world*, Pergamon Press, New York.

Hämäläinen, P.K. (1966), *The Nationality Struggle between the Finns and the Swedish-Speaking Minority in Finland 1917–1939*, Indiana University, Ann Arbor.

Hämäläinen, P.K. (1978), *In Time of Storm: revolution, civil war and the ethnolinguistic issue in Finland*, State University of New York Press, Albeny.

Hämäläinen, P.K. (1980), The Swedish Dilemma in Contemporary Finland, in: *Scandinavian Studies*, v.52, pp.414–422.

Hannum, H. (1990), *Autonomy, Sovereignty and Self-Determination: the accommodation of conflicting rights*, University of Pennsylvania Press, Philadelphia.

Hannum, H. (ed.) (1993), *Documents on Autonomy and Minority Rights*, Martinus Nijhoff, Dordrecht.

Hechter, M. (1975), *Internal Colonialism: the Celtic Fringe in British national development*, Routledge & Kegan Paul, London.

Heisler, M. (1990), Hyphenating Belgium: changing state and regime to cope with cultural division, in: Montville, J.V. (ed.), *Conflict and Peacemaking in Multiethnic Societies*, pp.177–195, Lexington Books, Lexington / Toronto.

Hellemans, S. and Schepers, R. (1992), De Ontwikkeling van Corporatieve Verzorgingsstaten in België en Nederland, in: *Sociologische Gids*, v.39, pp.346–364.

Heraclides, A. (1991), *The Self-Determination of Minorities in International Politics*, Frank Cass, London.

Hill, R.J. (1990), *Communist Politics under the Knife: surgery or autopsy?*, Pinter Publishers Ltd., London.

Hjeppe, R. (1993), Finland's Foreign Trade and Trade Policy in the 20th Century, in: *Scandinavian Journal of History*, v.18, pp.57–76.

Hobsbawm, E.J. (1990), *Nations and Nationalism since 1780: programme, myth, reality*, Cambridge University Press, Cambridge.

Hoensch, J.K. (1991), Tsjechoslowakije, in: Neeven, J., Ramkema, H. and Schaik, E. van (red.), *Van Tallinn tot Tirana: Oost Europa tijdens het interbellum*, pp.47–60, Werkgroep Oost-Europa Projecten, Utrecht.

Hooghe, L. (1991), *A Leap in the Dark: nationalist conflict and federal reform in Belgium*, Western Societies Program Occasional Paper no.27, Cornell University, Ithaca.

Hooghe, L. (1992), Nationalist Movements and Social Factors: a theoretical perspective, in: Coakley, J. (ed.), *The Social Origins of Nationalist Movements: the contemporary Western European Experience*, pp.21–44, Sage Publications, Newbury Park / London / New Delhi.

Hooghe, L. (1993), Belgium: from Regionalism to Federalism, in: *Regional Politics and Policy*, v.3, pp.44–68.

Höpken, W. (1987a), Modernisierung und Nationalismus: Sozialgeschichtliche Aspekte der bulgarischen Minderheitenpolitik gegenüber den Türken, in: Schönfeld, R. (hrsg.), *Nationalitätenprobleme in Südosteuropa*, pp.255–280, R.Oldenbourg Verlag, München.

Höpken, W. (1987b), Im Schatten der nationalen Frage: die bulgarisch-türkischen Beziehungen (I + II), in: *Südosteuropa*, v.36, pp.75–95, 178–194.

Höpken, W. (1990a), Politisches System, in: Grothusen, K.-D. (hrsg.), *Bulgarien* (Südosteuropa-Handbuch Band VI), pp.173 – 223, Vandenhoeck & Ruprecht, Göttingen.

Höpken, W. (1990b), Die Wahlen in Bulgarien – Ein Pyrrhus-Sieg für die Kommunisten?; in: *Südosteuropa*, v.39, pp.429 – 457.

Höpken, W. (1992), Emigration und Integration von Bulgarien-Türken seit dem Zweiten Weltkrieg, in: Seewann, G. (hrsg.), *Minderheitenfragen in Südosteuropa*, pp.359 – 376, R.Oldenbourg Verlag, München.

Hoppe, H.-J. (1986), Bulgarian nationalities policy in occupied Thrace and Aegean Macedonia, in: *Nationalities Papers*, v.14, pp.89 – 100.

Horak, S.M. (ed.) (1985), *East European National Minorities 1919 – 1980: a handbook*, Libraries Unlimited Inc., Littleton.

Horowitz, D.L. (1975), Ethnic Identity, in: Glazer, N. and Moynihan, D.P. (eds.), *Ethnicity: theory and experience*, pp.111 – 140, Harvard University Press, Cambridge.

Horowitz, D.L. (1985), *Ethnic Groups in Conflict*, University of California Press, Berkeley / Los Angeles / London.

Hristov, H. (1987), The Bulgarian Agrarian People's Union in the Political System of Socialist Bulgaria (1971 – 1980), in: *Bulgarian Historical Review*, v.15, pp.3 – 19.

Hroch, M. (1985), *Social Preconditions of National Revival in Europe: a comparative analysis of the social composition of patriotic groups among the smaller European nations*, Cambridge University Press, Cambridge.

Huyse, L. (1970), *Passiviteit, Pacificatie en Verzuiling in de Belgische Politiek*, Antwerpen.

Huyse, L. (1981), Political Conflict in Bicultural Belgium, in: Lijphart, A. (ed.), *Conflict and Coexistence in Belgium: the dynamics of a culturally divided society*, pp.107 – 126, Research Series no.46, Institute of International Studies, University of California, Berkeley.

Huyse, L. (1982), België: een wankele natie?, in: Rosenthal, U. (red.), *Politieke Stelsels: stabiliteit en verandering*, pp.57 – 88, Samson, Alphen aan de Rijn / Brussel.

Iliev, C.L. (1989), The Bulgarian Nation through the Centuries, in: *Journal Institute of Muslim Minority Affairs*, v.10, pp.1 – 20.

Illner, M. (1994), *Czechoslovak Federal Assembly and the Split of the Country* (comments on the paper of Ms.Krok-Pazkowska), in: Proceedings Workshop on Transformation Processes in Eastern Europe, 16 – 17 December 1993, NWO-ESR, The Hague.

Ionescu, G. (1967), *The Politics of the European Communist States*, Weidenfield and Nicolson, London.

Irwin, Z.T. (1984), The fate of Islam in the Balkans: a comparison of four state policies, in: Ramet, P. (ed.), *Religion and Nationalism in Soviet and East European Politics*, pp.207 – 225, Duke Press Policy Studies, Durham.

Jackson, M. (1987), Changes in Ethnic Populations of Southeastern Europe: Holocaust, Migration and Assimilation 1940 to 1970, in: Schönfeld, R. (hrsg.),

Nationalitätenprobleme in Südosteuropa, pp.73–104, R.Oldenbourg Verlag, München.

Javeau, C. (1989), De la Belgitude à l'Éclatement du Pays, in: Dumont, H. et al. (éd.), *Belgitude et Crise de l'Etat Belge*, pp.157–161, Publications des facultés universitaires Saint-Louis no.48, Bruxelles.

Jehlicka, P., Kostelecky, T., and Sykora, L. (1993), Czechoslovak Parliamentary Elections 1990: old patterns, new trends, and lots of surprises, in: O'Loughlin, J. and Wusten, H.H. van der (eds.), *The New Political Geography of Eastern Europe*, pp.235–254, Belhaven Press, London / New York.

Jelinek, Y.A. (1976), *The Parish Republic: Hlinka's Slovak People's Party 1939–1945*, East European Quarterly, Boulder.

Jelinek, Y.A. (1983), *The Lust for Power: nationalism, Slovakia, and the communists 1918–1948*, East European Monographs, Boulder.

Jičinskí, Z. (1969), *The Czechoslovak Federation*, Prague.

Johnson, O. (1985), *Slovakia 1918–1938: education and the making of a nation*, East European Monographs, Boulder.

Johnston, R.J. (1982), *Geography and the State: an essay in political geography*, MacMillan Press Ltd., London / Basingstoke.

Johnston, R.J. (1989), The State, Political Geography and Geography, in: Peet, N. and Thrift, N. (eds.), *New Models in Geography*, pp.292–309, Unwin Hyman, London.

Jong, F. de (1980), The Muslim Minority in Western Thrace, in: Ashworth, G. (ed.), *World Minorities in the Eighties: a third volume in the series*, pp.95–100, Quartermaine House Ltd., Sunbury.

Kalibova, K., Haisman, T. and Gjuricova, J. (1993), Gypsies in Czechoslovakia: demographic developments and policy perspectives, in: O'Loughlin, J. and Wusten, H.H. van der (eds.), *The New Political Geography of Eastern Europe*, pp.133–144, Belhaven Press, London / New York.

Kalvoda, J. (1985), National Minorities in Czechoslovakia 1919–1980, in: Horak, S.M. (ed.), *Eastern European National Minorities 1919–1980: a handbook*, pp.108–159, Libraries Unlimited Inc., Littleton.

Kamenka, E (1976), *Nationalism: the nature and evolution of an idea*, Edward Arnold, London.

Karpat, K. (1990), Introduction, in: Karpat, K. (ed.), *The Turks of Bulgaria: the history, culture, and fate of a minority*, pp.1–42, The Isis Press, Istanbul.

Kauppi, M. (1984), The Resurgence of Ethno-Nationalism and Perspectives on State-Society Relations, in: *Canadian Review of Studies on Nationalism*, v.11, pp.119–132.

Keating, M. (1990), Minority Nationalism and the State: the European case, in: Watson, M. (ed.), *Contemporary Minority Nationalism*, pp.174–194, Routledge, London / New York.

Keating, M. (1991), Regionalism, Nationalism and the State in Western Europe: a political model, in: *Canadian Review of Studies on Nationalism*, v.18, pp.117–129.

Kesteloot, C., De Lannoy, W., Saey P., Swyngedouw, E. and Vandermotten, C. (Werkgroep Mort Subite) (1990), *Barsten in België: een geografie van de Belgische maatschappij*, EPO, Berchem.

Kettani, M. Ali (1988), Islam in post-Ottoman Balkans: a review essay, in: *Journal Institute of Muslim Minority Affairs*, v.9, pp.391–403.

King, R. (1973), *Minorities under Communism: nationalities as a source of tension among Balkan communist states*, Harvard University Press, Cambridge.

Kirby, A. (1989), State, Local State, Context, and Spatiality: a reappraisal of state theory, in: Caporaso, J.A. (ed.), *The Elusive State: international and comparative perspectives*, pp.204–227, Sage Publications, Newbury Park / London / New Delhi.

Kirisci, K. (1991), Refugee movements and Turkey, *International Migration*, v.29, pp.545–559.

Kirschbaum, S.J. (1989), Slovak Nationalism in the First Czechoslovak Republic 1918–1938, in: *Canadian Review of Studies on Nationalism*, v.14, pp.169–187.

Klein, G. (1975), The Role of Ethnic Politics in the Czechoslovak Crisis of 1968 and the Yugoslav Crisis of 1971, in: *Studies in Comparative Communism*, v.8, pp.339–369.

Klinge, M. (1993), Finland: from Napoleontic legacy to Nordic co-operation, in: Teich, M. and Porter, R. (eds.), *The National Question in Europe in Historical Context*, pp.317–331, Cambrige University Press, Cambridge.

Knight, D.B. (1982), Identity and Territory: geographical perspectives on nationalism and regionalism, in: *Annals of the American Association of Geographers*, v.72, pp.514–531.

Knippenberg, H. (1991), The 'Nationalities Question' in the Soviet Union, in: Amersfoort, H. van, and Knippenberg, H. (eds.), *States and Nations: the rebirth of the 'nationalities question' in Europe*, pp.42–58, Koninklijk Nederlands Aardrijkskundig Genootschap, Amsterdam.

Kohn, H. (1971), *Nationalism: its meaning and history (rev. ed.)*, Van Nostrand, Princeton.

Kolossov, V.A., Glezer, O. and Petrov, N. (1992), *Ethno-Territorial Conflicts and Boundaries in the Former Soviet Union*, Territory Briefing 2, International Bounderies Research Unit Press, Durham.

Konstantinov, Y. (1992), An account of Pomak Conversions in Bulgaria (1912–1990), in: Seewann, G. (hrsg.), *Minderheitenfragen in Südosteuropa*, pp.343–357, R.Oldenbourg Verlag, München.

Konstantinov, Y., Alhaug, G. and Igla, B. (1991), *Names of the Bulgarian Pomaks*, Nordlyd Tromsø University Working Papers on Language & Linguistics no.17, Tromsø.

Koopmans, R. and Duyvendak, W. (1991), Gegen die Herausforderer: neue soziale Bewegungen und Gegenbewegungen in der Bundesrepublik Deutschland, den Niederlanden und Frankreich, in: *Forschungsjournal neue sozialen Bewegungen*, v.2, pp.17–30.

Kopačka, L. (1994), Industrialization and Regional Industrial Structures, in: Barlow, M., Dostál, P. and Hampl, M. (eds.), *Territory, Society and Administration: the Czech Republic and the Industrial Region of Liberec*, pp.41–56, Instituut voor Sociale Geografie, Universiteit van Amsterdam, Amsterdam.

Kossmann, E.H. (1976), *De Lage Landen 1780–1940: anderhalve eeuw Nederland en België*, Elsevier, Amsterdam.

Kosta, J. (1984), Regionalprobleme in einer sozialistischen Planwirtschaft als Testbeispiel: die Slowakei, in: *Osteuropa-Wirtschaft*, v.29, pp.118–126.

Kostanick, H.L. (1957), *Turkish Resettlement of Bulgarian Turks 1950 – 1953*, University of California Publications in Geography no.8, Berkeley, Los Angeles.

Koulov, B. (1992), Tendencies in the Administrative Territorial Development of Bulgaria (1878–1990), in: *Tijdschrift voor Economische en Sociale Geografie*, v.83, pp.390–401.

Kraas-Schneider, F. (1989), *Bevölkerungsgruppen und Minoritäten: Handbuch der ethnischen, sprachlichen und religiösen Bevölkerungsgruppen der Welt*, Franz Steiner, Stuttgart.

Krasner, S.D. (1989), Sovereignty: an institutional perspective, in: Caporaso, J.A. (ed.), *The Elusive State: international and comparative perspectives*, pp.69–96, Sage Publications, Newbury Park / London / New Delhi.

Krasteva, A. (1992), *National identity and citizenship: the Bulgarian case*; paper presented at "The Conference on Nation-Building", August 2–6, Blagoevgrad, Bulgaria.

Krejčí, J. (1990), De Sociale en Economische Ontwikkelingen van Tsjechoslowakije na 1945, in: Mercks, K. and Ramkema, H. (red.), *Republiek aan de Moldau: de Tsjechoslowaakse erfenis*, pp.21–30, Werkgroep Oost-Europa Projecten, Utrecht.

Krejčí, J. and Velímský, V. (1981), *Ethnic and Political Nations in Europe*, St. Martin's Press, New York.

Kusin, V.V. (1972), *Political Groupings in the Czechoslovak Reform Movement*, MacMillan, London / Basingstoke.

Kusin, V.V. (1978), *From Dubček to Charter 77*, St.Martin's Press, New York.

Kusin, V.V. (1981), *Slovak Communist Party Congress in March 1981*, Radio Free Europe Research Background Report 96, 3 April.

Kusin, V.V. (1983), *A Slovak Panorama*, Radio Free Europe Research Situation Report 5, 16 March.

Lammich, S. and Schmid, K. (1979), *Die Staatsordnung der Tschechoslowakei*, Berlin Verlag, Berlin.

Lampe, J.R. (1986), *The Bulgarian Economy in the Twentieth Century*, Croom Helm, London.

Lane, J.-E. and Ersson, S. (1991), *Politics and Society in Western Europe (2nd ed.)*, Sage Publications, London / Newbury Park / New Delhi.

Leff, C.S. (1988), *National Conflict in Czechoslovakia: the making and remaking of a state 1918–1987*, Princeton University Press, Princeton.

Lettrich, J. (1955), *History of Modern Slovakia*, Praeger, New York.

Liebkind, K. (1984), *Minority Identity and Identification Processes: a social psychological study*, Commentationes Scientiarum Socialum no.22, Societas Scientiarum Fennica, Helsinki.

Lijphart, A. (1977a), Political Theories and the Explanation of Ethnic Conflict in the Western World: falsified predictions and plausible postdictions, in: Esman, M. (ed.), *Ethnic Conflict in the Western World*, pp.46–64, Cornell University Press, Ithaca / London.

Lijphart, A. (1977b), *Democracy in Plural Societies: a comparative exploration*, Yale University Press, New Haven / London.

Lijphart, A. (1981), Introduction: the Belgian example of cultural coexistence in comparative perspective, in: Lijphart, A. (ed.), *Conflict and Coexistence in Belgium: the dynamics of a culturally divided society*, pp.1–12, Research Series no.46, Institute of International Studies, University of California, Berkeley.

Lind, M. (1994), In Defense of Liberal Nationalism, in: *Foreign Affairs*, v.73, pp.87–99.

Linz, J. and Stepan, A. (1992), Political Identities and Electoral Sequences: Spain, the Soviet Union and Yugoslavia, in: *Daedalus*, v.121, pp.123–139.

Lipset, S.M. and Rokkan, S. (1967), Party Systems and Voter Alignments: an introduction, in: Lipset, S.M. and Rokkan, S. (eds.), *Party Systems and Voter Alignments: cross-national perspectives*, pp.1–64, The Free Press, New York.

Lorwin, V. (1966), Belgium: religion, class, and language in national politics, in: Dahl, R. (ed.), *Political Opposition in Western Democracies*, pp.147–187, Yale UP, New haven / London.

Luchterhandt, O. (1990), Regierungssystem, in: Grothusen, K.-D. (hrsg.), *Bulgarien* (Südosteuropa-Handbuch Band VI), pp.136–172, Vandenhoeck & Ruprecht, Göttingen.

Mackie, T.T. and Rose, R. (1991), *The International Almanac of Electoral History* (3rd fully rev. ed.), MacMillan, London.

Mamatey, V.S. (1979), The Birth of Czechoslovakia: union of two peoples, in: Brisch, H. and Volgyes, I. (eds.), *Czechoslovakia: the heritage of ages past*, pp.75–88, East European Monographs no.51, Boulder.

Mann, M. (1984), The Autonomous Power of the State: its origins, mechanisms and results, in: *Archives européennes de Sociologie*, v.25, pp.185–213.

McGarry, J. and O'Leary, B. (1993), Introduction: the macro-political regulation of ethnic conflict, in: McGarry, J. and O'Leary, B. (eds.), *The Politics of Ethnic Conflict Regulation*, pp.1–40, Routledge, London / New York.

McKay, J. (1982), An exploratory synthesis of primordial and mobilizationist approaches to ethnic phenomena, in: *Ethnic and Racial Studies*, v.5, pp.395–417.

McRae, K.D. (1974), Introduction, in: McRae, K.D. (ed.), *Consociational Democracy: political accommodation in segmented societies*, pp.1–28, McClelland and Stewart Limited, Toronto.

McRae, K.D. (1975), The Principle of Territoriality and the Principle of Personality in Multilingual States, in: *Linguistics: an interdisciplinary journal of the language sciences*, v.13, pp.33–54.

McRae, K.D. (1986), *Conflict and Compromise in Multilingual Societies: Belgium*, Wilfried Laurier University Press, Waterloo / Ontario.

McRae, K.D. (1990), Theories of Power-Sharing and Conflict Management, in: Montville, J.V. (ed.), *Conflict and Peacemaking in Multiethnic Societies*, pp.177–195, Lexington Books, Lexington / Toronto.

Meinardus, R. (1985), Die griechisch-türkische Minderheitenfrage, in: *Orient (Hamburg)*, v.26, pp.48–61.

Meštrović, S.G., Letica, S. and Goreta, M. (1993), *Habits of the Balkan Hart: social character and the fall of communism*, Texas A & M University Press, College Station.

Mikesell, M.W. and Murphy, A.B. (1991), A Framework for Comparative Study of Minority-Group Aspirations, in: *Annals of the American Association of Geographers*, v.81, pp.581–604.

Minority Rights Group (1990), *World Directory of Minorities*, Minority Rights Group, London.

Minority Rights Group (ed.) (1993), Minorities in Central and Eastern Europe, Minority Rights Group, London.

Molitor, A. (1981), The Reform of the Belgian Constitution, in: Lijphart, A. (ed.), *Conflict and Coexistence in Belgium: the dynamics of a culturally divided society*, pp.139–153, Research Series no.46, Institute of International Studies, University of California, Berkeley.

Mollahüseyin, H. (1984), Muslims in Bulgaria: a status report, in: *Journal Institute of Muslim Minority Affairs*, v.5, pp.136–144.

Moynihan, D.P. (1993), *Pandaemonium: ethnicity in international politics*, Oxford University Press, New York.

Murphy, A.B. (1988a), *The Regional Dynamics of Language Differentiation in Belgium: a study in cultural-political geography*, Geography Research Paper 227, University of Chicago Press, Chicago.

Murphy, A.B. (1988b), Evolving Regionalism in Linguistically Divided Belgium, in: Johnston, R.J., Knight, D.B. and Kofman, E. (eds.), *Nationalism, Self-Determination and Political Geography*, pp.135–150, Croom Helm, London.

Murphy, A.B. (1989), Territorial Policies in Multiethnic States, in: *Geographical Review*, v.79, pp.410–421.

Murphy, A.B. (1990a), *Urbanism and the Diffusion of Substate Nationalist Ideas in Western Europe*, paper presented at the conference of the International Society for the Study of European Ideas, 3–8 September, Leuven.

Murphy, A.B. (1990b), Electoral Geography and the Ideology of Place: the making of regions in Belgian electoral politics, in: Johnston, R.J., Shelley, F.M. and Taylor, P.J. (eds.), *Developments in Electoral Geography*, pp.227–241, Routledge, London / New York.

Musil, J. (1992), Czechoslovakia in the Middle of Transition, in: *Czechoslovak Sociological Review*, v.28, pp.5–21.

Musil, J. (1993), Czech and Slovak Society: the outline of the comparative study, in: *Czech Sociological Review*, v.29, pp.1–18.

Nahaylo, B. and Svoboda, V. (1990), *Soviet Disunion: a history of the nationalities problem in the USSR*, Free Press, New York.

Nairn, T. (1977), *The Break-Up of Britain: crisis and neo-nationalism*, New Left Books, London.

Nationalities (1989), Nationalities update: the ethnic Turks in Bulgaria, in: *Nationalities Papers*, v.16, pp.106–110.

Nettl, J.P. (1969), The State as a Conceptual Variable, in: *World Politics*, v.21, pp.559–592.

Newman, S. (1994), Ethnoregional Parties: a comparative perspective, in: *Regional Politics and Policy*, v.4, pp.28–66.

Niederhauser, E. (1981), The Rise of Nationality in Eastern Europe, Kner Printing House, Gyoma.

Nielsson, G.P. (1985), States and 'Nation-Groups': a global taxonomy, in: Tiryakian, E.A. and Regowski, R. (eds.), *New Nationalisms of the Developed West: towards explanation*, pp.27–56, Allan & Unwin, Boston.

Niznansky, L. and Robinson, W.F. (1979), *Slovakia after a Decade of Federation*, Radio Free Europe Research Background Report 5, 10 January.

NRC Handelsblad, various editions.

Olson, D.M. (1993), Dissolution of the State: Political Parties and the 1992 election in Czechoslovakia, in: *Communist and Post-Communist Studies*, v.26, pp.301–314.

Olzak, S. and Nagel, J. (eds.) (1986), *Competitive Ethnic Relations*, Academic Press, Orlando.

Orridge, A.W. (1981), Varieties of Nationalism, in: Tivey, L. (ed.), *The Nation-State: the formation of modern politics*, pp.39–58, Martin Robertson, Oxford.

Orridge, A.W. (1982), Separatist and Autonomist Nationalisms: the structure of regional loyalties in the modern state, in: Williams, C.H. (ed.), *National Separatism*, pp.43–74, University of British Columbia Press, Ithaca.

Orridge, A.W. and Williams, C.H. (1982), Autonomous Nationalism: a theoretical framework for spatial variations in its genesis and development, in: *Political Geography Quarterly*, v.1, pp.19–39.

Oschlies, W. (1986), *Bulgariens Bevölkerung Mitte der 80-er Jahre: eine demographische und sozialpolitische Skizze*, Berichte des Bundesinstituts für ostwissenschaftliche und internationale Studien 17, Köln.

Paasi, A. (1992), The Construction of Socio-Spatial Consciousness: geographical perspectives on the history and context of Finnish nationalism, in: *Nordisk Samhällsgeografisk Tidskrift nr. 15*, pp.79–100.

Paddison, R. (1983), *The Fragmented State: the political geography of power*, Basil Blackwell, Oxford.

Palley, C. (1978), *Constitutional Law and Minorities*, Minority Rights Group Report no.36, London.

Paul, D.W. (1985), Slovak Nationalism and the Hungarian State 1870–1910, in: Brass, P. (ed.), *Ethnic Groups and the State*, pp.117–155, Croom Helm, Londen/Sydney.

289

Paul, L. (1991), The Hungarians in Romania: portrait of an explosive minority issue, in: Amersfoort, H. van, and Knippenberg, H. (eds.), *States and Nations: the rebirth of the 'nationalities question' in Europe*, pp.59–78, Koninklijk Nederlands Aardrijkskundig Genootschap, Amsterdam.

Pavlínek, P. (1992), Regional Transfromation in Czechoslovakia: towards a market economy, in: *Tijdschrift voor Economische en Sociale Geografie*, v.83, pp.361–371.

Pentikaeinen, J. et al. (1985), *Cultural Minorities in Finland: an overview towards cultural policy*, Publications of the Finnish National Commission for UNESCO, no.32, Helsinki.

Pesonen, P. and Rantala, O. (1985), Outlines of the Finnish Party System, in: Alapuro, R. et al. (eds.), *Small States in Comparative Perspectives: essays for Erik Allardt*, pp.211–227, Norwegian University Press, Oslo.

Pithart, P. (1993), *The Split of Czechoslovakia and the Changing Perception of Czech Identity: nationalism or regional separatism*, paper presented at the conference on 'Nations and Borders in the New European Architecture', 6–8 May, Brussels.

Poggi, G. (1990), *The State: its nature, development, and prospects*, Stanford University Press, Stanford.

Polasky, J. (1981), Liberalism and Biculturalism, in: Lijphart, A. (ed.), *Conflict and Coexistence in Belgium: the dynamics of a culturally divided society*, pp.34–45, Research Series no.46, Institute of International Studies, University of California, Berkeley.

Popov, P. and Demerdjiev, Z. (1989), Bulgaria: administrative division and territorial management, in: Bennett, R. (ed.), *Territory and Administration in Europe*, pp.180–190, Pinter Publishers, London.

Popovic, A. (1986a), *L'Islam Balkanique: les Musulmans du Sud-est Européen dans la période post-Ottomane*, Osteuropa Institut an der Freien Universität, Berlin.

Popovic, A. (1986b), The Turks of Bulgaria (1878–1985), in: *Central Asian Survey*, v.5, no. 2, pp.1–32.

Poulsen, H. (1987), The Nordic States, in: Mühlberger, D. (ed.), *The Social Basis of European Fascist Movements*, Croom Helm, London / New York / Sydney.

Poulton, H. (1991), *The Balkans: minorities and states in conflict*, Minority Rights Publications, London.

Pufflerová, Š. (1994), National Minorities in Slovakia, in: *Helsinki Monitor*, v.5, pp.52–63.

Puister, T.E. (1994), De Turken in Bulgarije, in: Ramkema, H. and Schaik, E. van (red.), *Tussen Recht en Repressie: minderheden in Oost-Europa*, pp.131–146, Instituut voor Publiek en Politiek, Amsterdam.

Pundeff, M. (1984), Church – State Relations in Bulgaria under Communism, in: Ramet, P. (ed.), *Religion and Nationalism in Soviet and Eastern European Politics*, pp.328–350, Duke Press, Durham.

Ra'anan, U., Mesner M., Armes, K. and Martin, K. (eds.) (1991), *State and Nation in Multi-Ethnic Societies: the breakup of multinational states*, Manchester University Press, Manchester / New York.

Rabushka, A. and Shepsle, K.A. (1972), *Politics in Plural Societies: a theory of democratic instability*, Charles E. Merill Publishing Company, Columbus.

Radicova, I. (1993), The Velvet Divorce, in: *Uncaptive Minds*, v.6, pp.51–62.

Ragin, C.C. (1989), *The Comparative Method: moving beyond qualitative and quantitative strategies*, University of California Press, Berkeley.

Raikin, S. (1989), Nationalism and the Bulgarian Orthodox Church, in: Ramet, P. (ed.), *Religion and Nationalism in Soviet and East European Politics (rev. ed.)*, pp.352–377, Duke University Press, Durham.

Ramet, P. (1984), The interplay of religious policy and nationalities policy in the Soviet Union and Eastern Europe, in: Ramet, P. (ed.), *Religion and nationalism in Soviet and East European politics*, pp.3–30, Duke Press Policy Studies, Durham.

Reban, M.J. (1981), Czechoslovakia: the new federation, in: Klein, G. and Reban, M.J. (eds.), *The Politics of Ethnicity in Eastern Europe*, pp.215–246, East European Monographs, Boulder.

Regowski, R. (1985), Conclusion, in: Tiryakian, E.A. and Regowski, R. (eds.), *New Nationalisms of the Developed West: towards explanation*, pp.374–384, Allan & Unwin, Boston.

Remington, R.A. (1969), *Winter in Prague: documents on Czechoslovak communism in crisis*, The MIT Press, Cambridge / London.

Renner, H. and Závodský, P. (1991), Communistische Metamorfosen: het voorbeeld van de CP van Tsjechoslowakije, in: *Internationale Spectator*, v.45, pp.227–233.

Res Publica: tijdschrift voor politicologie, various editions.

Reuter, J. (1985), Die Entnationalisierung der Türken in Bulgarien, in: *Südosteuropa*, v.34, pp.169–177.

RFE/RL, Radio Free Europe / Radio Liberty Research Reports, various editions.

Riedel, S. (1993), Die türkische Minderheit im parlementarischen System Bulgariens, in: *Südosteuropa*, v.42, pp.100–124.

Riezebos, C. and Tang, G.F.M. van der (1992), Bevoegdheid en Controle in Federale Staten, in: Munneke, H.F, Riezebos, C. and Tang, G.F.M. van der, *Federalisme*, pp.1–55, Publikaties van de Staatsrechtkring no. 3, Tjeenk Willink, Zwolle.

Roeder, P.G. (1991), Soviet Federalism and Ethnic Mobilization, in: *World Politics*, v.43, pp.196–232.

Roessingh, M.A. (1991), The Interaction of States and Ethnic Groups: emergence, persistance or disappearance of primordial manifestations, in: Amersfoort, H. van, and Knippenberg, H. (eds.), *States and Nations: the rebirth of the 'nationalities question' in Europe*, pp.172–189, Koninklijk Nederlands Aardrijkskundig Genootschap, Amsterdam.

Roessingh, M.A. and Sytsema, B. (1993), The Turkish Minority in Greece and Bulgaria: a comparative perspective on the interaction between minorities and governments, paper presented at the international conference on "The Diaspora Networks", 25–28 April, Nicosia/Larnaca.

Rokkan, S. and Urwin, D.W. (eds.) (1982), *The Politics of Territorial Identity: studies in European regionalism*, University of Chicago Press, Chicago.

Rokkan, S. and Urwin, D.W. (1983), *Economy, Territory, Identity: politics of West-European peripheries*, Sage Publications, Beverly Hills / London / New Delhi.

Rothschild, J. (1981), *Ethnopolitics: a conceptual framework*, Columbia University Press, New York.

Rothschild, J. (1989), *Return to Diversity: a political history of East Central Europe since World War II*, Oxford University Press, Oxford / New York.

Rudolph Jr., J.R. (1989), Belgium: variations on the theme of territorial accommodation, in: Rudolph Jr., J.R. and Thompson, R.J. (eds.), *Ethnoterritorial Politics, Policy and the Western World*, pp.91–113, Lynne Riener Publishers, Boulder / London.

Rudolph Jr., J.R. and Thompson, R.J. (1985), Ethnoterritorial Movements and the Policy Process: accommodating nationalist demands in the developed world, in: *Comparative Politics*, v.17, pp.291–311.

Ruostetsaari, I. (1993), The Anatomy of the Finnish Power Elite, in: *Scandinavian Political Studies*, v.16, pp.305–337.

Ryan, S. (1990), *Ethnic Conflict and International Relations*, Dartmouth, Aldershot / Brookfield.

Sack, R.D. (1986), *Human Territoriality: its meaning and history*, Cambridge University Press, Cambridge.

Safran, W. (1991), Ethnicity and Pluralism: comparative and theoretical perspectives, in: *Canadian Review of Studies on Nationalism*, v.18, pp.1–12.

Schendelen, M.P.C.M. van (ed.) (1984), *Consociationalism, Pillarization and Conflict-Management in the Low Countries* (Acta Politica, v.19, pp.1–178), Boom, Meppel.

Schöpflin, G. (1993), Culture and Identity in Post-Communist Europe, in: White, S., Batt, J. and Lewis, P.G. (eds.), *Developments in East European Politics*, pp.16–34, The MacMillan Press Ltd., Basingstoke / London.

Senelle, R. (1989), Constitutional Reform in Belgium: from unitarism towards federalism, in: Forsyth, M. (ed.), *Federalism and Nationalism*, pp.51–95, Leicester University Press, Leicester / London.

Seton-Watson, H. (1977), *Nations and States*, Methuen & Co. Ltd., London.

Seyppel, T. (1992), Das Interesse an der muslimischen Minderheit Westthrakien (Griechenland) 1945–1990, in: Seewann, G. (hrsg.), *Minderheitenfragen in Südosteuropa*, pp.377–392, R.Oldenbourg Verlag, München.

Shils, E. (1957), Primordial, Personal, Sacred and Civil Ties, in: *British Journal of Sociology*, v.8, pp.207–226.

Shoup, P. (1981), *The East European and Soviet Data Handbook: political, social and developmental indicators 1945–1975*, Columbia University Press, New York.

Šik, O. (1981), *The Communist Power System*, Praeger Publishers, New York.

Şimşir, B.N. (1988), *The Turks of Bulgaria (1878–1985)*, Rustem, London.

Şimşir, B.N. (1990), The Turkish minority in Bulgaria: history and culture, in: Karpat, K. (ed.), *The Turks of Bulgaria: the history, culture, and fate of a minority*, pp.43–82, The Isis Press, Istanbul.

292

Singleton, F. (1989), *A Short History of Finland*, Cambridge University Press, Cambridge.

Skalický, K. (1989), The Vicissitudes of the Catholic Church in Czechoslovakia 1918-1988, in: Stone, N. and Strouhal, E. (eds.), *Czechoslovakia: crossroads and crisis 1918–1988*, pp.297–324, MacMillan, Basingstoke / London.

Skilling, H.G. (1976), *Czechoslovakia's Interrupted Revolution*, Princeton University Press, Princeton.

Skilling, H.G. (1981), *Charter 77 and Human Rights in Czechoslovakia*, George Allen and Unwin, London.

Skocpol, T. (1985), Bringing the State Back, in: Strategies of analysis in current research, in: Evans, P.B., Rueschemeyer, D. and Skocpol, T. (eds.), *Bringing the State Back In*, pp.3–37, Cambridge University Press, Cambridge NY.

Smith, A.D. (1981), *The Ethnic Revival in the Modern World*, Cambridge University Press, Cambridge.

Smith, A.D. (1982), Nationalism, Ethnic Separatism, and the Intelligentsia, in: Williams, C.H. (ed.), *National Separatism*, pp.17–41, University of British Columbia Press, Ithaca.

Smith, A.D. (1984), Ethnic Myths and Ethnic Revivals, in: *Archives européennes de Sociologie*, v.25, pp.283–305.

Smith, A.D. (1986), *The Ethnic Origin of Nations*, Blackwell, Oxford.

Smith, A.D. (1991), *National Identity*, Penguin Books, London.

Smith, G. (1989), Administering Ethnoregional Stability: the Soviet state and the nationalities question, in: Williams, C.H. and Kofman, E. (eds.), *Community Conflict: partition and nationalism*, pp.224–251, Routledge, London.

Smith, G. (1990), The Soviet Federation: from corporatist to crisispolitics, in: Chisholm, M. and Smith, D.M. (eds.), *Shared Space, Divided Space: essays on conflict and territorial organization*, pp.84–105, Unwin Hyman, London.

Snyder, L.L. (1983), Nationalism and the Flawed Concept of Ethnicity, in: *Canadian Review of Studies on Nationalism*, v.10, pp.253–265.

Snyder, L.L. (1990), *Encyclopedia of Nationalism*, St.James Press, Chicago / London.

Staar, R.F. (1982), *Communist Regimes in Eastern Europe (4th ed.)*, Hoover Institution Press, Stanford.

Stanovčić, V. (1992), Problems and Options in Institutionalizing Ethnic Relations, in: *International Political Science Review*, v.13, pp.359–379.

Statistical Yearbook of Finland (1993), v.88, Tilastokeskus, Helsinki.

Steiner, E. (1973), *The Slovak Dilemma*, Cambridge University Press, Cambridge.

Stengers, J. (1981), Belgian National Sentiments, in: Lijphart, A. (ed.), *Conflict and Coexistence in Belgium: the dynamics of a culturally divided society*, pp.46–60, Research Series no.46, Institute of International Studies, University of California, Berkeley.

Stepan, A. (1978), *The State and Society: Peru in comparative perspective*, Princeton University Press, Princeton.

Swyngedouw, M. (1992), The Extreme Right in Belgium: the breakthrough of the extreme right in Flanders, in: *Regional Politics and Policy*, v.2, pp.62–75.

Symmons-Symonolewicz, K. (1985), The Concept of Nationhood: toward a theoretical clarification, in: *Canadian Review of Studies on Nationalism*, v.12, pp.215–222.

Taaffe, R.N. (1990), Population Structure, in: Grothusen, K.-D. (hrsg.), *Bulgarien* (Südosteuropa-Handbuch Band VI), pp.433–457, Vandenhoeck & Ruprecht, Göttingen.

Tarrow, S. (1977), *Between Center and Periphery: grassroots politicians in Italy and France*, Yale University Press, New Haven / London.

Taylor, P.J. (1989), *Political Geography: world economy, nation-state and locality (3rd ed.)*, Longman Scientific & Technical, Harlow.

Thibaut, F. (1990), *La Finlande: politique intérieure et neutralité active*, Librairie Générale de Droit et de Jurisprudence, Paris.

Tilly, C. (ed.) (1975), *The Formation of National States in Western Europe*, Princeton University Press, Princeton.

Tilly, C. (1992), *Coercion, Capital and European States, AD. 990–1992 (rev. paperback ed.)*, Blackwell, Cambridge / Oxford.

Toonen, T.A.J. (1993), Bestuur op Niveau: regionalisatie in een ontzuilend bestuur, in: *Acta Politica*, v.28, pp.295–325.

Troebst, S. (1990), Nationale Minderheiten, in: Grothusen, K.-D. (hrsg.), *Bulgarien* (Südosteuropa-Handbuch Band VI), pp.474–489, Vandenhoeck & Ruprecht, Göttingen.

Troebst, S. (1992), Nationalismus als Demokratisierungshemnis in Bulgarien: von der Verfassungsdiskussion zur Präsidentschaftswahl (Mai 1991 – Januar 1992), in: *Südosteuropa*, v.41, pp.188–227.

Troebst, S. (1994), Ethnopolitics in Bulgaria: the Turkish, Macedonian, Pomak and Gypsy Minorities, in: *Helsinki Monitor*, v.5, pp.32–42.

Ulč, O. (1974), *Politics in Czechoslovakia*, W.H.Freeman and Company, San Fransisco.

Ulč, O. (1982), Legislative Politics in Czechoslovakia, in: Nelson, D. and White, S. (eds.), *Communist Legislatures in Comparative Perspective*, pp.111–124, MacMillan, London / Basingstoke.

Urwin, D.W. (1982), Perspectives on Conditions of Regional Protest and Accommodation, in: Rokkan, S. and Urwin, D.W. (eds.), *The Politics of Territorial Identity: studies in European regionalism*, pp.425–435, University of Chicago Press, Chicago.

Van Damme, M. (1984), *Constitutionele en Politieke Systemen: een typologische benadering*, Kluwer, Antwerpen.

Van den Berghe, P.L. (1981), *The Ethnic Phenomenon*, Elsevier, New York, Oxford.

Van den Brande, L. (1993), Beslissingsbevoegdheden van de Nieuwe Belgische Instituties, in: *Internationale Spectator*, v.47, pp.556–559.

Van Haegendoren, M. (1962), *De Vlaamse Beweging Nu en Morgen: na honderddertig jaar*, deel I, Heideland, Hasselt.

Van Impe, H. (1983), Van Cultuurraad tot Vlaamse Raad, in: Peeters, Y.J.D. (red.), *Over Volksopvoeding en Staatsvorming*, pp.183–187, De Nederlanden, Antwerpen.

Van Istendael, G. (1989), *Het Belgisch Labyrint: de schoonheid der wanstaltigheid*, De Arbeiderspers, Amsterdam.

Van Velthoven, H. (1987), The Process of Language Shift in Brussels: historical background and mechanisms, in: Witte, E. and Baetens Beardsmore, H. (eds.), *The Interdisciplinary Study of Urban Bilingualism in Brussels*, pp.15–45, Multilingual Matters Ltd., Clevedon.

Vasileva, D. (1991), Bulgarian-Turkish Emigration and Return, in: *International Migration Review*, v.26, pp.342–352.

Vidláková, O. and Zářecký, P. (1989), Czechoslovakia: the development of public administration, in: Bennett, R. (ed.), *Territory and Administration in Europe*, pp.168–179, Pinter Publishers Ltd., London.

Vnuk, F. (1983), Slovak-Czech Relations in Post-War Czechoslovakia 1945–1948, in: Kirschbaum, S.J. (ed.), *Slovak Politics: essays on Slovak history in honour of Joseph M. Kirschbaum*, Slovak Institute, Cleveland / Rome.

Vos, L. (1993), Shifting Nationalism: Belgians, Flemings and Walloons, in: Teich, M. and Porter, R. (eds.), *The National Question in Europe in Historical Context*, pp.128–147, Cambridge University Press, Cambridge.

Vucinich, W.S. (1969), Islam in the Balkans, in: Arberry, A.J. (ed.), *Religion in the Middle East: three religions in concord and conflict, vol.2 Islam*, pp.236–252, Cambridge University Press, Cambridge.

Wädekin, K.-E. (1982), *Agrarian Policies in Communist Europe: a critical introduction*, Martinus Nijhoff, The Hague.

Wallerstein, I. (1991), Typology of Crisis in the World System, in: Wallerstein, I., *Geopolitics and Geoculture: essays on the changing world-system*, pp.104–122, Cambridge University Press, Cambridge / New York.

Waterman, S. (1989), Partition and Modern Nationalism, in: Williams, C.H. and Kofman, E. (eds.), *Community Conflict: partition and nationalism*, pp.117–132, Routledge, London.

Watson, M. (ed.) (1990), *Contemporary Minority Nationalism*, Routledge, London.

Wheaton, B. and Kavan, Z. (1992), *The Velvet Revolution: Czechoslovakia 1988–1991*, Westview Press, Boulder / San Fransico / Oxford.

Whitaker, R. (1990), Social Structure, in: Grothusen K.-D. (hrsg.), *Bulgarien* (Südosteuropa-Handbuch Band VI), pp.474–489, Vandenhoeck & Ruprecht, Göttingen.

Wightman, G. (1993), The Czech and Slovak Republics, in: White, S., Blatt, J. and Lewis, P.G. (eds.), *Developments in East European Politics*, pp.51–65, MacMillan, Basingstoke / London.

Wilkinson, H.R. (1951), *Maps and politics: a review of the ethnographic cartography of Macedonia*, University Press of Liverpool, Liverpool.

Williams, C.H. (1980), Ethnic Separatism in Western Europe, in: *Tijdschrift voor Economische en Sociale Geografie*, v.71, pp.142–158.

Williams, C.H. (1985), Conceived in Bondage – Called into Liberty: reflections on nationalism, in: *Progress in Human Geography*, v.9, pp.331–355.

Wils, L. (1993), Natievorming in België: Vlamingen en Walen in wisselwerking, in: *Internationale Spectator*, v.47, pp.552–555.

Witte, E. (1987), Bilingual Brussels as an Indication of Growing Political Tensions (1960–1985), in: Witte, E. and Baetens Beardsmore, H. (eds.), *The Interdisciplinary Study of Urban Bilingualism in Brussels*, pp.47–74, Multilingual Matters Ltd., Clevedon.

Witte, E. (1992), Belgian Federalism: towards complexity and asymmetry, in: *West European Politics*, v.15, pp.95–117.

Witte, E. (1993), Taal en Territorialiteit: een overzicht van de ontwikkelingen in België sinds 1830, in: *Tijdschrift voor Geschiedenis*, v.106, pp.208–229.

Witte, E. and Craeybeckx, J. (1983), *Politieke Geschiedenis van België sinds 1830: spanningen in een burgerlijke democratie (2nd edition)*, Standaard Wetenschappelijke Uitgeverij, Antwerpen.

Witte, E., Craeybeckx, J. and Meynen,.A. (1990), *Politieke Geschiedenis van België van 1830 tot heden (5th rev. ed.)*, Standaard, Antwerpen.

Wolchik, S. (1991), *Czechoslovakia in Transition: politics, economics and society*, Pinter Publishers, London / New York.

Wolf, K. (1986), Ethnic Nationalism: an analysis and defence, in: *Canadian Review of Studies on Nationalism*, v.13, pp.99–109.

Wright, A.W. (1981), Socialism and Nationalism, in: Tivey, L. (ed.), *The Nation-State: the formation of modern politics*, pp.148–170, Martin Robertson, Oxford.

Wusten, H.H. van der (1988), The Occurrence of Successful and Unsuccessful Nationalisms, in: Johnston, R.J., Knight, D.B. and Kofman, E. (eds.), *Nationalism, Self-Determination and Political Geography*, pp.189–202, Croom Helm, London.

Wusten, H.H. van der (1993), Les symboles de la future carte géopolitique de l'Europe, in: Philippart, E. (éd.), *Nations et Frontières dans la nouvelle Europe: l'impact croisé*, pp.127–140, Editions Complexe, Bruxelles.

Yapou, E. (1981), The Autonomy that Never Was: the autonomy plans for the Sudeten in 1938, in: Dinstein, Y. (ed.), *Models of Autonomy*, pp.97–122, Transaction Books, New Brunswick / London.

Yerasimos, S. (1991), Balkans: frontières d'aujourd'hui, d'hier et de demain?, in: *Hérodote*, nr. 63, pp.80–98.

Yin, R.K. (1989), *Case Study Research: design and method (rev. ed.)*, Sage Publications, Newbury Park / London / New Delhi.

Zagarov, O. (1987), *The Truth*, Sofia Press, Sofia.

Zariski, R. (1989), Ethnic Extremism among Ethnoterritorial Minorities in Western Europe: dimensions, causes, and institutional responses, in: *Comparative Politics*, v.21, pp.253–272.

Zartman, I.W. (1990), Negotiations and Prenegotiations in Ethnic Conflict: The Beginning, The Middle, and the Ends, in: Montville, J.V. (ed.), *Conflict and*

Peacemaking in Multiethnic Societies, Lexington Books, pp.511 – 534, Lexington / Toronto.

Zolberg, A. (1977), Splitting the Difference: federalization without federalism in Belgium, in: Esman, M.J. (ed.), *Ethnic Conflict in the Western World*, pp.103 – 142, Cornell University Press, Ithaca.

Zwemer, S.M. (1927), Islam in South Eastern Europe, in: *The Moslem World*, v.17, pp.331 – 358.

Abbreviations

BKP	=	Bulgarian Communist Party
BSP	=	Bulgarian Socialist Party (reformed communists)
BZNS	=	Bulgarian National Agrarian Union
CVP	=	Christian People's Party (Dutch-language)
DPS	=	Movement for Rights and Freedom (Turkish Bulgarians)
FDF	=	Francophone Democratic Front (Brussels)
FN	=	National Front (Wallonia)
HSLS	=	Hlinka Slovak Populist Party
HZDS	=	Movement for a Democratic Slovakia
IKL	=	People's Patriotic Movement
KSČ	=	Communist Party of Czechoslovakia
KSS	=	Communist Party of Slovakia
MPW	=	Walloon People's Movement
ODS	=	Civic Democratic Party
OF	=	Civic Forum
PRL	=	Liberal Reform Party
PS	=	Socialist Party (French-language)
PSC	=	Christian Social Party (French-language)
PVV	=	Party of Liberty and Progress (Dutch-language)
RAD/UDRT	=	Democratic Union for the Respect of Labour
RW	=	Walloon Rally
SDS	=	Union of Democratic Forces
SFP	=	Swedish People's Party
SKDL	=	Democratic League of the People of Finland (or Left-Wing Alliance)
SNR	=	Slovak National Council
SNS	=	Slovak National Party
SP	=	Socialist Party (Dutch-language)
SSP	=	Social Democratic Party of Finland
VMRO	=	Internal Macedonian Revolutionary Organization
VNV	=	Flemish National Union
VPN	=	Public Against Violence
VU	=	People's Union (Flemish)

Tables, figures and maps

Index